# IN THIS SERIES

*Socio-Economic Surveys of Three Villages in Andhra Pradesh:*
*A Study of Agrarian Relations*
Edited by V. K. Ramachandran, Vikas Rawal, Madhura Swaminathan

*Socio-Economic Surveys of Two Villages in Rajasthan:*
*A Study of Agrarian Relations*
Edited by Madhura Swaminathan and Vikas Rawal

*Socio-Economic Surveys of Three Villages in Karnataka:*
*A Study of Agrarian Relations*
Edited by Madhura Swaminathan and Arindam Das

# SOCIO-ECONOMIC SURVEYS OF
# Three Villages in Karnataka

## A STUDY OF AGRARIAN RELATIONS

*Edited by*

Madhura Swaminathan and Arindam Das

Foundation for
Agrarian
Studies

Tulika Books

Published by

**Tulika Books**

www.tulikabooks.in

*in association with*

**Foundation for Agrarian Studies**

www.agrarianstudies.org


© Foundation for Agrarian Studies 2017

First published in India 2017

ISBN: 978-93-82381-88-4


**Designed by M. V. Bhaskar, TNQ**

Printed at Chaman Enterprises, Delhi 110 002

# Preface

In 2005, the Foundation for Agrarian Studies (FAS) initiated the Project on Agrarian Relations in India (PARI) with the aim of studying village-level production, production systems, and livelihoods, and the socio-economic characteristics of different strata of the rural population, by means of detailed village surveys. To date, this Project has covered 25 villages in 10 States of India. The Project was conceptualised and is guided by V. K. Ramachandran.

In the Karnataka round of surveys in 2009, three villages were surveyed: Alabujanahalli in Mandya district, Siresandra in Kolar district, and Zhapur in Kalaburagi district. The choice of villages was made so as to capture some of the differences between agro-ecological regions in the State. Alabujanahalli, in Maddur taluk of Mandya district, is a village belonging to the Cauvery-irrigated region of southern Karnataka. At the time of the survey, the major crops grown in this village were sugarcane, rice, and finger millet. The village is located very close to a major sugar factory of the district. Siresandra, in Kolar taluk of Kolar district, belongs to the semi-dry, rainfed region of south-eastern Karnataka. Cultivation in the village was mainly rainfed, supplemented by irrigation by means of borewells and drip irrigation. Sericulture and dairying were important occupations in this village. Zhapur, in Kalaburagi taluk of Kalaburagi district, falls in the dry, rainfed region of northern Karnataka. The cropping pattern followed here was that of a single mixed crop of rainfed cereals and oilseeds. Many workers of Zhapur were employed as daily workers in a stone quarry located on the boundaries of the village.

Census surveys were conducted in the three selected villages. A special feature of these surveys was the estimation of household incomes from detailed information on incomes from crop production, animal resources, agricultural and non-agricultural wage labour, salaries, business and trade, rent, interest earnings, pensions, remittances, scholarships, and other sources.

In 2014, we revisited the villages and conducted case studies in all three villages: we covered 16 households in Alabujanahalli, 10 households in Siresandra, and 11 households in Zhapur.

Preliminary findings from the village surveys were presented at a workshop held at Bengaluru on November 8–9, 2014. We are grateful to V. Sridhar, Maruti Manpade, G. N. Nagaraj, C. Gopinath, U. Basavaraja, G. C. Byya Reddy, Gouramma Patil, Jayakumar, and other participants from the Karnataka Pranta Raitha Sangha (KPRS) and the All India Agricultural Workers Union (AIAWU), for their comments and suggestions.

We are grateful to the Rosa Luxemburg Stiftung, New Delhi, for their support for the re-survey of 2014 as well as the Bengaluru workshop.

This volume is a survey report, and the third in a series of field reports based on village surveys. The report draws on the work of field investigators, data entry assistants, data analysts, and social scientists. There are, however, three chapters dealing with issues at the State level: on the agrarian economy of Karnataka, on famer suicides, and on rural banking.

We thank Indira Chandrasekhar and the staff of Tulika Books for their efforts in getting the manuscript ready for print. This book has been designed by M. V. Bhaskar of TNQ Books and Journals Pvt. Ltd., and we thank him and TNQ for their continued support to FAS publications. We thank *The Hindu* group of publications for permission to use the cover photographs.

Madhura Swaminathan is grateful to the Indian Statistical Institute Bangalore for providing an excellent environment for research and writing.

*Bengaluru*  
*August 31, 2016*

Madhura Swaminathan  
Arindam Das

# Contents

Preface
*Madhura Swaminathan and Arindam Das*                          v

1 The Agrarian Economy of Karnataka
  *R. Ramakumar*                                               1

  APPENDIX: A Note on Sericulture in Karnataka
  *Yoshifumi Usami*                                            31

2 Agrarian Crisis and Farmer Suicides in Karnataka
  *T. N. Prakash Kammardi, H. Chandrashekar,*
  *K. J. Parameshwarappa, Harsha V. Torgal, Gireesh P. S.,*
  *Mali Patil Vijay Kumar, Nagendra*                           37

3 An Introduction to the Survey Villages
  *Arindam Das*                                                60

4 Socio-Economic Classes in the Three Villages
  *V. K. Ramachandran*                                         69

5 Literacy and Schooling in Three Villages of Karnataka
  *Venkatesh Athreya, with T. Sivamurugan*                     86

6 Landholdings and Irrigation in the Study Villages
  *Deepak Kumar*                                               121

7  Features of Asset Ownership in the Three
   Study Villages
   *Madhura Swaminathan and Yasodhara Das*                    140

8  Cropping Pattern, Yields, and Crop Incomes:
   Findings from Three Villages Surveyed in Karnataka
   *Biplab Sarkar*                                            162
   APPENDIX: Shri Chamundeshwari Sugars Limited:
   A Note
   *Arindam Das*                                              190

9  Manual Workers in Rural Karnataka: Evidence
   from Three Villages
   *Niladri Sekhar Dhar, Arindam Das,
   and T. Sivamurugan*                                        193

10 Household Incomes in the Three Study Villages
   *Aparajita Bakshi and Arindam Das*                         218
   APPENDIX: A Note on Sericulture in Two Study Villages
   *Arindam Das*                                              250

11 State of Rural Banking in Karnataka:
   With Special Reference to the Three Study Districts
   *Pallavi Chavan*                                           256

12 Rural Indebtedness in Karnataka: Findings from
   Three Village Surveys
   *R. V. Bhavani*                                            271

13 Condition of Housing and Access to Basic
   Household Amenities
   *Shamsher Singh*                                           295

   List of Contributors                                       317

# 1

# The Agrarian Economy of Karnataka

R. Ramakumar

The State of Mysore (renamed Karnataka in 1973) was formed in 1956 by bringing together a diverse set of regions: namely, the old Mysore State, the Coorg State, and the Kannada-speaking areas of Bombay Presidency, the Nizam's Hyderabad, and Madras Presidency (see Figures 1 and 2). These regions represented a diversity of agrarian relations as well as agrarian legislations. Also, implementation of some land reform measures had already begun in some of these regions. For example, the Bombay Tenancy and Agricultural Land Act of 1948 was already being implemented in the areas of Bombay Presidency added to the State of Mysore, and the Mysore (Religious and Charitable) Inams Abolition Act of 1954 was already being implemented in the old Mysore State. The need for uniform agrarian legislation led to the passage of the Mysore Land Reforms Act in 1961.

In the 1950s and 1960s, the distribution of operational landholdings was highly unequal in Mysore State as a whole (Table 1). In 1961–62, 9 per cent of all operational holdings were larger than 20 acres in size, and accounted for 45 per cent of the total area of operational holdings. About 22 per cent of all holdings accounted for roughly 70 per cent of the total area of operational holdings.

Table 1 provides the status of distribution of operational landholdings in the State as a whole, but there were strong regional differences across the State. First, the extent of tenancy varied between districts. In 1957, of the roughly 18 lakh registered tenancies in the State, about 7 lakh tenancies (i.e. more than a third) were in the two coastal districts of Dakshina Kannada and Uttara Kannada, which came from the Madras and Bombay Presidencies respectively (Damle 1989). The four districts of Belgaum, Dharwad, Shimoga, and Bijapur had another 6 lakh tenancies. Thus, the above six districts

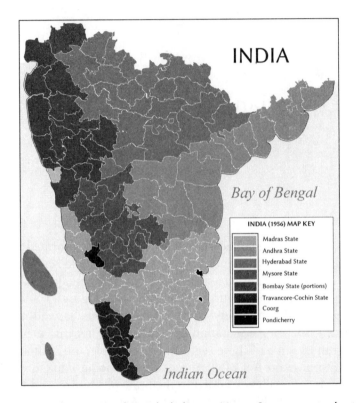

**Figure 1** *Map of the larger region from which the new Mysore State was carved out in 1956*

accounted for about 13 lakh registered tenancies out of the State total of 18 lakhs. Of course, oral leases were prevalent in all districts of the State.

Secondly, the nature of tenancy relations also varied between districts. In the coastal and southern districts, tenancy involved landlords and larger landholders leasing out land to smaller landholders or to those who were landless (Kohli 1988). In the eastern and northern districts, tenancy additionally involved "reverse tenancy" in large measure, i.e. larger landholders leasing in from smaller landholders. Kohli cites data from the early 1970s to argue that, in the eastern districts (undivided Chikkamagalur, Coorg, Hassan, and Shimoga) and northern districts (undivided Belgaum, Bellary, Bidar, Bijapur, Chitradurga, Dharwar, Kalaburagi, and Raichur), about 28 to 29 per cent of the total area leased in was by those who owned more than 10 acres of land. These differences were to have a long-term

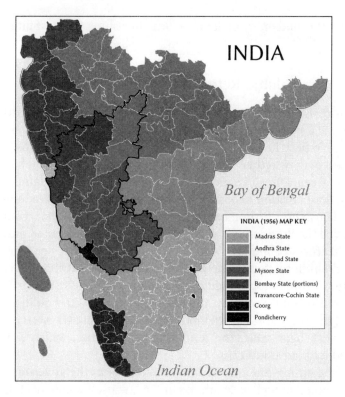

**Figure 2** *Map showing the borders of the new Mysore State of 1956 within the larger region*

**Table 1** *Distribution of operational holdings by size-class, Karnataka, 1960–61 and 1971–72 in per cent*

| Size-class of holdings | 1960–61 | | 1971–72 | |
|---|---|---|---|---|
| | Share of holdings | Share of area | Share of holdings | Share of area |
| < 1 acre | 34.2 | 0.2 | 34.4 | 0.4 |
| 1 to 2.5 acres | 9.8 | 2.4 | 15.6 | 4.7 |
| 2.5 to 5 acres | 13.2 | 6.7 | 16.0 | 10.7 |
| 5 to 10 acres | 21.3 | 21.3 | 17.9 | 23.0 |
| 10 to 20 acres | 12.6 | 24.3 | 9.9 | 24.8 |
| > 20 acres | 8.9 | 45.0 | 6.2 | 36.4 |
| All holdings | 100.0 | 100.0 | 100.0 | 100.0 |

*Source*: Kohli (1988).

impact on the outcomes of land reform measures in the State over the years.

## Land Reforms in Mysore State

The Mysore Land Reforms Bill was passed after prolonged discussions between 1956 and 1961, and after the submission of the B. D. Jatti Committee report in 1958. A major reason for this delay was persistent differences over whether landlords from the erstwhile Bombay regions should be given a fresh chance, under the new law, to reclaim land from tenants whose position had already been secured as "protected tenants" by the 1948 legislation in Bombay (Planning Commission 1966). Though the Bill received the President's assent in 1962, it was implemented only in 1965.

Three features of the law were important (for details, see below). First, it allowed landlords to resume half the area leased out to tenants, up to a maximum of three family holdings measuring up to 18 standard acres for personal cultivation. Secondly, the ceiling on ownership holdings was kept at very high levels. Thirdly, exemptions from ceiling laws were provided to cooperatives, sugar mills, and joint farming societies, which were mostly controlled by landed interests.

Given the strong presence of landed interests in the government and in the bureaucracy, as well as loopholes in the law itself, implementation of the Land Reforms Act of 1961 was a major failure across the State of Mysore. Quoting the Deputy Commissioner of Mandya, the Planning Commission (1966) notes that "in many cases landlords had seen to it that the names of tenants were not entered" in the *pahani* (a revenue record of rights over land and crops). Later studies from across Karnataka show that a very large number of tenants were evicted by landlords between 1956 and 1965. A 1964 report of the Planning Commission noted, from visits to villages, that "lands still continue to change hands from tenant to tenant or from tenant to owners." Karanth (1995) presents detailed case studies from Rajapura village in Bangalore district on how evictions were rampant: "The Kudur landowner, a Brahmin and a government servant, held about 20 acres of land. ... Five tenants had been cultivating his land. All but one among them were evicted."

> The Lingayat landowner ... had about 12 tenants cultivating his lands. ... Anticipating difficulty in evicting the tenants, he approached the headman for help. The headman, in turn, advised the tenants to give up the occupancy of the land. It was pointed out to them that the landowner and his dependants

will be left without a source of income if the land was taken away from him. It was also pointed out to the tenants that they would have little chances of establishing their claims legally as the *pahani* records had been maintained to suit the landowner's interests ... all the tenants agreed not to press their claims.

Another reason for the failure of the 1961 Land Reforms Act was the high levels of ceiling on land ownership, which ensured that very little land was available for redistribution. The ceiling on ownership for what was defined as Class I double-cropped land was fixed at 27 standard acres. The limit for other types of land translated into very large extents: 36 acres for Class II wet/garden lands, 45 acres for Class III wet/garden lands, 54 acres for Class IV Malanad land, 108 acres for Class V dry/garden lands, 162 acres for Class VI dry land, and 216 acres for Class VII dry land. In addition, if a household had more than five members, it was allowed to legally hold land up to a maximum of twice the ceiling area (Lakshman, Ramadas, and Kanthi 1973). *In other words, a household of 10 members could hold up to 432 acres of land.* Exceptions were also made for sugar factories to hold sugarcane land of up to one-sixth the total land required by the factory; Rajan (1979) notes that in 1971, a sugar factory was allowed to retain 25,000 acres of sugarcane land.

The second round of land reforms in Mysore State, by then renamed Karnataka, began in 1974, when the Devraj Urs government passed an amended land reform law. This new law was significantly different from the 1961 Act, even as there were continuities. Thimmaiah and Aziz (1983) list the differences as follows:

> Some notable features of this Act are: a total ban on the resumption of leased land by the landlords; abolition of tenancy except in the case of soldiers and seamen; reduction of land ceilings to ten standard acres; and the constitution of Land Tribunals in each taluk (with the Assistant Commissioner serving as chairman, the Tahsildar as secretary, and including the local MLA and three non-official members, one of whom should belong to a Scheduled Caste or Scheduled Tribe) to decide on the claims of the tenants on the land cultivated by them. (*Ibid.*: 823)

There are several studies which argue that the implementation of the 1974 law was a success. However, there are also a number of studies which show that this claim of success is highly overstated.

First, according to Kohli (1988) and Damle (1989), the 1974 law could be termed a success only in the coastal districts. This was because in the coastal districts, as compared to other districts, tenancy was widely prevalent. In 1971, the share of the number of tenant holdings in all holdings was 54.4 per cent in Dakshina Kannada and 68.2 per cent in Uttara Kannada. Shimoga occupied a distant third position with a corresponding share of 21.5 per cent, while the State average was 11.2 per cent. In both the coastal districts, the share of applications decided in favour of the tenant was also higher as compared to other districts. As a result, by 1981, the share of the number of tenant holdings in all holdings in the two coastal districts had declined to just about 2 per cent.

Secondly, some authors who have examined data on the share of applications that were approved in favour of tenants in the non-coastal districts of the State argue that the 1974 tenancy reforms were a success. A normal method used to measure the success of tenancy reforms in the State is to take the number of applicants granted occupancy rights under the 1974 law as a share of the number of tenants recorded in the Agricultural Census of 1971. Damle (1989) argues that this method is highly erroneous for two reasons: one, the 1971 survey is known to have heavily underestimated the number of tenants; two, most of the tenants had been evicted by landlords before 1971. As a result, the denominator from 1971 used in many studies was considerably lower than what it should have been, and inflated the success rate of the 1974 law.

Thirdly, as earlier noted, there was widespread prevalence of "reverse tenancy" in the northern and eastern districts. As a result, Kohli (1988) argues, uniform application of the 1974 law is likely to have led to a situation in these districts whereby some members of landed groups benefited from tenancy reforms by managing to hold on to their leased-in land. He notes:

> ... of the tenanted land that was transferred to the tenants, only a part went from the rich to the poor. For the rest, given the pattern of tenancy in the early 1970s, some of the already well-off members must have gained and some of the less well-off must have lost. [*Ibid*.: 178]

Fourthly, as Pani (1982) argues, the reduction of the ceiling limit from 17 acres to 10 acres was largely meaningless, as the change accompanied a redefinition of a standard acre. The 1961 method was abandoned; under the new method, Classes A, B, and C, which invited lower ceilings, were defined as those lands receiving "assured irrigation from government canals and government tanks." As a result, "land which was privately irrigated received a tremendous concession" (*ibid*.: 50). Pani further argues: "a farm with the best quality of land and fully irrigated through private sources now faced a ceiling of 25 acres. This is hardly a drastic reduction from the ceiling of 27 acres by the 1961 Act."

The redefinition of what constitutes a family was another weakness of the 1974 Act. Adult sons were kept out of the definition of a family, allowing them to claim more land by claiming that they belonged to a different family. Pani points out:

> by the original legislation, a family of 10 members could own 54 acres of the best quality land irrigated through private sources. Under the 1974 legislation, on the other hand, the same family often, if it had five adult sons, could own 150 acres (25 × 6) of the best quality privately irrigated land. (*Ibid.*: 50)

To conclude, detailed studies show that the 1974 Land Reforms Act did not lead to successful implementation of land reforms in Karnataka. According to Pani, the 1974 law was "an aggressive attempt at retaining a more efficient *status quo*" (*ibid.*: 53). Damle (1989: 1905) argues that "land reform measures in Karnataka have failed to achieve the avowed ideal of creating an egalitarian agrarian society." And Kohli (1988: 178) notes:

> On balance, then, how does one assess Karnataka's land reforms? In any assessment it is important to re-emphasise that little effort has been made to appropriate and redistribute the "above ceiling" lands. The policies have focused on tenancy reform. These reforms touch a small but not insignificant proportion of the rural poor. While mildly redistributive, tenancy reforms mainly contribute to the emergence of an owner-producer mode of production. Even with reference to this issue, however, the success in Karnataka has been limited.

In spite of its many failures, however, it is a fact that the extent of implementation of tenancy reforms in Karnataka was better than in the non-Left-ruled States of the country. Thus, by the 1970s, the stage was clearly set in the State for the growth of capitalist agriculture. It is on this basis that much of the recent agricultural growth in Karnataka has progressed. However, while older, pre-capitalist forms of landlordism do not exist any longer, the starting point for modern agricultural growth in Karnataka was not the synergy of small peasant agriculture, as in a State like West Bengal. As a result, high levels of land concentration remain a reality in many regions of the State, landlessness continues to be high, and the material conditions for discrimination based on caste remain in place. The persistence of landlessness is also, in some measure, related to the massive number of tenant evictions that took place between 1956 and 1965.

## Land Distribution in Karnataka: Contemporary Period

I use two sets of data to understand the contemporary distribution of land in Karnataka. First, data for 2003–04 from the National Sample Survey Organisation (NSSO), which allow us to estimate three indicators of landlessness (see Rawal 2008). It is clear that landlessness in Karnataka by these three definitions is either close to or higher than the Indian average.

- If we define landlessness as neither owning any land other than homestead, nor cultivating owned homestead land, about 30.8 per cent of households in Karnataka were landless in 2003–04. In India as a whole, the corresponding share was 31.1 per cent.
- If we define landlessness as not owning non-homestead land, i.e. households that do not own any land other than homestead, about 40.5 per cent of households in Karnataka were landless in 2003–04. In India as a whole, the corresponding share was 41.6 per cent.
- If we define landlessness as not owning any land including homestead land, about 14.1 per cent of households in Karnataka were landless in 2003–04. In India as a whole, the corresponding share was 10 per cent.

Secondly, given the first definition above, NSSO data show that about 0.7 per cent of holdings accounted for 11 per cent of the area under ownership

**Table 2** *Distribution of ownership holdings of land by size-class, India and Karnataka, 2003–04 in per cent*

| Size-class (acres) | Karnataka | | India | |
|---|---|---|---|---|
| | Share of holdings | Share of area | Share of holdings | Share of area |
| Landless | 30.8 | 0.0 | 31.1 | 0.0 |
| Less than 1 acre | 18.0 | 1.7 | 29.8 | 5.1 |
| 1 to 2.5 acres | 22.5 | 14.4 | 19.0 | 16.9 |
| 2.5 to 5 acres | 13.9 | 19.3 | 10.7 | 20.5 |
| 5 to 7.5 acres | 6.7 | 16.2 | 4.2 | 13.9 |
| 7.5 to 12.5 acres | 5.1 | 21.0 | 3.1 | 16.6 |
| 12.5 to 25 acres | 2.3 | 16.1 | 1.6 | 15.2 |
| More than 25 acres | 0.7 | 11.4 | 0.5 | 11.8 |
| Total | 100.0 | 100.0 | 100.0 | 100.0 |

*Source*: Rawal (2008).

holdings in Karnataka in 2003–04 (Table 2). Considering all land above 12.5 acres, 3 per cent of holdings accounted for 27.5 per cent of the area under ownership holdings. If we take the corresponding criterion for India as a whole, 2.1 per cent of holdings accounted for 27 per cent of the area under ownership holdings in 2003–04.

Thirdly, data from the Agricultural Census 2005–06 indicate that there are distinct regional differences in the average size of holdings. From 1956 onwards, the northern districts of Karnataka were marked by the presence

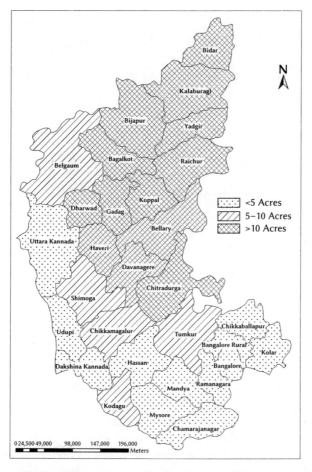

**Figure 3** *Distribution of districts by size-classes of average size of landholdings, Karnataka, 1970–71*
*Source*: Agricultural Census, Karnataka State, 1970–71.

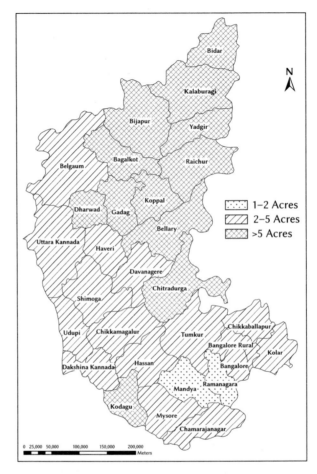

**Figure 4** *Distribution of districts by size-class of average size of landholding, Karnataka, 2005–06*
*Source*: Agricultural Census, Karnataka State, 2005–06.

of large landholdings, while the southern regions were marked by relatively small landholdings. As Figure 3 shows, in a distinct set of northern districts including Bijapur, Kalaburagi, Bellary, Raichur, Chitradurga, and Dharwad, the average size of holdings was above 10 acres in 1970–71. In the three coastal districts and southern districts of Mandya, Mysore, and Kolar, the average size of holdings was less than 5 acres. These differences are also reflected in the number of ceiling declarations the government received under the land reform laws. For example, in Bijapur, 23,470 declarations were received amounting to 12.5 lakh acres; in Raichur, 19,784 declarations were received amounting to 9.3 lakh acres; in Kalaburagi, 18,608 declarations were received amounting to 11.7 lakh acres. In contrast, in Mandya, only 2,200 declarations were received amounting to 59,325 acres; in Kolar, only 1,458 declarations were received amounting to 75,973 acres; and in Tumkur, only 2,465 declarations were received amounting to 1.5 lakh acres. These differences have persisted till now.

Between 1970–71 and 2005–06, the average size of holdings in the State as a whole came down from 8 acres to 4 acres. However, regional differences in the average size of holdings have persisted. The northern regions continue to have a higher average size of holdings than the southern regions. As Figure 4 shows, the average size of holdings was above 5 acres in the northern districts (and Coorg), while many southern districts moved down to the size-class of 2–5 acres or even less than 2 acres (as in Mandya and Ramanagara) by 2005–06.

## Distribution of Cultivators and Agricultural Labourers

There seem to be clear regional differences in the extents to which cultivators and agricultural labourers are represented in the work force of Karnataka. These also appear to be roughly correlated to the regional differences in the average size of landholdings.

Census data from 2011 show that, relatively speaking, there is a higher concentration of cultivators in the work force in the southern districts (see Figure 5). In most of the southern districts and Belgaum, the share of cultivators in the work force stood at above 40 per cent. In Mandya and Hassan districts, the share stood at above 50 per cent. In all the northern districts except Belgaum, the share of cultivators was less than 40 per cent. In Koppal, Kalaburagi, and Bidar, the share was less than 30 per cent.

On the other hand, in most northern districts, the share of agricultural labourers in the work force was above 40 per cent in 2011 (see Figure 6). In Raichur, the share stood at above 50 per cent. In most southern districts, the share of agricultural labourers in the work force was relatively low. In districts like Mandya, Hassan, Chikkamagalur, and Ramanagara, the share of agricultural labourers in the work force was less than 30 per cent.

In the two coastal districts of Dakshina Kannada and Udipi, the shares of both cultivators and agricultural labourers in the work force were the lowest in the State.

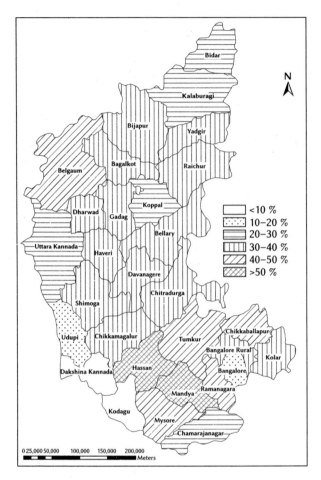

**Figure 5** *Distribution of districts by size-class of share of cultivators in work force, Karnataka, 2011*
*Source*: Census of India, 2011.

# The Spread of Irrigation

A major feature of change in the agricultural sector of Karnataka between the 1950s and 2000s was the spread of irrigation in large parts of the State. Between 1970–71 and 2011–12, the net irrigated area in the State rose from 1,137,000 hectares to 3,440,000 hectares, and the share of gross irrigated area in gross cropped area rose from 12.4 per cent to 34.3 per cent. It is important to note that much of this rise occurred after 2003–04 (see Figure

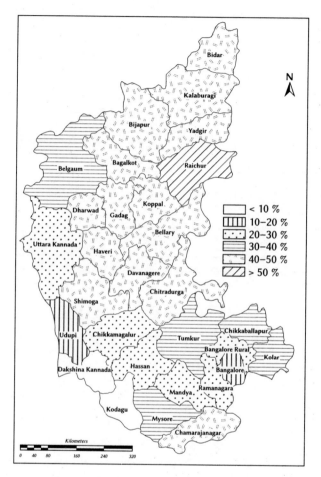

**Figure 6** *Distribution of districts by size-class of share of agricultural labourers in work force, Karnataka, 2011*
*Source*: Census of India, 2011.

7). Canals and wells were the major source for the rise in irrigated area in the 1970s, while tube wells and bore wells were the major source for the rise in irrigated area in the 2000s.

In the 1960s, the northern parts of Karnataka were dry regions with poor irrigation facilities; this was considered to be one of the reasons for the relative backwardness of the northern regions as compared to the southern regions of the State. If we look at data for 1973–74, we see that the share of net irrigated area in net sown area was 2.2 per cent in Kalaburagi, 4.3 per

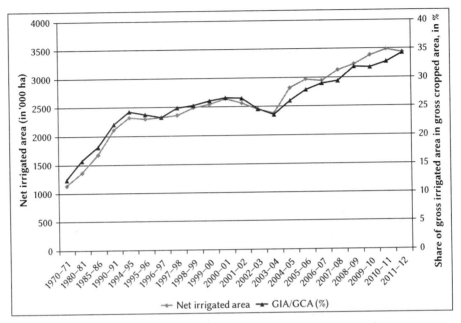

**Figure 7** *Net irrigated area, and share of gross irrigated area in gross cropped area,*
*Karnataka, 1970–71 to 2011–12* in '000 ha and per cent
*Source: Economic Survey,* various issues.

cent in Bidar, 4.7 per cent in Bijapur, 6.5 per cent in Dharwad, 9.9 per cent
in Bellary, and 12.7 per cent in Belgaum (see Figure 8). On the other hand,
the share of net irrigated area in net sown area was higher, on average, in
the southern districts of Karnataka, with some pockets of extremely well-
irrigated districts. For 1973–74, the shares were 44.2 per cent in Shimoga,
40 per cent in Dakshina Kannada, 32 per cent in Mandya, and 21 per cent in
Kolar. The districts of Shimoga and Mandya were largely irrigated by canals
from the Tungabhadra and Kaveri rivers.

By 2011–12, the situation had drastically changed. If 42.2 per cent of the
land area in the southern dry zone was irrigated, the northern dry zone was
also irrigated to the extent of 38 per cent (see Figure 9). Irrigation had also
spread significantly in the southern transition zone. The only regions that
continued to remain poorly irrigated were the north-eastern transition zone
and the northern transition zone.

In 2011–12, more than 50 per cent of land in Belgaum, Bagalkote, Bellary,

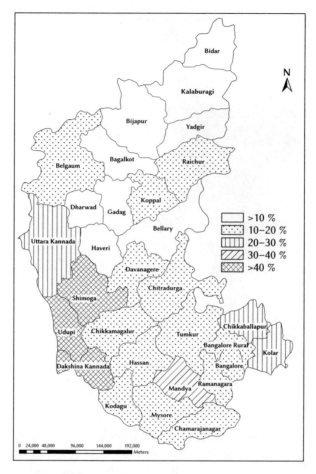

**Figure 8** *Distribution of districts by size-class of share of irrigated area in total cropped area, Karnataka, 1973–74*
*Source*: Season *and Crop Report, Karnataka, 1973–74.*

and Davanagare was irrigated (see Figures 10 and 11), and more than 40 per cent of land was irrigated in Bijapur, Yadgir, Raichur, and Koppal. Shimoga and Mandya were the best irrigated districts with shares of above 60 per cent. Some of these shifts are important: between 1973–74 and 2011–12, the share of irrigated land in Bellary rose from 9.9 per cent to 54.2 per cent; in Belgaum, it rose from 12.7 per cent to 51.7 per cent; in Bijapur, it rose from 4.7 per cent (in undivided Bijapur) to 49.7 per cent and 41.6 per cent in the

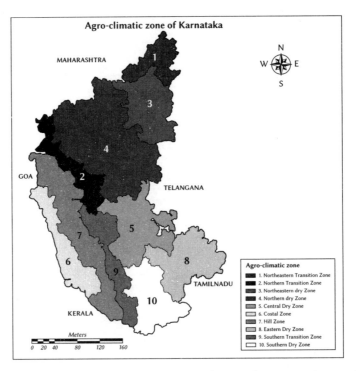

**Figure 9** *Distribution of zones by size-class of share of irrigated area in total cropped area, Karnataka, 2011–12*

newly created districts of Bagalkote and Bijapur respectively; in Raichur, it rose from 14 per cent (in undivided Raichur) to 44 per cent and 40 per cent in the newly created districts of Raichur and Koppal respectively; and in Kalaburagi, it rose from 2.2 per cent (in undivided Kalaburagi) to 39.7 per cent in the newly created district of Yadgir (though in the other new district of Kalaburagi, the share remained at 10.2 per cent).

Over the years, these shifts in the irrigation pattern have changed the face of agriculture in Karnataka. How did they take place? In 1974–75, of the gross irrigated area in the State, 39.1 per cent was drained by canals, 27.7 per cent was drained by tanks, and 24.6 per cent was drained by wells. In 2011–12, of the gross irrigated area, while 35.6 per cent was drained by canals, only 5.2 per cent was drained by tanks and 11.7 per cent by wells. At the same time, 36.3 per cent of the gross irrigated area was drained by tube wells or bore wells. *In other words, the major sources of additional irrigated area between 1974–75 and 2011–12 have been canals and tube/bore wells.*

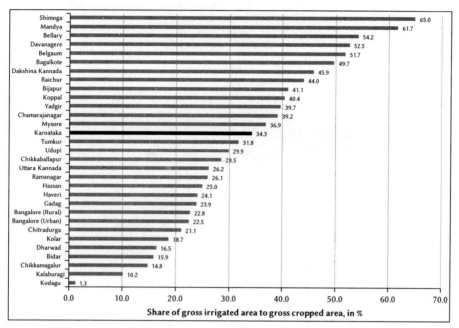

**Figure 10** *District-wise shares of gross irrigated area in gross cropped area, Karnataka, 2011–12* in per cent
*Source*: Economic Survey, 2013–14.

First, the explanation for the sharp rise in irrigated area in the northern districts of the State, such as Bagalkote, Bijapur, Yadgir, Raichur, and Koppal, appears to lie in the completion of Phases 1 and 2 of the Upper Krishna irrigation project (UKP), which was initiated in 1964. The Alamatti dam is the major reservoir of the UKP, which is located on the border of Bagalkote and Bijapur (see Figure 12). Downstream from Alamatti, there is also the Narayanpur dam. The irrigation potential of the UKP in 2011 was estimated at about 6 lakh hectares.

Secondly, the rise in irrigated area in Belgaum and Bijapur appears linked to the Ghataprabha and Malaprabha irrigation projects. As of 2013, according to claims by the government, the Ghataprabha project irrigates about 3 lakh hectares of land, and the Malaprabha dam irrigates another 2 lakh hectares in the northern region.

Thirdly, the rise in irrigated area in Shimoga, Davanagare, Bellary, and Koppal is linked to projects undertaken in the Tungabhadra sub-basin of

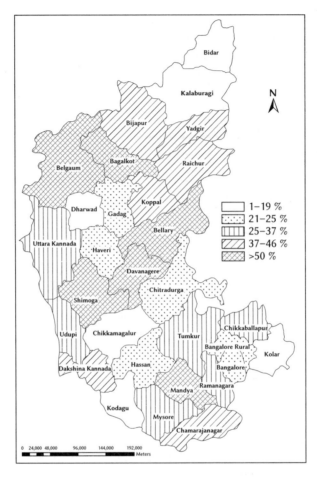

**Figure 11** *Distribution of districts by size-class of share of irrigated area in total cropped area, Karnataka, 2011–12*

the larger Krishna basin. The Tungabhadra dam (the largest reservoir) and the Bhadra dam, as well as the Tunga anicut, Bhadra anicut, Rajolibanda anicut, and Vijayanagar anicut, irrigate large areas of land in this sub-basin (see Figure 13).

Fourthly, there has been a major spread of tube wells and bore wells in Chitradurga, Tumkur, Chikkaballapur, Kolar, Bangalore Rural, and Ramanagara districts (see Figure 14). More than 86 per cent of the area irrigated in these districts in 2011–12 was through tube/bore wells. Tube/bore wells were also the major sources of irrigation in Chamarajanagar,

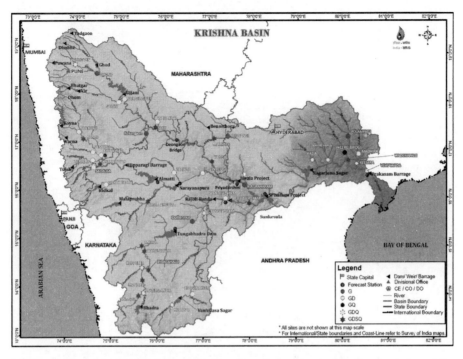

**Figure 12** *Map of the Krishna basin in Maharashtra, Karnataka, and Andhra Pradesh, and the dams therein*

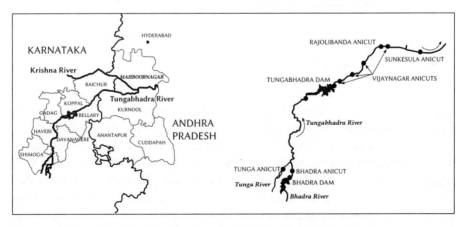

**Figure 13** *Maps of the Tungabhadra river route and the dams/anicuts therein*

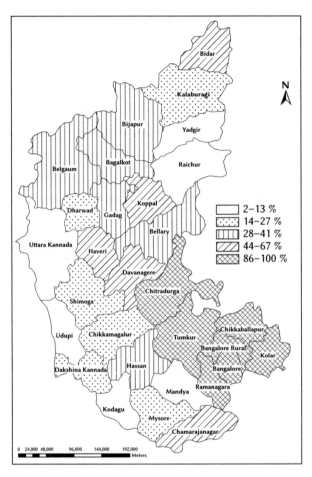

**Figure 14** *Distribution of districts by size-class of share of area irrigated by tube/bore wells in total cropped area, Karnataka, 2011–12*
*Source*: Economic Survey. 2013–14.

Davanagare, Haveri and Koppal, Bidar and Gadag districts. The increase in tube/bore wells has taken place in districts outside the best irrigated districts, historically speaking. In 2011–12, the districts in Karnataka that continued to be irrigated predominantly by canals were Raichur, Yadgir, Dharwad, Mandya, Mysore, and Coorg. It was only in Shimoga, Hassan, Chikkamagalur, and Uttara Kannada that tanks irrigated a significant extent of land. Wells remained an important source of irrigation only in Udipi, Dakshina Kannada, Bidar, Uttara Kannada, Kalaburagi, Bijapur, and Belgaum.

# Changes in the Cropping Pattern

If we examine the changes in cropping pattern in Karnataka in the context of the sharp rise in irrigated area between the 1960s and 2000s, two interesting phenomena come to light.

First, six crops – sorghum (jowar), pulses, rice, finger millet (ragi), groundnut, and cotton – occupied 82 per cent of the cropped area in the State in 1960–61. Sorghum was cultivated in about 30 per cent of the area; pulses in about 13 per cent; and rice, finger millet, and cotton in about 10 per cent each (see Table 3). In 2012–13, these six crops occupied only 65.4 per cent of the total cropped area in the State. On the one hand, there was a sharp reduction in the share of land under sorghum: a decline by 17.1 percentage points between 1960–61 and 2011–12. Further, the share of land under cotton cultivation fell from 10 per cent to 5 per cent, groundnut cultivation from 9 per cent to 6 per cent, and finger millet cultivation from

Table 3 *Share of area under major crops to total cropped area, Karnataka, 1960–61 to 2012–13 in per cent*

| Crop | Share of area under each crop (%) | | | | | |
|---|---|---|---|---|---|---|
| | 1960–61 | 1970–71 | 1980–81 | 1990–91 | 2000–01 | 2012–13 |
| Pulses | 13.1 | 14.4 | 15.3 | 16.2 | 20.5 | 22.7 |
| Pigeon pea | 3.0 | 3.0 | 3.4 | 4.6 | 5.8 | 6.6 |
| Maize | 0.1 | 0.6 | 1.6 | 2.5 | 6.7 | 13.2 |
| Rice | 10.3 | 11.7 | 11.1 | 11.7 | 14.8 | 12.8 |
| Sorghum | 29.7 | 22.2 | 19.9 | 21.6 | 12.4 | 12.6 |
| Finger millet | 10.0 | 10.7 | 10.6 | 10.6 | 10.2 | 6.5 |
| Groundnut | 9.2 | 10.3 | 7.9 | 12.1 | 10.6 | 5.9 |
| Sunflower | 0.0 | 0.0 | 0.4 | 9.0 | 4.8 | 5.1 |
| Cotton | 9.8 | 11.4 | 10.1 | 6.0 | 5.5 | 5.0 |
| Sugarcane | 0.7 | 1.0 | 1.5 | 2.7 | 4.2 | 4.3 |
| Bajra | 5.0 | 5.6 | 5.6 | 4.3 | 4.6 | 2.8 |
| Wheat | 3.3 | 3.4 | 3.2 | 2.0 | 2.7 | 2.3 |
| Sesamum | 0.6 | 0.9 | 1.2 | 1.4 | 1.0 | 0.7 |
| Small millets | 4.4 | 5.4 | 3.7 | 1.6 | 0.7 | 0.2 |
| All crops | 100.0 | 100.0 | 100.0 | 100.0 | 100.0 | 100.0 |

*Note*: The figures in the columns may not add to 100 as many minor crops have been excluded.

*Source*: Compiled from different official sources.

## Box: Cultivation of Pigeon Pea (*Arhar* or *Tur Dal*) in Karnataka

*Arhar dal* or pigeon pea, according to the World Health Organisation, is an excellent source of nutrients and plant protein, as well as a source of carbohydrates. India produces almost 73 per cent of the world's pigeon pea, followed by Myanmar (15 per cent), Kenya (3 per cent), Uganda (3 per cent), Malawi, Tanzania, and Nepal. However, India's productivity per hectare is the third lowest among the major pigeon pea-producing countries. Uganda and Myanmar (11 quintals per hectare) report the highest productivity.

According to the latest data of the Directorate of Economics and Statistics, in 2011–12, the total area under pigeon pea cultivation in India was 3.9 million hectares, which was nearly double that in 1950–51 (2 million hectares). Much of this increase took place in the 1970s and 1980s; after 1990, there has been very little increase in the area under pigeon pea cultivation, and the share of area under pigeon pea in total cultivated area has declined. Yields have been stagnant with some year to year variation. In 1950–51, the yield of pigeon pea was 8 quintals per hectare; and it was the same in 2011. There has clearly been no technological or productivity breakthrough in the cultivation of pigeon pea. The increase in total production, from 1.7 million tonnes in 1950–51 to 2.9 million tonnes in 2011 was mainly on account of changes in area cultivated.

If we were to rank the States of India based on share of pigeon pea production in total national production, Maharashtra (32 per cent) would be ranked first, followed by Karnataka (13 per cent), Madhya Pradesh (12 per cent), Uttar Pradesh (11 per cent), Gujarat (9 per cent), Andhra Pradesh (8 per cent), Jharkhand (7 per cent), and Odisha (4 per cent). So, Karnataka is the second largest pigeon pea-producing State in the country. However, average yields in Karnataka (6 quintals per hectare) were low, as compared to the higher yields in Uttar Pradesh, Jharkhand, and Gujarat (almost 10 quintals per hectare).

The five northern Karnataka districts of Kalaburagi (55 per cent), Bidar (18 per cent), Bijapur (11 per cent), Raichur (1 per cent), and Yadgir (1 per cent) accounted for almost 95 per cent of the total pigeon pea production of Karnataka (2.8 lakh tonnes) in 2009–10. Kalaburagi alone produced more than half of the State's production. Average yield, however, was the highest in Bidar (7.4 quintals per hectare), followed by Kalaburagi (4.6 quintals per hectare), Bijapur (3 quintals per hectare), and Raichur (2.8 quintals per hectare).

**Biplab Sarkar**

10 per cent to 7 per cent. On the other hand, the share of land cultivated with pulses rose from 13.1 per cent to 22.7 per cent, and rice from 10 per cent to 13 per cent. Within pulses, the area under *tur dal* (pigeon pea) rose from 3 per cent to 7 per cent.

Outside the six major crops discussed above, three changes were notable. Maize, sunflower, and sugarcane emerged as important new crops between 1960–61 and 2011–12. The area under maize cultivation rose from 0.1 per cent to 13.2 per cent, sunflower from 0 to 5.1 per cent, and sugarcane from 0.7 per cent to 4.3 per cent.

In which districts of Karnataka have the new crops been introduced?

- About 64 per cent of the area cultivated with pigeon pea in 2011–12 was in two districts of the State: Kalaburagi and Bijapur. Kalaburagi alone accounted for 42 per cent of the area cultivated with pigeon pea in 2011–12. In addition, Bidar, Yadgir, and Raichur also had limited areas under pigeon pea cultivation.
- About 52 per cent of the area cultivated with maize was in five districts: Davanagare, Belgaum, Haveri, Chitradurga, and Bellary. In addition, Bagalkote, Bijapur, and Shimoga also had limited areas under maize cultivation.
- About 71 per cent of the area cultivated with sugarcane was in three districts: Belgaum, Bagalkote, and Bijapur. Belgaum alone accounted for 44 per cent of the area cultivated with sugarcane in Karnataka in 2011–12. Mandya, Bidar, and Kalaburagi also had limited areas under sugarcane cultivation.
- About 74 per cent of the area cultivated with sunflower was in seven districts: Bijapur, Raichur, Bellary, Koppal, Gadag, Bagalkote, and Kalaburagi.

As is clear, the increase in land area cultivated with the new crops – maize, pigeon pea, sugarcane, and sunflower – has been in districts where the extent of irrigated area sharply increased between the 1970s and 2000s.

Secondly, there has been a major expansion of cultivation of horticultural crops in Karnataka in recent years. Historically, spices and plantation crops like coffee have been a major part of Karnataka agriculture. However, the more recent growth has taken place in fruit, vegetables, and commercial flowers, and not in traditional plantation crops (see also chapter 2 in this volume).

Between 2005–06 and 2010–11, the area under horticultural crops in India rose by 6.42 lakh hectares; within this, Karnataka is estimated to have ranked fifth by contributing about 57,000 hectares or 8.9 per cent. If we consider the total area under horticultural crops in Karnataka in 2008–09, about 44 per cent was cultivated with plantation crops, 23 per cent with vegetables, 18 per cent with fruit, 14 per cent with spices, and 1.5 per cent with commercial flowers. Within fruit, much of the growth was in two crops: mango and banana. In 1990–91, the area cultivated with mango and banana constituted 54.5 per cent of the total area under fruit in the State. In 2011–12, the corresponding share stood at 71 per cent. If we consider the total value

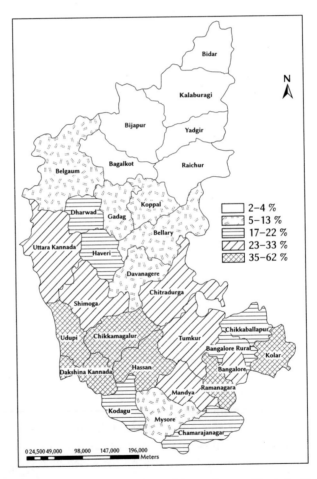

**Figure 15** *Distribution of districts by size-class of share of area cultivated with horticultural crops in the total cropped area, Karnataka, 2011–12*
*Source*: Department of Horticulture, Government of Karnataka.

of production of horticultural crops in 2008–09, 33 per cent was contributed by fruit, 32 per cent by plantation crops, 23 per cent by vegetables, 9 per cent by spices, and 3 per cent by commercial flowers.

Data provided by the Department of Horticulture in the State show that area under horticultural crops constitutes a significant share of the total cultivated area in the districts of Uttara Kannada (62.7 per cent), Kolar (50.1 per cent), Udipi (44.3 per cent), Hassan (36.9 per cent), Ramanagara (35.8 per cent), and Chikkamagalur (34.9 per cent) (see Figure 15). Area under horticultural crops does not constitute a significant share of the cropped area in the northern districts.

Despite the general shift in the cropping pattern of Karnataka in favour of high-value crops, the levels and growth in the per hectare value of agricultural production in the State remain poor by national standards. Bhalla and Singh (2010) have computed growth rates of the value of agricultural production for all composite districts of India between 1962 and 2006 (see Table 4). Their data show that, first, very few districts moved up the output-per-hectare ladder between 1962 and 2006. Secondly, in most districts, the growth rate of output appears to have declined between the period 1980–83 to 1990–93 and 1990–93 to 2003–06. Chand, Garg, and Pandey (2009) also classify most Karnataka districts under the "very low" or "low" value of production per hectare categories for the year 2004–05, as below:

Very high yield per hectare: Dakshina Kannada, Kodagu
High yield per hectare: Mandya, Shimoga, Udipi, Bangalore, Kolar
Average yield per hectare: Uttara Kannada, Mysore
Low yield per hectare: Belgaum, Chitradurga, Bellary, Chamrajnagar, Tumkur, Hassan, Devanagare, Chikmagalur
Very low yield per hectare: Bijapur, Gadag, Kalaburagi, Raichur, Bidar, Dharwad, Bagalkot, Koppal, Haveri

## Agriculture in the Macroeconomy

In 2011–12, the primary sector contributed about 16 per cent to the state domestic product (SDP) of Karnataka. In the same year, according to NSSO estimates, about 50 per cent of usual status workers in the State were employed in the primary sector. The falling share of income from agriculture, unaccompanied by a concomitant fall in the share of the work force dependent on agriculture, has led to increased pressure on land and water resources in the State.

**Table 4** *Cross-classification of districts by output growth and value of yield (output/ha) levels in per cent*

| Output/ha in the terminal year at 1990–93 prices (Rs) | Number of districts in Karnataka with output growth rate over the period at (N=19 districts): | | | |
|---|---|---|---|---|
| | More than 3.5 % | 1.5 to 3.5 % | Less than 1.5 % | All |
| Period 1: 1962–65 to 1980–83 | | | | |
| More than Rs 10,200 | 1 | 3 | 0 | 4 |
| Rs 6,250 to Rs 10,200 | 1 | 4 | 0 | 5 |
| Less than Rs 6,250 | 0 | 7 | 3 | 10 |
| Total | 2 | 14 | 3 | 19 |
| Period 2: 1980–83 to 1990–93 | | | | |
| More than Rs 10,200 | 1 | 4 | 1 | 6 |
| Rs 6,250 to Rs 10,200 | 4 | 2 | 0 | 6 |
| Less than Rs 6,250 | 3 | 3 | 1 | 7 |
| Total | 8 | 9 | 2 | 19 |
| Period 3: 1990–93 to 2003–06 | | | | |
| More than Rs 10,200 | 0 | 5 | 1 | 6 |
| Rs 6,250 to Rs 10,200 | 0 | 2 | 5 | 7 |
| Less than Rs 6,250 | 1 | 2 | 3 | 6 |
| Total | 1 | 9 | 9 | 19 |

*Source*: Bhalla and Singh (2010).

Neither the rise in irrigated area over the years nor the shift to high-value crops in the cropping pattern appears to have raised agricultural incomes in Karnataka's districts commensurate with the rise of incomes in other sectors. To illustrate this point, we may consider a simple cross-tabulation: in Table 5, the 30 districts of Karnataka have been arranged in different boxes based on two indicators, the district per capita income (PCI) and the share of agriculture in the district domestic product (ag. share) in 2011–12. These 30 districts were ranked according to the two indicators and classified into groups Q1 to Q5, each group consisting of six districts. Districts belonging to Q1 are the top six and those belonging to Q5 are the bottom six, with respect to that variable.

First, except for plantation-rich Coorg, all the districts in the top six with

**Table 5** *Cross-classification of districts based on their ranks in per capita income (PCI) and share of agriculture in district domestic product (ag. share), Karnataka, 2011–12*

| PCI/Ag. Share | Ag. Share: Q1 | Ag. Share: Q2 | Ag. Share: Q3 | Ag. Share: Q4 | Ag. Share: Q5 |
|---|---|---|---|---|---|
| PCI: Q1 | Coorg | – | – | – | Udipi, Dharwad, Bangalore (R), Bangalore (U), Dakshina Kannada |
| PCI: Q2 | Chikkamagalur | – | Kolar, Bellary | Ramanagara, Shimoga | Mysore |
| PCI: Q3 | Bagalkote | Koppal, Hassan, Davanagare | Belgaum | Uttara Kannada | – |
| PCI: Q4 | Chakkaballapur | Mandya, Bijapur | Tumkur, Kalaburagi | Gadag | – |
| PCI: Q5 | Chamaraja Nagar, Haveri | Raichur | Chitradurga | Bidar, Yadgir | – |

*Note*: Movement from Q1 to Q5 is in descending rank order.
*Source*: Computed from *Economic Survey*, 2013–14.

respect to per capita income are in the bottom six with respect to share of agriculture to district domestic product. Most districts in the top six in per capita income are either dominated by the services sector, such as Bangalore, or heavily dependent on remittances, such as Dakshina Kannada and Udupi.

Secondly, as we move from higher to lower ranks of per capita income, the number of districts with higher ranks in the share of agriculture in district domestic product increases.

Thirdly, as irrigation has greatly expanded in the northern districts, most of their respective district incomes continue to be contributed by agriculture; yet, their ranks in per capita income remain low. Examples are Kalaburagi, Bijapur, and Raichur.

These phenomena need more discussion and research than is possible within the scope of this article. Appendix 1 takes up another important sector of the agrarian economy of Karnataka, namely sericulture.

# Neoliberalism and Karnataka Agriculture:
# Two Issues for Discussion

## *Reversal of Land Reform Laws*

New economic policies in Indian agriculture are premised on a rejection of the need for a basic institutional transformation in rural areas. It is no surprise, then, that one of the most important features of these policies has been a rejection, and reversal, of state-led land reforms.

The new policies aim at a shift in India's cropping pattern from less remunerative foodgrains to high-value and export-oriented crops. Such a change in cropping pattern is to be achieved by promoting economies of scale in agriculture, allowing free leasing-in and leasing-out of land, boosting agro-processing, and facilitating the development of private post-harvest and marketing infrastructure in rural areas. The new organisation of production demands possession of large tracts of land with private firms, which was constrained by the ceilings on land possession imposed by the land reform laws. Post-1991 policies have aimed at removing the ceiling limits by amending the law to allow private firms to cultivate unlimited areas of land (see Ramachandran and Ramakumar 2000; Athreya 2003).

In a country like India with a bad track record of land reforms, the removal of land ceilings may be widely expected to encourage absentee farming by large farmers and corporations. It is also likely to reduce the extent of ceiling-surplus land while a substantial proportion of rural households remains landless.

Government of Karnataka was the first State government to actually push through a land reform amendment Bill in its Legislative Assembly in the 1990s.[1] The Bill was remarkable as a sweeping piece of counter-legislation. First, it raised the land ceiling from a range of 10–54 acres to a range of 40–216 acres. Secondly, it legalised leasing, which had been banned by the original land reform Act. The government legalised leasing in order to allow large owners to lease in from small owners. Thirdly, restrictions on the acquisition of agricultural land by "non-agricultural sources," individual or corporate, were removed. Fourthly, the Bill gave landholders wide powers to convert agricultural land to non-agricultural land. Agricultural land could now be used for industry, urban housing, educational institutions, places of worship, and for any other purpose that the government deemed to be in public interest.

---

[1] I draw liberally here from Ramachandran and Ramakumar (2000).

The amended Act was criticised by political parties of the Left in Karnataka and peasant unions for surrendering peasants' welfare to business houses, multinational corporations, private real estate developers, and private entrepreneurs in the field of higher education. The general secretary of the Karnataka Prantha Raitha Sangha said that the Act ensured "free entry" to multinational corporations. He warned that:

land prices are going to increase drastically. Small and marginal farmers will be forced to sell out, as land prices will increase while agriculture will become unremunerative because of the increase in the prices of fertilizers and seeds. This will spell disaster for the peasantry and for agriculture as a whole. (Quoted in Menon 1995).

Much of this forecast came true in the following years. In 2014, a new amendment to the land reforms law was introduced in the Karnataka Assembly that seeks to further ease the conditions for converting agricultural land to non-agricultural uses. According to a report in the *Business Standard*:

The amendment to the Act would make it easy for promoters of industries, floriculture, horticulture and agro industries or owners of educational institutions, housing projects, places of worship. They would no longer have to run from pillar to post in the government offices for conversion of the agricultural land they have purchased.

The reversal of land reforms is indeed one of the pressing issues that Karnataka agriculture faces today. This is a topic that demands more discussion.

### Persistence of Farmers' Suicides

Even as the agricultural sector of Karnataka has been registering impressive growth rates in the 2000s, these growth rates sit rather uncomfortably with the number of farmers reported to be committing suicide in the State every year. Data from the National Crime Records Bureau (NCRB) show that about 2,000 farmers annually committed suicide in the State between 1995 and 2012. Cumulatively, between these years, about 40,000 farmers have been reported to have committed suicide in Karnataka; this accounts for about 13 per cent of all farmers' suicides in India as a whole in the same period.

Why do we observe rising growth rates in agriculture, increasingly large extents of irrigated land, and shifts to high-value crops, on the one hand, and at least 2,000 farmers committing suicide every year, on the other hand? This is another topic that demands more discussion (see chapter 2).

# References

Athreya, Venkatesh (2003), "Redistributive Land Reforms in India: Some Reflections in the Current Context," paper presented at the All-India Conference on Agriculture and Rural Society in Contemporary India, Barddhaman, December 17–20.

Bhalla, G. S., and Singh, Gurmail (2010), *Growth of Indian Agriculture: A District Level Study*, Final Report on Planning Commission Project, Centre for the Study of Regional Development, Jawaharlal Nehru University, New Delhi.

Chand, Ramesh, Garg, Sanjeev, and Pandey, Lalmani (2009), *Regional Variations in Agricultural Productivity: A District Level Study*, National Professor Project, National Centre for Agricultural Economics and Policy Research, Indian Council of Agricultural Research, New Delhi.

Damle, C. B. (1989), "Land Reforms Legislation in Karnataka: Myth of Success," *Economic and Political Weekly*, 24 (33), August 19, pp. 1896–1906.

Karanth, G. K. (1995), *Change and Continuity in Agrarian Relations*, Concept Publishing House, New Delhi.

Kohli, Atul (1988), *The State and Poverty in India: The Politics of Reform*, Cambridge University Press, Cambridge.

Lakshman, T. K., Ramadas, K. L., and Kanthi, Mahendra S. (1973), "Land Ceilings in Karnataka: A Case Study," *Economic and Political Weekly*, 8 (39), September 29, pp. A111–A115.

Menon, Parvathi (1995), "Acting for Change: Amendments to the Karnataka Land Reforms Act," *Frontline*, Chennai, December 15, pp. 39–41.

Pani, Narendar (1982), "Legislating against Fundamental Change: Land Legislation in Karnataka," *Social Scientist*, 10 (8), August, pp. 45–54.

Planning Commission (1966), Implementation of Land Reforms: A Review by the Land Reforms Implementation Committee of the National Development Council, Government of India, New Delhi.

Rajan, M. A. S. (1979), *Land Reforms in Karnataka*, Hindustan Publishing Corporation, New Delhi.

Ramachandran, V. K., and Ramakumar, R. (2000), "Agrarian Reforms and Rural Development Policies in India: A Note," paper presented at the International Conference on Agrarian Reform and Rural Development, Government of the Philippines and the Philippines Development Academy, Tagaytay City, Philippines, December 5–8.

Thimmaiah, G., and Aziz, Abdul (1983), "The Political Economy of Land Reforms in Karnataka: A South Indian State," *Asian Survey*, 23 (7), July, pp. 810–29.

## Appendix

# A Note on Sericulture in Karnataka

### *Yoshifumi Usami*

India is the second largest producer of raw silk in the world. In 2011, raw silk production in India was 23,000 tonnes, accounting for 17.5 per cent of world production (131,500 tonnes). China's raw silk production was 104,000 tonnes, accounting for 79.1 per cent of world production. India produces four varieties of silk, namely, mulberry, *tasar*, *eri* and *muga*. Mulberry silk production is the highest, accounting for 73.5 per cent (19,476 tonnes) of total silk production. Karnataka, Andhra Pradesh, Tamil Nadu, and West Bengal are the major Indian States producing mulberry silk. The leading States in the production of non-mulberry silk are Jharkhand and Chhattisgarh (*tasar*), Assam and other North-Eastern States (*eri* and *muga*).

Figure 1 shows the production, imports, and prices of raw silk in India during the last 25 years. As domestic production of raw silk lagged behind the demand, which grew due to the growth in export from the mid-1990s, the import of raw silk from China increased. In addition, a decline in raw silk production due to droughts in 2002 and 2003 gave an impetus to the import of raw silk from China. The import of Chinese raw silk reached 9,200 tonnes, accounting for 40 per cent of total domestic supplies, in 2003. Availability of a large quantity of better quality raw silk at low prices depressed the local market price, as shown in Figure 1. The price of raw silk was more than Rs 1,000 per kg (at 1993–94 prices) during the mid-1990s, but it fell to less than Rs 600 per kg in 2002. Cocoon prices, which are closely tied to raw silk prices, fell to Rs 97.25 per kg in 2002–03 from Rs 130 per kg in 2001–02.

The fall in raw silk and cocoon prices seriously affected sericulture farms and the reeling industry. The Indian government imposed an anti-dumping duty on raw silk (of 2A and below) in 2003 to protect domestic producers of raw silk. (This duty has been extended twice, up to 2014.) To cope with the anti-dumping duty on raw silk, China started increasing exports of silk yarn and silk fabrics; and the anti-dumping duty was again imposed on Chinese silk fabrics in 2006. (This duty too has been extended, up to 2016.) As a result of these policy interventions, the import of raw silk started decreasing and the fall in real prices of raw silk was controlled. The prices of raw silk in real terms started rising from a trough of Rs 507 per kg in 2008–09. Mulberry raw silk production also gradually increased to reach 20,000 tonnes in 2013–14.

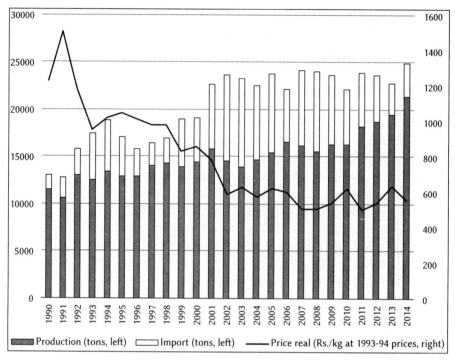

**Figure 1** *Production, imports, and prices of raw silk, 1990–2014*
Source: Central Silk Board, *Compendium of Statistics of Silk Industry*, 1999; Central Silk
Board, *Sericulture and Silk Industry Statistics*, 2007 and 2012; and Central Silk Board,
*Annual Report*, 2012–13 and 2013–14.

Karnataka is the largest producer of mulberry raw silk in India, followed
by Andhra Pradesh, West Bengal, and Tamil Nadu. Table 1 shows the area
under mulberry, production of reeling cocoons, and raw silk in the major
mulberry silk producing States. Karnataka produced 55,900 tonnes of
mulberry reeling cocoons in 2011–12, accounting for 40 per cent of 139,800
tonnes of total production, followed by Andhra Pradesh (51,100 tonnes). In
recent years, cocoon production in Karnataka has declined much below the
peak level of 80,000 tonnes in 2001–02 because of a large fall in mulberry
area. The area under mulberry has been subject to substantial fluctuations,
mainly due to monsoon conditions: the area under mulberry was 116,000
hectares in 2001–02, and it fell to less than 80,000 hectares in 2002–03 and
2003–04. It is argued that about 30 per cent of the area under mulberry was

**Table 1** *Area under mulberry, and production of reeling cocoon and raw silk in hectares and tonnes*

| year | Area under Mulberry (ha) | | | | Production of Reeling Cocoons (tonnes) | | | | Production of Raw silk (tonnes) | | | |
|---|---|---|---|---|---|---|---|---|---|---|---|---|
| | Karnataka | Andhra Pradesh | Tamil Nadu | Total | Karnataka | Andhra Pradesh | Tamil Nadu | Total | Karnataka | Andhra Pradesh | Tamil Nadu | Total |
| 1999–00 | 120,119 | 44,641 | 10,953 | 227,151 | 68,920 | 34,194 | 6,383 | 124,531 | 8,121 | 3,757 | 672 | 13,944 |
| 2000–01 | 112,557 | 48,442 | 11,060 | 215,921 | 66,518 | 37,651 | 6,400 | 124,663 | 8,200 | 4,183 | 711 | 14,432 |
| 2001–02 | 116,158 | 52,225 | 13,096 | 232,076 | 73,860 | 42,982 | 5,882 | 139,616 | 8,728 | 4,775 | 655 | 15,842 |
| 2002–03 | 88,903 | 54,384 | 5,394 | 194,463 | 55,851 | 50,664 | 4,005 | 128,181 | 6,760 | 5,629 | 490 | 14,617 |
| 2003–04 | 79,778 | 57,231 | 4,025 | 185,120 | 44,652 | 54,304 | 2,124 | 117,471 | 5,949 | 6,054 | 285 | 13,970 |
| 2004–05 | 77,998 | 44,885 | 5,073 | 171,959 | 54,210 | 45,453 | 3,101 | 120,027 | 7,302 | 5,084 | 443 | 14,620 |
| 2005–06 | 87,734 | 39,533 | 6,614 | 179,065 | 55,493 | 48,024 | 5,225 | 126,261 | 7,471 | 5,375 | 739 | 15,445 |
| 2006–07 | 97,647 | 42,458 | 10,043 | 191,893 | 58,697 | 49,350 | 7,931 | 135,462 | 7,883 | 5,526 | 1,125 | 16,525 |
| 2007–08 | 91,434 | 35,180 | 15,148 | 184,928 | 60,796 | 40,068 | 17,415 | 132,039 | 8,240 | 4,485 | 1,660 | 16,245 |
| 2008–09 | 77,329 | 33,325 | 15,563 | 177,943 | 53,377 | 40,157 | 16,352 | 124,838 | 7,238 | 4,492 | 1,809 | 15,610 |
| 2009–10 | 82,098 | 36,384 | 14,220 | 183,773 | 54,282 | 45,858 | 8,588 | 131,661 | 7,360 | 5,119 | 1,233 | 16,322 |
| 2010–11 | 62,697 | 37,010 | 12,545 | 170,314 | 52,709 | 48,105 | 8,157 | 130,714 | 7,338 | 5,161 | 1,182 | 16,360 |
| 2011–12 | 70,958 | 40,314 | 13,557 | 181,089 | 55,957 | 51,186 | 17,274 | 139,871 | 7,796 | 6,447 | 1,924 | 18,272 |
| 2012–13 | | | | 186,015 | | | | 144,434 | 8,219 | 6,550 | 1,185 | 18,715 |
| 2013–14 | | | | 203,023 | | | | 142,487 | 8,574 | 6,911 | 1,120 | 19,476 |
| 2014–15 | | | | 219,819 | | | | 159,259 | | | | 21,390 |

*Source:* Same as Figure 1.

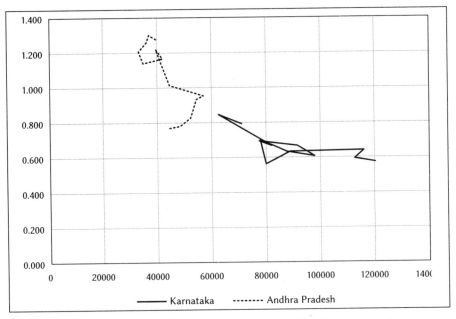

**Figure 2** *Relationship between mulberry area and cocoon yield in Karnataka and Andhra Pradesh*
*Source:* Same as Figure 1.

abandoned due to severe droughts during 2002–04. Mulberry area recovered to some extent by 2006–07, but fell again over the next few years and in another drought year, 2010–11.

Similarly, cocoon production has fluctuated, though modestly, in recent years. Raw silk production in Karnataka stood at 8,574 tonnes in 2013–14, almost the same level (8,728 tonnes) as in 2001–02. This indicates an improvement in cocoon yield and renditta (kg of cocoon per kg of raw silk). The cocoon yield per hectare of mulberry area was 0.64 tonne in 2001–02 and it rose to 0.79 tonne in 2011–12. Renditta also improved from 8.46 to 7.18 during the same period. To sum up, while the area under mulberry fell during the last decade, production of mulberry raw silk fell in 2003–04 but recovered in 2013–14 to the same level as at the turn of the century on account of improved yields.

Figure 2 shows the change in mulberry area and cocoon yield in Karnataka and Andhra Pradesh from 1999 to 2011. It is evident that cocoon yield in Karnataka was much below that in Andhra Pradesh (and Tamil Nadu). Interestingly, the figure shows a sort of inverse relationship between

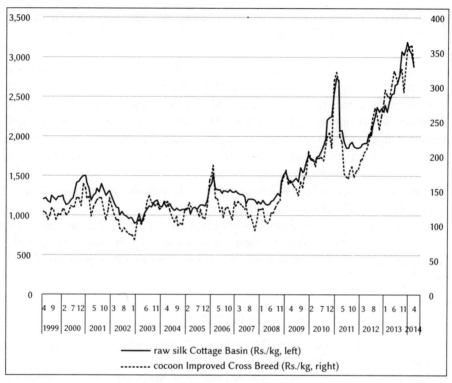

**Figure 3** *Prices of reeling cocoon and raw silk* in Rs per kg
*Note:* Reeling cocoon refers to Improved Crossbreed at Ramanagaram; raw silk refers to Cottage Basin at Bangalore Silk Exchange.
*Source:* Same as Figure 1.

changes in mulberry area and cocoon yield. The decrease in mulberry area in a drought year was accompanied by a rise in cocoon yield in the same or next year. Similarly, an increase in mulberry area was accompanied by a fall in cocoon yield. This inverse relationship suggests that farms in unirrigated areas and hence with lower yields abandoned sericulture in a period of drought, and, as a result, cocoon yield at an aggregated state level appears to have risen. (A similar relation could be observed in Andhra Pradesh as well.)

These data suggest that there existed a substantial gap between potential and actual farm level productivity. The situation, however, seems to have changed, although this cannot be confirmed for area under mulberry and cocoon production because state-level data are not available for recent years. However, raw silk production in Karnataka has increased during the last four to five years, as shown in Table 1, suggesting an improvement in productivity at the farm level. Farmers engaged in sericulture responded positively to prices (Lakshmanan 2007) and are supposed to have adopted improved techniques during the recent period of rise in prices (Figure 3). The monthly prices of raw silk and cocoon have shown an upsurge since 2008–09, when import of raw silk from China started decreasing. Though seasonal fluctuations are large, it appears that the price of raw silk rose substantially in real terms, and that sericulture farms responded to profitability by adopting recommended technologies. It is also noteworthy that the production of bivoltine raw silk in Karnataka more than doubled from 364 tonnes in 2011–12 to 808 tonnes in 2013–14.

Based on this quick analysis of secondary data, I argue that sericulture in Karnataka has withstood hardships brought about by monsoon failure and dumping (import) of Chinese raw silk, and has begun a new phase of steady growth.

# References

Government of Karnataka (2004), "Sericulture and Silk Filatures," *Revenue Reforms Commission Final Report*, Chapter 4, Bangalore.

Lakshmanan S. (2007), "Yield Gaps in Mulberry Sericulture in Karnataka: An Econometric Analysis," *Indian Journal of Agricultural Economics*, vol. 62, no. 4, pp. 623–36.

# 2

# Agrarian Crisis and Farmer Suicides in Karnataka[1]

T.N. Prakash Kammardi, H. Chandrashekar, K.J. Parameshwarappa,
Harsha V. Torgal, Gireesh P. S., Mali Patil Vijay Kumar, Nagendra

## Background

During the last six-and-a-half decades after Independence, one visible achievement of Indian agriculture at the macro level has been in terms of achieving a surplus in the production of several crops, and large buffer stocks of rice and wheat. While the success of Indian agriculture in achieving self-sufficiency in food production is widely acknowledged, the various risks and uncertainties that undermine the stability and predictability of incomes of farmers have not drawn equal attention from policy makers. The country is yet to ensure its farmers a decent standard of living by means of assured and adequate incomes.

The returns from agriculture have declined due to a variety of reasons, such as increase in cost of production, inadequate market mechanism, unremunerative prices, weak government intervention, and unsustainability of productive systems due to fall in water table, decline of soil fertility, occurrence of pests and diseases, and so on (Prakash 2011). All these have adversely affected the farm economy, and have manifested in agrarian crises and the occurrence of farmers' suicides in different parts of India. In the state of Karnataka the agrarian crisis has become very severe in recent years, as a result of which farmers' suicides have risen to alarming levels. The next section of this chapter analyses the data on farmer suicides in Karnataka in 2015, as reported by the Department of Agriculture of the Government of Karnataka.

[1] The views expressed in this chapter do not reflect the views of Karnataka Agriculture Prices Commission.

## Farmers' Suicides in Karnataka

Farmers' suicides are not a new phenomenon in Karnataka. Nonetheless, there has been a startling rise in the deaths of peasants due to suicide in the State in the year 2015. As of December 2015, as per the data maintained by the State Department of Agriculture, nearly 1,000 farmers had committed suicide in Karnataka. Suicide is a multifaceted and complex phenomenon, and the factors associated with it are both psycho-neurobiological and socio-economic (Mishra 2007). In this chapter, an attempt is made to analyse the socio-economic as well as environmental background of farmers who committed suicide in Karnataka during the calendar year of 2015.

For convenience of analysis, the state of Karnataka is divided into five broad agro-ecological regions: viz., Old Mysore, Coastal and Malnad region, and the parts of the State falling under Central, Mumbai, and Hyderabad regions. These five regions have clearly discernable agro-ecological and socio-cultural features.

An analysis of the data reveals that Old Mysore accounts for the largest proportion (27 per cent) of suicides that occurred in the State in 2015 (Table 1). In fact, suicides were first reported in the Old Mysore region among farmers cultivating sugarcane, farmers who are well endowed with irrigation facilities and technology, and also receive a high degree of government support in terms of minimum support price and procurement price. The Hyderabad and Central Karnataka regions, which are relatively less developed, accounted for 21 per cent and 20 per cent, respectively, of suicides during 2015. Surprisingly, the Coastal and Malnad (hilly) region, which is considered to be relatively well developed in terms of income, literacy, and other parameters, as well as endowed with rich natural resources, accounted for 15 per cent of the total number of farmers' suicides that took place in the State during 2015. The remaining 17 per cent of suicides occurred in the Mumbai region of Karnataka. In short, farmers' suicides in 2015 were widely spread across the regions of the State, though they were first reported in the Old Mysore region.

The distribution of farmers' suicides across the regions of Karnataka has remained more or less the same over the years. The Expert Committee appointed by the Government of Karnataka, headed by Dr G. K. Veeresh, which submitted its report in April 2002, pointed out a similar distribution of farmers' suicides prior to 2003 (Table 1). As per the Veeresh Committee report, the Old Mysore region stood first, accounting for around 27 per cent of farmers' suicides that occurred between 1996 and 2003, followed by the

**Table 1** *Region-wise distribution of farmers' suicides, 1996–2003 and 2015* in number and per cent

| Region | District | 1996–2003 | | 2015 | |
|---|---|---|---|---|---|
| | | Number | Per cent | Number | Per cent |
| Old Mysore | Tumkur, Kolara, Bangalore Urban, Bangalore Rural, Mandya, Mysore, Chamarajanagar, Ramnagar, Chikballapur | 2991 | 27 | 265 | 27 |
| Central Karnataka | Gadag, Haveri, Chitradurga, Davanagere | 2078 | 19 | 192 | 20 |
| Hyderabad Karnataka | Kalaburagi, Bidar, Raichur, Koppal Bellary, Yadgir | 1417 | 13 | 208 | 21 |
| Malnad and Coastal Karnataka | Uttara Kannada, Shimoga, Udupi Chikmagalur, Hassan, Kodagu, Dakshina Kannada, | 2902 | 26 | 145 | 15 |
| Mumbai Karnataka | Belgaum, Bagalkote, Bijapur, Dharwad | 1669 | 15 | 168 | 17 |
| Overall | | 11,057 | 100 | 978 | 100 |

*Source:* Veeresh Committee Report (2002) and Department of Agriculture.

Malnad and Coastal region (26 per cent), and Central Karnataka (19 per cent). An unasked question is why the Malnad and Coastal region, which is socio-economically well developed and endowed with rich natural resources, witnessed a larger number of suicides than the relatively backward regions of Central and Hyderabad?

An analysis of the cropping patterns of farmers who committed suicide reveals that nearly 44 per cent of the victim-farmers were growing commercial and vegetable crops, and another one-third were cultivating cereal crops. Farmers growing sugarcane and cotton together accounted for 22 per cent of total suicides in 2015. Farmers growing pulses, oilseeds, plantation crops, and fruit crops too committed suicide, and accounted for around 22 per cent of total suicides in the state (Table 2). It is disturbing to note that there was increasing occurrence of suicides among farmers who were socio-economically better off, growing market-oriented commercial crops with assured irrigation.

In the Old Mysore region, more than half of suicide-victim farmers had grown commercial crops like sugarcane and vegetables, and 26 per cent had grown cereal crops. On the other hand, in the Central Karnataka region, 44

**Table 2** *Cropping patterns among suicide-victim farmers, by region, 2015* in per cent

| Region | Crop | | | | | |
|--------|---------|--------|----------|---------------------------------|------------------------------|-----|
| | Cereals | Pulses | Oilseeds | Commercial Crops and Vegetables | Plantation Crops and Fruits | All |
| Old Mysore | 26 | 2 | 5 | 56 | 11 | 100 |
| Central Karnataka | 44 | 3 | 11 | 40 | 2 | 100 |
| Hyderabad Karnataka | 30 | 25 | 8 | 36 | 1 | 100 |
| Malnad and Coastal Karnataka | 56 | 0 | 4 | 24 | 17 | 100 |
| Mumbai Karnataka | 16 | 13 | 10 | 57 | 3 | 100 |
| Overall | 33 | 8 | 7 | 44 | 7 | 100 |

*Note*: Commercial crops include sugarcane, cotton, tobacco, and mulberry.

per cent of suicide victims had grown cereals, and an equal proportion had grown commercial and vegetable crops. Oilseed-growing farmers accounted for 11 per cent of suicides in the region. In the Hyderabad Karnataka region, one-fourth of victim farmers had also grown pulses. Red gram is a major pulse crop of the region, often affected by drought and pest attacks.

In the Coastal region, surprisingly, the majority of farmers who committed suicide were growing cereal crops. Though plantation and fruit crops are relatively less vulnerable to fluctuations in yield and price, 17 per cent of plantation crop farmers also succumbed to suicide. In the Mumbai Karnataka region, 57 per cent of farmers who committed suicide had grown commercial and vegetable crops, and the remaining 40 per cent had grown cereals, pulses, and oilseed crops.

Thus, while at the aggregate level it appears that farmers cultivating commercial crops became easy victims of suicide, trends at the regional level were different. In the Old Mysore region, farmers who committed suicide cultivated commercial and vegetable crops, but also cereals. In the Malnad and Coastal region, farmers who committed suicide mainly cultivated cereals, followed by commercial crops and vegetables. It is distressing to note that in addition to farmers cultivating commercial and vegetable crops, cereal farmers also took the unfortunate decision to end their lives.

In the year 2000, as shown by the Veeresh Committee report, cereals like jowar, maize, and paddy were the main crops cultivated by farmers who had succumbed to suicide. In fact, the phenomenon of suicides began

**Table 3** *Size-class distribution of landholdings among suicide-victim farmers, 2015* in number and per cent

| Sl. No. | Size-class | Number | Per cent |
|---------|------------|--------|----------|
| 1 | Marginal (< 1 ha) | 415 | 42 |
| 2 | Small (1 to 2 ha) | 277 | 28 |
| 3 | Medium (2 to 4 ha) | 123 | 13 |
| 4 | Big (> 4 ha) | 53 | 5 |
| 5 | No land / Information Not Available | 110 | 11 |
| All | | 978 | 100 |

during the late 1990s among farmers growing red gram in the Hyderabad Karnataka region. The deadly pest *Heliothis bollworm* had destroyed their crop, and was seen as the main culprit at that time.

The changes in cropping patterns among suicide-victim farmers in the different agro-ecological regions of Karnataka deserve further investigation. Data on the size-class of landholdings of suicide-victim farmers are presented in Table 3. It is clear that the problem of suicides mainly affected marginal and small farmers, who accounted for nearly 70 per cent of the total number of suicide cases recorded in 2015. Medium and big farmers accounted for 13 per cent and 5 per cent, respectively, of suicide cases. The pattern was different during 2000, when almost 50 per cent of the suicide victims had landholdings of between 2 and 10 hectares, and an average holding of 5.44 hectares (Government of Karnataka 2002).

The observation that small and marginal farmers predominated among the suicide victims is cause for concern to all those who are interested in the equitable development of agriculture in Karnataka.

Table 4 shows the major crops grown across size-classes by the suicide-victim farmers. Commercial crops like sugarcane, cotton, and vegetables were the common predominant crops across size-classes of landholdings. Of course, it must be noted that in Karnataka, farmers are shifting their crop pattern from traditional food crops towards commercial and horticulture crops. Though this may be a good sign from the point of view of modernizing and commercializing agriculture, it increases the vulnerability of farmers as they have to depend more on the market (for supply of inputs and for remunerative prices). This vulnerability is likely to be greater among small and marginal farmers who have taken up cultivation of commercial and vegetable crops.

**Table 4** *Major crops grown by size-class of landholding among suicide-victim farmers, 2015* in per cent of cropped area

| Size-class of landholdings | Share of Gross Cropped Area | | | | | Total |
|---|---|---|---|---|---|---|
| | Cereals | Pulses | Oilseeds | Commercial crops and Vegetables | Plantation and Fruit crops | |
| Marginal (< 1 ha) | 36 | 8 | 5 | 44 | 7 | 100 |
| Small (1 to 2 ha) | 31 | 8 | 6 | 47 | 8 | 100 |
| Medium (2 to 4 ha) | 31 | 11 | 12 | 38 | 8 | 100 |
| Big (> 4 ha) | 25 | 10 | 18 | 45 | 3 | 100 |

An attempt was made to analyse the age distribution of farmers who committed suicide (Table 5). The results of the analysis showed that although the suicide victims were distributed across all age-groups, there was a large concentration in the age-group of 31 to 60 years, with nearly 75 per cent of the victims belonging to this age-group. Farmers below 30 years accounted for 11 per cent of total suicides, while 10 per cent were above 60 years. These results reinforce the findings of earlier studies, which concluded that middle-aged farmers were more prone to suicide as this was an age-group responsible for making a good number of decisions not only pertaining to farming, but also to social obligations such as marriage and education of their children (Deshpande 2002). Middle-aged farmers may be more vulnerable to external stresses and shocks, and the inability to cope with these may push them to suicide.

The literature on agrarian distress points to indebtedness as the foremost proximate cause of suicide among farmers in India (Desphande and Prabhu 2005). Data from the National Sample Survey (NSS) 59th Round show that nearly one-half of farming households in the country were indebted, and with significant liabilities. Further, more than 70 per cent of farmers who owned less than 2 hectares of land were indebted.

Farmers availed credit from both formal and informal sources. Formal sources included commercial banks, regional rural banks, cooperative societies, and other financial institutions like new generation banks. Informal sources of credit were local moneylenders, commission agents, traders, relatives, and friends. Data on indebtedness show that the majority of suicide-victim farmers had borrowed from multiple sources (Table 6). Commercial banks and regional rural banks (RRBs), two important formal credit institutions, accounted for half of the loans of the suicide-victim

**Table 5** *Age distribution of suicide-victim farmers, 2015* in number and per cent

| Age-group | Number | Per cent |
|-----------|--------|----------|
| 20–30 | 109 | 11 |
| 31–40 | 252 | 26 |
| 41–50 | 284 | 29 |
| 51–60 | 219 | 22 |
| 61–70 | 91 | 9 |
| > 70 | 14 | 1 |
| Not known | 9 | 1 |
| All | 978 | 100 |

**Table 6** *Number and proportion of indebted suicide-victim farmers, by source of credit*

| Institution | Number | Per cent |
|-------------|--------|----------|
| Commercial banks | 274 | 28 |
| Regional rural banks | 190 | 19 |
| Cooperative banks | 53 | 5 |
| Cooperative societies | 141 | 14 |
| Private financial institutions | 46 | 5 |
| Moneylenders | 127 | 13 |
| No loan | 87 | 9 |
| Information not available | 60 | 6 |
| All | 978 | 100 |

farmers. Farmers who had not borrowed from any source accounted for only 9 per cent of the victims. Cooperative societies and cooperative banks were not a major source of finance for suicide victims. Moneylenders provided loans to 13 per cent of the victim farmers. However, loans taken from unauthorised rural moneylenders may have been concealed for fear of legal action, and hence full information in this regard was not readily available.[1] In fact, as per the available evidence, there are instances of marginal farmers with outstanding loans of a few lakh rupees borrowed from different sources including local moneylenders.

Farmers were in a debt crisis because of multiple factors: crop failure due to drought and natural calamities, a crash in prices, and delayed payments

---

[1] These are data collected by the Department of Agriculture.

(in the case of sugarcane farmers). When they became defaulters of sources of institutional credit and were left with no alternative, they borrowed from non-institutional sources including private moneylenders.

## Genesis of Agrarian Crisis

The present crisis faced by the farmers of Karnataka is on account of technological, ecological, institutional, and socio-economic factors. The State has not experienced a significant breakthrough in the productivity of many crops, and there is an urgent need to break yield barriers. Farmers need to be encouraged to shift from resource-depleting technologies to resource-augmenting technologies. Depletion of natural resources is taking place at a much faster pace than in earlier years. Unscientific use of water in command areas has resulted in an increase of saline and alkaline patches in these areas, besides denying water to farmers at the tail-end of the command. Groundwater exploitation is taking place at an alarming rate without much attention being paid to recharging groundwater. Almost 60 per cent of the arable land is affected by soil erosion, alkalinity, salinity, and other problems. Loss of bio-diversity and soil degradation have further exacerbated the situation. Agriculture is becoming more and more knowledge-driven, and existing institutions are not in a position to cope with the situation. There is a growing gap between scientific know-how and field-level "do-how." Fragmented holdings, increase in input prices, reduced ability of farmers to invest in future growth, lack of proximity to output markets, asymmetric information, and reduced investment by the public sector have resulted in a decline in the profitability of agricultural enterprises. Thus, the current agrarian crisis has its origin in several problems and impediments that Karnataka agriculture has experienced in recent years (Prakash *et al.* 2013). Here, we elaborate on two of these: the shifts in cropping pattern and the profitability of crop cultivation.

## Shifts in Cropping Pattern

From 2005–06 to 2014–15, the area under agriculture crops in Karnataka registered a decline of 11 per cent, while the area under horticulture crops registered an increase of 19 per cent. The details are given in Appendix Tables 1 and 2, and Figure 1.

Among cereal crops, except for maize which registered an area increase of 43 per cent, all the other crops – viz., paddy, sorghum, finger millet,

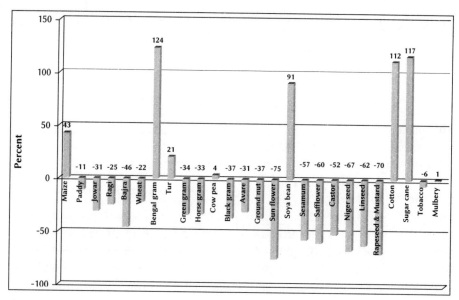

**Figure 1** *Decadal change in area under agricultural crops in Karnataka, 2005–06 to 2014–15*

bajra, and other millets – experienced a decline in area during this period. In respect of pulses, except for Bengal gram, pigeon pea, and cowpea, all the other pulse crops showed a decline in area during the same period. The area under Bengal gram more than doubled (to 124 per cent), from 4.18 lakh hectares to 9.39 lakh hectares. There was a drastic reduction, of 52 per cent, in the area under oilseeds: the area under oilseeds was around 28.63 lakh hectares in 2005–06 and it declined to 13.72 lakh hectares in 2014–15.

In addition to maize, there was a phenomenal increase in the area under cotton and sugarcane. The area under cotton increased from 4.13 lakh hectares in 2005–06 to 8.76 lakh hectares in 2014–15, registering an increase of 112 per cent. Similarly, the area under sugarcane nearly doubled, from 2.21 lakh hectares to 5.80 lakh hectares, during the decade.

In horticulture, almost all crops except potato, dry chilli, and spices exhibited a phenomenal increase in area over the last decade. As a group, fruit crops showed an increase of 58 per cent, followed by plantation crops (17 per cent) and vegetables (15 per cent). Arecanut (40 per cent), mango (51 per cent), banana (89 per cent), tomato (47 per cent), and onion (11 per cent) were the major horticulture crops that registered high growth in absolute area during the last decade (see Figure 2).

The changes in cropping pattern indicate an expansion of market-

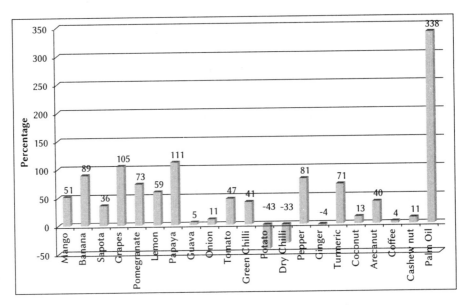

**Figure 2** *Decadal change in area under horticultural crops in Karnataka, 2005–06 to 2014–15*

dependent crops: viz., maize, Bengal gram, pigeon pea, soyabean, cotton, sugarcane, and horticulture crops. Some of these crops, including maize, cotton, sugarcane, and oilseeds, are tied to and are affected by global markets. Price volatility is also important for horticulture crops.

## Yield Gap and Extension Failure

Yield gap or sub-optimal yield as compared to potential yield is a bottleneck that needs immediate attention. Yield gaps may be caused by multiple factors: for instance, inadequate R&D efforts, improper extension services, inadequate irrigation and infrastructure, and inefficiency in delivering credit, agro-inputs and services to farmers. Figure 3 depicts yield gap, taken as the difference between potential yields that can be realised through scientific methods of farming as prescribed in "package of practices" of State Agricultural Universities, and actual yields realised by farmers in the case of principal agricultural and horticultural crops, during 2009–10 (Prakash *et al.* 2013). The figure shows that farmers cultivating major field crops were not able to achieve even 50 per cent of the potential yield in Karnataka.

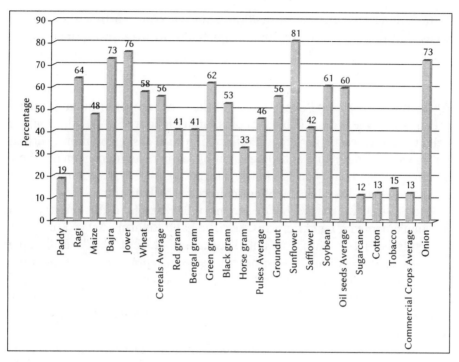

**Figure 3** *Yield gap in principal agricultural and horticultural crops of Karnataka, 2009–10*

## Unremunerative Agriculture

This section draws on the report titled *Assured Prices and Stable Market for Principal Agriculture and Horticulture Crops in the State*, submitted by the Karnataka Agriculture Price Commission in December 2015. In this report, cost of cultivation was estimated for 15 crops – paddy, sorghum, finger millet, maize, pearl millet, pigeon pea, Bengal gram, groundnut, sunflower, soybean, tomato, onion, potato, dry chilli, and cotton – for the year 2014–15. Within paddy, high-yielding varieties (HYV) and rainfed paddy were taken separately; similarly, hybrid sorghum and local (*Maldandi*) sorghum were taken separately. Thus the total number of crops were 17, and these together accounted for 72 per cent of net sown area in Karnataka. This exercise thus throws light on the economic conditions of a majority of farmers of the State. The results are summarised in Table 7.

To estimate the cost of cultivation, paid-out costs, such as the costs of seeds, fertilizers, labour, etc., that are actually incurred by farmers, were taken into account. Besides, direct cash payments, depreciation on machinery and farm buildings, and interest on working capital were also included. While declaring the minimum support price (MSP), the Commission for Agricultural Costs and Prices (CACP) of the Government of India normally calculates all these costs (Cost A1) plus family labour (FL). In addition, we need to include costs that are not reflected in such cost estimations, such as rental value of own land and time spent by farmers on management. There are termed opportunity costs. Hence, total cost (Cost C3) is a comprehensive cost that reflects the viability of agriculture in the long run.

The State of Karnataka is one among a few States in the country that has implemented a Land Reforms Act. The Land Reforms Act of Karnataka prohibits both the leasing-in and leasing-out of land. While estimating the cost of cultivation using different cost concepts, the CACP assumes the rental value of leased-in land as zero for Karnataka. Thus Cost A1 and Cost A2, which includes rent for leased-in land, work out to be the same in Karnataka. Hence, we use Cost A1 + FL and total Cost (C3) for our analysis in this chapter.

On average, the cost incurred on labour (human, mechanical, and animal put together) accounted for 38 per cent of the total cost of cultivation of principal agriculture and horticulture crops in the State. This formed the single largest cost component in crop cultivation (Figure 4). Input costs came second, accounting, on average, for 26 per cent of the total cost incurred by farmers to produce the 17 major crops in Karnataka. Imputed value of rent on land with a share of around 20 per cent was the next important cost item.

The estimates of profitability for the 17 principal crops of Karnataka are given in Table 7. If paid-out costs are taken into account, rainfed paddy, finger millet, hybrid sorghum, pearl millet, Bengal gram, and potato showed a negative net return or loss. The loss was highest for potato, at Rs 9,238 per acre. The net return over paid-out costs was positive and highest for onion (Rs 51,286 per acre), followed by dry chilli (Rs. 24,467 per acre) and irrigated paddy (Rs 12,666 per acre). However, the surplus or profit dissipates drastically for almost all the crops if total cost (Cost C3) is used.

To sum up, if Cost C3 is considered, which includes imputed rental value of owned land and managerial cost, except for onion, the cultivation of all other crops in the State turned out to be loss-making during 2014–15. The loss was ranged from Rs 3,208 per acre for soybean to Rs 48,723 for tomato. The results reinforce the findings of an earlier study by Prakash *et al.* (2013),

**Table 7** *Cost of cultivation of major crops in Karnataka, 2014–15 in rupees and per cent*

| Sl.No. | Crops | Productivity Q/acre | MSP 2015–16 Rs/Q | Cost of Production (Rs/Qtl) | | Per Acre Profit/Loss over (in Rs) | | Sold through APMC (per cent) | Sales Above MSP 2015–16 (per cent) | Difference between MSP and Cost C3 (per cent) |
|---|---|---|---|---|---|---|---|---|---|---|
| | | | | Cost A1+FL | Total Cost (C3) | A1 + Family Labour cost | Total Cost (C3) | | | |
| 1 | Paddy (Irrigated) | 26 | 1450 (Grade-A) | 1030 | 1671 | 12666 | –3768 | | | |
| 2 | Paddy (Rainfed) | 16 | 1410 (Avg.) | 1189 | 1985 | –301 | –12730 | 49 | 98 | –13 |
| 3 | Ragi | 13 | 1650 | 1881 | 2781 | –2808 | –14380 | 7 | 20 | –44 |
| 4 | White Jowar | 5 | 1590 | 1712 | 2922 | 3029 | –3260 | | | –46 |
| 5 | Hybrid Jowar | 8 | 1570 | 1307 | 1919 | –299 | –4923 | 5 | 53 | –18 |
| 6 | Maize | 15 | 1325 | 915 | 1425 | 3996 | –3842 | 59 | 0 | –7 |
| 7 | Bajra | 6 | 1275 | 1639 | 2324 | –2687 | –6936 | 41 | 61 | –45 |
| 8 | Bengal gram | 4 | 3500 | 3456 | 4963 | –59 | –5621 | 26 | 56 | –29 |
| 9 | Red gram | 3 | 4625 | 4009 | 6286 | 3537 | –3293 | 75 | 63 | –26 |
| 10 | Groundnut | 4 | 4030 | 3966 | 6186 | 572 | –8196 | 39 | 45 | –35 |
| 11 | Sunflower | 5 | 3800 | 3022 | 4416 | 1144 | –5214 | 30 | 0 | –14 |
| 12 | Soyabean | 6 | 2600 | 2324 | 3647 | 5127 | –3208 | 21 | 100 | –29 |
| 13 | Tomato | 176 | No MSP | 742 | 1086 | 11879 | –48723 | 24 | – | – |
| 14 | Onion | 76 | No MSP | 575 | 1.21 | 51286 | 17417 | 44 | – | – |

*(continued)*

**Table 7** (continued) Cost of cultivation of major crops in Karnataka, 2014–15 in rupees and per cent

| Sl.No. | Crops | Productivity Q/acre | MSP 2015–16 Rs/Q | Cost of Production (Rs/Qtl) | | Per Acre Profit/Loss (in Rs) over | | Sold through APMC (per cent) | Sales Above MSP 2015–16 (per cent) | Difference between MSP and Cost C3 (per cent) |
|---|---|---|---|---|---|---|---|---|---|---|
| | | | | Cost A1+FL | Total Cost (C3) | A1 + Family Labour cost | Total Cost (C3) | | | |
| 15 | Potato | 35 | No MSP | 1378 | 1906 | –9238 | –27960 | 75 | – | – |
| 16 | Dry chilli | 9 | No MSP | 7598 | 11679 | 24467 | –13482 | 49 | – | – |
| 17 | Cotton | 9 | 3800 (Med. Staple) 4100 (Long Staple) | 2915 | 4528 | 8701 | –5684 | 28 | 89 | –16 |
| | Average | | | | | | | 41 | 53 | –27 |

*Note:* While announcing MSP for any year, it is normal practice to consider cost of cultivation (CoC) of the previous year and adjust for inflation, as MSP for crops is announced before the sowing season. Hence, CoC per quintal for 2014–15 is compared with the declared MSP for 2015–16.

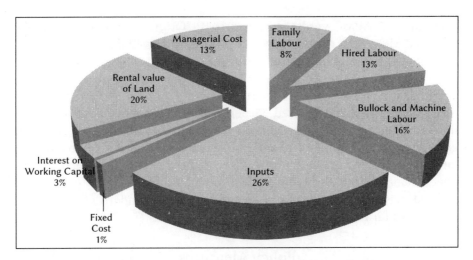

**Figure 4** *Components of cost of cultivation of agricultural and horticultural crops in Karnataka* in per cent

which examined the cost of cultivation of 19 principal crops of Karnataka for the year 2009–10. This study found that barring red gram and cash crops, no other crop was profitable. Unremunerativeness of agriculture on such a scale is of concern as it is has a direct bearing on the income and livelihoods of farmers in the State.

Prakash *et al.* (2013) also found that the principal field crops, which occupied 70 per cent of the gross cropped area, contributed no more than 40 per cent of farmers' incomes. The proportion was lower (18 per cent) for marginal farmers. Further, if income from farming alone was taken, the majority of farmers fell below the poverty line in Karnataka.

The data in Table 7 show that the MSP declared by the Union Government was less than the actual cost incurred by farmers for a majority of crops during 2014–15 (columns 4, 5, and 6). On average, the MSP could cover only 73 per cent of the cost of production. Even in paddy, where the government undertakes direct procurement, the MSP covered 87 per cent of the C3 cost of production. In the last two years, the Union Government has enhanced MSP by only 3.12 per cent annually.

The disquieting fact is not merely the inadequacy of MSP with respect to full cost of cultivation, but the inability to guarantee MSP to farmers of the State. Only 41 per cent of the produce of the 17 crops studied here was bought and sold in regulated markets (Agriculture Produce Market

Committee or APMC yards) during 2014–15. Of the total produce brought to the APMC yards, only 53 per cent received prices higher than the MSP and the rest was sold below the MSP. This is a classic case of "intervention failure" in agriculture. To put it differently, the market failed to transfer a fair share of the consumer's rupee to the farmer. According to an earlier study, farmers received 35 per cent of the payment made by the final consumer for most agricultural commodities in Karnataka (Prakash *et al.* 2013). Plugging the yield and market gaps are thus crucial to enhance farmers' incomes from agriculture. Even if these gaps are plugged, due to uneconomic and small holding sizes, the additional income that can be realised may not be sufficient to provide a decent standard of living to a majority of farmers.

## Policy Measures

We briefly list below, some of the policy measures required to enhance farmers' incomes.

1. *Enhance the collective bargaining power of farmers.* Generate collective action through cooperative avenues – for example, through Farmer Producer Organisation or Group Crop Insurance – to overcome the problem of small and uneconomical landholdings,
2. *Guarantee prices and effective procurement.* The Karnataka Agriculture Price Commission, in its recent report (2015), has recommended giving statutory status to MSP. Specifically, the KAPC suggested the following measures.
   - Consider the minimum support price announced by the Union Government or paid-out cost including family labour (A1 + FL), whichever is higher, as the State's statutory minimum transaction price (SMTP).
   - Enact legislation to ensure that any formal transaction, including the sale that takes place within APMCs, is not below the SMTP.
   - Impose restrictions on informal transactions taking place outside regulated markets for all agriculture and horticulture produce in the State.
   - Ensure that farmers receive a price not below total cost (C3) while procuring for the State's public distribution system, or in any procurement made by cooperatives and big retail outlets.
   - Expand the 'Food Security Basket' of the *Anna Bhagya* scheme by

including pigeon pea, onion, boiled rice, and other essential agriculture commodities for distribution. The Food Security Act, 2013 needs to be reoriented towards this end.

- To compensate for the loss incurred by farmers due to a fall in prices, new mechanisms like Price Compensation and Deficiency Payment may be put in place.
- The State Government should create a Rs 5,000-crore Price Stabilization Revolving Fund.
- The government should bear the costs of transportation, and supply quality bags and containers to bring produce to market. The Primary Agriculture Cooperative Societies (PACS) need to be strengthened and extended to villages for on-site procurement of farm produce in the vicinity of the farmers.
- The Union Government should implement the recommendation of the Dr M. S. Swaminathan-led National Commission on Farmers, to ensure a 50 per cent profit margin while fixing the MSP and to bring a legislation on the Right to Remunerative Prices. It is also time to extend MSP to horticulture crops and give statutory status to the Commission for Agriculture Cost and Prices.

3. *Diversify incomes.* The Official Group of the Government of Karnataka recommended a policy for diversification of agriculture with the motto that there shall be "no field with one crop, and no farmer with one income." Farmers should be encouraged to have multiple sources of income by adopting crop diversification appropriate to prevailing agro-climatic conditions, and adopt income-generating subsidiary occupations like dairying, poultry, sericulture, and farm forestry that can provide an assured income throughout the year.

4. *Exclusive focus on cost reduction.* Mechanical innovations like harvesters for finger millet and transplanting machines for paddy can reduce the costs of cultivation. To enable sharing of farm machinery, an online aggregation system (on the lines of that for taxi aggregators) may be developed. The Rural Employment Guarantee Programme (MGNREGA) can be used for soil and water conservation activities, and land development, especially in dry land conditions.

5. *Institutional sources of finance including crop insurance.* To prevent farmers from being caught in a debt trap, institutional sources of finance need to be strengthened with renewed focus on cooperative credit. Credit should be made available not only for production and investment purposes, but also for consumption needs, as well as social obligations like education

and marriage. Self-help groups of farmers can be established and given adequate revolving funds for immediate credit needs.

6. *Farmers' welfare.* In order to improve the income and welfare of farmers, it is essential to adopt the recommendations of the National Commission on Farmers (headed by M. S. Swaminathan) immediately. In addition, the State Government needs a separate Farmers' Income Commission, along the lines of the Pay Commission, to plan, enforce, and oversee all aspects of income and livelihood security of farmers.

7. Finally, an Index of Farmers' Livelihood Security can be constructed and used to gauge changes in the income and livelihood status of farmers consequent upon changes in agricultural prices. Government support by means of subsidy or income transfers can be provided as soon as the Index falls below a threshold level.

To conclude, the analysis of farmers' suicides and associated factors such as cost of cultivation in this chapter brings out the precariousness of income from farming, and the urgent need to address the problem of farmers' distress.

**Appendix Table 1** *Decadal change in area under agricultural crops in Karnataka, 2005–06 to 2014–15 in lakh ha and per cent*

| Sl. No. | Crops | 2005–06 | | 2014–15 | | Decadal Change | | |
|---|---|---|---|---|---|---|---|---|
| | | Area | Per cent | Area | Per cent | Area | Per cent | CAGR |
| 1 | Maize | 9.36 | 8 | 13.37 | 13 | 4.01 | 43 | 4.54 |
| 2 | Paddy | 14.85 | 13 | 13.27 | 13 | -1.59 | -11 | -1.19 |
| 3 | Jowar | 15.20 | 13 | 10.46 | 10 | -4.74 | -31 | -3.59 |
| 4 | Ragi | 9.39 | 8 | 7.08 | 7 | -2.30 | -25 | -2.20 |
| 5 | Bajra | 4.31 | 4 | 2.34 | 2 | -1.97 | -46 | -5.77 |
| 6 | Wheat | 2.53 | 2 | 1.98 | 2 | -0.55 | -22 | -3.35 |
| 7 | Other Cereals | 0.52 | N | 0.23 | N | -0.30 | -56 | -8.54 |
| **Total Cereals** | | **56.16** | **50** | **48.73** | **48** | **-7.43** | **-13** | **-1.15** |
| 1 | Bengal gram | 4.18 | 4 | 9.39 | 9 | 5.21 | 124 | 7.89 |
| 2 | Tur | 6.00 | 5 | 7.28 | 7 | 1.28 | 21 | 3.07 |
| 3 | Green gram | 4.01 | 4 | 2.63 | 3 | -1.38 | -34 | -6.26 |
| 4 | Horse gram | 2.69 | 2 | 1.81 | 2 | -0.89 | -33 | -5.59 |
| 5 | Cow pea | 0.69 | 1 | 0.72 | 1 | 0.03 | 4 | 1.13 |
| 6 | Black gram | 1.11 | 1 | 0.70 | 1 | -0.41 | -37 | -5.36 |
| 7 | Carpet legume | 0.87 | 1 | 0.60 | 1 | -0.27 | -31 | 0.06 |
| 8 | Other Pulses | 0.94 | 1 | 0.08 | N | -0.86 | -92 | -8.21 |
| **Total Pulses** | | **20.50** | **18** | **23.21** | **23** | **2.71** | **13** | **1.48** |
| 1 | Groundnut | 10.40 | 9 | 6.54 | 6 | -3.86 | -37 | -4.77 |
| 2 | Sunflower | 14.27 | 13 | 3.56 | 4 | -10.72 | -75 | -15.16 |
| 3 | Soya bean | 1.33 | 1 | 2.56 | 3 | 1.22 | 91 | 7.82 |

*(continued)*

**Appendix Table 1** (continued) Decadal change in area under agricultural crops in Karnataka, 2005–06 to 2014–15 in lakh ha and per cent

| Sl. No. | Crops | 2005–06 | | 2014–15 | | Decadal Change | | |
|---|---|---|---|---|---|---|---|---|
| | | Area | Per cent | Area | Per cent | Area | Per cent | CAGR |
| 4 | Sesamum | 1.03 | 1 | 0.44 | N | -0.59 | -57 | -7.68 |
| 5 | Safflower | 0.81 | 1 | 0.33 | N | -0.48 | -60 | -8.96 |
| 6 | Castor | 0.25 | N | 0.12 | N | -0.13 | -52 | -8.29 |
| 7 | Niger seed | 0.33 | N | 0.11 | N | -0.22 | -67 | -11.54 |
| 8 | Linseed | 0.13 | N | 0.05 | N | -0.08 | -62 | -10.97 |
| 9 | Rapeseed and Mustard | 0.07 | N | 0.02 | N | -0.05 | -70 | -9.77 |
| | **Total Oilseeds** | **28.63** | **25** | **13.72** | **14** | **-14.91** | **-52** | **-8.17** |
| 1 | Cotton | 4.13 | 4 | 8.76 | 9 | 4.63 | 112 | 8.15 |
| 2 | Sugarcane H | 2.21 | 2 | 4.80 | 5 | 2.59 | 117 | 8.08 |
| 3 | Tobacco | 1.01 | 1 | 0.94 | 1 | -0.06 | -6 | -0.22 |
| 4 | Mulberry | 0.88 | 1 | 0.88 | 1 | 0.01 | 1 | -1.69 |
| | **Total Commercial Crops** | **8.25** | **7** | **15.39** | **15** | **7.16** | **87** | **6.45** |
| | **Total** | **113.54** | **100** | **101.04** | **100** | **-12.49** | **-11** | **-1.15** |

*Note:* N = Negligible.

**Appendix Table 2** *Decadal change in area under horticultural crops in Karnataka, 2005–06 to 2014–15 in lakh ha and per cent*

| Sl. No. | Crops | 2005–06 | | 2014–15 | | Decadal Change | | |
|---|---|---|---|---|---|---|---|---|
| | | Area | Per cent | Area | Per cent | Area | Per cent | CAGR |
| 1 | Mango | 1.21 | 6 | 1.83 | 8 | 0.62 | 51 | 4.68 |
| 2 | Banana | 0.56 | 3 | 1.07 | 5 | 0.50 | 89 | 7.14 |
| 3 | Sapota | 0.23 | 1 | 0.31 | 1 | 0.08 | 36 | 2.70 |
| 4 | Grapes | 0.10 | 1 | 0.21 | 1 | 0.11 | 105 | 7.74 |
| 5 | Pomegranate | 0.11 | 1 | 0.19 | 1 | 0.08 | 73 | 5.45 |
| 6 | Lemon | 0.08 | N | 0.12 | 1 | 0.05 | 59 | 6.24 |
| 7 | Papaya | 0.04 | N | 0.08 | N | 0.04 | 111 | 7.45 |
| 8 | Guava | 0.06 | N | 0.07 | N | 0.00 | 5 | –0.06 |
| 9 | Other Fruit Crops | 0.18 | 1 | 0.19 | 1 | 0.01 | 6 | –0.25 |
| | **Total Fruit Crops** | **2.58** | **14** | **4.07** | **18** | **1.49** | **58** | **4.96** |
| 1 | Onion | 1.48 | 8 | 1.65 | 7 | 0.17 | 11 | 0.51 |
| 2 | Tomato | 0.44 | 2 | 0.64 | 3 | 0.21 | 47 | 4.27 |
| 3 | Green chilli | 0.32 | 2 | 0.45 | 2 | 0.13 | 41 | 3.49 |
| 4 | Potato | 0.76 | 4 | 0.43 | 2 | –0.32 | –43 | –7.37 |
| 5 | Other Vegetables | 1.04 | 6 | 1.46 | 7 | 0.41 | 39 | 3.13 |
| | **Total Vegetables** | **4.03** | **22** | **4.63** | **21** | **0.59** | **15** | **0.91** |

(continued)

**Appendix Table 2** (continued) Decadal change in area under horticultural crops in Karnataka, 2005–06 to 2014–15 in lakh ha and per cent

| Sl. No. | Crops | 2005–06 | | 2014–15 | | Decadal Change | | |
|---|---|---|---|---|---|---|---|---|
| | | Area | Per cent | Area | Per cent | Area | Per cent | CAGR |
| 1 | Dry chilli | 1.23 | 7 | 0.83 | 4 | -0.40 | -33 | -7.86 |
| 2 | Pepper | 0.16 | 1 | 0.30 | 1 | 0.13 | 81 | 7.95 |
| 3 | Ginger | 0.25 | 1 | 0.24 | 1 | -0.01 | -4 | 0.81 |
| 4 | Turmeric | 0.12 | 1 | 0.20 | 1 | 0.08 | 71 | 7.64 |
| 5 | Other Spices | 0.55 | 3 | 0.52 | 2 | -0.03 | -5 | -1.45 |
| | **Total Spices** | **2.32** | **12** | **2.09** | **9** | **-0.23** | **-10** | **-2.61** |
| 1 | Coconut | 4.55 | 24 | 5.15 | 23 | 0.60 | 13 | 1.25 |
| 2 | Arecanut | 1.87 | 10 | 2.61 | 12 | 0.74 | 40 | 3.75 |
| 3 | Coffee | 2.22 | 12 | 2.30 | 10 | 0.08 | 4 | 0.42 |
| 4 | Cashewnut | 0.67 | 4 | 0.75 | 3 | 0.08 | 11 | 0.63 |
| 5 | Palm Oil | 0.03 | N | 0.13 | 1 | 0.10 | 338 | 17.53 |
| 6 | Other Plantation Crops | 0.22 | 1 | 0.27 | 1 | 0.06 | 27 | 2.07 |
| | **Total Plantation Crops** | **9.56** | **51** | **11.22** | **50** | **1.66** | **17** | **1.66** |
| | **Others***  | **0.23** | **1** | **0.34** | **2** | **0.12** | **50** | **4.35** |
| | **State Total** | **18.72** | **100** | **22.35** | **100** | **3.64** | **19** | **1.60** |

*Notes:* * Others includes flowers, medicinal and aromatic plants. N = Negligible.

# References

Deshpande, R. S. (2002), "Suicide by Farmers in Karnataka, Agrarian Distress and Possible Alleviatory Steps," *Economic and Political Weekly*, vol. 37, no. 26.

Deshpande, R. S., and Prabhu, Nagesh (2005), "Farmers' Distress: Proof beyond Question," *Economic and Political Weekly*, vol. 44, no. 45, pp. 4663–65.

Government of Karnataka (GoK) (2002), *Farmers' Suicides in Karnataka: A Scientific Analysis*, Report of the Expert Committee for Study on Farmers' Suicides (Chairman: G. K. Veeresh), Department of Agriculture, Government of Karnataka.

Hazell, Peter (2010), "The Role of Markets for Managing Agricultural Risks in Developing Countries," in Keijiro Otsuka and Kaliappa Kalirajan (eds.), *Community, Market, and State in Development*, Palgrave Macmillan, U. K.

Jeromi, P. D. (2007), "Farmers' Indebtedness and Suicides: Impact of Agricultural Trade Liberalisation in Kerala," *Economic and Political Weekly*, vol. 42, no. 31.

Kammardi, T. N. Prakash (2011), "Indian Agriculture and Ashok Mehta," Janata, vol. 66, no. 41.

Kammardi, T. N. Prakash, Ashok Kumar, H. A., Aditya, K. S., and Chandrakanth, M.G. (2013), "Income and Livelihood Security of Farmers in the Era of Economic Reforms," in P. K. Shetty and M. V. Srinivasa Gowda (eds.), *Innovations in Agricultural Policy*, National Institute of Advanced Studies, Indian Institute of Science, Bangalore.

Mishra, Srijit (2007), "Risks, Farmers' Suicides and Agrarian Crisis in India: Is There A Way Out?" Working Paper 2007-014, Indira Gandhi Institute of Development Research, Mumbai, September.

Nadkarni, M. V. (1988), "Crisis of Increasing Costs in Indian Agriculture: Is There A Way Out?" *Economic and Political Weekly*, vol. 23, no. 39, September 24, p. A-114.

Sowndarya, D. C. (2012), "Utilisation of Benefits from Governmental Programmes/Schemes by Farmers in Karnataka: An Institutional Economic Analysis," M.Sc. (Agri) thesis, University of Agriculture Science, Bangalore.

# 3

# An Introduction to the Survey Villages

Arindam Das

In the Karnataka round of the Project on Agrarian Relations in India (PARI), in May–June 2009, census surveys were conducted in three villages of the State. To undertake follow-up case studies, all three villages were revisited five years later, in October–November 2014. Details of the household questionnaire and the manual for income calculation are available at http://fas.org.in/survey-method-toolbox.

The choice of villages, as in other PARI surveys, was made so as to represent different agro-climatic regions of the State. The selected villages were: Alabujanahalli village of Mandya district from the Southern Dry region, Siresandra village of Kolar district from the Eastern Dry region, and Zhapur village of Kalaburagi district from the Northeastern Dry region (Figure 1).[1]

A brief description follows of the three villages surveyed in Karnataka.

## Alabujanahalli

Alabujanahalli village is in Maddur taluk of Mandya district, in southern Karnataka. It is located at a distance of 25 km from Mandya town and 95 km from Bengaluru city. The nearest railway station is at Maddur, at a distance of 15 km. At the time of the survey, while there was a *pucca* approach road to the village, there was no bus stop in Alabujanahalli. The nearest bus stop was at Kalamudandoddi (K. M. Doddi), at a distance of 1.5 km, and motor vans from there passed through the village. There was an *anganwadi* centre, a primary school, and a milk procurement centre in the village. But the

[1] The agro-climatic zones are as per the classification of the University of Agricultural Sciences (UAS), Bengaluru.

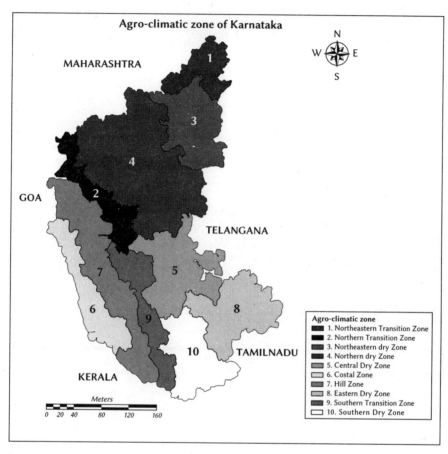

**Figure 1** *Agro-climatic zones of Karnataka*

nearest post office and commercial bank were located at K. M. Doddi; and for medical services, people had to go to either K. M. Doddi or Mandya town.

Alabujanahalli belongs to the Cauvery-irrigated region of Karnataka. Channels leading from a system tank that is fed by canals from the Krishnarajasagar dam irrigate the village. At the time of the survey, the major crops grown in the village were sugarcane, rice, and finger millet (*ragi*). Alabujanahalli is located very close to a major sugar factory of Mandya district, Sri Chamundeswari Sugars Limited (see Chapter 8). The sugarcane produced in the village is procured by the sugar factory as raw material, and the factory and its owners have a substantial hold over the economy of the village. A large number of medium-peasant and small-

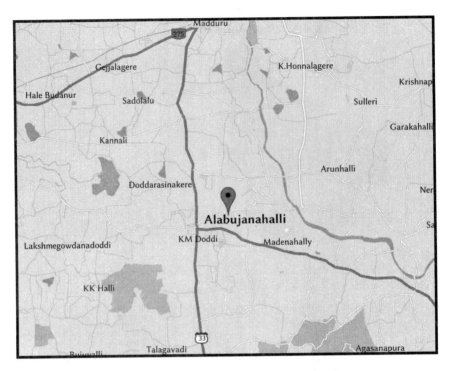

**Figure 2** *Location of Alabjuanahalli village, Mandya district, Karnataka*

peasant households of the village practise sericulture and livestock-raising, which contribute significantly to household incomes.

At the Census of 2011, the population of the village stood at 1,458 persons and 294 households. The PARI survey of the Foundation for Agrarian Studies (FAS) covered a population of 1,258 persons and 248 households. However, due to incomplete data, the analysis in this book is confined to 243 households only. The average number of persons per household in the village was 4.9. The distribution of households by social group is shown in Table 1, and Table 2 shows the detailed caste composition of the village population.

As shown in Table 1, 85 per cent of households in the village belonged to Backward Classes (BC) and 14 per cent to Scheduled Castes (SC). Among the Backward Classes, a large section belonged to the Vokkaliga caste, a major landowing caste (Table 2). The other castes were Adi Karnataka (SC), Besthar (BC), Madivala (BC), and Vaishnava (Other Caste Hindu). At the Census of 2011, the SC population in the village was 16.9 per cent, while in the FAS survey, the SC population was 13.5 per cent.

**Table 1** *Distribution of households by social group, Alabujanahalli, 2009* in number and per cent

| Social group | Number of households | As percentage of all households |
|---|---|---|
| Backward Class | 206 | 84.8 |
| Hindu | 1 | 0.4 |
| Scheduled Caste | 35 | 14.4 |
| Scheduled Tribe | 1 | 0.4 |
| All | 243 | 100.0 |

**Table 2** *Distribution of population by caste, Alabujanahalli, 2009* in number and per cent

| Caste | Females | Males | Total | As percentage of total population |
|---|---|---|---|---|
| Barber | 1 | 3 | 4 | 0.3 |
| Gangamatha/Besthar | 40 | 30 | 70 | 5.9 |
| Lingayat | 5 | 5 | 10 | 0.8 |
| Madivala (Dhobi) | 27 | 30 | 57 | 4.8 |
| Thigala | 7 | 10 | 17 | 1.4 |
| Vokkaliga | 425 | 431 | 856 | 72.4 |
| Backward Class | 505 | 509 | 1014 | 85.8 |
| Vaishnava | 1 | 2 | 3 | 0.3 |
| Other Caste Hindu | 1 | 2 | 3 | 0.3 |
| Scheduled Caste | 82 | 76 | 158 | 13.4 |
| Scheduled Tribe | 5 | 2 | 7 | 0.6 |
| All | 593 | 589 | 1182 | 100.0 |

*Note*: The Scheduled Caste population of the village belonged to Adi Karnataka group; the sole Scheduled Tribe household was from the Lambada group.

While the sex ratio of the adult population was favourable, at 1,007, the child sex ratio was very low, at 776 females per 1,000 males.

# Siresandra

Siresandra is a revenue village in Huttur Block of Kolar taluk, in Kolar district in eastern Karnataka. It is a small village with a geographical area of 265 hectares as per the revenue records. The nearest town is Kolar, 20 km

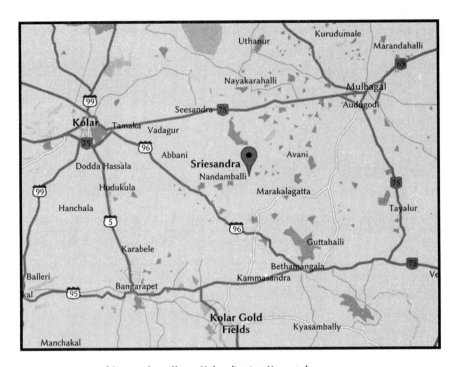

**Figure 3** *Location of Siresandra village, Kolar district, Karnataka*

away. The nearest railway stations are Kolar Gold Fields and Bangarapet, 15 km from the village. At the time of the PARI survey, there was a metalled approach road, a bus stop, and a primary school in Siresandra, but no post office or bank. The nearest primary health centre was located at Shapur, at a distance of 5 km, and the nearest district hospital and private nursing home were in Kolar town. There was an *anganwadi* centre and a milk procurement centre in the village.

At the Census of 2011, the population of Siresandra stood at 514 in 105 households with a sex ratio of 912. As per the 2009 PARI survey the population of the village was 992, and the survey covered 79 households. Of these 79 households, 50 were Backward Class (BC) households and 29 were Scheduled Caste (SC) households (Table 3). At the Census of 2011, 38 per cent of the population of the village was Scheduled Caste; the corresponding proportion in the PARI survey was 36.4 per cent. There were no Scheduled Tribe (ST) households. The major caste group in the village was Vokkaliga, which was also the major landowning caste. The other caste groups were Bhovi (SC), Kapu (BC), Madivala (BC), and Mala (SC).

**Table 3** *Distribution of households by social group, Siresandra, 2009* in number and per cent

| Social group | Number of households | As percentage of all households |
|---|---|---|
| Scheduled Caste | 29 | 36.7 |
| Backward Class | 50 | 63.3 |
| All | 79 | 100.0 |

**Table 4** *Distribution of population by caste and sex, Siresandra, 2009* in number and per cent

| Caste | Females | Males | Total | As percentage of total population |
|---|---|---|---|---|
| Kapu | 6 | 3 | 9 | 1.9 |
| Madivala (Dhobi) | 3 | 7 | 10 | 2.1 |
| Vokkaliga | 134 | 141 | 275 | 58.8 |
| **Backward Class** | **143** | **151** | **294** | **62.8** |
| Adi Karnataka | 69 | 65 | 134 | 28.6 |
| Bhovi | 20 | 16 | 36 | 7.7 |
| Mala | 2 | 2 | 4 | 0.9 |
| **Scheduled Caste** | **91** | **83** | **174** | **37.2** |
| All | 234 | 234 | 468 | 100.0 |

The sex ratio of the population, defined as the number of females per 1,000 persons, was exactly 1,000 in Siresandra in 2009, at the time of the PARI survey. The gender balance for the age-group of 0 to 6 years was healthy, with 23 girls to 22 boys in this age-group. The sex ratio for Siresandra in 2011, as per the Census of India, was 912.

The average household size in the village was 5.9. Around 45 per cent of all households had six or more members, and they accounted for five-eighths of the total population of the village. There was no single-person household in Siresandra. Households with four or fewer members accounted for 36.7 per cent of all households, but only 21.2 per cent of the total population of the village. Fifteen very large households, with an average household size of 11.1 and constituting 19 per cent of all households in the village, accounted for 35.5 per cent of the total population.

Siresandra belongs to the semi-dry, rainfed region of eastern Karnataka – Southern Plateau and Hills region as per the NARP (National Agricultural Research Project) classification. Cultivation in the village was mainly rainfed, supplemented by irrigation by means of borewells and drip irrigation. Since Siresandra is situated on the banks of the Palar river, a very small area in the village was irrigated by water from the river, which was available only during the rainy season. The cropping pattern of the village included kharif *ragi* (finger millet), followed by vegetables (potato, tomato, carrot, cauliflower, beetroot, radish), fodder maize and fodder grass, condiments, and tree crops. *Ragi* (finger millet) was often intercropped with *jowar* (sorghum), pigeon pea, and sesamum. Apart from crop cultivation, sericulture and dairying were also important occupations, and contributed significantly to household incomes.

At the time of our revisit in 2014, agriculture in the village was mainly rainfed. The water level had fallen to 1,200 ft and there were only five functional borewells. There had been a significant expansion in the scale of sericulture in Siresandra over the previous five years.

## Zhapur

Zhapur is a small village in Kalaburagi taluk of Kalaburagi district, in northeastern Karnataka. The village is located at a distance of 15 km from Kalaburagi town. The nearest railway station and primary health centre were both at Nandur, at a distance of 5 km, at the time of the 2009 PARI survey. There was a metalled approach road to the village, and a bus stop. The nearest commercial bank and cooperative bank were in Kalaburagi. There was an *anganwadi* centre and a primary school within the village.

In November 2014, we returned to the village to conduct some case studies. By then the region had seen a major infrastructural change with the construction of an 8-km-long *pucca* road leading to Kalaburagi town, on account of a proposed new airport. This development has not only increased connectivity between Zhapur and Kalaburagi town, but also affected land prices. The price of land in Zhapur has risen ten-fold in these five years, from Rs 1 lakh per acre in 2009 to Rs 10 lakh per acre in 2014. There has also been an increase in quarrying activity in the region.

The PARI survey of Zhapur in 2009 covered 113 households resident in the village with a population of 729 persons. The overall sex ratio was 970, but a healthier 1,145 girls per 1,000 boys for children below 6 years. At the Census of 2011, the village reported a population of 129 households and 838 persons. In 2011, the sex ratio of the village population was 940. On average, there were six persons in a household. Households with seven or more members constituted 37 per cent of all households.

Scheduled Caste (SC) and Backward Class (BC) households were equal in number. The dominant landowning caste was Lingayat. The distribution of

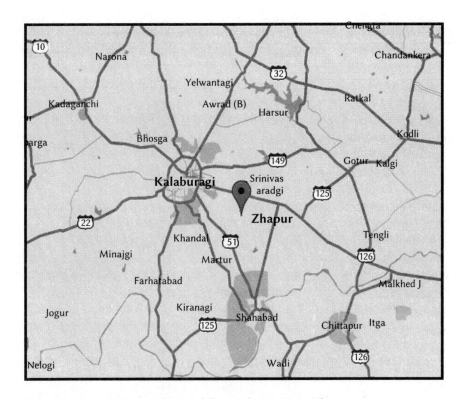

**Figure 4** *Location of Zhapur village, Kalaburagi district, Karnataka*

**Table 5** *Distribution of households by social group, Zhapur, 2009* in number and per cent

| Social group | Number of households | As percentage of all households |
| --- | --- | --- |
| Scheduled Caste | 46 | 42.2 |
| Scheduled Tribe | 14 | 12.8 |
| Backward Class | 46 | 42.2 |
| Other Caste Hindu | 2 | 1.8 |
| Muslim | 1 | 0.9 |
| All | 109 | 100.0 |

population by caste is shown in Table 6. In addition to cultivation and wage labour in agriculture, many workers were employed as daily labourers in a stone quarry located partially on the boundaries of the village. This was a major source of non-agricultural employment for manual workers in Zhapur.

Zhapur falls in the dry rainfed region of northeastern Karnataka. The

**Table 6** *Distribution of population by caste, Zhapur, 2009* in number and per cent

| Caste | Females | Males | Total | As percentage of total population |
|---|---|---|---|---|
| Lingayat | 40 | 47 | 87 | 13.0 |
| Kuruba | 48 | 52 | 100 | 15.0 |
| Kabbaliga | 18 | 17 | 35 | 5.2 |
| Kabbilagaru | 18 | 9 | 27 | 4.0 |
| Madivala (Dhobi) | 12 | 9 | 21 | 3.1 |
| Jangama | 5 | 3 | 8 | 1.2 |
| Bhajanthri | 2 | 2 | 4 | 0.6 |
| Barber | 5 | 2 | 7 | 1.0 |
| **Backward Class** | **148** | **141** | **289** | **43.3** |
| **Muslim** | **8** | **6** | **14** | **2.1** |
| Holeya | 55 | 72 | 127 | 19.0 |
| Vaddaru | 70 | 70 | 140 | 21.0 |
| Madiga | 2 | 7 | 9 | 1.3 |
| Bhovi | 1 | 4 | 5 | 0.7 |
| Kuravan | 2 | 1 | 3 | 0.4 |
| **Scheduled Caste** | **130** | **154** | **284** | **42.6** |
| Beda | 37 | 34 | 71 | 10.6 |
| Badige | 5 | 4 | 9 | 1.3 |
| **Scheduled Tribe** | **42** | **38** | **80** | **12.0** |
| Total | 328 | 339 | 667 | 100.0 |

village has a geographical area of 628 hectares, of which 84 per cent was under cultivation – most of it rainfed. The cropping pattern followed was that of a single mixed crop of rainfed cereals and oilseeds. Most cultivators grew pigeon pea intercropped with maize, sesamum, *bajra* (pearl millet), and green gram. They also cultivated *jowar* (sorghum) and safflower, either as mono crops or mixed crops.

In the last five years, groundwater irrigation has expanded due to the intervention of a local NGO. Cotton is now being cultivated by different sections of the peasantry.

# 4

## Socio-Economic Classes
## in the Three Villages

### V. K. Ramachandran

The three main sets of criteria that have classically been used to differentiate classes in the countryside are the ownership and control by households of the means of production (particularly, though not exclusively, land); the relative use of different forms of family and hired labour (particularly, though not exclusively, in the process of production in agriculture); and the surplus that a household is able to generate in a working year. It is immediately clear, of course, that these are factors that have changed greatly over time and vary greatly over space, and are influenced by circumstances within the village and without.

This chapter deals with the classification of households from our field data in Karnataka into socio-economic classes, and the criteria we have used for such classification.

## Characterisation of Classes in Contemporary Rural India

This section is drawn from Ramachandran (2011).

### *Landlords*

Landlord households own the most land and generally the best land in most Indian villages, and the members of landlord households do not participate in the major agricultural operations on the land. Their land is cultivated either by tenants, to whom land is leased out on fixed rent or share, or by means of the labour power of hired workers.[1] Landlord families are,

---

[1] Those landlords whose surpluses come mainly from the labour of hired manual workers are called capitalist landlords.

in general, historical participants in the system of land monopoly in the village. Landlords dominate not just economic, but also traditional social and modern political hierarchies in the village. It is absolutely essential to remember that – to quote E. M. S. Namboodiripad – "landlordism is not only an economic category but also social and political."

Capitalist farmers also do not participate in the major manual operations on the land. The main difference between capitalist farmers and landlords is that the former did not traditionally belong to the class of landlords. Some of them came from rich peasant or upper-middle peasant families that had a tradition of family labour, whose members, in fact, actually worked at major manual tasks even in the present or previous generation. Such families invested the surplus they gained from agriculture or other activities – including moneylending, salaried employment, trade and business – in land. Agriculture was or became the focal point of their activity, and the basis of their economic power.

The basis of the power of landlords and rich capitalist farmers is their control over land.

### Manual Workers

At the other end of the spectrum of classes involved in agricultural production is the class of manual workers, whose major income comes from working as hired workers on the land of others and at tasks outside crop production.

In general, manual workers work on a wide range of tasks, and the set of skills necessary for most tasks in, say, a village are found among most manual labourers in that village.

Notably, I use the term "manual workers" rather than "agricultural workers," because it is no longer possible (nor particularly helpful) to separate a *class* of non-agricultural workers from the larger pool of manual workers – that is, to recognise rural farm and non-farm workers as discrete categories – in most villages. The typical rural manual worker today can be characterised more as a "miscellaneous worker in rural society" than as solely an agricultural worker.

Most manual workers are casual workers who work at daily-rated tasks or for piece-rates. Some, however, are annual workers: farm servants who do agricultural, non-agricultural, and some domestic tasks for a single employer for a monthly wage (and generally on an annual contract).

Manual workers can also have other sources of income. These can include, for instance, animal husbandry, petty vending, domestic work, and miscellaneous low-remuneration jobs in the private sector.

For historical reasons, in most regions, a majority or a large proportion of Dalit households and households belonging to other region-specific oppressed castes belong to the class of manual workers. Nevertheless, since manual work remains the rural occupation of last resort, manual labour tends to be the most caste-heterogeneous class in village society.

## The Peasantry

Peasant households, whose members work on all or some of the major manual operations on the land, constitute the sector of petty producers that lies between landlords and rich capitalist farmers on the one hand, and manual workers on the other. While peasants have shown great resilience as a social category, having existed continually under different historical social formations, the hallmark of the modern peasantry is its subjugation to the capitalist market.

As part of our research, using the classical texts as guideposts, we have tried to work out broad criteria for the classification of peasants in the modern rural Indian context into different class categories. These criteria are as follows:

1. Ownership of the means of production and other assets.
2. The labour ratio – defined as the ratio between the sum of number of days of family labour and the number of days of labouring out – of members of the household in agricultural and non-agricultural work (in the numerator), and the number of days of labour hired in by the household (in the denominator).
3. Rent exploitation: that is, rent received or paid by the household.
4. Net income of the household, making separate note of the gross value of output from agriculture and the investment in agriculture per hectare.
5. The sources of income of the household.

We emphasise here the problems of classifying the peasantry on the basis of a single year's data, when socio-economic circumstances typically fluctuate from year to year. We use, in other words, static data to study dynamic circumstances. This problem affects income particularly, since peasant incomes typically fluctuate from year to year.

With regard to the labour ratio, the extent of participation of working members of peasant households in the labour process in agriculture depends on the nature of land use and cropping pattern in each village, on economic and social status. In every village, cropping pattern and technological processes are such that there are substantial variations in labour absorption per crop, and the relative ratios in which family labour, exchange labour (if it exists at all), and different types of hired labour are deployed.[2]

We then classified households into rich, upper-middle, lower-middle, and poor, on the basis of their ownership of the means of production, labour ratios, and incomes. This was in itself a complex effort, and the point to remember is that the purpose here is not to provide a universal, one-size-fits-all scheme, but to try to apply the existing Marxist literature, and village-level data and observation, to construct criteria (or identify guidelines) for identifying classes in different socio-economic and agricultural environments.

Rich peasant households have the highest levels of ownership of means of production, particularly land and other productive assets, while, at the other end of the spectrum, poor peasants hardly have any productive assets at all other than small plots of land. In some villages, poor and lower-middle peasants are tenants, so do not own any land. With respect to the labour ratio, in general, the coefficient is above 0 but very low for rich peasants, generally in the vicinity of 1 among middle peasants (less than 1 for upper-middle and greater than 1 for lower-middle peasants), and greater than 1 among poor peasants.

Incomes can vary from high surpluses based on relatively heavy investments among the rich, to subsistence and even negative incomes among the poor (this is discussed in greater detail below). The income criterion was particularly important in resolving borderline problems in the classification of the middle peasantry into upper and lower sections.

## Socio-Economic Classes in Three Villages of Karnataka

Our survey – the Project on Agrarian Relations in India (PARI) survey – was conducted in 2009, so the data pertain to the agricultural year 2008–09. The income data pertain to one year – and as income fluctuates, often sharply, from year to year, households cannot be classified solely on the basis of incomes. Secondly, given cropping pattern, farming practices, and the specific features of the labour market in the villages, the labour criterion too could not be the sole basis for classification.

Once we had separated the peasantry in general from other classes on the basis of general income, labour, and asset criteria, we differentiated classes among the peasantry on the basis of categories of ownership of all means of production, that is, land and other means of production.

[2] Labour ratios are also affected by year-to-year fluctuations.

The class of manual workers was identified on the basis of share of income from wage labour.

Finally, we identified the major non-agricultural classes in each village.

### *Alabujanahalli*

In the village of Alabujanahalli, there was no farmer who belonged to the traditional class of landlords. There were, however, households with relatively large holdings that did not engage in any family labour. These households belong to the highest landholding and asset-holding bracket of the village.

Over time, these rich capitalist farmer households themselves have split, so the individual holdings are smaller than earlier. In 2009, 25 acres was the largest holding, and when we returned in 2014, this holding had been split into three. Clearly, we cannot call an 8-acre farmer a big landlord! However, what has happened is that these households have incomes other than incomes from land. Incomes from land came mainly from sugarcane and paddy. Of the two, sugarcane is a more lucrative crop. Other incomes were from poultry farming, tree cultivation, grain mills, and businesses in Maddur and towns in Kerala. Members of these households, men and women, do not work at any major manual operations. While economic inequality has grown over five years, the old type of landlordism has changed.

Then we come to the peasantry, households whose earnings are primarily from cultivation. Their major sources of income are agriculture, animal husbandry, and sericulture. The households were initially grouped on the basis of landholding (ownership and operational holdings), income sources, and asset-holding. As there were some variations by the three criteria, the final categories used in this chapter are as follows:

*Peasant 1*: The value of household assets is above Rs 50 lakhs (Rs 5 million).

*Peasant 2*: The value of household assets ranges from Rs 20 lakhs to Rs 50 lakhs (Rs 2 million to Rs 5 million).

*Peasant 3*: The value of household assets ranges from Rs 10 lakhs to Rs 20 lakhs (Rs 1 million to Rs 2 million).

*Peasant 4*: The value of household assets is below Rs 10 lakhs (Rs 1 million).

In other words, there was very wide variation in the asset base of the peasant households. The major change between the two surveys, particularly among richer sections of the peasantry, was the expansion of sericulture.

There were three types of manual workers in the village.

*Manual worker 1:* These were households for whom the major source of income was manual work, but who also had small operational holdings of land.

*Manual worker 2:* These were households for whom the major source of income was manual work, but who also gained small incomes from other sources (animal husbandry, old age pensions, etc.).

*Manual worker 3:* These were households for whom the only major source of income was manual work, agricultural and non-agricultural.

Lastly, we classified households into some other categories.

*Rents/remittances:* Households for whom the major sources of income were rents from agricultural land or commercial land, or remittances.

*Business activities:* Households whose major source of income was business activity other than crop production.

*Salaried households:* Households whose major source of income was salaries.

The distribution of all households in Alabujanahalli village by socio-economic class is shown in Table 1.

There were only two rich capitalist farmer households in the village, but they held 6 per cent of the land and 19 per cent of the assets of all village households (Tables 1 and 2). There were nine Peasant 1 households (the wealthiest among our categories of peasants), and they held 16 per cent of total land and assets. The lowest rung of the peasantry, Peasant 4 households, comprised 24 per cent of households resident in the village, and held 15 per cent of ownership and operational holdings of land (Table 3). Their share of total assets, however, was only 3 per cent. Manual workers of all three types together comprised 30 per cent of households. Manual workers accounted for 5 per cent of ownership and operational holdings of land, and of total assets.

The data in Appendix Table 1 show that the correlation between socio-economic class and caste remained strong. Scheduled Caste (SC) households were concentrated among Peasant 4, Manual worker 1, and Manual worker 2 categories. Conversely, 100 per cent of Rich capitalist farmer, Peasant 1, and Peasant 2 households were from among Caste Hindus – Backward Class (BC) or other Caste Hindu. Caste Hindus were also the majority among Peasant 3 and Peasant 4 households. There were only nine Scheduled

**Table 1** *Number of households and share in assets, by socio-economic class, Alabujanahalli*

| Socio-economic class | Number of households | Per cent of total households | Per cent of total assets |
|---|---|---|---|
| Rich capitalist farmer | 2 | 0.8 | 19.0 |
| Peasant 1 | 9 | 3.7 | 15.7 |
| Peasant 2 | 39 | 16 | 29.5 |
| Peasant 3 | 30 | 12.3 | 11.5 |
| Peasant 4 | 58 | 23.9 | 8.9 |
| Manual worker 1 | 40 | 16.5 | 3.3 |
| Manual worker 2 | 22 | 9.1 | 1.2 |
| Manual worker 3 | 11 | 4.5 | 0.5 |
| Business/self-employment | 11 | 4.5 | 2 |
| Rents/remittances | 7 | 2.9 | 2.1 |
| Salaried persons | 14 | 5.8 | 6.3 |
| All | 243 | 100 | 100 |

**Table 2** *Household ownership holdings owned by each class as a proportion of all ownership holdings in the village, Alabujanahalli, 2009* in per cent

| Class | Number of households | Percentage of total households | Extent of ownership holdings | Percentage of all ownership holdings |
|---|---|---|---|---|
| Rich capitalist farmer | 2 | 1 | 39.1 | 6 |
| Peasant 1 | 9 | 4 | 99.8 | 16 |
| Peasant 2 | 39 | 16 | 212.7 | 33 |
| Peasant 3 | 30 | 12 | 100.9 | 16 |
| Peasant 4 | 58 | 24 | 97.5 | 15 |
| Manual worker 1 | 40 | 16 | 26.5 | 4 |
| Manual worker 2 | 22 | 9 | 9.1 | 1 |
| Manual worker 3 | 11 | 5 | 1.1 | 0 |
| Business/ self-employment | 11 | 5 | 9.3 | 1 |
| Rents/remittances | 7 | 3 | 11.0 | 2 |
| Salaried persons | 14 | 6 | 31.7 | 5 |
| Total | 243 | 100 | 638.8 | 100 |

**Table 3** *Household operational holdings owned by each class as a proportion of all operational holdings in the village, Alabujanahalli, 2009* in per cent

| Class | Number of households | Percentage of total households | Extent of operational holdings | Percentage of all operational holdings |
|---|---|---|---|---|
| Rich capitalist farmer | 2 | 1 | 37.0 | 7 |
| Peasant 1 | 9 | 4 | 92.5 | 17 |
| Peasant 2 | 39 | 16 | 184.2 | 34 |
| Peasant 3 | 30 | 12 | 87.1 | 16 |
| Peasant 4 | 58 | 24 | 84.3 | 15 |
| Manual worker 1 | 40 | 16 | 28.2 | 5 |
| Manual worker 2 | 22 | 9 | 0.4 | 0 |
| Manual worker 3 | 11 | 5 | 0.0 | 0 |
| Business/self-employment | 11 | 5 | 6.6 | 1 |
| Rents/remittances | 7 | 3 | 7.6 | 1 |
| Salaried persons | 14 | 6 | 17.3 | 3 |
| Total | 243 | 100 | 545.1 | 100 |

Tribe (ST) households in the village and all of them belonged to the class of Manual worker 3.

Over the period 2009–14, incomes of peasant households had improved on account of expansion of sericulture. For manual workers, the main new activity was construction.

### Siresandra

There were no landlords or rich capitalist farmers in this village.[3] The peasantry was classified into three categories:

*Peasant 1*: The value of household assets is above Rs 50 lakhs (Rs 5 million).

*Peasant 2*: The value of household assets ranges from Rs 15 lakhs (Rs 1.5 million) to Rs 50 lakhs (Rs 5 million).

*Peasant 3*: The value of household assets is below Rs 15 lakhs (Rs 1.5 million).

[3] One limitation of our survey was that there was a landlord in the next village and this landlord owned large holdings of land in Siresandra. In retrospect, the survey should have covered him though he was not a resident of the selected village.

*Manual worker:* Households for whom the main source of income was from manual work at agricultural and non-agricultural tasks.

Lastly, we classified the remaining households in the category:

*Business/small self-employment:* Households whose major source of income was business activity other than crop production including small-scale self-employment.

The distribution of all households in Siresandra by socio-economic class is shown in Table 4.

There were four Peasant 1 households in the village. Even in the richest Peasant 1 household, whose asset holdings were valued at Rs 20 million, all family members worked in sericulture. The household members not only undertook supervisory work, but also some manual work. Peasant

**Table 4** *Number of households and share in assets, by socio-economic class, Siresandra*

| Socio-economic class | Number of households | Per cent of total households | Per cent of total assets |
|---|---|---|---|
| Peasant 1 | 4 | 5.1 | 28.8 |
| Peasant 2 | 24 | 30.4 | 47.5 |
| Peasant 3 | 32 | 40.5 | 18.8 |
| Manual worker | 13 | 16.5 | 2.4 |
| Business/small self-employment | 6 | 7.6 | 2.6 |
| All | 79 | 100 | 100 |

**Table 5** *Household ownership holdings owned by each class as a proportion of all ownership holdings in the village, Siresandra, 2009* in acres and per cent

| Class | Number of households | Percentage of total households | Extent of ownership holdings | Percentage of all ownership holdings |
|---|---|---|---|---|
| Peasant 1 | 4 | 5 | 108.8 | 30 |
| Peasant 2 | 24 | 30 | 152.4 | 42 |
| Peasant 3 | 32 | 41 | 83.5 | 23 |
| Manual worker | 13 | 16 | 10.7 | 3 |
| Business/small self-employment | 6 | 8 | 11.6 | 3 |
| Total | 79 | 100 | 367.0 | 100 |

**Table 6** *Household operational holdings owned by each class as a proportion of all operational holdings in the village, Siresandra, 2009* in acres and per cent

| Class | Number of households | Percentage of total households | Extent of operational holdings | Percentage of all operational holdings |
|---|---|---|---|---|
| Peasant 1 | 4 | 5 | 108.0 | 30 |
| Peasant 2 | 24 | 30 | 147.9 | 41 |
| Peasant 3 | 32 | 41 | 84.9 | 24 |
| Manual worker | 13 | 16 | 11.3 | 3 |
| Business/small self-employment | 6 | 8 | 5.5 | 2 |
| Total | 79 | 100 | 357.6 | 100 |

1 households accounted for 5 per cent of all households, and 30 per cent of ownership and operational holdings (Tables 5 and 6). Among Peasant 1 households, we saw a major change between 2009 and 2014. One household had improved in a big way because they had access to water and they had made quite a lot of money from sericulture, benefiting from the Government of Karnataka subsidy given in the first year of sericulture cultivation. This household also reported salary incomes. The case of this household shows how a clear improvement in its economic position (and as a result new inequality in the village) was built on profits based on subsidies from the government. In fact, smaller cultivators have not benefited from subsidies in sericulture.

Peasant 2 and Peasant 3 households together constituted 70 per cent of all households, and accounted for 65 per cent of the land owned and operated by residents of the village.

There was a small section of Manual workers: 13 households, accounting for 16.5 per cent of all households. In Siresandra, we have not divided manual workers into further categories as the manual workers did not have much land; also, the percentage of manual workers in this village is small.

Of the three villages, Siresandra had the least inequality in terms of asset-holdings. Nevertheless, 5 per cent of households (Peasant 1 households) owned almost 29 per cent of all assets. Manual workers comprised 16.5 per cent of all households but owned less than 3 per cent of total assets.

The distribution of households by socio-economic class and caste (Appendix Table 2) shows that there was no Scheduled Caste (SC) family among Peasant 1 households. By contrast, 69 per cent of Manual worker households were SC households. Also, Scheduled Castes were the majority in the Business/small self-employment category, that is, of households engaged in petty business.

## Zhapur

The definitions and criteria that we used to classify households in Zhapur were as follows:

*Landlord households*: Households belonging to the highest landholding and asset-holding bracket of the village, and owning the best quality of crop land. Members of landlord households did not participate in any major agricultural operation. Cultivation was done with the help of hired labour or by leasing out land to tenant cultivators.

*Peasant households*: These are households whose major source of income was from agriculture and animal husbandry. The final categories used in this chapter are as follows:

*Peasant 1*: The value of household assets is above Rs 25 lakhs (Rs 2.5 million).

*Peasant 2*: The value of household assets ranges from Rs 10 lakhs to Rs 25 lakhs (Rs 1 million to Rs 2.5 million).

*Peasant 3*: The value of household assets is below Rs 10 lakhs (Rs 1 million).

*Manual worker*: These are households for whom the major source of income was manual work.

Lastly, we classified households into some other categories.

*Rents/remittances*: Households for whom the major sources of income were rents from agricultural land or commercial land, remittances, pensions or other handouts.

*Business activity/self-employed*: Households whose major source of income was business activity other than crop production.

*Salaried persons*: Households whose major source of income was salaries.

The distribution of all households in Zhapur by socio-economic class is shown in Table 7.

In Zhapur, there was one traditional dominant landlord family, which now comprises four households. These four landlord households accounted for 34 per cent of ownership holdings and 47 per cent of assets of all village

**Table 7** *Distribution of households by socio-economic class, Zhapur*

| Class | Number of households | Percentage of total households |
|---|---|---|
| Landlord | 4 | 4 |
| Peasant 1 | 2 | 2 |
| Peasant 2 | 7 | 6 |
| Peasant 3 | 28 | 26 |
| Manual worker | 51 | 47 |
| Business/self-employment | 6 | 6 |
| Rents, remittances | 5 | 5 |
| Salaried persons | 6 | 6 |
| Total | 109 | 100 |

**Table 8** *Household ownership holdings owned by each class as a proportion of all ownership holdings in the village, Zhapur, 2009* in acres and per cent

| Class | Number of households | Percentage of total households | Extent of ownership holdings | Percentage of all ownership holdings |
|---|---|---|---|---|
| Landlord | 4 | 4 | 205.1 | 34 |
| Peasant 1 | 2 | 2 | 80.2 | 13 |
| Peasant 2 | 7 | 6 | 68.2 | 11 |
| Peasant 3 | 28 | 26 | 117.4 | 20 |
| Manual worker | 51 | 47 | 60.3 | 10 |
| Business/self-employment | 6 | 6 | 7.1 | 1 |
| Rents, remittances | 5 | 5 | 36.6 | 6 |
| Salaried persons | 6 | 6 | 25.7 | 4 |
| Total | 109 | 100 | 600.7 | 100 |

households (Tables 7 and 8). However, they controlled only 19 per cent of operational holdings (Table 9).

The traditional landlord family (comprising four households) in Zhapur is one that has taken advantage of opportunities for salaried educated employment that arose in post-Independence India. One person was the head of the state-run transport corporation in Bangalore; others opened small businesses, obtained salaried employment, and so on. By the time of our survey in 2009, most of the family had left the village. The largest

**Table 9** *Household operational holdings owned by each class as a proportion of all operational holdings in the village, Zhapur, 2009* in acres and per cent

| Class | Number of households | Percentage of total households | Extent of operational holdings | Percentage of all operational holdings |
|---|---|---|---|---|
| Landlord | 4 | 4 | 109 | 19 |
| Peasant 1 | 2 | 2 | 110 | 20 |
| Peasant 2 | 7 | 6 | 110 | 20 |
| Peasant 3 | 28 | 26 | 218 | 39 |
| Manual worker | 51 | 47 | 5 | 1 |
| Business/ self-employment | 6 | 6 | 2 | 0 |
| Rents, remittances | 5 | 5 | 1 | 0 |
| Salaried persons | 6 | 6 | 4 | 1 |
| Total | 109 | 100 | 560 | 100 |

landholder in the family who is still in the village owns 70 acres. Their land is the best land in the village, irrigated by groundwater. Additionally, because of the new airport and the city coming closer, they have gained hugely in terms of the rise in land value. Land valued at Rs 20,000 earlier has now risen to Rs 25 lakhs, or a hundred-fold increase over a few years. The family has leased out all their land to a Peasant 1 family.

We now turn to the two Peasant 1 households in the village who controlled 20 per cent of operational holdings. On household in this category is of particular interest. The economic status of this household (let us call the head of household AB) and its cultivation practices changed completely between our studies of 2009 and 2015. While the household's ownership holding has not changed, its operational holding has changed completely: from 45 acres to 130 acres, because AB has now leased in land from the landlord. His main sources of finance for cultivation have been agricultural surpluses, bank loans, and funds channelled into the village by different categories of non-governmental organisations (NGOs). AB now cultivates the major irrigated holdings in the village, and controls the flour mill and some village shops. His brother is a member of the panchayat board. Another brother is a salaried employee in the Transport Department in Bengaluru. Farming practices have improved, and family incomes have diversified. AB's household is now rapidly on the rise.

At the other end of the spectrum, there were 51 Manual worker households in the village, accounting for almost one-half of all households. Peasant 3 and Manual worker households together accounted for 72 per cent of all households, but only 23 per cent of the ownership of assets in the village.

Non-agricultural classes comprised 15 per cent of households resident in Zhapur, and accounted for around 10 per cent of ownership and operational holdings of land.

Finally, there were clear patterns in respect of the distribution of households by socio-economic class and caste (Appendix Table 3). There was no Scheduled Caste (SC) or Scheduled Tribe (ST) household among Landlord, Peasant 1, and Peasant 2 classes. Of all SC households, 61 per cent were Manual workers; the corresponding proportion for ST households was similar, at 57 per cent.

# Reference

Ramachandran, V. K. (2011), "The State of Agrarian Relations in India Today," *The Marxist*, vol. 27, nos. 1–2, January–June.

**Appendix Table 1** *Distribution of households by socio-economic class and caste, Alabujanahalli, 2008–09 in per cent*

| Class | Scheduled Caste (SC) | | | Scheduled Tribe (ST) | | | Caste Hindu | | | All | | |
|---|---|---|---|---|---|---|---|---|---|---|---|---|
| | No. | % of row total | % of column total | No. | % of row total | % of column total | No. | % of row total | % of column total | No. | % of row total | % of column total |
| Rich capitalist farmer | 0 | 0 | 0 | 0 | 0 | 0 | 2 | 100 | 1 | 2 | 100 | 1 |
| Peasant 1 | 0 | 0 | 0 | 0 | 0 | 0 | 9 | 100 | 4 | 9 | 100 | 4 |
| Peasant 2 | 0 | 0 | 0 | 0 | 0 | 0 | 39 | 100 | 19 | 39 | 100 | 16 |
| Peasant 3 | 1 | 3 | 3 | 0 | 0 | 0 | 29 | 97 | 14 | 30 | 100 | 12 |
| Peasant 4 | 7 | 12 | 21 | 0 | 0 | 0 | 51 | 88 | 25 | 58 | 100 | 24 |
| Rents/remittances | 2 | 29 | 6 | 0 | 0 | 0 | 5 | 71 | 2 | 7 | 100 | 3 |
| Salaried persons | 3 | 21 | 9 | 0 | 0 | 0 | 11 | 79 | 5 | 14 | 100 | 6 |
| Business/ self-employment | 0 | 0 | 0 | 0 | 0 | 0 | 11 | 100 | 5 | 11 | 100 | 5 |
| Manual worker 1 | 14 | 35 | 41 | 0 | 0 | 0 | 26 | 65 | 13 | 40 | 100 | 16 |
| Manual worker 2 | 6 | 27 | 18 | 0 | 0 | 0 | 16 | 73 | 8 | 22 | 100 | 9 |
| Manual worker 3 | 1 | 9 | 3 | 1 | 9 | 100 | 9 | 82 | 4 | 11 | 100 | 5 |
| Total | 34 | 14 | 100 | 1 | 9 | 100 | 208 | 86 | 100 | 243 | 100 | 100 |

**Appendix Table 2** *Distribution of households by socio-economic class and caste, Siresandra, 2008–09 in per cent*

| Class | Scheduled Caste (SC) | | | Other Backward Classes (OBC) | | | All | | |
|---|---|---|---|---|---|---|---|---|---|
| | No. | % of row total | % of column total | No. | % of row total | % of column total | No. | % of row total | % of column total |
| Peasant 1 | 0 | 0 | 0 | 4 | 100 | 8 | 4 | 100 | 5 |
| Peasant 2 | 3 | 13 | 10 | 21 | 87 | 42 | 24 | 100 | 30 |
| Peasant 3 | 12 | 37 | 41 | 20 | 63 | 40 | 32 | 100 | 41 |
| Business/small self-employment | 5 | 83 | 17 | 1 | 17 | 2 | 6 | 100 | 8 |
| Manual workers | 9 | 69 | 31 | 4 | 31 | 8 | 13 | 100 | 16 |
| Total | 29 | 37 | 100 | 50 | 63 | 100 | 79 | 100 | 100 |

**Appendix Table 3** *Distribution of households by socio-economic class and caste, Zhapur, 2009*

| Class | Scheduled Caste (SC) | | | Scheduled Tribe (ST) | | | Other Caste Hindu | | | All | | |
|---|---|---|---|---|---|---|---|---|---|---|---|---|
| | No | % of row total | % of column total | No | % of row total | % of column total | No | % of row total | % of column total | No | % of row total | % of column total |
| Landlord | 0 | 0 | 0 | 0 | 0 | 0 | 4 | 100 | 8 | 4 | 100 | 4 |
| Peasant 1 | 0 | 0 | 0 | 0 | 0 | 0 | 2 | 100 | 4 | 2 | 100 | 2 |
| Peasant 2 | 0 | 0 | 0 | 0 | 0 | 0 | 7 | 100 | 14 | 7 | 100 | 6 |
| Peasant 3 | 14 | 50 | 30 | 3 | 11 | 21 | 11 | 39 | 22 | 28 | 100 | 26 |
| Rents, remittances, pensions | 1 | 20 | 2 | 1 | 20 | 7 | 3 | 60 | 6 | 5 | 100 | 5 |
| Salaried persons | 2 | 33 | 4 | 0 | 0 | 0 | 4 | 67 | 8 | 6 | 100 | 6 |
| Business activity/ self-employed | 1 | 17 | 2 | 2 | 33 | 14 | 3 | 50 | 6 | 6 | 100 | 6 |
| Manual workers | 28 | 55 | 61 | 8 | 16 | 57 | 15 | 29 | 31 | 51 | 100 | 47 |
| Total | 46 | 42 | 100 | 14 | 13 | 100 | 49 | 45 | 100 | 109 | 100 | 100 |

# 5

## Literacy and Schooling in Three Villages of Karnataka

Venkatesh Athreya, with T. Sivamurugan

The discussion on literacy and schooling in this chapter will cover the following indicators: school attendance; literacy rates among the population aged 7 years and above; literacy among adults aged above 18 years; mean and median years of schooling; and distribution of children by work status and school attendance status. Following international norms, any person up to the age of 18 is defined as a child.

### Alabujanahalli

#### School Attendance

Table 1 and Appendix Tables 1 and 2 show, in succession, the school attendance ratios in 2009 for children, boys and girls, in Alabujanahalli village, in the age-group 6 to 18 years.

School attendance was not universal in Alabujanahalli in 2009, even for children in the age-group 6 to 14 years. While all children in the age-group 6 to 10 years were in school, six out of 69 children in the age-group 11 to 14 years (of whom four were boys and two were girls) were not in school. In the age-group 15 to 16 years, eight out of 49 children, of whom only one was a boy, were out of school. In the age-group 17 to 18 years, 33 out of 57 children were not in school. There were no children in school in this age-group from Manual worker 2 and Manual worker 3 households.

Turning to attendance ratios for girls, nearly all girls in the age-group 11 to 14 years were in school, with only two girls – both from Manual worker 3 households – out of school. Beyond the age of 14 years, attendance ratios

**Table 1** *Children attending school, by age-group and socio-economic class, Alabujanahalli, 2009*

| Socio-economic class | | 6 to 10 years | 11 to 14 years | 15 to 16 years | 17 to 18 years | All |
|---|---|---|---|---|---|---|
| Rich capitalist farmer | Number | 0 | 1 | 0 | 1 | 2 |
| | Per cent | – | 100 | – | 100 | 100 |
| Peasant 1 | Number | 6 | 5 | 1 | 1 | 13 |
| | Per cent | 100 | 100 | 100 | 50 | 92.9 |
| Peasant 2 | Number | 19 | 7 | 8 | 3 | 37 |
| | Per cent | 100 | 87.5 | 88.9 | 60 | 90.2 |
| Peasant 3 | Number | 14 | 4 | 5 | 4 | 27 |
| | Per cent | 100 | 100 | 100 | 50 | 87.1 |
| Peasant 4 | Number | 15 | 18 | 11 | 7 | 51 |
| | Per cent | 100 | 94.7 | 78.6 | 38.9 | 77.3 |
| Manual worker 1 | Number | 15 | 11 | 6 | 5 | 37 |
| | Per cent | 100 | 100 | 75 | 35.7 | 77.1 |
| Manual worker 2 | Number | 7 | 5 | 3 | 0 | 15 |
| | Per cent | 100 | 83.3 | 100 | 0 | 83.3 |
| Manual worker 3 | Number | 6 | 1 | 1 | 0 | 8 |
| | Per cent | 100 | 25 | 33.3 | 0 | 53.3 |
| Business/self-employment | Number | 3 | 4 | 3 | 1 | 11 |
| | Per cent | 100 | 100 | 100 | 50 | 91.7 |
| Salaried persons | Number | 2 | 2 | 1 | 2 | 7 |
| | Per cent | 100 | 100 | 100 | 100 | 100 |
| Rents/remittances | Number | 4 | 5 | 2 | 0 | 11 |
| | Per cent | 100 | 100 | 100 | – | 100 |
| All | Number | 91 | 63 | 41 | 24 | 219 |
| | Per cent | 100 | 91.3 | 83.7 | 42.1 | 82.6 |

falls steeply for girls from poor peasant and manual worker households (Appendix Table 2).

Overall, one can say that there is a distinct correlation between socio-economic class status and school attendance ratios, with the top segments of the agrarian population and the non-agrarian households doing better than those in the lower segments of the agrarian population.

## School Attendance and Social Group

Tables 2 to 4 present the distribution of attendance ratios by age-group and social group. All the children in the age-group 6 to 10 years were attending school in Alabujanahalli in 2009. However, in the next age-group of 11 to 14 years, four out of 57 children from Backward Class (BC) households and both the children from Scheduled Tribute (ST) households were out of school, whereas all the ten children from Scheduled Caste (SC) households were in school.

There were no tribal children in the age-group 15 to 18 years. Of the 42 children from BC households aged 15 to 16 years, only 35 were in school as compared to six out of seven among SC households. In the age-group 17 to 18 years, 19 out of 48 children from BC households and five out of eight children from SC households were attending school. Among boys, four out of 26 boys from BC households in the age-group 11 to 14 years were not in school, whereas all three children from SC households were in school. In the

**Table 2** *Children attending school, by age-group and caste, Alabujanahalli, 2009*

| Age-group | Backward Class (BC) | | Scheduled Caste (SC) | | Scheduled Tribe (ST) | | All | |
|---|---|---|---|---|---|---|---|---|
| | Number | Per cent | Number | Per cent | Number | Per cent | Number | Per cent |
| 6 to 10 years | 81 | 100 | 8 | 100 | 2 | 100 | 91 | 100 |
| 11 to 14 years | 53 | 93 | 10 | 100 | 0 | 0 | 63 | 91.3 |
| 15 to 16 years | 35 | 83.3 | 6 | 85.7 | 0 | – | 41 | 83.7 |
| 17 to 18 years | 19 | 39.6 | 5 | 62.5 | 0 | – | 24 | 42.9 |
| All | 188 | 82.5 | 29 | 87.9 | 2 | 50 | 219 | 82.6 |

**Table 3** *Boys attending school, by age-group and caste, Alabujanahalli, 2009*

| Age-group | Backward Class (BC) | | Scheduled Caste (SC) | | Scheduled Tribe (ST) | | All | |
|---|---|---|---|---|---|---|---|---|
| | Number | Per cent | Number | Per cent | Number | Per cent | Number | Per cent |
| 6 to 10 years | 42 | 100 | 2 | 100 | 1 | 100 | 45 | 100 |
| 11 to 14 years | 22 | 84.6 | 3 | 100 | – | – | 25 | 86.2 |
| 15 to 16 years | 15 | 93.8 | 3 | 100 | 0 | – | 18 | 94.7 |
| 17 to 18 years | 10 | 45.5 | 3 | 75 | 0 | – | 13 | 50 |
| All | 89 | 84 | 11 | 91.7 | 1 | 100 | 101 | 84.9 |

**Table 4** *Girls attending school, by age-group and caste, Alabujanahalli, 2009*

| Age-group | Backward Class (BC) | | Scheduled Caste (SC) | | Scheduled Tribe (ST) | | All | |
|---|---|---|---|---|---|---|---|---|
| | Number | Per cent | Number | Per cent | Number | Per cent | Number | Per cent |
| 6 to 10 years | 39 | 100 | 6 | 100 | 1 | 100 | 46 | 100 |
| 11 to 14 years | 31 | 100 | 7 | 100 | 0 | 0 | 38 | 95 |
| 15 to 16 years | 20 | 76.9 | 3 | 75 | 0 | – | 23 | 76.7 |
| 17 to 18 years | 9 | 34.6 | 2 | 50 | 0 | – | 11 | 36.7 |
| All | 99 | 81.1 | 18 | 85.7 | 1 | 33.3 | 118 | 80.8 |

age-group 15 to 16 years, all but one of 19 children were in school, with only one BC household reporting one boy out of school. Finally, in the age-group 17 to 18 years, 10 out of 22 boys from BC households and three out of four boys from SC households were out of school.

As with boys, in the case of girls too, SC children did better than BC children in the age-group 15 to 18 years in terms of school attendance ratios, while both castes reported 100 per cent attendance in the age-group 6 to 14 years. Alabujanahalli in 2009 was one of the few villages surveyed by the Foundation for Agrarian Studies (FAS) where the SCs did distinctly better than the BCs in respect of school attendance ratios.

## School Attendance and Work

It is clear from the foregoing that there is some degree of correlation between socio-economic class status and school attendance, at least in the age-group 15 to 18 years, and that children of poorer manual workers were the most deprived with regard to schooling. Likewise, STs fared poorly and BCs did not do as well as SCs in schooling in Alabujanahalli in 2009. We turn now to the linkages between school attendance and work status of children. Table 5 shows the distribution of children aged 6 to 18 years by school attendance and work status in Alabujanahalli in 2009.[1]

Nearly one-fifth of the girls and one-sixth of the boys were out of school. Over 6 per cent of girls and nearly 27 per cent of boys were working children even within the narrow definition adopted in this study. If one treats all children out of school as working – which is not unreasonable

---

[1] Work here is defined as paid or unpaid work outside the household for an employer, work on household operational holding, and work in any household enterprise other than relating to animal resources.

**Table 5** *School attendance and work status among children aged 6 to 18 years, Alabujanahalli, 2009*

| Children | Not attending school | | | | Attending school | | | |
|---|---|---|---|---|---|---|---|---|
| | Not working | | Working | | Not working | | Working | |
| | Number | Per cent | Number | Per cent | Number | Per cent | Number | Per cent |
| Girls | 21 | 14.4 | 7 | 4.8 | 116 | 80 | 2 | 1.4 |
| Boys | 1 | 0.8 | 17 | 14.3 | 86 | 72.3 | 15 | 12.6 |
| All | 22 | 8.3 | 24 | 9.1 | 202 | 76 | 17 | 6.4 |

given that all but one out of the 22 out-of-school children reported as not working were girls engaged in household chores – then, as many as 63 out of a total of 265 children, or nearly one-fourth of the child population, were working children in Alabujanahalli in 2009. Thus, even in a village relatively favourably placed with respect to agricultural productivity and agrarian activity, there was a high incidence of child work.

*Literacy*

Notwithstanding its limitations, literacy is an important indicator of educational achievement. Table 6 shows the literacy status of the population aged 7 years and above by socio-economic class in Alabujanahalli in 2009.

The PARI (Project on Agrarian Relations in India) surveys of FAS counted members of respondent households as literate only if the persons reported that they could both read and write. Using this criterion, the overall literacy rate for the population aged 7 years and above in Alabujanahalli in 2009 was a modest 64.5 per cent. The male literacy rate was 71.8 per cent and the female literacy rate was much lower, at 57.5 per cent. There were, as one might expect, significant differences across socio-economic classes. The top three agrarian classes reported literacy rates in excess of 75 per cent, while the three Manual worker categories together reported a literacy rate of less than 50 per cent. The female literacy rate was below the male rate for all classes except Rich capitalist farmers, among whom all persons were literate. Households dependent mainly on salaries, as also those dependent on rents and remittances, reported higher literacy rates than manual workers, poor peasants, and small business households. There was a distinct correlation between socio-economic class status and literacy status.

The variation in literacy rates of the population aged 7 years and above by social group is shown in Table 7.

**Table 6** *Percentage of population aged 7 years and above, who can read and write, by socio-economic class, Alabujanahalli, 2009*

| Socio-economic class | Number of literate persons | | | Literacy rate (per cent) | | |
|---|---|---|---|---|---|---|
| | Females | Males | Persons | Females | Males | Persons |
| Rich capitalist farmer | 6 | 6 | 12 | 100 | 100 | 100 |
| Peasant 1 | 23 | 28 | 51 | 85.2 | 96.6 | 91.1 |
| Peasant 2 | 70 | 93 | 163 | 67.3 | 83 | 75.5 |
| Peasant 3 | 48 | 49 | 97 | 66.7 | 70 | 68.3 |
| Peasant 4 | 68 | 88 | 156 | 55.3 | 72.1 | 63.7 |
| Manual worker 1 | 39 | 49 | 88 | 44.3 | 56.3 | 50.3 |
| Manual worker 2 | 14 | 11 | 25 | 35 | 55 | 41.7 |
| Manual worker 3 | 8 | 9 | 17 | 34.8 | 42.9 | 38.6 |
| Business/self-employment | 13 | 12 | 25 | 54.2 | 60 | 56.8 |
| Salaried persons | 14 | 23 | 37 | 60.9 | 79.3 | 71.2 |
| Rents/remittances | 12 | 13 | 25 | 66.7 | 86.7 | 75.8 |
| All | 315 | 381 | 696 | 57.5 | 71.8 | 64.5 |

Although we saw earlier that school attendance rates for the age-group of 6 to 18 years were higher for SCs as compared to BCs, it was otherwise with respect to literacy rates. Leaving aside the very small number of Other Caste Hindus and STs, we can see that the literacy rates for the SCs were well below that for the BCs in respect of both females and males. This is the general pattern across rural India.

*Adult literacy*

Table 8 presents the variation in literacy rates of the adult population (defined to include all persons above the age of 18 years) in Alabujanahalli in 2009 across socio-economic classes. The overall adult literacy rate, at 57.6 per cent, was distinctly lower than that for the population aged 7 years and above, which stood at 64.5 per cent. The difference was much higher in the case of female literacy rates, at 10.3 percentage points, as against a difference of 3 percentage points in the male literacy rates between the adult population and the age-group of 7 years and above. As one would expect, adult literacy rates were lower than the corresponding rates for the age-group of 7 years and above in the case of the various socio-economic classes. The differential was generally greater for female literacy, since improvements in access to schooling for women have come later than for men.

**Table 7** *Percentage of population aged 7 years and above, who can read and write, by social group, Alabujanahalli, 2009*

| Social group | Number of persons | | | Number of literate persons | | | Literacy rate (per cent) | | |
|---|---|---|---|---|---|---|---|---|---|
| | Females | Males | Persons | Females | Males | Persons | Females | Males | Persons |
| Backward Class (BC) | 467 | 458 | 925 | 277 | 337 | 614 | 59.3 | 73.6 | 66.4 |
| Other Caste Hindu | 1 | 2 | 3 | 0 | 2 | 2 | 0 | 100 | 66.7 |
| Scheduled Caste (SC) | 76 | 69 | 145 | 37 | 42 | 79 | 48.7 | 60.9 | 54.5 |
| Scheduled Tribe (ST) | 4 | 2 | 6 | 1 | 0 | 1 | 25 | 0 | 16.7 |
| All | 548 | 531 | 1079 | 315 | 381 | 696 | 57.5 | 71.8 | 64.5 |

**Table 8** *Percentage of population aged 18 years and above, who can read and write, by socio-economic class, Alabujanahalli, 2009*

| Socio-economic class | Number of literate persons | | | Literacy rate (per cent) | | |
|---|---|---|---|---|---|---|
| | Females | Males | Persons | Females | Males | Persons |
| Rich capitalist farmer | 5 | 5 | 10 | 100 | 100 | 100 |
| Peasant 1 | 17 | 24 | 41 | 81 | 96 | 89.1 |
| Peasant 2 | 53 | 77 | 130 | 60.9 | 82.8 | 72.2 |
| Peasant 3 | 31 | 43 | 74 | 56.4 | 68.3 | 62.7 |
| Peasant 4 | 46 | 63 | 109 | 46.5 | 65.6 | 55.9 |
| Manual worker 1 | 19 | 32 | 51 | 28.4 | 46.4 | 37.5 |
| Manual worker 2 | 6 | 6 | 12 | 19.4 | 42.9 | 26.7 |
| Manual worker 3 | 3 | 6 | 9 | 18.8 | 40 | 29 |
| Business/self-employment | 6 | 9 | 15 | 35.3 | 52.9 | 44.1 |
| Salaried persons | 10 | 22 | 32 | 52.6 | 78.6 | 68.1 |
| Rents/remittances | 7 | 8 | 15 | 53.8 | 80 | 65.2 |
| All | 203 | 295 | 498 | 47.2 | 67.8 | 57.6 |

**Table 9** *Percentage of population aged 18 years and above, who can read and write, by social group, Alabujanahalli, 2009*

| Social group | Number of literate persons | | | Literacy rate (per cent) | | |
|---|---|---|---|---|---|---|
| | Females | Males | Persons | Females | Males | Persons |
| Backward Class (BC) | 182 | 258 | 440 | 49.3 | 69.7 | 59.5 |
| Other Caste Hindu | 0 | 2 | 2 | 0 | 100 | 66.7 |
| Scheduled Caste (SC) | 21 | 35 | 56 | 35.6 | 56.5 | 46.3 |
| Scheduled Tribe (ST) | 0 | 0 | 0 | 0 | 0 | 0 |
| All | 203 | 295 | 498 | 47.2 | 67.8 | 57.6 |

The variation in adult literacy rates by social group in Alabujanahalli in 2009 is shown in Table 9.

As expected, the differences in literacy rates between the 7+ and the adult populations were much larger for females than males. The other point to note is that the difference between literacy rates among females of BC and SC households was somewhat lower for the 7+ population as compared to the adult population. In the case of males, no such narrowing of the differential in literacy rates among BCs and SCs was seen. This suggests a more rapid improvement in female school attendance ratios for SCs than for BCs, but no such improvement in the case of male attendance ratios.

## Years of Schooling

In addition to the literacy rate, one can use years of schooling as an indicator of educational achievement/deprivation. Two such measures are average and median years of schooling. Table 10 presents the variation in the mean years of schooling of the population aged above 16 years in Alabujanahalli, by socio-economic class status. Table 11 shows the corresponding variation in median years of schooling.

The overall picture is one of rather modest achievement with regard to formal schooling. The mean years of schooling for all males above 16 years of age were only seven, and that for women they were substantially lower, at 4.8 years. The median years of schooling for females were as low as three years, meaning that half or more of females aged above 16 years in Alabujanahalli in 2009 had not completed even three years of formal schooling. It is true that many other villages surveyed by PARI have done even more poorly, but the fact remains that these are not figures that warrant any celebration.

In terms of variation across socio-economic classes with respect to both median and mean years of schooling, it is clear that the Rich capitalist farmer households and the upper sections of the peasantry were able to obtain a significantly greater extent of formal schooling than manual workers and the poorer sections of the peasantry. Half or more of women from the

**Table 10** *Average number of completed years of schooling for population above 16 years, by socio-economic class, Alabujanahalli, 2009*

| Socio-economic class | Females | Males | Persons |
|---|---|---|---|
| Rich capitalist farmer | 9.6 | 8.8 | 9.2 |
| Business/self-employment | 3.9 | 5.1 | 4.5 |
| Manual worker 1 | 3.1 | 4.6 | 3.9 |
| Manual worker 2 | 2.0 | 3.6 | 2.5 |
| Manual worker 3 | 2.4 | 4.5 | 3.4 |
| Peasant 1 | 7.5 | 11.1 | 9.5 |
| Peasant 2 | 6.4 | 8.2 | 7.3 |
| Peasant 3 | 5.8 | 7.4 | 6.7 |
| Peasant 4 | 4.4 | 6.5 | 5.5 |
| Rents/remittances | 5.5 | 8.4 | 6.8 |
| Salaried persons | 5.7 | 8.9 | 7.5 |
| All | 4.8 | 7.0 | 5.9 |

**Table 11** *Median number of completed years of schooling for population above 16 years, by socio-economic class, Alabujanahalli, 2009*

| Socio-economic class | Females | Males | Persons |
|---|---|---|---|
| Rich capitalist farmer | 10.0 | 10.0 | 10.0 |
| Peasant 1 | 9.0 | 12.0 | 10.0 |
| Peasant 2 | 8.0 | 9.0 | 8.0 |
| Peasant 3 | 7.0 | 9.0 | 8.0 |
| Peasant 4 | 0.0 | 7.5 | 6.0 |
| Manual worker 1 | 0.0 | 2.0 | 0.0 |
| Manual worker 2 | 0.0 | 1.0 | 0.0 |
| Manual worker 3 | 0.0 | 0.0 | 0.0 |
| Business/self-employment | 0.0 | 4.0 | 0.0 |
| Rents/remittances | 5.0 | 9.5 | 8.0 |
| Salaried persons | 6.5 | 10.0 | 10.0 |
| All | 3.0 | 8.0 | 7.0 |

**Table 12** *Average number of completed years of schooling for population above 16 years, by social group, Alabujanahalli, 2009*

| Social group | Females | Males | Persons |
|---|---|---|---|
| Backward Class (BC) | 5.0 | 7.2 | 6.1 |
| Other Caste Hindu | 0.0 | 6.5 | 4.3 |
| Scheduled Caste (SC) | 3.7 | 5.7 | 4.7 |
| Scheduled Tribe (ST) | 0.0 | 0.0 | 0.0 |
| All | 4.8 | 7.0 | 5.9 |

poorest peasant category or "Peasant 4," and from the three Manual worker categories, did not have even one completed year of formal schooling. Thus, there is a clear correlation between socio-economic class status and schooling, with the Manual worker and poor peasant households suffering much higher levels of deprivation than the Rich capitalist farmer and rich peasant households.

The variation in mean years of schooling by social group in Alabujanahalli in 2009 among the population aged above 16 years is shown in Table 12. The corresponding table for median years of schooling is Table 13.

We may leave out of the discussion the "Other Caste Hindu" households and STs, in view of the very small number of observations for these two social groups. With regard to both the mean and the median years of

**Table 13** *Median number of completed years of schooling for population above 16 years, by social group, Alabujanahalli, 2009*

| Social group | Females | Males | Persons |
|---|---|---|---|
| Backward Class (BC) | 4 | 9 | 7 |
| Other Caste Hindu | 0 | 6.5 | 4 |
| Scheduled Caste (SC) | 0 | 6.5 | 0.5 |
| Scheduled Tribe (ST) | 0 | 0 | 0 |
| All | 3 | 8 | 7 |

schooling among those aged above 16 years, the BCs were much better off than the SCs in Alabujanahalli in 2009. Half or more of the SC women aged above 16 years had not completed even one year of formal schooling.

## Siresandra

Let us now turn to the same indicators for Siresandra village.

### *School Attendance and Socio-Economic Class Status*

Table 14 shows the variations in school attendance ratios of children by socio-economic class status of households in Siresandra in 2009; the corresponding figures for boys and girls in the age-group of 6 to 18 years are given in Appendix Tables 3 and 4.

The data show that as far as children in the age-group 6 to 14 years are concerned, almost all the children are in school. Only one girl and one boy, out of 44 children consisting of 23 girls and 21 boys, in this age-group were not attending school in Siresandra in 2009. The boy belonged to a household classified as Peasant 3 and the girl to a Peasant 2 family. In the age-group 15 to 16 years, 18 out of 21 children were in school. All ten boys in this age-group were in school, but three out of the 11 girls were not. In the age-group 17 to 18 years, only 12 out of 21 children – five out of 10 girls and seven out of 11 boys – were in school. Given the rather small numbers involved, it is not possible to draw any conclusions about the relationship between school attendance and socio-economic class status.

### *School Attendance and Social Group*

Variations in school attendance ratios across social groups are shown in Tables 15 and 16.

**Table 14** *Children attending school, by socio-economic class and age-group, Siresandra, 2009*

| Socio-economic class | | Age-group | | | | |
|---|---|---|---|---|---|---|
| | | 6 to 10 years | 11 to 14 years | 15 to 16 years | 17 to 18 years | All |
| Peasant 1 | Number | 2 | 0 | 0 | 2 | 4 |
| | Per cent | 100 | – | – | 66.7 | 80 |
| Peasant 2 | Number | 14 | 16 | 9 | 1 | 40 |
| | Per cent | 93.3 | 100 | 100 | 33.3 | 93 |
| Peasant 3 | Number | 17 | 11 | 7 | 6 | 41 |
| | Per cent | 94.4 | 100 | 87.5 | 60 | 87.2 |
| Manual workers | Number | 6 | 4 | 2 | 1 | 13 |
| | Per cent | 100 | 100 | 66.7 | 33.3 | 81.3 |
| Business/small self-employment | Number | 3 | 4 | 0 | 2 | 9 |
| | Per cent | 100 | 100 | 0 | 100 | 90 |
| All | Number | 42 | 35 | 18 | 12 | 107 |
| | Per cent | 95.5 | 100 | 85.7 | 57.1 | 88.4 |

**Table 15** *Boys attending school, by social group, Siresandra, 2009*

| Age-group | Scheduled Caste (SC) | | Backward Caste (BC) | |
|---|---|---|---|---|
| | Number | Per cent | Number | Per cent |
| 6 to 10 years | 12 | 100.0 | 9 | 100.0 |
| 11 to 14 years | 3 | 100.0 | 7 | 100.0 |
| 15 to 16 years | 3 | 100.0 | 7 | 100.0 |
| 17 to 18 years | 1 | 50.0 | 5 | 62.5 |
| All | 19 | 95.0 | 28 | 90.3 |

**Table 16** *Girls attending school, by social group, Siresandra, 2009*

| Age-group | Scheduled Caste (SC) | | Backward Caste (BC) | |
|---|---|---|---|---|
| | Number | Per cent | Number | Per cent |
| 6 to 10 years | 13 | 100.0 | 9 | 100.0 |
| 11 to 14 years | 11 | 100.0 | 14 | 100.0 |
| 15 to 16 years | 2 | 40.0 | 6 | 100.0 |
| 17 to 18 years | 0 | 0.0 | 5 | 62.5 |
| All | 26 | 83.9 | 34 | 91.9 |

The data suggest that, in the age-group 6 to 14 years, there was little difference in school attendance percentages as between SC and BC households in Siresandra, in the case of both boys and girls. However, in the next age-group of 15 to 16 years, while all three SC boys were in school, three out of the five girls were out of school. Among BCs, all seven boys and all six girls in this age-group were attending school. In the next age-group of 17 to 18 years, of the two girls and two boys from SC households, only one boy was in school. The situation was better among the BCs, with five out of eight boys and five out of eight girls in school. Overall, the BCs did better than the SCs in the matter of school attendance among children aged 6 to 18 years in Siresandra in 2009.

### School Attendance and Work

Table 17 shows the distribution of children aged 6 to 18 years by their status with respect to school attendance and work.

Out of 68 girls in the age-group 6 to 18 years, as many as 14, or a little over one-fifth, were working children, even by the restricted definition of work used in this study which excludes work with animal resources.[2] The proportion of working children among boys in the same age-group was a little lower, at nine out of 51 or a little more than one-sixth. Nearly one in eight of girls and one in 13 of boys in the age-group of 6 to 18 years were not attending school. The incidence of working children as well as children not attending school in Siresandra in 2009 seems to have been small in comparison with some of the other villages surveyed by PARI, but it is hardly negligible.

Table 17 *School attendance and work status among children aged 6 to 18 years, Siresandra, 2009*

| Children | Not attending school | | | | Attending school | | | |
|---|---|---|---|---|---|---|---|---|
| | Not working | | Working | | Not working | | Working | |
| | Number | Per cent | Number | Per cent | Number | Per cent | Number | Per cent |
| Girls | 3 | 4.4 | 5 | 9.8 | 51 | 72.5 | 9 | 13.2 |
| Boys | 0 | 0 | 4 | 9.5 | 42 | 80.7 | 5 | 9.8 |
| All | 3 | 2.5 | 9 | 9.7 | 93 | 76 | 14 | 11.8 |

[2] Even among the 51 girls categorised as attending school and not working, 12 or just under one-fourth were reported as doing house work. On the other hand, not a single boy was reported as doing house work, and this is of course not surprising in our patriarchal society.

## Literacy

From a discussion of school attendance and work, and their correlation with socio-economic class and social status, we now turn to a discussion of the state of deprivation/achievement with regard to literacy, first among the population aged 7 years and above, and then among adults. As noted earlier, respondents in the PARI survey were divided in terms of literacy, not in a binary manner as literate/non-literate, but into four mutually exclusive categories: "cannot read or write," "can only sign name," "can read but not write," "can read and write" – and it is only the last category we treat as literate in the discussion that follows. Table 18 presents the data in respect of literacy among those aged 7 years and above.

The literacy rates for Siresandra show that nearly two-fifths of its population aged 7 years and above were not literate in 2009. Nearly half of all females in this age-group were not literate. Clearly, there was considerable deprivation in terms of possession of literacy skills in the village.

**Table 18** *Distribution of population aged 7 years and above, by literacy status, Siresandra, 2009*

| Literacy status | Females | | Males | | Persons | |
|---|---|---|---|---|---|---|
| | Number | Per cent | Number | Per cent | Number | Per cent |
| Cannot read or write | 58 | 27.5 | 37 | 17.5 | 95 | 22.5 |
| Can only sign name | 40 | 19 | 22 | 10.4 | 62 | 14.7 |
| Can read but cannot write | 1 | 0.5 | 3 | 1.4 | 4 | 0.9 |
| Can read and write | 112 | 53.1 | 147 | 69.7 | 259 | 61.4 |
| Unspecified | 0 | 0 | 2 | 0.9 | 2 | 0.5 |
| All | 211 | 100 | 211 | 100 | 422 | 100 |

**Table 19** *Percentage of population aged 7 years and above, who can read and write, by socio-economic class, Siresandra*

| Socio-economic class | Number of literate persons | | | Literacy rate (per cent) | | |
|---|---|---|---|---|---|---|
| | Females | Males | Persons | Females | Males | Persons |
| Peasant 1 | 8 | 17 | 25 | 50 | 81 | 67.6 |
| Peasant 2 | 43 | 65 | 108 | 54.4 | 82.3 | 68.4 |
| Peasant 3 | 37 | 41 | 78 | 48.1 | 57.7 | 52.7 |
| Manual workers | 15 | 15 | 30 | 57.7 | 62.5 | 60 |
| Business/small self-employment | 9 | 9 | 18 | 69.2 | 56.3 | 62.1 |
| All | 112 | 147 | 259 | 53.1 | 69.7 | 61.4 |

The variation across socio-economic classes in this regard is shown in Table 19. The top two peasant classes recorded the highest rates of literacy, and the poor peasants the lowest rates. Manual workers did better than poor peasants in respect of male literacy rates, and, what is more surprising, did even better than all the peasant classes with regard to female literacy rates. It is also noteworthy that the gender differential in literacy rates was the lowest for the socio-economic class of manual workers and the widest for the top two peasant classes taken together. This reflects, in part, the fact that any general improvement in society accrues first to the males in a patriarchal society, as also the fact that patriarchal values are generally more strongly entrenched among the peasantry than among the wage-earning sections.

The variation in literacy rates for the population aged 7 years and above across social groups is presented in Table 20.

As is the case across most of rural and urban India, the literacy rates of SCs were significantly lower than those for BCs, among both females and males. The differences between males and females in literacy rates were much higher for BCs than for SCs, reflecting the substantially lower male literacy rate among SCs as compared to BCs.

How did Siresandra perform in terms of adult literacy rates? Table 21 shows the variation in literacy rates across socio-economic classes for the population aged above 18 years.

It is interesting to note that male literacy rates for the adult population were not very different from those for the population aged 7 years and above, except for the  socio-economic class of Business/small self-employment. It was quite otherwise with female literacy rates except for the socio-economic class of Business/small self-employment, in which category there was practically no difference between the two rates. This reflects the fact that female literacy rates have caught up with those of males in the age-group of 7 to 18 years, as school attendance rates for girls have improved more rapidly over time than for boys, whose attendance rates were much higher than that for girls in earlier years.

Table 22 presents the variation in adult literacy rates across the two major social groups in Siresandra, namely SCs and BCs. The difference in literacy rates between adult males and all males aged 7 years and above was very small for BCs and a little larger for SCs. Even for SCs, however, the difference was only 8 percentage points.

When it came to females, however, the difference between literacy rates for adults and those for the population aged 7 years and above was substantial for both BCs and SCs, at 11.7 and 19.8 percentage points respectively. This

**Table 20** *Percentage of population aged 7 years and above, who can read and write, by social group, Siresandra, 2009*

| Social group | Number | | | Literacy rate (per cent) | | |
|---|---|---|---|---|---|---|
| | Females | Males | Persons | Females | Males | Persons |
| Scheduled Caste (SC) | 39 | 40 | 79 | 49.4 | 57.1 | 53.0 |
| Backward Class (BC) | 73 | 107 | 180 | 55.3 | 75.9 | 65.9 |
| All | 112 | 147 | 259 | 53.1 | 69.7 | 61.4 |

**Table 21** *Percentage of population aged 18 years and above, who can read and write, by socio-economic class, Siresandra, 2009*

| Socio-economic class | Number of literate persons | | | Literacy rate (per cent) | | |
|---|---|---|---|---|---|---|
| | Females | Males | Persons | Females | Males | Persons |
| Peasant 1 | 5 | 17 | 22 | 38.5 | 81 | 64.7 |
| Peasant 2 | 22 | 50 | 72 | 39.3 | 76.9 | 59.5 |
| Peasant 3 | 17 | 29 | 46 | 30.4 | 51.8 | 41.1 |
| Manual workers | 9 | 11 | 20 | 45 | 61.1 | 52.6 |
| Business/small self-employment | 7 | 5 | 12 | 70 | 45.5 | 57.1 |
| All | 60 | 112 | 172 | 38.7 | 65.5 | 52.8 |

**Table 22** *Proportion of population aged 18 years and above, who can read and write, by social group, Siresandra, 2009*

| Social group | Number | | | Adult literacy rate (per cent) | | |
|---|---|---|---|---|---|---|
| | Females | Males | Persons | Females | Males | Persons |
| Scheduled Caste (SC) | 16 | 26 | 42 | 29.6 | 49.1 | 39.3 |
| Backward Class (BC) | 44 | 86 | 130 | 43.6 | 72.9 | 59.4 |
| All | 60 | 112 | 172 | 38.7 | 65.5 | 52.8 |

brings out the more rapid increase in school attendance rates, in general, among females, and particularly, the more rapid increase for SC females who started from a lower rate than that for BC females. Thus, over time, there was a tendency for literacy rates to rise as well as for literacy rate differentials to fall, both between social groups, and between males and females, provided the rate of school attendance improved overall, and more rapidly for SCs and females than for BCs and males.

## Years of Schooling

We can use the indicators of mean and median years of schooling as measures of educational achievement. Table 23 shows the distribution of mean years of schooling by socio-economic class status for the population aged above 16 years.

Educational achievement as measured by mean years of schooling was modest in Siresandra even among the better-off sections of the agrarian population. Among males aged above 16 years, the highest achievement was nine years of schooling, which was the average among males in this age-group from the category of Peasant 1 households. The lowest was 5.3 years for manual workers, with Peasant 3 households reporting almost the same figure. Among females in this age-group, the highest figure was 7.5 years among Business/small self-employment households, and the lowest was 3.3 years among the poor peasant (Peasant 3) households. In general, manual worker and peasant households had lower mean years of schooling than the other socio-economic classes.

Table 24 shows the distribution of median years of schooling by socio-economic class.

Table 23 *Average number of completed years of schooling for population aged above 16 years, by socio-economic class, Siresandra, 2009*

| Socio-economic class | Females | Males | Persons |
|---|---|---|---|
| Peasant 1 | 5.1 | 9 | 7.4 |
| Peasant 2 | 4 | 7.7 | 6 |
| Peasant 3 | 3.3 | 5.4 | 4.4 |
| Manual workers | 4.1 | 5.3 | 4.7 |
| Business/small self-employment | 7.5 | 5.2 | 6.3 |

Table 24 *Median number of completed years of schooling for population aged above 16 years, by socio-economic class, Siresandra, 2009*

| Socio-economic class | Females | Males | Persons |
|---|---|---|---|
| Peasant 1 | 0 | 10 | 10 |
| Peasant 2 | 0 | 9 | 6 |
| Peasant 3 | 0 | 5 | 0 |
| Manual workers | 3 | 6 | 5 |
| Business/small self-employment | 9.5 | 5 | 7 |

The record in respect of median years of schooling was also modest. Among males aged above 16 years, it was somewhat correlated with agrarian class, with the top two categories of peasants doing much better than poor peasants and manual workers. Among females, all socio-economic classes of the agrarian population did badly, with half or more of females aged above 16 years among the peasantry not completing even one year of formal schooling. Clearly, while the levels of educational deprivation observed in Siresandra in 2009 may be much lower than those in the other surveyed villages, they are still unacceptably high.

Tables 25 and 26 present respectively the variation in mean and median years of schooling in Siresandra in 2009 among those aged above 16 years, by social group.

The mean years of schooling were low for both BCs and SCs in Siresandra in 2009, in the specified age-group. SCs fared even more poorly than BCs among both males and females. Males fared a little better than females, especially among the BCs. The situation with regard to median years of schooling was that only males aged above 16 years from BC households reported completion of some years of schooling; and even among these males, half of them did not have more than nine years of schooling. Among all male SCs aged above 16 years, half or more had not completed even one year of formal schooling. This was true for females aged above 16 years among both SCs and BCs. Taking the entire population aged above 16 years in Siresandra, half or more of them had not completed even five years of school in 2009.

**Table 25** *Average number of completed years of schooling for population above 16 years, by social group, Siresandra, 2009*

| Social group | Females | Males | Persons |
|---|---|---|---|
| Scheduled Caste (SC) | 5.3 | 5.8 | 5.6 |
| Backward Class (BC) | 6.8 | 8.2 | 7.5 |
| All | 6.3 | 7.4 | 6.9 |

**Table 26** *Median number of completed years of schooling for population above 16 years, by social group, Siresandra, 2009*

| Social group | Females | Males | Persons |
|---|---|---|---|
| Scheduled Caste (SC) | 0 | 0 | 0 |
| Backward Class (BC) | 0 | 9 | 8 |
| All | 0 | 8 | 5 |

# Zhapur

This section discusses literacy and schooling in Zhapur.

### School Attendance by Socio-Economic Class Status

The picture in respect of school attendance across different classes in Zhapur village is shown in Table 27, and Appendix Tables 5 and 6.

One would *a priori* expect that there would be some variation in school attendance ratios across classes, with the better-off socio-economic classes doing better than the other classes. There is, indeed, a clear correlation between class status and school attendance as far as the agrarian population is concerned. Children aged between 6 and 18 years from the Landlord category households, and Peasant 1 and Peasant 2 category households, were all in school.

Table 27 *Children attending school, by age-group and socio-economic class, Zhapur, 2009*

| Socio-economic class | | Age-group | | | | |
|---|---|---|---|---|---|---|
| | | 6 to 10 years | 11 to 14 years | 15 to 16 years | 17 to 18 years | All |
| Landlord | Number | 3 | 2 | 2 | 2 | 9 |
| | Per cent | 100 | 100 | 100 | 100 | 100 |
| Peasant 1 | Number | 3 | 0 | 0 | 1 | 4 |
| | Per cent | 100 | NA | NA | 100 | 100 |
| Peasant 2 | Number | 4 | 4 | 3 | 1 | 12 |
| | Per cent | 100 | 80 | 100 | 33.3 | 80 |
| Peasant 3 | Number | 22 | 14 | 4 | 4 | 44 |
| | Per cent | 88 | 77.8 | 44.4 | 40 | 71 |
| Manual workers | Number | 37 | 12 | 6 | 4 | 59 |
| | Per cent | 80.4 | 57.1 | 37.5 | 28.6 | 60.8 |
| Business activity/ self-employed | Number | 12 | 2 | 0 | 0 | 14 |
| | Per cent | 100 | 66.7 | 0 | 0 | 82.4 |
| Salaried persons | Number | 2 | 1 | 0 | 1 | 4 |
| | Per cent | 66.7 | 100 | - | 50 | 66.7 |
| Rents, remittances, pensions, handouts | Number | 0 | 0 | 0 | 0 | 0 |
| | Per cent | 0 | 0 | 0 | 0 | 0 |
| All | Number | 83 | 35 | 15 | 13 | 146 |
| | Per cent | 85.6 | 70 | 48.4 | 40.6 | 69.5 |

The situation was different with respect to poor peasant (Peasant 3) and manual worker households. Here, the attendance ratios were less than 100 per cent even in the age-group of 6 to 14 years. Around 30 per cent of all children from Peasant 3 households and 40 per cent of those from Manual worker households in the age-group of 6 to 18 years were out of school.

### School Attendance by Social Group

One may reasonably expect, given the social inequalities and hierarchies that characterise Indian villages, that attendance ratios may vary systematically with social group status. Tables 28 to 30 throw some light on this issue.

Leaving out of the discussion the small number of children from Muslim and Other Caste Hindu households, and age-groups beyond 14 years where the numbers involved are again rather small, let us examine the pattern of attendance ratios in the age-group of 6 to 14 years across SCs, BCs, and

**Table 28** *Children attending school, by social group, Zhapur, 2009*

| Age-group | Scheduled Caste (SC) | | Scheduled Tribe (ST) | | Backward Class (BC) | | Other Caste Hindu | | Muslim | |
|---|---|---|---|---|---|---|---|---|---|---|
| | No. | Per cent | No. | Per cent | No. | Per cent | No. | Per cent | No. | Per cent |
| 6 to 10 years | 37 | 78.7 | 10 | 90.9 | 33 | 91.7 | 0 | NA | 3 | 100.0 |
| 11 to 14 years | 14 | 60.9 | 5 | 71.4 | 15 | 78.9 | 1 | 100.0 | 0 | NA |
| 15 to 16 years | 4 | 30.8 | 2 | 50.0 | 8 | 61.5 | 1 | 100.0 | 0 | NA |
| 17 to 18 years | 3 | 37.5 | 2 | 66.7 | 7 | 36.8 | 1 | 100.0 | 0 | 0.0 |
| All | 58 | 63.7 | 19 | 76.0 | 63 | 72.4 | 3 | 100.0 | 3 | 75.0 |

**Table 29** *Boys attending school, by social group, Zhapur, 2009*

| Age-group | Scheduled Caste (SC) | | Scheduled Tribe (ST) | | Backward Class (BC) | | Other Caste Hindu | | Muslim | |
|---|---|---|---|---|---|---|---|---|---|---|
| | No. | Per cent | No. | Per cent | No. | Per cent | No. | Per cent | No. | Per cent |
| 6 to 10 years | 23 | 79.3 | 6 | 85.7 | 16 | 84.2 | 0 | NA | 0 | NA |
| 11 to 14 years | 5 | 45.5 | 4 | 66.7 | 3 | 100.0 | 1 | 100.0 | 0 | NA |
| 15 to 16 years | 3 | 37.5 | 0 | 0.0 | 7 | 70.0 | 0 | NA | 0 | NA |
| 17 to 18 years | 3 | 60.0 | 1 | 100.0 | 4 | 57.1 | 0 | NA | 0 | 0.0 |
| All | 34 | 64.2 | 11 | 73.3 | 30 | 76.9 | 1 | 100.0 | 0 | 0.0 |

**Table 30** *Girls attending school, by social group, Zhapur, 2009*

| Age-group | Scheduled Caste (SC) | | Scheduled Tribe (ST) | | Backward Class (BC) | | Other Caste Hindu | | Muslim | |
|---|---|---|---|---|---|---|---|---|---|---|
| | No. | Per cent | No. | Per cent | No. | Per cent | No. | Per cent | No. | Per cent |
| 6 to 10 years | 14 | 77.8 | 4 | 100.0 | 17 | 100.0 | 3 | 100.0 | 0 | NA |
| 11 to 14 years | 9 | 75.0 | 1 | 100.0 | 12 | 75.0 | 0 | NA | 0 | NA |
| 15 to 16 years | 1 | 20.0 | 2 | 66.7 | 1 | 33.3 | 0 | NA | 1 | 100.0 |
| 17 to 18 years | 0 | 0.0 | 1 | 50.0 | 3 | 25.0 | 0 | NA | 1 | 100.0 |
| All | 24 | 63.2 | 8 | 80.0 | 33 | 68.8 | 3 | 100.0 | 2 | 100.0 |

STs. There was not much of a gap between the BCs and the STs in respect of attendance ratios. However, the SCs had a consistently lower attendance ratio than the BCs and STs. This links up, in part, with the prevalence of child labour in the age-group 6 to 14 years. Of the 15 working children in this age-group, as many as 12 belonged to SC households. Of course, being a working child in the sense in which the term is used here does not rule out the possibility that the child may also be in school. But a link can nevertheless be hypothesised. This gets strengthened when one looks at the attendance ratio for SC boys in the age-group of 11 to 14 years, which was as low as 45.5 per cent. Six SC boys in this age-group were working for an employer outside the household, as against to two girls. The likelihood of not going to school was greater when the child was working for an employer outside the household since such work was more likely to be full-time.

It is obvious that while all social groups in the age-group of 6 to 18 years fared poorly in respect of school attendance, the SCs were the most severely deprived.

## School Attendance and Work

We have seen above that attendance ratios vary by socio-economic class and by social group in fairly systematic ways. Let us probe further the question of the relationship between school attendance and children being engaged in work. Table 31 provides a four-way classification of the children of Zhapur in the age-group of 6 to 18 years: working and not attending school; attending school and not working; attending school and working; neither attending school nor working.

Several points emerge from the data. First, 42 children out of a total of 210 – that is, one in five – were working children. Secondly, if we include

**Table 31** *School attendance and work status among children aged 6 to 18 years, Zhapur, 2009*

| Children | Not attending school | | | | Attending school | | | |
|---|---|---|---|---|---|---|---|---|
| | Not working | | Working | | Not working | | Working | |
| | Number | Per cent | Number | Per cent | Number | Per cent | Number | Per cent |
| Girls | 13 | 12.9 | 18 | 26.1 | 69 | 60.1 | 1 | 1.0 |
| Boys | 12 | 11.0 | 21 | 28.4 | 74 | 58.8 | 2 | 1.8 |
| All | 25 | 11.9 | 39 | 27.3 | 143 | 59.4 | 3 | 1.4 |

the seven boys and two girls engaged in work with animal resources, the proportion goes up to 51 out of 210 or approximately one in four. Thirdly, many of the children, mostly girls, whether in school or not, were engaged in household chores, which are not treated as work here. Such chores included not just routine physical house work including fetching water from some distance from the homestead, but also such things as minding senior elders or younger siblings.

Twenty-seven girls, of whom eleven were out of school, reported doing house work. If their numbers are added, working children as a proportion of the total amounts to 78 out of 210, or 37 per cent. By far the largest segment of the set of working children came from SC households. They also came predominantly from poor peasant and manual worker households.

## Literacy

Having examined school attendance and child labour at some length, let us turn now to the issue of literacy and other indicators of educational achievement among Zhapur's population, in the context child well-being. Table 32 presents the distribution of the population of Zhapur aged 7 years and above by level of literacy.

With literates being defined to include only those reporting that they could both read and write, the overall literacy rate in Zhapur for the population aged 7 years and above was just under 40 per cent. There was a large differential between the literacy rates of males and females, with the female literacy proportion not reaching one-third and the male literacy proportion not reaching one in two.

How did the literacy rates vary across socio-economic classes? The evidence is presented in Table 33.

Excluding from our analysis the households dependent on pensions, remittances, and handouts, on account of the very small number of

**Table 32** *Distribution of population aged 7 years and above, by literacy status, Zhapur, 2009*

| Literacy status | Females | | Males | | Persons | |
|---|---|---|---|---|---|---|
| | Number | Per cent | Number | Per cent | Number | Per cent |
| Cannot read and write | 135 | 49.3 | 85 | 29.2 | 220 | 38.9 |
| Can only sign name | 42 | 15.3 | 66 | 22.7 | 108 | 19.1 |
| Can read but cannot write | 3 | 1.1 | 7 | 2.4 | 10 | 1.8 |
| Can read and write | 90 | 32.8 | 133 | 45.7 | 223 | 39.5 |
| Unspecified | 4 | 1.5 | 0 | 0.0 | 4 | 0.7 |
| All | 274 | 100.0 | 291 | 100.0 | 565 | 100.0 |

**Table 33** *Proportion of population aged 7 years and above, who can read and write, by socio-economic class, Zhapur, 2009*

| Socio-economic class | Number of literate persons | | | Literacy rate (per cent) | | |
|---|---|---|---|---|---|---|
| | Females | Males | Total | Females | Males | Total |
| Landlord | 11 | 12 | 23 | 73.3 | 92.3 | 82.1 |
| Peasant 1 | 0 | 9 | 9 | 0 | 64.3 | 42.9 |
| Peasant 2 | 10 | 12 | 22 | 50 | 57.1 | 53.7 |
| Peasant 3 | 26 | 41 | 67 | 36.6 | 46.6 | 41.8 |
| Manual workers | 26 | 35 | 61 | 21.3 | 30.4 | 25.3 |
| Business activity/self-employed | 13 | 12 | 25 | 56.5 | 52.2 | 54.3 |
| Salaried persons | 4 | 10 | 14 | 40 | 90.9 | 66.7 |
| Rents, remittances, pensions, handouts | 0 | 2 | 2 | 0 | 33.3 | 16.7 |
| All | 90 | 133 | 223 | 32.8 | 45.7 | 39.5 |

observations involved, there is a clear correlation between socio-economic class status and levels of literacy achievement. Only the Landlord class reported a literacy rate exceeding 80 per cent. It is followed at some distance by the Salaried households. All the peasant classes did poorly, and the Manual workers were the most deprived in terms of literacy.

The variation in literacy rates across social groups is shown in Table 34. Leaving aside the small number of Other Caste Hindus and Muslims, let us focus on the SCs, STs, and BCs. It is clear that the literacy rates among BCs were distinctly higher than those among the SCs and STs. The SCs did marginally better than the STs in respect of both females and males. Female literacy rates were significantly lower than male rates for all three social groups. The sex differential was highest among the BCs. Overall, it is a

**Table 34** *Proportion of population aged 7 years and above, who can read and write, by social group, Zhapur, 2009*

| Social group | Number of literates | | | Literacy rate (per cent) | | |
|---|---|---|---|---|---|---|
| | Females | Males | Total | Females | Males | Total |
| Scheduled Caste (SC) | 27 | 46 | 73 | 25.2 | 36.2 | 31.2 |
| Scheduled Tribe (ST) | 7 | 11 | 18 | 21.9 | 33.3 | 27.7 |
| Backward Class (BC) | 48 | 71 | 119 | 38.7 | 57.7 | 48.2 |
| Other Caste Hindu | 3 | 1 | 4 | 75.0 | 33.3 | 57.1 |
| Muslim | 5 | 4 | 9 | 71.4 | 80.0 | 75.0 |
| All | 90 | 133 | 223 | 32.8 | 45.7 | 39.5 |

dismal picture, with the literacy rate being less than 50 per cent for all the three major social groups in the village, and hovering around 30 per cent in the case of two of them: the SCs and the STs.

*Adult literacy*

Moving from the population aged 7 years and above, let us take a look at the literacy profile of the adult population in Zhapur. The relevant data, by socio-economic class status, are presented in Table 35.

Except for the socio-economic classes of Landlord and Salaried persons, who historically have relatively higher rates of literacy, in the case of all the other socio-economic classes (with the exception of Peasant 1), there is clear evidence that literacy rates improved over the years, as shown by the much higher literacy rates for the 7+ population as compared to the 18+ population. The class of Peasant 1 has shown the least improvement.

The picture in respect of variation in adult literacy rates across social groups is brought out in Table 36. There has been improvement in school attendance rates over the years. Given this, and the fact that the 7+ age-group includes those currently in schools, most of whom would be reported as literate, the literacy rates for adults, males as well as females, were naturally much lower than those for the population aged 7 years and above, for every social group.

Comparing the corresponding literacy rates in the two age-groups by the category of social groups, we find that the differential was higher with respect to female literacy rates in every social group. With respect to male literacy rates, the highest difference between the two age-groups was recorded by STs, while BCs and SCs report more modest differences. With respect to female literacy rates, it is evident that both BCs and SCs showed

Table 35 *Proportion of population aged 18 years and above, who can read and write, by socio-economic class, Zhapur, 2009*

| Socio-economic class | No of literate persons | | | Literacy rate (per cent) | | |
|---|---|---|---|---|---|---|
| | Females | Males | Total | Females | Males | Total |
| Landlord | 8 | 9 | 17 | 72.7 | 90 | 81 |
| Peasant 1 | 0 | 8 | 8 | 0 | 61.5 | 40 |
| Peasant 2 | 2 | 7 | 9 | 16.7 | 43.8 | 32.1 |
| Peasant 3 | 9 | 23 | 32 | 18.4 | 39.7 | 29.9 |
| Manual workers | 6 | 17 | 23 | 7.1 | 22 | 14.2 |
| Business activity/self-employed | 6 | 8 | 14 | 42.9 | 44.4 | 43.8 |
| Salaried persons | 4 | 8 | 12 | 40 | 88.9 | 63.2 |
| Rents, remittances, pensions, handouts | 0 | 1 | 1 | 0 | 20 | 9 |
| All | 35 | 81 | 116 | 18 | 39.3 | 29 |

Table 36 *Proportion of population aged 18 years and above, who can read and write, by social group, Zhapur, 2009*

| Social group | Number of literates | | | Literacy rate (per cent) | | |
|---|---|---|---|---|---|---|
| | Females | Males | Persons | Females | Males | Persons |
| Scheduled Caste (SC) | 7 | 25 | 32 | 9.5 | 29.8 | 20.3 |
| Scheduled Tribe (ST) | 3 | 5 | 8 | 12.0 | 23.8 | 17.4 |
| Backward Class (BC) | 21 | 47 | 68 | 23.6 | 50.0 | 37.2 |
| Other Caste Hindu | 2 | 0 | 2 | 66.7 | 0.0 | 40.0 |
| Muslim | 2 | 4 | 6 | 50.0 | 80.0 | 66.7 |
| All | 35 | 81 | 116 | 17.9 | 39.3 | 28.9 |

a higher differential between the 7+ and 18+ age-groups than the STs. As a result, the gender differentials in literacy rates were much smaller in the population aged 7 years and above than in the adult population for both BCs and SCs. In the case of STs, the gender difference in literacy rates was more or less the same in both age-groups.

## Years of Schooling

A useful measure of adult achievement with respect to school education is the average number of years of schooling in a group. The distribution of median and mean years of schooling for the population of Zhapur aged above 16 years by socio-economic class status is presented in Tables 37 and 38.

It is clear that the socio-economic class of Landlord was truly a class

**Table 37** *Average number of completed years of schooling for population above 16 years, by socio-economic class, Zhapur, 2009*

| Socio-economic class | Females | Males | Persons |
|---|---|---|---|
| Landlord | 7.7 | 11.1 | 9.4 |
| Peasant 1 | 0.0 | 6.2 | 4.1 |
| Peasant 2 | 1.6 | 4.2 | 3.1 |
| Peasant 3 | 1.9 | 4.1 | 3.1 |
| Manual workers | 0.8 | 2.5 | 1.6 |
| Business activity/self-employed | 2.9 | 2.4 | 2.6 |
| Salaried persons | 4.5 | 8.4 | 6.4 |
| Rents, remittances, pensions, handouts | 0.0 | 4.0 | 1.8 |

**Table 38** *Median number of completed years of schooling for population above 16 years, by socio-economic class, Zhapur, 2009*

| Socio-economic class | Females | Males | Persons |
|---|---|---|---|
| Landlord | 9.5 | 12 | 11 |
| Peasant 1 | 0 | 7 | 0 |
| Peasant 2 | 0 | 3 | 0 |
| Peasant 3 | 0 | 3 | 0 |
| Manual workers | 0 | 0 | 0 |
| Business activity/self-employed | 0 | 0 | 0 |
| Salaried persons | 1.5 | 9 | 5 |
| Rents, remittances, pensions, handouts | 0 | 0 | 0 |

apart, with a huge distance separating it from all the other socio-economic classes. The Salaried persons class came next, but at a far distance. Among Manual workers, half or more of women and men aged above 16 years had not completed even one year of formal schooling. Women fared worse than men in all the socio-economic classes.

Tables 39 and 40 show the variations in mean and median years of schooling, respectively, among men and women aged above 16 years across social groups. We have not separately given the figures for Other Caste Hindus and Muslims in view of their small numbers, but data relating to them have been taken into account in calculating the numbers in the category "All."

Among males, median and mean years of schooling in the specified age-group were highest for BCs and lowest for SCs, with STs in between. When

**Table 39** *Average number of completed years of schooling for population above 16 years, by social group, Zhapur, 2009*

| Social group | Females | Males | Persons |
|---|---|---|---|
| Scheduled Caste (SC) | 1.5 | 4.3 | 3.1 |
| Scheduled Tribe (ST) | 4.8 | 5.0 | 4.9 |
| Backward Class (BC) | 4.5 | 6.7 | 5.8 |
| All | 3.2 | 5.5 | 4.5 |

**Table 40** *Median number of completed years of schooling for population above 16 years, by social group, Zhapur, 2009*

| Social group | Females | Males | Persons |
|---|---|---|---|
| Scheduled Caste (SC) | 0 | 3 | 0 |
| Scheduled Tribe (ST) | 5 | 4 | 4 |
| Backward Class (BC) | 3.5 | 7 | 6 |
| All | 0 | 5 | 4 |

it comes to females, however, STs had a significantly higher median and a marginally higher mean value than BCs for completed years of schooling. In both cases, SCs were at the bottom. Half of SC women above 16 years of age had not completed even one year of schooling. On average, SC women in this age-group received only a year-and-a-half of formal schooling. The record was modest enough for BCs and STs, but it was even worse for SCs. The overall figures of four years of schooling as the median value, and 4.5 years as the mean value, confirm that Zhapur was educationally quite deprived. The extreme level of deprivation among SCs has a clear socio-economic class implication: most SCs in Zhapur were manual workers, and this segment, which contributed substantially to production in the village, remained the most deprived.

# Concluding Observations

## *School Attendance*

It is sobering to note that school attendance was not universal in the three villages of Karnataka, even for the age-group 6 to 14 years. Siresandra was the best performer among the three villages in this regard, with only one girl and one boy out of 23 girls and 21 boys in this age-group being out of school. Zhapur was the poorest performer.

Around 40 per cent of children aged 15 to 18 years were out of school in Alabujanahalli, a relatively advanced village in terms of agricultural productivity. Siresandra fared somewhat better, with 30 out of 42 children in this age-group in school. In Zhapur, as many as 36 out of 64 children (56 per cent) in the age-group of 15 to 18 years were out of school.

### Working Children

In all three villages, in 2009, a section of the children in the age-group 6 to 18 years were working children. Over one-fifth of the children in Zhapur were working children. If children engaged in work with animal resources and those doing house work are included, the proportion goes up substantially to 37 per cent. The overall proportion of working children, using the narrow definition that excludes work with animals, and household chores and care functions, was a little lower than one-fifth in Siresandra. The presence of stone quarries in the neighbourhood of Zhapur had facilitated boys of poor households being sent to work in the quarries by their parents. In Zhapur, child labour took the form of boys being engaged as wage workers in quarries, in addition to employment in household operational holdings. In Siresandra, children were not engaged in work for employers outside the household. Over 6 per cent of girls and nearly 27 per cent of boys were working children in Alabujanahalli. If one treats all children out of school as working, one-fourth of the children in the age-group 6 to 18 years in Alabujanahalli were at work. Thus, even in a village relatively favourably placed with respect to agricultural productivity, there was a high incidence of child labour.

### Literacy and Years of Schooling

The literacy rates in the three villages remind us of the unacceptably high levels of educational deprivation in rural India even after decades of GDP growth rates in excess of 6 per cent per annum. In 2009, Zhapur had a literacy rate, for its population aged 7 years and above, of less than 40 per cent, with that for females at just under 33 per cent. Siresandra performed better, with an overall literacy rate of 61.4 per cent (males 69.7 per cent, females 53.9 per cent). Alabujanahalli fared a little better than Siresandra, with the male literacy rate at 71.8 per cent, the female rate at 57.5 per cent, and an overall rate at 64.5 per cent. Nearly seventy years after Independence, and three decades and more of rapid GDP growth, universal literacy seems a long way off in rural Karnataka – as also in India, going by the nearly 30 village studies carried out by FAS between 2005 and 2015.

## Years of Schooling

The overall picture with regard to formal schooling was poor in all the three villages of Karnataka studied by the FAS in 2009. Even in Alabujanahalli, the best performer among the three, the mean years of schooling for all males above 16 years of age was only seven, and that for women was substantially lower at 4.8 years. The median years of schooling for females was as low as three years, meaning that half or more of the women aged above 16 years in Alabujanahalli in 2009 had not completed even three years of formal schooling.

The other two villages fared much more poorly. In Zhapur, the mean years of schooling for males and females aged 16 years or older were, respectively, 5.5 and 3.2 years. The median years of schooling for this group were five years for males and zero for females, meaning that half or more of the women in the specified age-group in Zhapur had not completed even one year of schooling.

While Siresandra fared better than Zhapur with regard to mean years of schooling, it fared no better with regard to median years of schooling for women in the specified age-group. These figures testify to the overall levels of deprivation. Given the substantial inequalities across class and caste, the extent of deprivation was much greater for those who were economically or socially disadvantaged.

## Class, Caste, and Educational Inequality

In all the three villages, the richest sections – the Landlord class – fared much better with respect to educational indicators such as school attendance, literacy rates, and mean and median years of schooling. Children from this class were generally not to be found in the category of working children. By contrast, poor peasant and manual labour households fared very poorly. In both Alabujanahalli and Zhapur, the class of Manual workers had the lowest mean and median years of schooling in the village concerned among those over 16 years of age. Interestingly, the picture in Siresandra was different in this regard, with manual workers doing better than poor peasants.

In terms of social groups, Caste Hindus other than BCs were not present in Zhapur and Siresandra. Even in Alabujanahalli, they were only marginally present. The population in the three villages, for all practical purposes, can be seen as belonging to the categories of ST, SC, and BC. In Alabujanahalli, STs were small in number, and the main social groups were SC and BC. The BCs generally fared better than the SCs (and STs) in terms of literacy rates and years of schooling. In Siresandra, the population consisted only of SCs and BCs. The BCs fared better than the SCs on all educational indicators. The same was the case in Zhapur, where the STs fared a little worse than the SCs, and the BCs were relatively less deprived than the other two groups.

## Summing Up

To sum up, it is clear that measures to improve the incomes of the poor, to eliminate social oppression and inequality, and to ensure social provision of care services, are essential to address educational deprivation in rural Karnataka. These require strong political commitment to transform the ownership and distribution of assets in the countryside, as well as to make adequate provision of educational infrastructure and services in the villages. Finding the resources to do this is far from being an impossible proposition, provided the fiscal policies of the Central and State governments are modified to tax the richer sections effectively.

# Appendix Tables

**Appendix Table 1** *Boys attending school, by socio-economic class and age-group, Alabujana-halli, 2009*

| Socio-economic class | | Age-group | | | | |
|---|---|---|---|---|---|---|
| | | 6 to 10 years | 11 to 14 years | 15 to 16 years | 17 to 18 years | All |
| Rich capitalist farmer | Number | 0 | 0 | 0 | 1 | 1 |
| | Per cent | – | – | – | 100 | 100 |
| Peasant 1 | Number | 1 | 1 | 1 | 1 | 4 |
| | Per cent | 100 | 100 | 100 | 50 | 80 |
| Peasant 2 | Number | 11 | 3 | 3 | 1 | 18 |
| | Per cent | 100 | 75 | 100 | 33.3 | 85.7 |
| Peasant 3 | Number | 4 | 2 | 1 | 1 | 8 |
| | Per cent | 100 | 100 | 100 | 25 | 72.7 |
| Peasant 4 | Number | 8 | 10 | 5 | 5 | 28 |
| | Per cent | 100 | 90.9 | 100 | 55.6 | 84.8 |
| Manual worker 1 | Number | 9 | 4 | 4 | 3 | 20 |
| | Per cent | 100 | 100 | 100 | 60 | 90.9 |
| Manual worker 2 | Number | 2 | 3 | 1 | 0 | 6 |
| | Per cent | 100 | 75 | 100 | – | 85.7 |
| Manual worker 3 | Number | 5 | 0 | 0 | 0 | 5 |
| | Per cent | 100 | 0 | 0 | 0 | 62.5 |
| Business/self-employment | Number | 2 | 0 | 1 | 0 | 3 |
| | Per cent | 100 | – | 100 | – | 100 |
| Salaried persons | Number | 1 | 0 | 1 | 1 | 3 |
| | Per cent | 100 | – | 100 | 100 | 100 |
| Rent/remittance | Number | 2 | 2 | 1 | 0 | 5 |
| | Per cent | 100 | 100 | 100 | – | 100 |
| All | Number | 45 | 25 | 18 | 13 | 101 |
| | Per cent | 100 | 86.2 | 94.7 | 50 | 84.9 |

**Appendix Table 2** *Girls attending school, by socio-economic class and age-group, Alabujanahalli, 2009*

| Socio-economic class | | Age-group | | | | |
|---|---|---|---|---|---|---|
| | | 6 to 10 years | 11 to 14 years | 15 to 16 years | 17 to 18 years | All |
| Rich capitalist farmer | Number | 0 | 1 | 0 | 0 | 1 |
| | Per cent | – | 100 | – | – | 100 |
| Peasant 1 | Number | 5 | 4 | 0 | 0 | 9 |
| | Per cent | 100 | 100 | – | – | 100 |
| Peasant 2 | Number | 8 | 4 | 5 | 2 | 19 |
| | Per cent | 100 | 100 | 83.3 | 100 | 95 |
| Peasant 3 | Number | 10 | 2 | 4 | 3 | 19 |
| | Per cent | 100 | 100 | 100 | 75 | 95 |
| Peasant 4 | Number | 7 | 8 | 6 | 2 | 23 |
| | Per cent | 100 | 100 | 66.7 | 22.2 | 69.7 |
| Manual worker 1 | Number | 6 | 7 | 2 | 2 | 17 |
| | Per cent | 100 | 100 | 50 | 22.2 | 65.4 |
| Manual worker 2 | Number | 5 | 2 | 2 | 0 | 9 |
| | Per cent | 100 | 100 | 100 | 0 | 81.8 |
| Manual worker 3 | Number | 1 | 1 | 1 | 0 | 3 |
| | Per cent | 100 | 33.3 | 50 | 0 | 42.9 |
| Business/self-employment | Number | 1 | 4 | 2 | 1 | 8 |
| | Per cent | 100 | 100 | 100 | 50 | 88.9 |
| Salaried persons | Number | 1 | 2 | 0 | 1 | 4 |
| | Per cent | 100 | 100 | – | 100 | 100 |
| Rent/remittance | Number | 2 | 3 | 1 | 0 | 6 |
| | Per cent | 100 | 100 | 100 | – | 100 |
| All | Number | 46 | 38 | 23 | 11 | 118 |
| | Per cent | 100 | 95 | 76.7 | 36.7 | 80.8 |

**Appendix Table 3** *Boys attending school, by socio-economic class and age-group, Siresandra, 2009*

| Socio-economic class | | Age-group | | | | |
|---|---|---|---|---|---|---|
| | | 6 to 10 years | 11 to 14 years | 15 to 16 years | 17 to 18 years | All |
| Peasant 1 | Number | 0 | 0 | 0 | 2 | 2 |
| | Per cent | – | – | – | 100 | 100 |
| Peasant 2 | Number | 7 | 5 | 4 | 1 | 17 |
| | Per cent | 100 | 100 | 100 | 50 | 94.4 |
| Peasant 3 | Number | 8 | 2 | 4 | 2 | 16 |
| | Per cent | 88.9 | 100 | 100 | 40 | 80 |
| Manual workers | Number | 3 | 0 | 2 | 1 | 6 |
| | Per cent | 100 | – | 100 | 100 | 100 |
| Business/small self-employment | Number | 2 | 3 | 0 | 1 | 6 |
| | Per cent | 100 | 100 | – | 100 | 100 |
| All | Number | 20 | 10 | 10 | 7 | 47 |
| | Per cent | 95.2 | 100 | 100 | 63.6 | 90.4 |

**Appendix Table 4** *Girls attending school, by socio-economic class and age-group, Siresandra*

| Socio-economic class | | Age-group | | | | |
|---|---|---|---|---|---|---|
| | | 6 to 10 years | 11 to 14 years | 15 to 16 years | 17 to 18 years | All |
| Peasant 1 | Number | 2 | 0 | 0 | 0 | 2 |
| | Per cent | 100 | – | – | 0 | 66.7 |
| Peasant 2 | Number | 7 | 11 | 5 | 0 | 23 |
| | Per cent | 87.5 | 100 | 100 | 0 | 92 |
| Peasant 3 | Number | 9 | 9 | 3 | 4 | 25 |
| | Per cent | 100 | 100 | 75 | 80 | 92.6 |
| Manual workers | Number | 3 | 4 | 0 | 0 | 7 |
| | Per cent | 100 | 100 | 0 | 0 | 70 |
| Business/small self-employment | Number | 1 | 1 | 0 | 1 | 3 |
| | Per cent | 100 | 100 | 0 | 100 | 75 |
| All | Number | 22 | 25 | 8 | 5 | 60 |
| | Per cent | 95.7 | 100 | 72.7 | 50 | 87 |

**Appendix Table 5** *Boys attending school, by socio-economic class and age-group, Zhapur, 2009*

| Socio-economic class | | Age-group | | | | |
|---|---|---|---|---|---|---|
| | | 6 to 10 years | 11 to 14 years | 15 to 16 years | 17 to 18 years | All |
| Landlord | Number | 1 | 0 | 2 | 1 | 4 |
| | Per cent | 100 | – | 100 | 100 | 100 |
| Peasant 1 | Number | 1 | 0 | 0 | 1 | 2 |
| | Per cent | 100 | – | – | 100 | 100 |
| Peasant 2 | Number | 2 | 0 | 3 | 0 | 5 |
| | Per cent | 100 | – | 100 | 0 | 83.3 |
| Peasant 3 | Number | 17 | 7 | 3 | 3 | 30 |
| | Per cent | 89.5 | 87.5 | 60 | 60 | 81.1 |
| Manual workers | Number | 18 | 3 | 2 | 2 | 25 |
| | Per cent | 75 | 30 | 22.2 | 40 | 52 |
| Business activity/ self-employed | Number | 4 | 2 | 0 | 0 | 6 |
| | Per cent | 100 | 100 | – | 0 | 85.7 |
| Salaried persons | Number | 2 | 1 | 0 | 1 | 4 |
| | Per cent | 66.7 | 100 | – | 100 | 80 |
| Rents, remittances, pensions, handouts | Number | 0 | 0 | 0 | 0 | 0 |
| | Per cent | 0 | – | – | – | 0 |
| All | Number | 45 | 13 | 10 | 8 | 76 |
| | Per cent | 81.8 | 61.9 | 52.6 | 53.3 | 69.1 |

**Appendix Table 6** *Girls attending school, by socio-economic class and age-group, Zhapur, 2009*

| Socio-economic class | | Age-group | | | | |
|---|---|---|---|---|---|---|
| | | 6 to 10 years | 11 to 14 years | 15 to 16 years | 17 to 18 years | All |
| Landlord | Number | 2 | 2 | 0 | 1 | 5 |
| | Per cent | 100 | 100 | – | 100 | 100 |
| Peasant 1 | Number | 2 | 0 | 0 | 0 | 2 |
| | Per cent | 100 | – | – | – | 100 |
| Peasant 2 | Number | 2 | 4 | 0 | 1 | 7 |
| | Per cent | 100 | 80 | – | 50 | 77.8 |
| Peasant 3 | Number | 5 | 7 | 1 | 1 | 14 |
| | Per cent | 83.3 | 70 | 25 | 20 | 56 |
| Manual workers | Number | 19 | 9 | 4 | 2 | 34 |
| | Per cent | 86.4 | 81.8 | 57.1 | 22.2 | 69.4 |
| Business activity/ self-employed | Number | 8 | 0 | 0 | 0 | 8 |
| | Per cent | 100 | 0 | 0 | – | 80 |
| Salaried persons | Number | 0 | 0 | 0 | 0 | 0 |
| | Per cent | – | – | – | – | – |
| Rents, remittances, pensions, handouts | Number | 0 | 0 | 0 | 0 | 0 |
| | Per cent | – | – | – | – | – |
| All | Number | 38 | 22 | 5 | 5 | 70 |
| | Per cent | 90.5 | 75.9 | 41.7 | 27.8 | 69.3 |

# 6

## Landholdings and Irrigation in the Study Villages

### Deepak Kumar

This chapter explores aspects of land and irrigation in the three study villages in Karnataka. The emphasis is primarily on patterns of distribution of land among households, inequality in ownership and operation of land, the social composition of land distribution, and the extent and form of tenancy. Although many of the issues dealt with here require more analytical study, this lies outside the scope of the present chapter. Our aim is to give an overview of access to land among households resident in the villages. We restrict ourselves, therefore, to rendering a socio-economic report of vital parameters with respect to access to land and irrigation.

## Overview of the Study Villages

The study villages vary considerably in their agro-ecological, as well as social and economic characteristics. Here, I confine myself to stating some basic characteristics of land use and irrigation.

The village of Alabujanahalli is located in Mandya district in southern Karnataka. Historically, the dominant form of land tenure in this region was *ryotwari*. Alabujanahalli is the largest of the study villages, both in terms of acreage and number of households. At the time of the survey, it had a total of 243 households that collectively owned 639 acres of land (Table 1). The village falls in the command area of the Krishnarajasagar dam on the Cauvery river. Canals from this irrigation project feed a network of system tanks, and field channels deliver water to the fields through gravity flow. Nearly all cultivable land in the village was partially or completely irrigated by this system. Two-thirds of the total acreage was irrigated solely by tanks, while the remaining one-third was irrigated through a combination of tanks

**Table 1** *Number of households and extent of land in the three study villages* in number and acres

| District | Taluk | Village | Number of households | Extent (acres) |
|---|---|---|---|---|
| Mandya | Maddur | Alabujanahalli | 243 | 639 |
| Kolar | Kolar | Siresandra | 79 | 365 |
| Kalaburagi | Kalaburagi | Zhapur | 109 | 603 |

**Table 2** *Land use in the three villages* in per cent

| Land type | Alabujanahalli | Siresandra | Zhapur |
|---|---|---|---|
| Crop land | 75 | 53 | 94 |
| Orchard land and plantations | 6 | 24 | 0 |
| Current fallow | 2 | 21 | 4 |
| Land put to non-agricultural use | 18 | 2 | 2 |
| All | 100 | 100 | 100 |

**Table 3** *Distribution of crop land by source of irrigation in the three villages* in per cent

| Source of irrigation | Alabujanahalli | Siresandra | Zhapur |
|---|---|---|---|
| Tubewell/borewell | 2 | 42 | 10 |
| Tank | 67 | 3 | 0 |
| Traditional open well | 0 | 0 | 5 |
| Multi-source | 31 | 0 | 0 |
| Rainfed | 0 | 55 | 85 |
| All | 100 | 100 | 100 |

and tubewell lift irrigation (Table 3). Three-fourths of all the land in the village was put to cultivation of crops – primarily sugarcane, paddy, and finger millet. There was considerable area under non-agricultural use as homestead; orchards and plantations covered about 6 per cent of all the land area, and consisted mainly of coconut and eucalyptus trees (Table 2).

Siresandra is comparatively a smaller village with 79 resident households that owned a total of 365 acres of land. It is located in the water-scarce district of Kolar in southeastern Karnataka. Crop land comprised 53 per cent of all land in the village, and was used primarily for cultivation of finger millet and an assortment of vegetables. One-fourth of all the land area was under eucalyptus orchards. A significant 21 per cent of land had been left fallow in the survey year on account of lack of irrigation. About 45 per cent of all the cultivated land was irrigated and 55 per cent was rainfed. The primary means of irrigation was tubewells (42 per cent of total area), followed by tank irrigation (3 per cent).

Zhapur, located in the dry region of Kalaburagi, is spread over 603 acres and comprised 109 households in the summer of 2009. A share of 85 per cent of all the land area in the village was under rainfed cultivation. The dominant crops were rainfed cereals and oilseeds. Only 4 per cent of all the land was under current fallow, while 94 per cent was put to crop production. The homestead sites were small compared to Alabujanahalli, and comprised most of the 2 per cent of land put to non-agricultural use.

## Landholdings among Households

In rural India, households form the most important social unit of production. The PARI (Project on Agrarian Relations in India) survey of 2009, therefore, was indexed by households, and most parameters captured in the survey are represented as household characteristics. In this section, we will examine some basic characteristics of landholdings among households in the three villages.

Rural households can have access to land either as owners or through the lease market. In our three study villages, the most important tenure was that of owner-cultivators, and tenant cultivation was relatively less important in two of the villages (Table 4). In both Alabujanahalli and Siresandra, an overwhelming share of land area was operated by owner-cultivators. In Zhapur, too, 65 per cent of the area was operated by owner-cultivators. Ownership of landholding, then, was an important parameter and we shall look at this more closely.

Table 5 provides an overview of ownership holdings among households in the three villages. Ownership holdings refers to all land *owned* or held under *owner-like possession* by households. It includes all categories of land

**Table 4** *Distribution of operated area by tenure* in per cent

| Village | Owned and self-operated | Leased in | Total |
|---|---|---|---|
| Alabujanahalli | 91 | 9 | 100 |
| Siresandra | 99 | 1 | 100 |
| Zhapur | 65 | 35 | 100 |

**Table 5** *Descriptive statistics on household ownership holdings* in acres

| Village | Largest holding | Average size | Coefficient of variation |
|---|---|---|---|
| Alabujanahalli | 25.1 | 2.6 | 1.26 |
| Siresandra | 48.1 | 4.6 | 1.43 |
| Zhapur | 62.0 | 5.5 | 2.05 |

**Table 6** *Descriptive statistics on household operational holdings* in acres

| Village | Largest holding | Average | Coefficient of variation |
|---|---|---|---|
| Alabujanahalli | 25.0 | 2.2 | 1.37 |
| Siresandra | 48.0 | 4.5 | 1.46 |
| Zhapur | 75.0 | 5.1 | 2.13 |

use listed in Table 2. In Alabujanahalli, the largest landowning household had ownership rights over 25.1 acres of land. The average size of ownership holdings was 2.6 acres, and the coefficient of variation was 1.26. In Siresandra, the size of household ownership holdings was in general larger than that in Alabujanahalli. The largest landholding in the village was 48.1 acres, the average holding was 4.6 acres, and the coefficient of variation was 1.43. In Zhapur, the largest ownership holding was 62 acres, while the average size of holdings was 5.5 acres. Holdings in Zhapur were comparatively more dispersed than in the other two villages.

Table 6 shows the characteristics of operational holdings among households resident in the study villages. Operational holding refers to the total extent of land under the management (or possession) of the household during the reference period without regard to tenure, a part of which was put to agricultural production. The pattern of distribution of operational holdings was the same as ownership, though the variation in distribution was greater. The same households that owned the largest holdings in Alabujanahalli and Siresandra also operated the largest holdings. However, in Zhapur, the largest landowning household – the traditional landlord family of the village – only cultivated a part of the holding, and leased out the rest of the land to the largest capitalist farmer in the village who operated the largest holding (75 acres) in the village (see chapter 4).

Table 7 shows the size-class distribution of operational holdings in the study villages. The size-classes employed are broadly those used by the

**Table 7** *Size-class distribution of operational holdings in the three villages* in per cent

| Size-class | Alabujanahalli | | Siresandra | | Zhapur | |
|---|---|---|---|---|---|---|
| | Household | Area | Household | Area | Household | Area |
| Landless (< 0.01 hectare) | 19 | 0 | 11 | 0 | 57 | 0 |
| Marginal (< 1 hectare) | 49 | 23 | 33 | 12 | 9 | 3 |
| Small (1 to 2 hectares) | 18 | 26 | 24 | 18 | 9 | 6 |
| Semi-medium (2 to 4 hectares) | 12 | 33 | 22 | 28 | 8 | 11 |
| Medium (4 to 10 hectares) | 2 | 14 | 8 | 21 | 9 | 27 |
| Large (> 10 hectares) | 0 | 5 | 3 | 22 | 7 | 53 |
| All | 100 | 100 | 100 | 100 | 100 | 100 |

Indian Council of Agricultural Research (ICAR), as well as the National Sample Surveys of Land and Livestock Holdings.[1]

The degree of landlessness was most severe in Zhapur, where 57 per cent of all households did not possess any land for agricultural production. A further 18 per cent of household had holdings smaller than 4.94 acres. Notwithstanding this, Zhapur is a village where large holdings predominate. More than half the total operated area in the village (53 per cent) was in holdings larger than 24.7 acres (10 hectares). A cumulative 80 per cent of the total operated area was in holdings larger than 9.88 acres (4 hectares and above).

In Alabujanahalli, landlessness with respect to operational holdings was comparatively low. A fifth of all households did not have any operational holding. Marginal and small holdings were the most important size-class, both as a share of household population and as a share of total extent. Two-thirds of all households possessed holdings that were marginal or small in acreage, and accounted for half the total area. A third of the total area, held by 12 per cent of households, was in holdings of 5 to 10 acres. Even with the dominance of small and marginal holdings, a fifth of the area was still in holdings larger than 10 acres.

Over a tenth of all households did not possess any land in Siresandra. Less than a third of all land area was in small and marginal holdings, and

---

[1] Though we have considered only two decimal points in extent of land, the NSSO presently records extent up to three decimal points. In this particular case, there is no significant difference in outcome on account of this difference.

was held by 57 per cent of households. Semi-medium holdings comprised 28 per cent of all land. About 43 per cent of all land area was in holdings larger than 10 acres, while more than a fifth was in holdings larger than 25 acres.

Significant inequality in ownership and operation of landholdings among households is implicit in the preceding tables. We shall analyse this at greater length in the next section.

## Inequality

Inequality in landholdings among rural households is an important indicator of inequality in their economic status. There exists a high correlation between the extent of land ownership and the stock of wealth of rural households. Owned land usually comprises the largest component of total value of assets of households. In like manner, possession of land as operational holdings is an important source of income – both money income and produce for self-consumption – in rural societies.[2] Inequality in the ownership and operation of land, then, are indicative of and instrumental to inequality in economic status among rural households.

All three study villages exhibited considerable inequality in both ownership and operation of land. Table 8 presents the Gini coefficient for both these parameters. Siresandra was the least unequal village, with a Gini coefficient of 0.54 in both ownership and operation of land. Alabujanahalli exhibited a slightly higher level of inequality, at 0.63 for ownership holdings and 0.60 in operational holdings. Inequality was most severe in Zhapur, where inequality in ownership holding was 0.76 and in operational holdings, 0.81.

Inequality in landholdings can also be observed by comparing the extent of land owned or operated by the top and bottom households in the village. Table 9 compares the percentage of land owned and land possessed by the

Table 8 *Gini coefficient of household ownership and operational holdings in the three villages*

| Village | Ownership holding | Operational holding |
|---|---|---|
| Alabujanahalli | 0.631 | 0.605 |
| Siresandra | 0.547 | 0.543 |
| Zhapur | 0.764 | 0.807 |

---

[2] The measure of its significance, of course, varies based on the level of development of other markets.

**Table 9** *Share of total extent of ownership and operational holdings held by bottom 50 and top 5 per cent of households in the three villages*

| Village | Tenure | Bottom 50 percentile | Top 5 percentile |
| --- | --- | --- | --- |
| Alabujanahalli | Ownership | 11 | 26 |
| | Operational | 9 | 28 |
| Siresandra | Ownership | 17 | 30 |
| | Operational | 21 | 31 |
| Zhapur | Ownership | 1 | 48 |
| | Operational | 0 | 53 |

bottom 50 per cent and top 5 per cent of all households resident in the village. In all three villages, the top 5 per cent of households owned *as well as* operated more land than the bottom 50 per cent. In Alabujanahalli, the bottom 50 per cent collectively owned only 11 per cent of all land, while the top 5 per cent owned more than 25 per cent. In Siresandra, the difference was less severe but still significant. The bottom half owned 17 per cent and operated 21 per cent. The corresponding figure for the top 5 per cent was 30 and 31 per cent respectively. In Zhapur, the bottom 50 per cent owned only 1 per cent of all land and operated close to zero. The top 5 per cent owned nearly half of all land and operated more than half.

## Social Composition of Land Ownership

This immense inequality corresponds to definite social categories. Here, we shall investigate the social composition of land possession that serves both as a basis and an indicator of the position of households in social hierarchies in rural India. We shall look at the distribution of ownership of *agricultural* land among different caste groups and socio-economic classes.

The majority of residents of Alabujanahalli belong to Backward Class (BC) households, which comprise 206 out of the total of 243 households in the village. Numerically, the largest caste is Vokkaliga, and there are a few Besthar and Madivala households. Nearly half of the households in this social group owned marginal holdings of agricultural land. About 18 per cent owned small holdings, while 15 per cent did not own any agricultural land. The only holding larger than 25 acres in the village was owned by a Vokkaliga household. Adi Karnataka was the only Scheduled Caste (SC) in the village. Nearly a third of all SC households did not own land, and the few who did, owned marginal holdings. There was only one Scheduled

**Table 10** *Distribution of ownership holdings of agricultural land by size-class and social group in Alabujanahalli* in per cent

| Size-class | Backward Class (BC) | Scheduled Caste (SC) | All social groups |
|---|---|---|---|
| Landless | 15.0 | 31.4 | 18.1 |
| Marginal | 49.0 | 65.7 | 51.0 |
| Small | 18.4 | 2.9 | 16.0 |
| Semi-medium | 14.1 | 0.0 | 11.9 |
| Medium | 2.9 | 0.0 | 2.5 |
| Large | 0.5 | 0.0 | 0.4 |
| All | 100.0 | 100.0 | 100.0 |
|  | (206) | (35) | (243) |

*Note*: One Other Caste Hindu household and one ST household are included in the "All" column.

**Table 11** *Social composition of ownership holdings of agricultural land in Siresandra* in per cent

| | Siresandra | | |
|---|---|---|---|
| Size-class | Backward Class (BC) | Scheduled Caste (SC) | All social groups |
| Landless | 4.0 | 24.1 | 11.4 |
| Marginal | 26.0 | 44.8 | 32.9 |
| Small | 22.0 | 27.6 | 24.1 |
| Semi-medium | 34.0 | 0.0 | 21.5 |
| Medium | 10.0 | 3.4 | 7.6 |
| Large | 4.0 | 0.0 | 2.5 |
| All | 100.0 | 100.0 | 100.0 |
|  | (50) | (29) | (79) |

Tribe (ST) household in the village and it did not own any agricultural land.

There were 50 BC households and 29 SC households in Siresandra at the time of the survey. Here too Vokkaligas were numerically the most important caste. Scheduled Castes were primarily Adi Karnataka, with a few Bhovi households. Only a small proportion (4 per cent) of BC households was landless, as compared to SC households (24 per cent). BC households were better represented in the higher size-classes. The two holdings larger than 25 acres were owned by BC households, while a tenth owned medium holdings (10 to 25 acres). There was only one SC holding that was larger

**Table 12** *Social composition of ownership holdings of agricultural land in Zhapur* in per cent

| Size-class | Backward Class (BC) | Scheduled Caste (SC) | Scheduled Tribe (ST) | All social groups |
|---|---|---|---|---|
| Landless | 28.3 | 54.3 | 71.4 | 45.0 |
| Marginal | 13.0 | 6.5 | 14.3 | 10.1 |
| Small | 6.5 | 28.3 | 0.0 | 15.6 |
| Semi-medium | 21.7 | 6.5 | 14.3 | 14.7 |
| Medium | 17.4 | 4.3 | 0.0 | 9.2 |
| Large | 13.0 | 0.0 | 0.0 | 5.5 |
| All | 100.0 | 100.0 | 100.0 | 100.0 |
|  | (46) | (46) | (14) | (109) |

*Note*: One Muslim household and two Other Caste Hindu households are included in the "All" column.

**Table 13** *Mean holdings and coefficient of variation (CV) of household distribution within caste groups in the three villages*

| Social group | Alabujanahalli | | Siresandra | | Zhapur | |
|---|---|---|---|---|---|---|
|  | Mean holdings | CV | Mean holdings | CV | Mean holdings | CV |
| Caste Hindu# | 2.9 | 0.8 | 6.0 | 0.8 | 10.1 | 0.6 |
| Scheduled Caste (SC) | 0.9 | 1.0 | 2.1 | 0.9 | 2.1 | 0.6 |
| Scheduled Tribe (ST) | * | * | - | - | 1.1 | 0.6 |

*Notes:* * Based on all land, not crop land.
# Includes BC and Other Caste Hindu households.

than 5 acres, while *all* other SC households were either landless or owned less than 5 acres of land.

Of all three study villages, Zhapur had the most severe landlessness and inequality in distribution of landholdings. It is also the most caste-heterogeneous of the study villages. More than half of SC households and 70 per cent of ST households in Zhapur did not own any agricultural land. The corresponding figure for BC households was 28 per cent. All large holdings, as was the case in other villages, were owned by BC households. In fact, one in every eight BC households had large holdings.

In all three villages, then, regardless of the size and caste composition of the household population, SCs and STs (where present) were disproportionately represented in the lower size-classes. The average size of holdings was larger for BC households than SC households, and the dispersion was similar (Table 13).

Next, we closely inspect the distribution of ownership and operational holdings among different socio-economic classes in the study villages.

Alabujanahalli is located close to an urban centre (K.M. Doddi), and shares a symbiotic relationship with it that largely influences the social and economic life of the village. This has a bearing on the class structure in the village in myriad ways and is reflected in its complexity. Notwithstanding the proximity to an urban centre, agriculture is an important source of income owing to favourable conditions of production, particularly the availability of irrigation, and a well-established and relatively stable market for produce – that is, the sugarcane factory – in the vicinity.

At the time of the survey, there were two Rich capitalist farmer households resident in the village. Their collective share in ownership and in operation of land was 7 per cent. The richest of the Peasant 1 households owned 18 per cent and operated 17 per cent of all land. Peasant 2 households had the single largest share in both ownership (34 per cent) and operation (34 per cent) of all land. Peasant 4 households, which constituted 24 per cent of all households in the village, owned 14 per cent of all land. Manual workers comprised nearly a third of all households, yet only owned 3 per cent of all land and 5 per cent of all operated area. The extent of land owned or operated by households who had little engagement with agriculture was very small.[3]

There is less complexity to the class structure in Siresandra (Table 15). There were no households currently resident in the village that belonged to a traditional landlord family. The richest households worked the land and the village was not as closely integrated with the urban economy as Alabujanahalli. The richest of the peasant households, Peasant 1 households, owned and operated 30 per cent of all land. Peasant 2 households had the single largest share, among all socio-economic categories, in both ownership (42 cent) and operational holdings (41 per cent). Peasant 3 households collectively held about a fourth of all land, while manual workers owned and operated a mere 3 per cent.

---

[3] This, of course, does not imply the converse, that is, households with agriculture as an important part of household economic activities not engaging in non-agricultural activities. In fact, the richest households in the village had many commercial interests in the neighbouring urban areas. The economic aspect of this relationship in the form of economic diversification has been analysed in chapter 10.

Table 14 *Area owned or operated by different socio-economic classes in Alabujanahalli in per cent*

| Socio-economic class (as percentage of population) | Ownership holdings (per cent of total area) | Operational holdings (per cent of total area) |
|---|---|---|
| Rich capitalist farmer (1) | 7 | 7 |
| Peasant 1 (4) | 18 | 17 |
| Peasant 2 (16) | 34 | 34 |
| Peasant 3 (12) | 16 | 16 |
| Peasant 4 (24) | 14 | 15 |
| Manual worker 1 (16) | 2 | 5 |
| Manual worker 2 (9) | 1 | 0 |
| Manual worker 3 (5) | 0 | 0 |
| Rents/remittances (3) | 2 | 1 |
| Business/self-employment (5) | 2 | 1 |
| Salaried person (6) | 4 | 3 |
| All | 100 | 100 |

*Note*: Number of households is shown in parentheses.

Table 15 *Area owned or operated by different socio-economic classes in Siresandra in per cent*

| Socio-economic class (as percentage of population) | Ownership holdings (per cent of total area) | Operational holdings (per cent of total area) |
|---|---|---|
| Peasant 1 (5) | 30 | 30 |
| Peasant 2 (30) | 42 | 41 |
| Peasant 3 (40) | 24 | 24 |
| Manual workers (16) | 3 | 3 |
| Business/small self-employment (8) | 2 | 2 |
| All | 100 | 100 |

*Note*: Same as in Table 14.

Zhapur is the most unequal of the study villages and this is exhibited in the distribution of land among socio-economic classes. Unlike the other two villages, the head of the landlord family was still resident in Zhapur. This household, along with the other landlord households, owned more than a third of all land and operated around a fifth. The rich peasant (Peasant 1) households owned 14 per cent and operated 20 per cent of all land. The numerically most significant socio-economic class, that of manual workers,

**Table 16** *Area owned or operated by different socio-economic classes in Zhapur* in per cent

| Socio-economic class (as percentage of population) | Ownership holdings (per cent of total area) | Operational holdings (per cent of total area) |
|---|---|---|
| Landlord (4) | 35 | 19 |
| Peasant 1 (2) | 14 | 20 |
| Peasant 2 (6) | 11 | 20 |
| Peasant 3 (26) | 19 | 39 |
| Manual workers (47) | 10 | 1 |
| Rents, remittances, pensions, handouts (5) | 7 | 0 |
| Business activity/self-employed (6) | 1 | 0 |
| Salaried persons (6) | 4 | 1 |
| All | 100 | 100 |

*Note*: Same as in Table 14.

which comprised nearly half of the village household population, owned only 10 per cent of the land and cultivated 1 per cent. There was considerable discrepancy in the household distribution in ownership and in operation holdings for all classes. This was on account of a fairly developed tenancy market in the village, and the direction of the discrepancy for each class is an indicator of some aspects of tenancy in the village. We will analyse this more closely in the next section.

# Tenancy

Tenancy is an important aspect of land relations in rural India, yet academic engagement in understanding this phenomenon has been incommensurate with its significance, particularly in recent years. This has been in large part due to a general lack of academic interest in rural India, particularly in the tradition of village studies. Macro-level sources of data on landholdings in India are notorious for under-reporting of tenancy, and severely distorting macro-analysis of the tenancy market. The complexity of social relations that characterise the tenancy market in rural India can only be untangled through concrete analysis of concrete conditions – the natural domain of village studies. Our task in this section, however, is more modest. We confine ourselves to a description of the tenancy arrangements in the study villages.

If the extent of tenancy is measured in terms of acreage of land under lease, it was not an important factor in Siresandra where only 1 per cent of all operated area was under lease, and only marginally more important in

Table 17 *Extent of tenancy in acreage in the study villages* in per cent

| Village | Leased in (as percentage of total operated area) | Leased out (as percentage of total agricultural land owned) |
|---|---|---|
| Alabujanahalli | 9 | 6 |
| Siresandra | 1 | 0 |
| Zhapur | 35 | 37 |

Table 18 *Extent of tenancy in terms of population in the study villages* in per cent

| Village | Households leasing in land (as percentage of population) | Households leasing out land (as percentage of population) |
|---|---|---|
| Alabujanahalli | 25 | 10 |
| Siresandra | 6 | 0 |
| Zhapur | 12 | 22 |

Table 19 *Extent of land under different forms of tenancy, two villages* in per cent

| Village | Fixed rent (%) | Rent-free (%) | Share rent (%) | Total |
|---|---|---|---|---|
| Alabujanahalli | 23 | 5 | 72 | 100 (49 acres) |
| Zhapur | 16 | 0 | 84 | 100 (198 acres) |

Alabujanahalli (9 per cent). However, in Zhapur, leased land comprised 35 per cent of all operated area and 37 per cent of all owned area (Table 17). If observed in terms of proportion of households (Table 18), a fourth of all households in Alabujanahalli leased land. In Siresandra, this proportion was relatively insignificant at 6 per cent of all households, while in Zhapur, 12 per cent of all households leased in land and 24 per cent leased out land. Fewer households leasing in land than those leasing out indicates concentration in operational holdings as compared to ownership holdings. While we have already noted this in the section on inequality, here we investigate it in greater detail.

Sharecropping was the most important form of tenancy in both villages where significant tenancy exists. In Alabujanahalli, 72 per cent of leased area was under sharecropping lease while 23 per cent was under fixed lease. There were seven lease agreements of a total of 2.5 acres that were leased in rent-free. These included small parcels leased in by long-term workers and relatives of landowners. In Zhapur, 84 per cent of all leased land (198 acres) was under sharecropping. We shall look at both these villages individually.

**Table 20** *Major crops grown on leased and owned land (as per cent of GCA by tenure),* *Alabujanahalli*

| Crop | Of total gross cropped area (GCA) under specified crop (in per cent) | |
|------|------|------|
| | Lease | Ownership |
| Paddy | 62 | 39 |
| Finger millet | 19 | 6 |
| Mulberry | 6 | 7 |
| Sugarcane | 13 | 40 |

In Alabujanahalli, a number of households participated in the tenancy market even though the total extent under lease was relatively small. A fourth of all households leased in 9 per cent of total operated area.[4] Out of the gross cropped area under tenancy, close to 80 per cent was used for cultivation of paddy (62 per cent) and finger millet (19 per cent), and only 13 per cent was used for cultivation of sugarcane.[5] The same figures for gross cropped area on owned land were 37 per cent for paddy and 6 per cent for finger millet. Leasing of land, therefore, was primarily for production of cereals.

The largest proportion of lessee households (40 out of 61) was poor peasants (Peasant 4) or manual workers, leasing in on average 0.67 acre per household. There were also a few Peasant 3 and Peasant 2 households, along with a few non-agricultural households, that leased in land. The most important lessee households were the poorer households or the non-agricultural households that did not accumulate surplus from agriculture. There was no clear pattern among lessor households in Alabujanahalli. The leased holdings were relatively small and were used for the production of

[4] There is some discrepancy in the reporting of land leased in by tenant households, and land leased out by landowning households. The magnitude of this discrepancy is of the order of a third of all extent leased in. This discrepancy can arise either due to lease of land from households resident in neighbouring villages or due to under-reporting of lease by landowning households.
[5] There is, of course, a methodological issue in drawing parity in gross cropped area of seasonal crops and an annual crop like sugarcane. A given extent would be counted multiple times when under seasonal crops depending on the number of crops grown per year, while being counted only once when under sugarcane – although the land is utilised for an equal duration. Even if we normalise for this, the significance of sugarcane cultivation on leased land does not exceed a quarter of all leased land.

**Table 21** *Tenancy among socio-economic classes in Alabujanahalli*

| Socio-economic class (number of total households) | Extent leased in (number of lessee households) | Extent leased out (number of lessor households) |
|---|---|---|
| Rich capitalist farmer | – (0) | 3 (2) |
| Peasant 1 | – (0) | 3 (4) |
| Peasant 2 | 11 (6) | 7 (3) |
| Peasant 3 | 5 (7) | 1 (2) |
| Peasant 4 | 11 (18) | 1 (2) |
| Manual worker 1 | 15 (21) | – (0) |
| Manual worker 2 | 0 (1) | 3 (5) |
| Business/self-employment | 1 (1) | 3 (2) |
| Rents/remittances | 4 (3) | 5 (1) |
| Salaried persons | 1 (4) | 7 (4) |
| Total | 49 (61) | 34 (25) |

**Table 22** *Tenancy among socio-economic classes in Zhapur*

| Socio-economic class (number of total households) | Extent leased in (number of lessee households) | Extent leased out (number of lessor households) |
|---|---|---|
| Landlord (4) | – (0) | 87 (3) |
| Peasant 1 (2) | 30 (1) | – (0) |
| Peasant 2 (6) | 55 (3) | 13 (1) |
| Peasant 3 (26) | 113 (9) | 6 (4) |
| Manual workers (47) | – (0) | 52 (10) |
| Rents, remittances, pensions, handouts (5) | – (0) | 36 (3) |
| Business activity/self-employed (6) | – (0) | 5 (1) |
| Salaried persons (6) | – (0) | 21 (2) |
| Total (100) | 198 (13) | 219 (24) |

cereals. It follows, then, that the primary purpose of lease was to service household consumption of cereals.

Tenancy in Zhapur was much more significant in terms of acreage than in Alabujanahalli. There was little discrepancy between the extent of land leased in as reported by tenant households and the extent of land leased out as reported by landowning households in Zhapur. This indicates that a comparative view of these two parameters among different socio-economic classes will provide a fairly accurate picture of the actual phenomenon.

The most important lessees of land were the poor peasant (Peasant 3) households. A total of nine households leased in 113 of the total 198 acres leased in the village. A total of 55 acres were leased in by three Peasant 2 households, while a single Peasant 1 household leased in 30 acres. Manual workers did not engage in any leasing in of land. The most important lessors of land belonged to the highest socio-economic class in the village – that of the Landlord and Rich capitalist farmers. Three households from this class leased out 87 (out of 219) acres of land. Interestingly, the second most important lessors were manual workers. A total of 10 Manual worker households (out of a total of 47) leased out land totalling up to 52 acres. Classes that were primarily reliant on non-agricultural sources of income, such as households with income from salaries, rents and remittances, and business activity, comprised the rest of the lessor households.

A prefatory overview of the socio-economic class composition of the tenancy market in Zhapur exhibits a somewhat striking feature. The *only* lessees of land were cultivator households that manually work the land – and therefore dedicate the most significant proportion of their time and effort, both in terms of manual work and supervision, to crop production – while the lessor households were spread over different socio-economic classes but found common cause in divesting themselves from agriculture to engage in non-farm work wholly (in the case of salaried, self-employed, and rent and remittance-receiving households), or at least partially (in the case of manual workers).

These two groups are, of course, internally heterogeneous in their social status and economic conditions. Land was leased in by both rich and poor households. The richer household that leased in 30 acres did so – and succeeded in doing so, as indicated by his class position – to accumulate. Meanwhile, the most significant lessees were poor peasants, who, despite leasing in an average of 12.5 acres of land per household, remained poor peasants. These two represent different *types* of tenancy. The relatively better off (agricultural) households leased in land in larger holdings from other well-off households, while a few poor peasant households leased in land from many poor households, such as manual worker households, to consolidate them and harness economies of scale. This was particularly significant in Zhapur as intensive cultivation on small holdings was not feasible in the given agro-ecological conditions. A common feature among lessee households in the village was the maintenance of draught animals for cultivation.

# Conclusion

Access to land is an important indicator and determinant of the social and economic well-being of rural households in underdeveloped countries. In this chapter, I have investigated the contours of distribution of this primary asset, in terms of ownership holdings as well as operational holdings, among households in the three study villages in Karnataka. I have also recorded the forms of tenancy arrangements where relevant. In addition, I have briefly investigated other village-level aspects related to landholdings, such as land use and irrigation.

The main findings of this investigation have been summarised here. The three study villages were characterised by significantly different land-use patterns and differential access to irrigation. While Alabujanahalli was well irrigated, both Siresandra and Zhapur were characterised by extensive dry-land agriculture. Cultivation on owned land was the most important form of access to land in all three villages, though there was significant tenancy in Zhapur and Alabujanahalli. Marginal, small, and semi-medium holdings dominated in Alabujanahalli. Notwithstanding this, nearly a fifth of the total land area was in holdings larger than 9.88 acres. In Siresandra, the total area was spread evenly across different size-classes. Nearly a third of all the area was in small and marginal holdings, while more than a fifth was in holdings larger than 24.7 acres. Zhapur had only 9 per cent of total extent under small and marginal holdings, while more than half of the total area was in holdings larger than 24.7 acres. Landlessness was most severe in Zhapur, where 57 per cent of all households did not possess any operational holdings. It was comparatively less in Alabujanahalli (19 per cent), followed by Siresandra (11 per cent).

All three villages were characterised by high levels of inequality in both ownership and operational holdings. This inequality was most acute in Zhapur, where the Gini coefficient of distribution of operational holdings was 0.807. The respective figures for Alabujanahalli and Siresandra were 0.605 and 0.543. In all three villages, the top 5 per cent of landowning and land-operating households had more land than the bottom 50 per cent.

In all three villages, SC and ST households were disproportionately represented in the lower size-classes. The average size of holdings was larger for BC households with a similar measure of dispersion.

The top socio-economic classes owned and operated the most land in all three villages. There was a significant proportion of land owned and/ or operated by middle peasant households in both Alabujanahalli and

Siresandra. Manual worker households owned very little land in all three villages, and cultivated small holdings if at all.

Tenancy was significant in both Zhapur and Alabujanahalli. More than a third of all operated area in Zhapur was leased in, while the respective figure for Alabujanahalli was 9 per cent. Sharecropping was the most important form of tenancy in both these villages. In Alabujanahalli, land was primarily leased in small holdings for cultivation of cereals. In Zhapur, many manual worker households and non-agricultural households would lease land to a few specialised sharecroppers who maintained draught animals and jointly cultivated the leased land.

**Appendix Figure** *Lorenz curves for ownership and operational holdings of land, three villages*

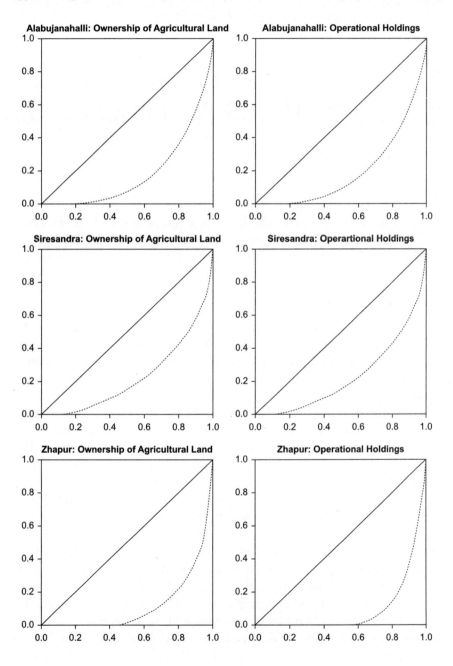

# 7

## Features of Asset Ownership in the Three Study Villages

Madhura Swaminathan and Yasodhara Das

In this chapter, we examine the level and composition of assets owned by households in the three villages of Alabujanahalli, Siresandra, and Zhapur, categorised by caste and socio-economic class. Assets here include agricultural land; non-agricultural land and buildings; animals; means of production; means of transport; and other assets, which include domestic durable goods, inventories in the form of grain, fodder, etc. We do not have information on financial assets and gold jewellery. While the former are not likely to be important except for very rich households, the latter are owned by all sections of households except the poorest. Accurate information on gold and jewellery is difficult to get, and hence was excluded from the questionnaire.

In 2009, the year of the PARI survey, an average household owned assets worth Rs 9.58 lakhs in Zhapur, Rs 15.9 lakhs in Alabujanahalli, and Rs 17.7 lakhs in Siresandra (at current prices). A median household owned less than the average (or mean) in each of the three villages (Table 1), indicating an unequal distribution of assets across households. The range of assets per household in each village was mind-boggling (see Appendix Tables 1 to 3). In Zhapur, for example, the range was between Rs 157 to Rs 200 lakhs.

In terms of the composition of assets, agricultural land, and non-agricultural land and buildings, were the two most important assets. In Zhapur, despite it being a rainfed area, agricultural land was clearly the most valuable asset, accounting for 79 per cent of the total asset value of households resident in the village (Table 2). In terms of the composition of assets, homestead land and buildings, followed by agricultural land, were the most important assets held by residents of Alabujanahalli. The location of this village is such, close to the town in Maddur taluk, that the price of

**Table 1** *Mean and median values of total assets owned by households in the three study villages, Karnataka, 2009* in Rs per household

| Village | Number of households | Mean value of assets | Median value of assets |
|---|---|---|---|
| Alabujanahalli | 243 | 15,99,582 | 6,42,702 |
| Siresandra | 79 | 17,73,099 | 10,60,560 |
| Zhapur | 109 | 9,58,823 | 2,59,825 |

*Source:* PARI survey data.

**Table 2** *Composition of assets in the three study villages, Karnataka, 2009* in per cent

| Category of asset | Alabujanahalli | Siresandra | Zhapur |
|---|---|---|---|
| Non-agricultural land and buildings | 56 | 42 | 16 |
| Agricultural land | 39 | 52 | 79 |
| Animals | 1 | 2 | 2 |
| Means of production | 1 | 2 | 0.8 |
| Means of transport | 1 | 1 | 0.5 |
| Other assets | 2 | 1 | 1 |
| All | 100 | 100 | 100 |

*Source:* PARI survey data.

homestead land here is quite high (Rs 462 per sq foot in Alabujanahalli, versus Rs 82 in Siresandra and Rs 25 in Zhapur). In Siresandra, agricultural land and non-agricultural land together accounted for 94 per cent of the value of assets owned by all households. Other assets comprised less than 6 per cent of assets owned in all three villages.

We now turn to the main features of asset ownership in the three villages.

## Inequality

The first and most striking feature of asset ownership in the three villages was the extremely high degree of inequality. The share of assets owned by households in the three villages, ranked in deciles of total asset ownership, is shown in Table 3. In Alabujanahalli and Zhapur, the richest decile cornered more than half of all the assets – 50 per cent in Alabujanahalli, and 67 per cent in Zhapur. In Siresandra, the top two deciles together accounted for 58 per cent of the assets owned by households resident in the village. Unlike the other two villages, wealth was not concentrated in the top decile but in the top two deciles in Siresandra. The top decile accounted for 38 per cent

**Table 3** *Share of assets by asset decile in the three study villages, Karnataka, 2009* in per cent

| Asset deciles | Alabujanahalli | Siresandra | Zhapur |
|---|---|---|---|
| D1 | 0.3 | 0.5 | 0.1 |
| D2 | 1 | 1.5 | 0.6 |
| D3 | 1.7 | 2.1 | 1 |
| D4 | 2.8 | 3.1 | 1.5 |
| D5 | 3.5 | 5.2 | 2.2 |
| D6 | 5 | 7.5 | 3.5 |
| D7 | 7.6 | 9.3 | 4.9 |
| D8 | 11.7 | 12.3 | 7 |
| D9 | 16.4 | 20.3 | 12.1 |
| D10 | 50 | 38.1 | 67.1 |

*Source:* PARI survey data.

of assets and the ninth decile for another 20 per cent of assets. At the other end of the distribution, the lowest three deciles or bottom 30 per cent of households owned between 2 and 4 per cent of all assets across the three villages surveyed.

The Gini coefficient of household asset ownership was 0.76 for Zhapur, 0.64 for Alabujanahalli, and 0.57 for Siresandra. Contrary to our findings from other States, of the three villages surveyed in Karnataka, inequality in asset ownership was highest in Zhapur (Kalaburagi district, north Karnataka) – the village with the least irrigation and relatively low agricultural productivity. Zhapur was the only village among the three villages which was characterised by the presence of the traditional landlord. There were four households in this socio-economic class, owning the highest quality of crop land.

## Inequality by Socio-Economic Class

The second striking feature of asset ownership in the three villages was that variations in asset ownership across households and inequalities in ownership closely followed the socio-economic class hierarchy.

In Alabujanahalli, the two Rich capitalist farmers in the village accounted for 0.8 per cent of all households and 19 per cent of total assets (Table 5). Peasant 4, the poorest class of peasants, comprised 24 per cent or about one quarter of all households, but owned only 5 per cent of assets. To put it

**Table 4** *Average value of assets per household, by socio-economic class, Alabujanahalli, 2009*

| Class | Number of households | Average value of assets (Rs) | Average level of asset-holding of each class as a percentage of average level of asset-holdings of "Rich capitalist farmers" (per cent) |
|---|---|---|---|
| Rich capitalist farmer | 2 | 3,69,97,969 | 100 |
| Peasant 1 | 9 | 62,05,621 | 17 |
| Peasant 2 | 39 | 29,35,927 | 8 |
| Peasant 3 | 30 | 14,92,605 | 4 |
| Peasant 4 | 58 | 5,97,066 | 2 |
| Manual worker 1 | 40 | 3,23,819 | 1 |
| Manual worker 2 | 22 | 2,08,327 | 1 |
| Manual worker 3 | 11 | 1,61,669 | 0.4 |
| Business/self-employment | 11 | 7,03,130 | 2 |
| Rents/remittances | 7 | 11,91,433 | 3 |
| Salaried persons | 14 | 17,47,595 | 5 |
| All | 243 | 15,99,582 | 4 |

*Source:* PARI survey data.

another way, if the assets of the two Rich capitalist farmers are valued at 100, the mean assets of Peasant 4 households was 4, and that of Manual workers was 1 or less than 1. In absolute terms, a Manual worker 3 household, that is, a household that did not engage in any cultivation, owned assets worth Rs 1.6 lakhs, as compared to a Peasant 1 household that owned Rs 67 lakhs.

Another way to examine the differences across classes is to compute the access index, that is, the relative share of a class in total assets as compared to its share in the population. The access index in this instance was higher than 1, implying disproportionate assets relative to population for Rich capitalist farmers (as high as 23), and Peasant 1 and Peasant 2 households (Table 5).

In Siresandra, there were no Landlords or Rich capitalist farmers. A Peasant 1 or rich peasant household owned on average assets worth Rs 95 lakhs, whereas a poor peasant or Peasant 3 household owned assets worth Rs 9 lakh and a Manual worker household had assets worth Rs 2.5 lakh (Table 6).

The access index was greater than 1 for Peasant 1 and Peasant 2

**Table 5** *Socio-economic class-wise distribution of households and total assets, and access index, Alabujanahalli, 2009*

| Socio-economic class | Households (per cent) | Assets (per cent) | Access index |
|---|---|---|---|
| Rich capitalist farmer | 0.8 | 19 | 23.7 |
| Peasant 1 | 3.7 | 15.7 | 4.2 |
| Peasant 2 | 16 | 29.5 | 1.8 |
| Peasant 3 | 12.3 | 11.5 | 0.9 |
| Peasant 4 | 23.9 | 8.9 | 0.4 |
| Manual worker 1 | 16.5 | 3.3 | 0.2 |
| Manual worker 2 | 9.1 | 1.2 | 0.1 |
| Manual worker 3 | 4.5 | 0.5 | 0.1 |
| Business/self-employment | 4.5 | 2 | 0.4 |
| Rents/remittances | 2.9 | 2.1 | 0.7 |
| Salaried persons | 5.8 | 6.3 | 1.1 |

*Note*: Access index = proportion of assets owned by a particular class in total assets as a ratio of the proportion of households belonging to that particular class.

*Source*: PARI survey data.

**Table 6** *Average value of assets per household, by socio-economic class, Siresandra, 2009*

| Socio-economic class | Number of households | Average value of assets (Rs) | Average level of asset-holding of each class as a percentage of average level of asset-holdings of "Peasant 1" households (per cent) |
|---|---|---|---|
| Peasant 1 | 6 | 95,00,103 | 100 |
| Peasant 2 | 13 | 27,14,103 | 29 |
| Peasant 3 | 4 | 9,31,261 | 10 |
| Manual workers | 32 | 2,50,773 | 3 |
| Business/small self-employment | 24 | 5,83,910 | 6 |

*Source*: PARI survey data.

households; that is, they held assets disproportionate to their shares in the population (Table 7).

In Zhapur too, among the agricultural classes, Manual workers were at the lowest rung of the asset ladder. Asset ownership rose exponentially as one moved up the class hierarchy from Peasant 3 to Peasant 1, and, finally, to the class of Landlords.

The access index was 0.1 for Manual workers and households with

**Table 7** *Distribution of households and assets, by socio-economic class, Siresandra, 2009* in per cent

| Socio-economic class | Households | Assets | Access index |
|---|---|---|---|
| Peasant 1 | 5 | 27 | 5.4 |
| Peasant 2 | 30 | 47 | 1.5 |
| Peasant 3 | 41 | 21 | 0.5 |
| Manual workers | 17 | 2 | 0.1 |
| Business/small self-employment | 8 | 3 | 0.3 |
| All | 100 | 100 | 1 |

*Note*: Access index = proportion of assets owned by a particular class in total assets as a ratio of the proportion of households belonging to that particular class.

*Source*: PARI survey data.

**Table 8** *Average value of assets, by socio-economic class, Zhapur, 2009*

| Socio-economic class | Number of households | Average value of assets (Rs) | Average level of asset-holding of each class as a percentage of average level of asset-holdings of "Landlords" (per cent) |
|---|---|---|---|
| Landlord | 4 | 1,24,14,963 | 100 |
| Peasant 1 | 2 | 43,27,915 | 35 |
| Peasant 2 | 7 | 13,93,551 | 11 |
| Peasant 3 | 28 | 4,45,115 | 4 |
| Manual workers | 51 | 2,22,994 | 2 |
| Business activity/ self-employed | 6 | 1,66,460 | 1 |
| Rents, remittances, pensions, handouts | 5 | 10,71,656 | 9 |
| Salaried persons | 6 | 10,39,154 | 8 |

*Source*: PARI survey data.

incomes from petty business. The access index was 13 for Landlords; 4.5 for Peasant 1 households; and above 1 for Peasant 2 households as well as Salaried persons, and those dependent on Rents and remittances. In other words, households in the latter classes owned assets disproportionate to their shares in the population (Table 9).

**Table 9** *Distribution of assets and access index, by socio-economic class, Zhapur, 2009* in per cent

| Socio-economic class | Households | Assets | Access index |
|---|---|---|---|
| Landlord | 3.7 | 47.4 | 12.9 |
| Peasant 1 | 1.8 | 8.4 | 4.5 |
| Peasant 2 | 6.4 | 9.3 | 1.4 |
| Peasant 3 | 25.7 | 12 | 0.5 |
| Manual workers | 46.8 | 10.9 | 0.2 |
| Business activity/self-employed | 5.5 | 1 | 0.2 |
| Rents, remittances, pensions, handouts | 4.6 | 5 | 1.1 |
| Salaried persons | 5.5 | 6 | 1.1 |
| All | 100 | 100 | 1 |

*Note*: Access index = proportion of assets owned by a particular class in total assets as a ratio of the proportion of households belonging to that particular class.

*Source*: PARI survey data.

## The Poorest and the Richest

It is instructive to examine the assets of the richest and poorest households, the destitute and super-rich households, in each of the three villages.

The poorest household in Alabujanahalli village – a Manual worker household without its own house – had assets worth Rs 1,178 (Table 10). The next poorest household held assets valued at Rs 3,839, which included a tiny plot of homestead land and a mud hut (Table 11).

In Siresandra, a Dalit hired manual worker household was ranked at the bottom. The head of the household earned a living by making stone slabs. The household was landless and lived in a rent-free house given by a relative. The asset composition of the household is given below.

The asset wealth of a poor household, but one owning some homestead land and a house constructed on that land, was a bit higher. This too was a Dalit hired manual worker household. The asset composition of this household is shown in Table 13.

In Zhapur, the poorest household was a single-woman household (placed in the Peasant 3 category on account of cultivation). The caretaker of a *dargah*, she lived in its premises and cultivated a few crops on the *dargah's* land. Her total assets were a few utensils and a clock worth Rs 200. The next poorest household in the village, a Manual worker household, owned a tiny plot of homestead land with a small *pucca* house (built with

**Table 10** *Asset composition of poorest household, Alabujanahalli, 2009*

| Category of asset | Description | Value (Rs) |
|---|---|---|
| Other assets | 25 kg rice and 1 kg wheat, one trunk, some kitchen utensils worth Rs 600 | 1,178 |

*Source*: PARI survey data.

**Table 11** *Asset composition of poorest household with a house, Alabujanahalli, 2009*

| Category of asset | Description | Value (Rs) |
|---|---|---|
| Other assets | 20 kg rice and 3 kg wheat, one bed, one watch and some kitchen utensils worth Rs 1,000 | 2,289 |
| Land | 0.00625 acre | |
| | Mud hut | 750 |
| House | | 800 |
| All | | 3,839 |

*Source*: PARI survey data.

**Table 12** *Asset composition of poorest household, Siresandra, 2009*

| Category of asset | Description | Value (Rs) |
|---|---|---|
| Inventories | 0.2 quintal of rice and 1 quintal of finger millet, | 1,774 |
| Other assets | one ceiling fan, one colour TV, one DVD player, one mixer-grinder, one mobile phone, one tape recorder, one transistor, one tubelight, one almirah, three chairs, one table, one TV stand, one trunk | 10,320 |
| All | | 12,094 |

*Source*: PARI survey data.

**Table 13** *Asset composition of poorest household with a house, Siresandra, 2009*

| Asset category | Description | Value (Rs) |
|---|---|---|
| Other assets | One clock, kitchen utensils, one transistor, one bed, one trunk, two bundles of fodder | 1,110 |
| Animals | One milch cow | 10,000 |
| Land | Homestead land of 544.5 sq. feet | 21,780 |
| House | | 10,000 |
| All | | 42,890 |

*Source*: PARI survey data.

**Table 14** *Asset composition of poorest household with a house, Zhapur, 2009*

|  | Description | Value (Rs) |
|---|---|---|
| Other assets | One table fan, one transistor, one cot, one trunk some kitchen utensils | 2,550 |
| Means of transport | One bicycle | 1,500 |
| Homestead land | 700 sq. feet | 17,500 |
| House | One small room | 5,000 |
| All |  | 26,550 |

*Source*: PARI survey data.

**Table 15** *Asset composition of richest household, Alabujanahalli, 2009*

| Category of asset | Description | Value (Rs) |
|---|---|---|
| Land and buildings | One house, 7 acres of orchard land, and 0.1 acre of homestead land | 5,09,30,000 |
| Trees | 4,000 eucalyptus trees | 66,66,600 |
| Agricultural land | 18 acres | 36,00,000 |
| Animals | Five bullocks, one calf, two milch buffalos, six sheep, two chickens | 1,34,000 |
| Means of production | Six pumps, six tubewells, two wooden ploughs, one leveller, one tractor, one tractor tiller, one bullock cart | 2,98,188 |
| Means of transport | One scooter and one bicycle | 55,600 |
| Other assets | Fridge, TV, cable connection, mobiles, etc | 47,650 |
| All | All | 6,17,32,038 |

*Source*: PARI survey data.

government assistance) on it, a bicycle, and a few household goods (Table 14). The household was entirely dependent on the stone-quarry work in which almost all its members are engaged.

Let us turn to the wealthy households. The richest of the Rich capitalist farmer households in Alabujanahalli owned assets valued at Rs 6 crores (Rs 61 million). As shown in Table 15, this included 18 acres of agricultural land, 7 acres of orchard land, 4,000 eucalyptus trees, and a range of farm machinery. The wealth of this household came from ownership of agriculture-related assets.

The richest household in Siresandra village, with assets worth Rs 2 crores (or Rs 20 million), was that a rich peasant. The family cultivated a variety

**Table 16** *Asset composition of richest household, Siresandra, 2009*

| Category of asset | Description | Value (Rs) |
|---|---|---|
| Land and building | Homestead land, land used for sericulture, orchard land, house | 65,52,150 |
| Agricultural land | 17 acres | 1,21,42,850 |
| Animals | One milch buffalo and two milch cows | 40,000 |
| Means of production | Tractor, borewell, plough, leveller, sprayer | 6,06,600 |
| Means of transport | Two motorcycles, one bicycle | 1,00,150 |
| Trees | 20 tamarind trees | 5,00,000 |
| Other assets | 10 quintals of finger millet, one tractor trolley of fodder, utensils, clock, watches, mixer grinder, cable connection, trunks, TV, etc. | 93,600 |
| All | | 2,00,35,350 |

*Source*: PARI survey data.

**Table 17** *Asset composition of richest household, Zhapur, 2009*

| Category of asset | Description | Value (Rs) |
|---|---|---|
| Animals | Two cow bullock, one cow calf, one milch cow | 55,500 |
| Other assets | Four bullock-carts of animal fodder, 25 kg of rice, 200 kg of wheat, 500 kg of sorghum, 100 kg of pigeon pea, one mobile phone, one transistor, one tubelight, two chairs, one bed, two trunks, one watch | 21,500 |
| Means of production | Electric pump, tubewell, plough, sprayer | 4,600 |
| Agricultural land | 60 acres | 1,55,50,000 |
| House | Jointly owned with brother | 50,000 |
| All | | 1,57,91,600 |

*Note*: Other assets are likely to be under-reported.

*Source*: PARI survey data.

of vegetable crops throughout the year. They also engaged in sericulture. The wealth of the household is reflected in their asset-base. They owned a tractor, two motorcycles, and a well-built house with modern electronic gadgets including communication and entertainment equipment.

The assets of the richest household in Zhapur were worth Rs 15 million (or Rs 1.5 crores). This traditional landlord household owned 60 acres of agricultural land, of which 20 acres were irrigated. They also owned a house that had been built almost a hundred years back and now jointly belonged to two brothers. The house consists of a courtyard and two kitchens. The main source of income of this household was from agricultural production. However, they have also expanded into hardware business in Kalaburagi.

This section brings out the huge disparity between the richest and the poorest households in each of the study villages. It shows that the poorest households were typically  landless and owned meagre assets, whereas the richest were invariably the biggest landowners in the village. In other words, wealth in the study villages was closely tied to ownership of land.

## Inequality and Caste

The fourth noteworthy feature of asset ownership is that inequality is clearly demarcated along caste lines in each of the three villages. Alabujanahalli and Siresandra had two main caste groups, Backward Class (BC) and Scheduled Caste (SC), while Zhapur had some Scheduled Tribe (ST) households as well.

The majority of households in Alabujanahalli belonged to the Vokkaliga caste (categorised as a Backward Class in Karnataka). Table 18 shows that there was huge inequality in asset ownership as between Adi Karnataka (SC) households and BC households in the village. On average, an SC household owned assets worth Rs 3.7 lakhs, whereas a BC household owned assets worth Rs 18.2 lakhs. The richest SC household owned Rs 28 lakhs of assets, whereas the richest BC household owned Rs 617 lakhs or Rs 6 crores of assets (a ratio of 1:22). In other words, differences existed between SC

Table 18 *Average and maximum value of asset-holdings per household, by social group, Alabujanahalli, 2009* in Rs

| Social group | Number of households | Mean value of asset-holdings | Maximum value of asset-holdings |
|---|---|---|---|
| Backward Class (BC) | 206 | 18,22,055 | 6,17,32,038 |
| Scheduled Caste (SC) | 35 | 3,77,775 | 28,53,055 |

*Source*: PARI survey data.

Table 19 *Distribution of households and assets, by social group, Alabujanahalli, 2009* in per cent

| Social group | Households | Assets | Access index |
|---|---|---|---|
| Backward Class (BC) | 84.8 | 96.6 | 1.14 |
| Scheduled Caste (SC) | 14.4 | 3.4 | 0.24 |

*Source*: PARI survey data.

**Table 20** *Average, minimum, and maximum values of asset-holdings per household, by social group, Siresandra, 2009* in Rs

| Social group | Number of households | Average value of asset-holdings | Minimum value of asset-holdings | Maximum value of asset-holdings |
|---|---|---|---|---|
| Backward Class (BC) | 50 | 24,37,528 | 1,66,230 | 2,00,35,350 |
| Scheduled Class (SC) | 29 | 6,27,531 | 12,094 | 20,20,225 |

*Source*: PARI survey data.

**Table 21** *Distribution of households and assets across caste groups, Siresandra, 2009* in per cent

| Social group | Households | Assets | Access index |
|---|---|---|---|
| Backward Class (BC) | 63.3 | 87 | 1.4 |
| Scheduled Caste (SC) | 36.7 | 13 | 0.3 |
| All | 100 | 100 | 1 |

*Source*: PARI survey data.

**Table 22** *Average and maximum values of asset-holdings per household, by social group, Zhapur, 2009* in Rs

| Social group | Number of households | Mean value of asset-holdings | Maximum value of asset-holdings |
|---|---|---|---|
| Backward Class (BC) | 46 | 18,98,352 | 1,57,91,600 |
| Scheduled Caste SC | 46 | 2,70,177 | 10,69,830 |
| Scheduled Tribe (ST) | 14 | 3,23,913 | 12,37,960 |
| All | 106 | 9,61,118 | 1,57,91,600 |

*Source*: PARI survey data.

**Table 23** *Distribution of households and share of total assets across social groups, Zhapur, 2009* in per cent

| Social group | Households | Assets | Access index |
|---|---|---|---|
| Backward Class (BC) | 42.2 | 83.4 | 2 |
| Scheduled Caste (SC) | 42.2 | 11.9 | 0.3 |
| Scheduled Tribe (ST) | 12.8 | 4.3 | 0.3 |
| Total | 100 | 100 | 1 |

*Source*: PARI survey data.

and BC households not only for average households, but also among the better-off households.

Adi Karnataka (SC) households had less wealth than BC households on average, but they also owned less of each individual type of asset (including animal resources). The richest SC household owned only 2.5 acres of agricultural land – and would officially be classified as marginal farmers.

There were similar stark differences across caste groups in Siresandra. BC households had assets valued at Rs 24 lakhs on average, as compared to Rs 6 lakhs among SC households. Further, a differential was observed for each type of asset. SC households comprised 37 per cent of all resident households, but owned only 13 per cent of assets. The difference in wealth persisted at the top too. The richest SC household had assets that were one-tenth that of the richest BC household.

The two major caste groups in Zhapur were Backward Classes (BC) and Scheduled Castes (SC). There were also some Scheduled Tribe (ST) households. BC households comprised 42 per cent of all households, but owned 83 per cent of all assets. This is reflected in an access index of 2. By contrast, the access index was 0.3 for SCs and STs. However, in terms of average asset holdings, ST households were a little better off than SC households. This was because one ST household owned a lorry, the only lorry in the village at that time. This was a business/self-employed household that owned homestead land and a house, along with animals and other durable domestic assets.

Again, differences across caste groups persisted even among the better-off households. The richest five BC households, for example, owned assets worth Rs 112 lakhs, whereas the richest five SC households owned assets worth Rs 7.6 lakhs.

## Composition of Assets

Fifthly, land remained a critical asset for rural households. Not only did land account for the major part of total assets, but ownership of land brought with it access to other assets (excluding, of course, gold jewellery). The value of land owned per household overshadowed all other assets. As the price of land increased, households owning land benefited disproportionately in terms of their asset wealth.

Due to its location close to the Bangalore–Mysore highway, non-agricultural land is also highly valuable in Alabujanahalli. The two Rich capitalist farmers in the village owned significant properties: one owned a rice mill and a printing press, and the other owned shops and commercial

**Table 24** *Share of different classes in asset values, by asset category, Alabujanahalli, 2009* in per cent

| Class | Land, buildings, and trees | Agricultural land | Animals | Means of production | Means of transport | Other assets |
|---|---|---|---|---|---|---|
| Rich capitalist farmer | 28.9 | 5.2 | 4.2 | 7.6 | 4.8 | 1 |
| Peasant 1 | 12.5 | 20.7 | 5.5 | 24.3 | 7.5 | 20.8 |
| Peasant 2 | 27.9 | 31.5 | 29.9 | 37.7 | 34.4 | 31.9 |
| Peasant 3 | 8.2 | 16.4 | 16.3 | 15.9 | 17.1 | 12.2 |
| Peasant 4 | 7.5 | 10.7 | 23 | 7.2 | 6.8 | 12 |
| Manual worker 1 | 3.8 | 2.2 | 12.7 | 2.8 | 1.5 | 4.8 |
| Manual worker 2 | 1.6 | 0.6 | 2.3 | 0 | 0.1 | 1.4 |
| Manual worker 3 | 0.7 | 0.1 | 0.6 | 0 | 0 | 0.5 |
| Business/ self-employment | 2 | 1.2 | 1.7 | 1.1 | 22.5 | 7 |
| Rents/remittances | 2.5 | 1.6 | 2.7 | 2 | 1.2 | 1.6 |
| Salaried persons | 4.4 | 9.8 | 1.1 | 1.4 | 4.1 | 6.8 |
| All | 100 | 100 | 100 | 100 | 100 | 100 |

*Source*: PARI survey data.

**Table 25** *Share of different assets in total asset value, by class, Siresandra, 2009* in per cent

| Class | Agricultural land | Land and buildings | Trees | Animals | Means of production | Means of transport | Other assets |
|---|---|---|---|---|---|---|---|
| Peasant 1 | 28 | 25 | 49 | 15 | 30 | 21 | 11 |
| Peasant 2 | 48 | 49 | 26 | 41 | 44 | 62 | 49 |
| Peasant 3 | 23 | 19 | 21 | 37 | 24 | 6.5 | 27 |
| Manual workers | 1 | 3 | 4 | 4 | 0 | 0.8 | 7 |
| Business/ small self-employment | 1 | 4 | 0 | 3 | 2 | 9.4 | 6 |
| All | 100 | 100 | 100 | 100 | 100 | 100 | 100 |

*Source*: PARI survey data.

establishments. This explains the relatively high share of land and buildings in the total assets of the two Rich capitalist farmers (Table 24).

In Siresandra, the two better-off peasant classes (Peasant 1 and Peasant

**Table 26** *Share of different classes in asset values, by asset category, Zhapur, 2009* in per cent

| Class | Land, buildings, and trees | Agricultural land | Animals | Means of production | Means of transport | Other assets |
|---|---|---|---|---|---|---|
| Landlord | 22 | 55 | 13 | 6 | 3 | 5 |
| Peasant 1 | 8 | 8 | 9 | 49 | 0 | 14 |
| Peasant 2 | 9 | 9 | 19 | 7 | 14 | 13 |
| Peasant 3 | 19 | 10 | 38 | 18 | 8 | 27 |
| Manual workers | 32 | 6 | 15 | 18 | 24 | 26 |
| Business activity/ self-employed | 3 | 0 | 2 | 2 | 49 | 6 |
| Rents, remittances, pensions, handouts | 2 | 6 | 1 | 0 | 0 | 2.5 |
| Salaried persons | 5 | 6 | 3 | 0.8 | 2 | 7 |
| All | 100 | 100 | 100 | 100 | 100 | 100 |

*Source*: PARI survey data.

2), comprising 35 per cent of all households, owned more than 50 per cent of assets. In the case of agricultural land, other·land and buildings, trees, means of production, and means of transport, the two peasant classes owned 75 per cent or more of each type of asset. To put it differently, the control over assets by the top two peasant classes extended to all types of assets.

In Zhapur, agricultural land accounted for 91 per cent of all assets among Landlord households. Other than homestead land and trees, animal resources were relatively equally distributed across classes, with poor peasants (Peasant 3) accounting for 38 per cent of all animal resources.

## Animal Wealth

Sixthly, there are two interesting features of animal wealth in the three villages. Draught animals are still used for agriculture in Karnataka, and so, ownership of draught animals is widespread among agrarian classes. As Table 27 shows, in Alabujanahalli, around 50 per cent of households among richer peasants (Peasant 1) and Rich capitalist farmers owned draught animals. Even a third of Manual worker households owned draught animals. Draught animals were widely used for agricultural operations and as means of transport in the village. The average value per draught animal, however,

**Table 27** *Distribution of draught and milch animals, by socio-economic class, Alabujanahalli, 2009*

| Socio-economic class | Draught animals | | Milch animals | |
|---|---|---|---|---|
| | Proportion of households (per cent) | Average value (Rs) | Proportion of households (per cent) | Average value (Rs) |
| Rich capitalist farmer | 50 | 18,000 | 100 | 18,000 |
| Peasant 1 | 44 | 5,000 | 89 | 13,900 |
| Peasant 2 | 64 | 12,500 | 82 | 12,511 |
| Peasant 3 | 50 | 9,333 | 77 | 9,645 |
| Peasant 4 | 24 | 7,890 | 72 | 9,572 |
| Manual worker 1 | 32 | 9,206 | 42 | 7,131 |

*Source*: PARI survey data.

**Table 28** *Proportion of households owning animals and average value per animal, Siresandra, 2009*

| Socio-economic class | Draught animals | | Milch animals | |
|---|---|---|---|---|
| | Proportion of households (per cent) | Average value (Rs) | Proportion of households (per cent) | Average value (Rs) |
| Peasant 1 | 50 | 10,625 | 100 | 17,500 |
| Peasant 2 | 70 | 14,028 | 71 | 18,272 |
| Peasant 3 | 25 | 10,312 | 65 | 15,428 |
| Manual workers | 7 | 12,500 | 23 | 17,667 |

*Source*: PARI survey data.

was very different across classes, with the highest value (representing better quality) prevailing among Rich capitalist farmers.

In Siresandra, a high proportion of peasant households owned draught animals, as they were used in agriculture (Table 28). Around 7 per cent of Manual worker households owned draught animals. The workers of these households were entirely dependent on agricultural and non-agricultural labouring out, and used these animals for agricultural operations like harvesting and threshing.

All Landlord households, and those belonging Peasant 1 and Peasant 2 classes, owned draught animals in Zhapur (Table 29). Only 61 per cent of Peasant 3 households owned draught animals, and the average value of the animals they owned was lower (at Rs 36,000) as compared to Peasant 1 households (Rs 90,000).

**Table 29** *Distribution of draught and milch animals, by socio-economic class, Zhapur, 2009*

| Socio-economic class | Draught animals | | Milch animals | |
|---|---|---|---|---|
| | Proportion of households (per cent) | Average value (Rs) | Proportion of households (per cent) | Average value (Rs) |
| Landlord | 100 | 65,000 | 100 | 10,000 |
| Peasant 1 | 100 | 90,000 | 100 | 18,500 |
| Peasant 2 | 100 | 44,714 | 86 | 11,083 |
| Peasant 3 | 61 | 36,000 | 57 | 9500 |
| Manual workers | 2 | 30,000 | 25 | 8461 |
| Rents, remittances, pensions, handouts | 0 | 0 | 40 | 10,000 |
| Business activity/self-employed | 0 | 0 | 17 | 10,000 |
| Salaried persons | 17 | 40,000 | 0 | 0 |

*Source*: PARI survey data.

The second feature of animal wealth relates to ownership of milch cattle. In the absence of land reforms, many poverty alleviation programmes in India sought to give landless households access to livestock assets. The ownership of livestock was expected to be more equal than that of other assets. What the data from these villages show is that even though livestock was not a means of production as are draught animals, but an independent source of income, ownership of livestock also followed socio-economic class hierarchies.

Cattle were mostly owned by those with access to land. In Alabujanahalli, ownership of milch animals was most widespread among poor peasants (Peasant 4), though, on average, the value of a milch animal owned by Peasant 4 households was one-half of that owned by Rich capitalist farmer households. Ownership of milch cattle was also widespread among the peasantry of Siresandra. In Zhapur, all Landlord and Peasant 1 households owned milch cattle, whereas 57 per cent of Peasant 3 households and 25 per cent of Manual worker households owned milch cattle. The average value of a milch animal owned by a manual worker, Rs 8,461, was less than the value of a milch animal owned by households in all other classes.

In other words, whether it was agricultural land or animals, there was a big difference across socio-economic classes, both in terms of the proportion of households owning an asset and the quality of asset owned (as shown by the average price).

## Postscript

In November 2014, the PARI team returned to the three villages for follow-up case studies. Since it was a short visit, it was not possible to collect accurate data on asset ownership, particularly on land and other property. Our interviews, however, clearly pointed to a huge rise in land prices over the previous five years. In Alabujanahalli, land prices had risen from Rs 3–4 lakhs per acre in 2009 to Rs 5–10 lakhs per acre in 2014. In Siresandra, the value of crop land had increased from about Rs 2 lakhs per acre in 2009 to Rs 6–7 lakh per acre in 2014. The steepest rise was seen in Zhapur, where the value of crop land had increased from Rs 1 lakh per acre in 2009 to Rs 5–10 lakhs per acre in 2014. This was on account of the construction of a new airport and a road to the airport from Kalaburagi town, which had increased land value in the neighbourhood. The rise in land value between 2009 and 2014 would, of course, have benefited all those owning land and large landowners the most.

During the 2014 survey, we also found that there was a general increase in the number of tubewells in all the three villages. This was because of a fall in the water table, especially in Siresandra. This had resulted in an increase in inequality in terms of ownership of the means of production, where the richer households were now able to bore new wells to generate the desired crop yield.

## Conclusions

The three study villages were each characterised by extremely high inequality in ownership of assets. Of the three villages, inequality, as measured by the Gini coefficient, was highest in Zhapur. Zhapur village belongs to a traditional zamindari area where almost 45 per cent of all households were landless (the highest incidence of landlessness among the three villages). Inequality was least in Siresandra, a village of only 79 households, where most households owned some land and only 11 per cent were landless. In absolute terms, in 2009, the asset wealth of the rich in Alabujanahalli and Siresandra was higher than that of those in Zhapur, as the value of irrigated land in the former two villages was much higher than that of rainfed land in the latter. Given the rapid development of infrastructure in Kalaburagi town, this difference may be narrowed in the future.

Ownership of assets or wealth showed clear differences along the axes of socio-economic class and caste. An examination of the composition of assets showed that landlords, rich capitalist farmers and rich peasants not only controlled the most crop land in each village, but also owned the best and most of other assets including livestock and non-agricultural assets. The asset ownership of a household is built on ownership of land, and inequalities in land-holdings get translated into inequalities in other assets as well. The observed increase in land prices will further strengthen the asset-base of the rural rich.

# Appendix Tables

**Appendix Table 1** *Minimum and maximum asset values by decile and share of each decile in total assets, Alabujanahalli, 2009* in Rs and per cent

| Asset decile | Minimum asset value | Maximum asset value | Percentage of assets |
|---|---|---|---|
| D1 | 1,178 | 1,00,140 | 0.3 |
| D2 | 1,02,110 | 2,21,048 | 1 |
| D3 | 2,22,365 | 3,47,300 | 1.7 |
| D4 | 3,66,310 | 5,00,445 | 2.8 |
| D5 | 5,03,222 | 6,42,702 | 3.5 |
| D6 | 6,50,280 | 9,63,650 | 5 |
| D7 | 9,70,450 | 14,49,600 | 7.6 |
| D8 | 15,30,300 | 22,58,254 | 11.7 |
| D9 | 22,76,800 | 32,51,927 | 16.4 |
| D10 | 35,24,478 | 6,17,32,038 | 50 |

*Source*: PARI survey data.

**Appendix Table 2** *Minimum and maximum asset values by decile and share of each decile in total assets, Siresandra, 2009* in Rs and per cent

| Asset decile | Minimum asset value | Maximum asset value | Percentage of assets |
|---|---|---|---|
| D1 | 12,094 | 1,67,892 | 0.5 |
| D2 | 1,98,123 | 3,19,213 | 1.5 |
| D3 | 3,37,150 | 4,11,490 | 2.1 |
| D4 | 4,29,980 | 7,05,050 | 3.1 |
| D5 | 7,58,320 | 10,60,560 | 5.2 |
| D6 | 11,85,488 | 14,59,506 | 7.5 |
| D7 | 14,62,120 | 18,37,565 | 9.3 |
| D8 | 18,59,490 | 24,13,813 | 12.3 |
| D9 | 26,48,800 | 41,53,225 | 20.3 |
| D10 | 41,64,097 | 2,00,35,350 | 38.1 |

*Source*: PARI survey data.

**Appendix Table 3** *Minimum and maximum asset values by decile and share of each decile in total assets, Zhapur, 2009* in Rs and per cent

| Asset decile | Minimum asset value | Maximum asset value | Percentage of assets |
|---|---|---|---|
| D1 | 200 | 33,800 | 0.1 |
| D2 | 41,910 | 73,920 | 0.6 |
| D3 | 74,260 | 1,17,720 | 1.0 |
| D4 | 1,25,450 | 1,60,235 | 1.5 |
| D5 | 1,60,520 | 2,69,910 | 2.2 |
| D6 | 2,73,250 | 3,91,010 | 3.5 |
| D7 | 4,07,068 | 5,10,645 | 4.9 |
| D8 | 5,21,482 | 8,08,850 | 7.0 |
| D9 | 8,19,335 | 14,99,000 | 12.1 |
| D10 | 16,30,820 | 1,57,91,600 | 67.1 |

*Source*: PARI survey data.

**Appendix Table 4** *Mean per asset-owning household, by category of assets and socio-economic class, Alabujanahalli, 2009* in Rs

| Socio-economic class | Land, buildings, and trees | Agricultural land | Animals | Means of production | Means of transport | Other assets |
|---|---|---|---|---|---|---|
| Rich capitalist farmer | 3,28,00,000 | 37,25,000 | 1,02,300 | 2,00,094 | 94,650 | 40,125 |
| Peasant 1 | 31,67,822 | 32,18,500 | 29,356 | 1,41,082 | 32,733 | 1,77,513 |
| Peasant 2 | 16,22,821 | 11,28,372 | 36,792 | 50,532 | 34,658 | 62,752 |
| Peasant 3 | 6,22,692 | 7,63,433 | 26,065 | 27,653 | 22473 | 31,155 |
| Peasant 4 | 2,93,966 | 2,57,224 | 19,058 | 6,500 | 4,612 | 15,867 |
| Manual worker 1 | 2,17,428 | 76,838 | 15,180 | 3,671 | 1,448 | 9,255 |
| Manual worker 2 | 1,62,775 | 35,568 | 4,995 | 0 | 150 | 4,838 |
| Manual worker 3 | 1,45,909 | 10,000 | 2,427 | 0 | 173 | 3,160 |
| Business/ self-employment | 4,08,727 | 1,52,500 | 7,520 | 5,200 | 80,400 | 48,783 |
| Rents/ remittances | 8,13,571 | 3,20,714 | 18,171 | 15,036 | 6,914 | 17,025 |
| Salaried persons | 7,07,407 | 9,82,357 | 3,682 | 5,089 | 11,536 | 37,523 |
| All | 9,34,900 | 5,75,665 | 19,738 | 21,514 | 16,192 | 31,575 |

*Source*: PARI survey data.

**Appendix Table 5** *Mean per asset-owning household, by category of assets and socio-economic class, Siresandra, 2009 in Rs*

| Socio-economic class | Agricultural land | Land, buildings, and trees | Animals | Means of production | Means of transport | Other assets |
|---|---|---|---|---|---|---|
| Peasant 1 | 42,48,213 | 45,58,070 | 86,175 | 1,90,588 | 39,113 | 40,495 |
| Peasant 2 | 13,25,400 | 13,08,768 | 54,460 | 58,309 | 21,744 | 33,027 |
| Peasant 3 | 3,28,952 | 3,81,558 | 35,273 | 23,429 | 1,752 | 13,490 |
| Manual workers | 55,462 | 1,76,303 | 9,355 | 588 | 542 | 8,523 |
| Business/small self-employment | 80,000 | 4,51,572 | 13,677 | 8,105 | 13,167 | 17,389 |
| Total | 7,78,815 | 8,57,989 | 38,017 | 38,008 | 10,638 | 20,518 |

*Source:* PARI survey data.

**Appendix Table 6** *Mean per asset-owning household, by category of assets and socio-economic class, Zhapur, 2009 in Rs*

| Socio-economic class | Land, buildings, and trees | Agricultural land | Animals | Means of production | Means of transport | Other assets |
|---|---|---|---|---|---|---|
| Landlord | 9,18,125 | 1,13,87,500 | 79,925 | 11,725 | 3,750 | 8,375 |
| Peasant 1 | 6,80,750 | 33,00,000 | 1,12,000 | 2,02,850 | 0 | 49,380 |
| Peasant 2 | 1,91,867 | 10,89,583 | 65,050 | 8,550 | 133 | 12,698 |
| Peasant 3 | 1,13,493 | 2,85,107 | 33,774 | 5,385 | 1,396 | 6,153 |
| Manual workers | 1,02,964 | 1,01,961 | 7,103 | 2,939 | 2,378 | 1,413 |
| Business activity/self-employed | 1,25,000 | 1,51,143 | 17,900 | 3,486 | 45,557 | 1,107 |
| Rents, remittances, pensions, handouts | 69,000 | 9,90,000 | 6,804 | 100 | 0 | 3,587 |
| Salaried persons | 1,40,917 | 8,70,000 | 12,250 | 1,158 | 1,667 | 3,240 |

*Source:* PARI survey data.

# 8

## Cropping Pattern, Yields and Crop Incomes: Findings from Three Villages Surveyed in Karnataka

Biplab Sarkar

An analysis of crop incomes in Karnataka shows that the average real income from crop production fell sharply over the last decade (see Narayanamoorthy 2013; Kannan 2015). However, as is well known, the main official source of data on incomes from crop production – the Comprehensive Scheme for Studying Cost of Cultivation of Principal Crops in India (known as the CCPC Scheme), conducted by agricultural universities under the supervision of the Directorate of Economics and Statistics of the Ministry of Agriculture – provides information at the crop level but cannot be used to study household incomes.

In this chapter, my focus is on estimation of incomes from crop production at the crop, operational holding, and household level in the three survey villages of Karnataka. Estimates of crop incomes used in this chapter refer to farm business incomes, that is, gross incomes (or gross value of output, GVO) net of costs incurred in the process of production. The items of cost broadly correspond to those collected by the Directorate of Economics and Statistics, Government of India under the CCPC. The cost of production or cost A2 includes the costs of home-produced and purchased seeds; the value of home-produced and purchased manure; the value of chemical fertilizer, plant protection, irrigation charges, hired labour; the costs of owned and hired animal labour; the costs of owned and hired machinery; rent paid for leased-in land; marketing expenses; land revenue; interest on working capital; depreciation of own machinery; and crop insurance expenses.

The chapter begins with a discussion of the cropping pattern and productivity of major crops in the three villages. It then goes on to examine the gross value of output, cost of production, and farm business incomes from the cultivation of major crops and on operational holdings of households belonging to different socio-economic classes.

The three villages – Alabujanahalli, Siresandra and Zhapur – that form a part of this study are in three different districts and three different agro-climatic regions of the State of Karnataka. The villages show substantial diversity in terms of the distribution of land, irrigation, cropping pattern, farming practices, and labour deployment. Given this diversity, we discuss them separately, and the concluding section of the chapter summarises the similarities and differences between the villages.

## Alabujanahalli Village, Mandya District

### Cropping Pattern

Alabujanahalli village was primarily irrigated by canals from the Krishnarajasagar dam. Tubewells were used for additional irrigation, particularly in the *rabi* season. Cropping intensity in the village was 133 per cent, slightly higher than the district average (117 per cent). The major crops grown were paddy, sugarcane, finger millet (*ragi*), and mulberry. *Kharif* and *rabi* paddy together accounted for 40 per cent of the total gross cropped area, followed by sugarcane (36 per cent), finger millet (7 per cent), and mulberry (7 per cent), during the agricultural year 2008–09. Sugarcane is cultivated in the village for a continuous period of more than six to seven months each year with a plentiful supply of water, either from canals or through borewell irrigation. Sugarcane is the most important commercial crop in the village.

A substantial amount of land was under annual and perennial crops in the village, and only 36 per cent of operational landholdings was available for seasonal crops. Paddy, sown on 32 per cent of operational holdings, was the most important crop cultivated during the *kharif* season. Other than paddy, about 2 per cent of the operated land was sown with horse gram and 1 per cent of land was sown with finger millet during this season (Table 1). In winter, paddy, which accounted for 19 per cent of operated land, and finger millet, which accounted for 6 per cent of operated land, were the important crops. Mango and coconut were also grown in the village.

Graph 1 show the major crop cycles in the village. The most important crop was sugarcane, cultivated throughout the year. Both planted and ratoon sugarcane were cultivated in the village. Normally farmers in this village

**Table 1** *Proportion of different crops in gross cropped area (GCA) and total operated land, Alabujanahalli, 2008–09*

| Crop name | Area (in acres) | As proportion of GCA (per cent) | As proportion of operational holding (per cent) |
|---|---|---|---|
| Paddy | 169.68 | 24 | 32 |
| Horse gram | 13.00 | 2 | 2 |
| Finger millet | 6.85 | 1 | 1 |
| **All *kharif* crops (rainy season)** | **191.23** | 27 | 36 |
| Paddy | 113.78 | 16 | 21 |
| Finger millet | 44.78 | 6 | 8 |
| **All *rabi* crops (winter)** | **180.29** | 25 | 34 |
| Sugarcane | 254.45 | 36 | 47 |
| Mulberry | 46.88 | 7 | 9 |
| Mango | 16.00 | 2 | 3 |
| Coconut (orchard) | 15.95 | 2 | 3 |
| **All annual and perennial crops** | **343.61** | 48 | 64 |
| Gross cropped area (GCA) | 715.10 | 100 | 133 |
| Operational holding | 537.63 | na | 100 |

*Source*: PARI survey data.

plant sugarcane on their field once in five years. After the first harvest of planted crops they leave the roots and lower parts of the plant, this process of cultivation is known as ratooning and we called the crop 'sugarcane ratoon'. The main benefit of ratooning is that farmers can save on the cost of preparing the field and planting. Ratoon crops also mature earlier than planted ones. Ratoon sugarcane takes 10 months to be ready for harvesting, while planted sugarcane takes 13 to 14 months. This method cannot be used endlessly as the yield of ratoon sugarcane declines after every harvest. In this village a common practice was to keep the sugarcane crop till the fourth ratoon.

The second important crop cycle was a combination of *kharif* paddy or *kharif* finger millet, and *rabi* paddy or *rabi* finger millet. The third important crop was mulberry, cultivated to feed the cocoons in sericulture. Sericulture was an important activity in this village for middle and poor peasant households (see chapter 10). It was not popular with rich peasants on account of the high family labour requirements. The fourth and fifth crop cycles, in terms of importance, involved cultivating one *rabi* or *kharif*

| Cycle | Jun-08 | Jul-08 | Aug-08 | Sep-08 | Oct-08 | Nov-08 | Dec-08 | Jan-09 | Feb-09 | Mar-09 | Apr-09 | May-09 | Area |
|---|---|---|---|---|---|---|---|---|---|---|---|---|---|
| 1 | Sugarcane | | | | | | | | | | | | 194.39 |
| 2 | Paddy or Finger millet or other kharif crops | | | | | | | Paddy or fingermillet or other rabi crops | | | | | 180.29 |
| 3 | Mulbery | | | | | | | | | | | | 46.88 |
| 4 | Sugarcane (ratoon) | | | | | | | Paddy or fingermillet or other rabi crops | | | | | 35.63 |
| 5 | Paddy or Finger millet or other kharif crops | | | | | Sugarcane (planted) | | | | | | | 24.43 |
| 6 | Mango | | | | | | | | | | | | 16.00 |
| 7 | Coconut (orchard) | | | | | | | | | | | | 15.95 |
| 8 | Paddy or Finger millet or other kharif crops | | | | | | | | | | | | 10.94 |

**Graph 1** *Major crop cycles, Alabujanahalli, 2008-09*
*Source:* PARI Survey data.

crop following a sugarcane ratoon. Two households in the village also had mango orchards: one was on 14 acres of land and the other one was on 2 acres of land. Almost 16 per cent of households in the village had coconut orchards on small plots of land, accounting for 3 per cent of total operational holdings. Coconut trees on the boundaries of fields were also very common; almost one-half of the households in the village had coconut trees on the boundaries of their fields. Although the village had substantial irrigation throughout the year, few farmers could access irrigation water in the *rabi* season; as a consequence, around 11 acres of land were kept fallow in the *rabi* season during 2008–09 (crop cycle 8).

### Productivity/Yield of Major Crops

Table 2 shows the average yield of major crops grown in Alabujanahalli in 2008–09, and the corresponding official data for Mandya district, Karnataka and India as a whole. Average yields of sugarcane and paddy in Alabhujanahalli were higher than the State and all-India averages, but lower than the district averages. An important feature of sugarcane production in Alabujanahalli was that the average yield for the planted crop was the highest (40,000 kg per acre), and the yield declined for subsequent ratoon crops (35,000 kg per acre for first ratoon, 34,667 kg for the second ratoon, and 34,167 kg for the third ratoon). A misleading feature of official statistics on sugarcane yields is that they do not provide separate data for planted and ratoon crops. As a result, we get misleading estimates of sugarcane output. In the case of finger millet (*ragi*), although cultivated only on 7 per cent of

**Table 2** *Average yield of major crops, Alabujanahalli, 2008–09* in kg per acre

| Crop | India | Karnataka (State) | Mandya (district) | Alabujanahalli (village) |
|------|-------|-------------------|-------------------|--------------------------|
| Sugarcane | 27,755 | 33,611 | 48,077 | 40,000 |
| Paddy (*kharif*) | 1,256 | 1,466 | 1,937 | 1,600 |
| Paddy (*rabi*) | 1,886 | 1,304 | 1,907 | 1,600 |
| Finger millet (*rabi*) | na | 583 | 866 | 1,500 |

*Source*: PARI survey data for Alabujanahalli; figures for India, Karnataka, and Mandya were taken from the Directorate of Economics and Statistics website.

the gross cropped area, average yield per acre was substantially higher than the district and State averages.

Sugarcane cultivated in Alabujanahalli is supplied to Chamundeshwari Sugars Limited, one of south India's largest sugar factories, located in nearby K. M. Doddi (see Appendix 8.1).

### Farm Business Incomes of Major Crops

In this section, we provide details of income from crop production for major crops grown in the village during 2008–09. Table 3 shows the average per acre gross value of output, cost A2, and net income for major crops grown in Alabujanahalli. Average farm business income per acre was highest for coconut orchards (Rs 19,072 per acre), followed by sugarcane (Rs 13,667 per acre), *kharif* paddy (Rs 4,387), *rabi* paddy (Rs 4,064), mango (Rs 3,472), and *rabi* finger millet (Rs 3,264). Farmers cultivating horse gram had incurred losses in the survey year. Coconut orchards, which gave the highest income per acre, were grown on only 3 per cent of operational holdings, and horse gram on only 2 per cent of operational holdings. Additionally, while comparing incomes across crops, we need to pay attention to crop duration. Incomes from sugarcane, coconut orchards, and mango are accounted for over 12 months; whereas incomes from paddy, horse gram, and finger millet are accounted for only 5 to 6 months. Even after taking crop duration into account, returns from coconut orchards and sugarcane were higher than from seasonal crops.

It is interesting to further differentiate between planted and ratoon sugarcane while studying the economics of crop production in detail. Table 4 shows that crop income from planted sugarcane was lower than from ratoon sugarcane. The average income from planted sugarcane was Rs 12,968 per acre. When sugarcane was cultivated as ratoon, the income

**Table 3** *Average gross value of output (GVO), paid-out cost (cost A2), and farm business income (FBI) for major crops, Alabujanahalli, 2008–09* in Rs per acre

| Crop season | Crop name | GVO | Cost A2 | FBI |
|---|---|---|---|---|
| *Kharif* | Paddy | 17,000 | 12,613 | 4,387 |
| *Kharif* | Horse gram | 633 | 719 | -85 |
| *Rabi* | Paddy | 16,160 | 12,091 | 4,069 |
| *Rabi* | Finger millet | 12,750 | 9,486 | 3,264 |
| Annual | Sugarcane | 38,936 | 26,040 | 13,667 |
| Perennial | Mango | 7,200 | 3,728 | 3,472 |
| Perennial | Coconut (orchard) | 23,349 | 4,277 | 19,072 |

*Source*: PARI survey data.

**Table 4** *Average gross value of output (GVO), paid-out cost (cost A2), and farm business income (FBI), planted and ratoon sugarcane, Alabujanahalli, 2008–09* in Rs per acre

| Crop | GVO | Cost A2 | FBI |
|---|---|---|---|
| Sugarcane (planted) | 44,000 | 31,032 | 12,968 |
| Sugarcane (ratoon) | 38,600 | 23,773 | 14,827 |

*Source*: PARI survey data.

was 14 per cent higher, at Rs 14,827 per acre. An analysis of costs of inputs shows that the lower cost of production in raising ratoon sugarcane as compared to planted sugarcane was mainly on account of not incurring expenditure towards seed costs and field preparation at the time of sowing (which was essential for planted sugarcane).

The discussion so far has focused on an average cultivator, but households belonging to different socio-economic classes are likely to obtain different returns from cultivation due to differential access to irrigation, quality of land, credit, and overall access to means of production. Table 5 presents data on the average gross value of output per acre for major crops across different socio-economic classes in Alabujanahalli. It shows that per acre average gross value of output was the same across classes for planted sugarcane and *rabi* finger millet. On the other hand, for sugarcane ratoon and paddy, the gross value of output per acre declined as one moved from rich peasants to middle peasants, and then to poor peasants. Take, for example, the case of sugarcane ratoon – average per acre gross value of output was Rs 40,255 for Rich capitalist farmers, Rs 39,996 for Peasant 1 households, and Rs 34,875 for Peasant 4 households. In the case of paddy, per acre gross value of output

**Table 5** *Average gross value of output, major crops, Alabujanahalli, 2008–09* in Rs per acre

| Socio-economic class | Sugarcane (planted) | Sugarcane (ratoon) | Paddy (*kharif*) | Paddy (*rabi*) | Finger millet (*rabi*) |
|---|---|---|---|---|---|
| Rich capitalist farmer | 44,000 | 40,255 | 15,385 | 13,878 | 12,750 |
| Peasant 1 | 44,000 | 39,996 | 20,000 | 17,750 | 12,750 |
| Peasant 2 | 44,000 | 38,523 | 18,520 | 16,160 | 12,750 |
| Peasant 3 | 44,000 | 34,875 | 16,160 | 16,160 | 12,750 |
| Peasant 4 | 44,000 | 35,200 | 15,880 | 16,160 | 12,750 |
| All classes | 44,000 | 38,600 | 17,000 | 16,160 | 12,750 |

*Source*: PARI survey data.

**Table 6** *Average cost of production (cost A2), major crops, Alabujanahalli, 2008–09* in Rs per acre

| Socio-economic class | Sugarcane (planted) | Sugarcane (ratoon) | Paddy (*kharif*) | Paddy (*rabi*) | Finger millet (*rabi*) |
|---|---|---|---|---|---|
| Rich capitalist farmer | 25,919 | 25,288 | 12,363 | 10,692 | 7,997 |
| Peasant 1 | 26,645 | 25,946 | 9,558 | 11,536 | 6,274 |
| Peasant 2 | 27,918 | 25,020 | 10,471 | 10,535 | 6,719 |
| Peasant 3 | 31,536 | 22,936 | 11,432 | 11,315 | 9,934 |
| Peasant 4 | 33,791 | 23,125 | 14,038 | 12,051 | 10,527 |
| All classes | 31,032 | 24,804 | 12,613 | 12,091 | 9,486 |

*Source*: PARI survey data.

for Rich capitalist farmers was lower than for the peasantry. This can be explained by the fact that Rich capitalist farmers cultivated fine-quality, *sonam* variety of paddy for own household consumption on some of their land, whose productivity was lower than for other paddy varieties. As we have not differentiated between paddy varieties, overall paddy output for Rich capitalist farmers was shown as lower due to the cultivation of *sonam* paddy.

The socio-economic advantage comes out more clearly when one looks at per acre cost of production. Table 6 shows that for all crops, cost of cultivation was lower for rich peasants than for poorer sections of the peasantry. In the case of *kharif* paddy, per acre cost of production was lowest (Rs 9,558 per acre) for Peasant 1 households, followed by Peasant 2 (Rs 10,471), Peasant 3 (Rs 11,432), and Peasant 4 (Rs 14,038) households. The higher cost of cultivation for poor peasants in comparison to rich peasants may be driven

**Table 7** *Average farm business incomes, major crops, Alabujanahalli, 2008–09* in Rs per acre

| Socio-economic class | Sugarcane (planted) | Sugarcane (ratoon) | Paddy (*kharif*) | Paddy (*rabi*) | Finger millet (*rabi*) |
|---|---|---|---|---|---|
| Rich capitalist farmer | 18081 | 14967 | 3022 | 3186 | 4753 |
| Peasant 1 | 17355 | 14050 | 10442 | 6214 | 6476 |
| Peasant 2 | 16082 | 13503 | 8049 | 5625 | 6031 |
| Peasant 3 | 12464 | 11939 | 4728 | 4845 | 2816 |
| Peasant 4 | 10209 | 12075 | 1842 | 4109 | 2223 |
| All classes | 12968 | 13796 | 4387 | 4069 | 3264 |

*Source*: PARI survey data.

by several cost items. Note that the cost of cultivation of ratoon sugarcane was lower than for planted sugarcane across socio-economic classes.

Table 7 provides summary data on average farm business incomes per acre for different crops by socio-economic class in Alabujanahalli. Although the average gross value of output was similar for planted sugarcane and *rabi* finger millet across classes, due to differences in cost of cultivation, farm business incomes fell as we moved from rich peasants to poor peasants. Take, for example, the case of planted sugarcane – the average farm business income was Rs 18,081 per acre for Rich capitalist farmers, while the corresponding figures were Rs 17,355 for Peasant 1, Rs 16,082 for Peasant 2, Rs 12,464 for Peasant 3, and Rs 10,209 for Peasant 4 households. A broadly similar pattern was observed in the case of ratoon sugarcane and paddy.

## Cost of Production of Major Crops

The data in Tables 8 to 10 show item-wise costs of production of planted sugarcane, ratoon sugarcane and *kharif* paddy in Alabujanahalli.

First, Table 8 shows that the high cost of cultivation incurred by poor peasants in planted sugarcane cultivation was on account of the systematically higher costs incurred by them for seed, manure, casual labour, and animal labour. For example, while the average per acre seed cost was Rs 2,970 for rich peasants (Peasant 1), the corresponding figures were Rs 3,406 for Peasant 2, Rs 4,855 for Peasant 3, and Rs 5,408 for poor peasant (Peasant 4) cultivators. In the case of paddy, the high cost of cultivation incurred by poor peasants was on account of the systematically higher costs incurred by them for seed, manure, fertilizer, animal labour, and rental payments on leased-in land (Table 10).

Secondly, Tables 8 to 10 show that expenditure on hired labour was the

**Table 8** *Average expenditure on different cost items, sugarcane (planted), Alabujanahalli, 2008–09* in Rs per acre

| Item | Socio-economic classes | | | | |
|---|---|---|---|---|---|
| | Rich capitalist farmer | Peasant 1 | Peasant 2 | Peasant 3 | Peasant 4 |
| Seed | 4200 | 2970 | 3406 | 4855 | 5408 |
| Manure | 1000 | 493 | 706 | 1155 | 2550 |
| Fertilizer | 3825 | 5982 | 4727 | 3161 | 5193 |
| Plant protection | 425 | 239 | 174 | 68 | 253 |
| Irrigation | 400 | 158 | 399 | 442 | 448 |
| Casual labour | 10205 | 11067 | 13280 | 14318 | 14217 |
| Long-term workers | 0 | 1156 | 680 | 974 | 0 |
| Animal labour | 894 | 356 | 1775 | 2396 | 1150 |
| Machine labour | 360 | 458 | 181 | 8 | 912 |
| Rent | 0 | 0 | 0 | 0 | 400 |
| Other costs | 4611 | 3767 | 2590 | 4159 | 3261 |
| Cost A2 | 25919 | 26645 | 27918 | 31536 | 33791 |

*Source*: PARI survey data.

**Table 9** *Average expenditure on different cost items, sugarcane (ratoon), Alabujanahalli, 2008–09* in Rs per acre

| Item | Socio-economic class | | | | |
|---|---|---|---|---|---|
| | Rich capitalist farmer | Peasant 1 | Peasant 2 | Peasant 3 | Peasant 4 |
| Seed | 0 | 0 | 0 | 0 | 0 |
| Manure | 0 | 445 | 1295 | 2036 | 1799 |
| Fertilizer | 6427 | 4274 | 5166 | 4739 | 5681 |
| Plant protection | 255 | 123 | 369 | 371 | 279 |
| Irrigation | 408 | 662 | 513 | 442 | 409 |
| Casual labour | 14894 | 15132 | 12775 | 10448 | 11430 |
| Long-term workers | 0 | 1454 | 336 | 493 | 0 |
| Animal labour | 0 | 421 | 1256 | 1754 | 1267 |
| Machine labour | 551 | 81 | 156 | 20 | 90 |
| Rent | 0 | 188 | 427 | 0 | 0 |
| Other costs | 2753 | 3165 | 2728 | 2633 | 2170 |
| Cost A2 | 25288 | 25946 | 25020 | 22936 | 23125 |

*Source*: PARI survey data.

**Table 10** *Average expenditure on different cost items, paddy (kharif), Alabujanahalli, 2008–09* in Rs per acre

| Item | Socio-economic class | | | | |
|---|---|---|---|---|---|
| | Rich capitalist farmer | Peasant 1 | Peasant 2 | Peasant 3 | Peasant 4 |
| Seed | 420 | 433 | 450 | 468 | 594 |
| Manure | 0 | 326 | 311 | 583 | 927 |
| Fertilizer | 1412 | 1155 | 1630 | 1665 | 1971 |
| Plant protection | 141 | 120 | 252 | 237 | 318 |
| Irrigation | 108 | 77 | 120 | 113 | 112 |
| Casual labour | 6933 | 4302 | 4309 | 4666 | 5657 |
| Long-term workers | 0 | 657 | 195 | 319 | 0 |
| Animal labour | 117 | 153 | 512 | 775 | 665 |
| Machine labour | 2059 | 1078 | 1104 | 978 | 1537 |
| Rent | 0 | 0 | 718 | 703 | 1488 |
| Other costs | 1173 | 1255 | 870 | 924 | 768 |
| Cost A2 | 12363 | 9558 | 10471 | 11432 | 14038 |

*Source*: PARI survey data.

largest cost component for all socio-economic classes and for all crops under discussion. While it is to be expected that rich farmers will be highly dependent on hired labour for cultivation, we see that even poor peasants incurred 40–50 per cent of their total costs on hired labour.

Lastly, rent payments were incurred by peasants (Peasant 2, Peasant 3, and Peasant 4 classes) in paddy cultivation, contrary to the official position that no land has been leased out or leased in after land reforms in Karnataka (see chapter 2).

## Farm Business Incomes from Operational Holdings

In Alabujanahalli, the average gross value of output per acre of operational holdings, counting all the seasons together in the agricultural year 2008–09, was Rs 27,746 (Table 11). The average farm business income, after deducting cost A2, was Rs 9,030. Variations across the main cultivating classes show that the average farm business income of Peasant 2 households was more than that of all other socio-economic classes. Variations in per acre farm business incomes accruing to households from different socio-economic classes can be explained by differences in cropping pattern.

First, Rich capitalist farmers devoted a larger proportion (57 per cent of gross cropped area) of their land to paddy cultivation (paddy was less profitable than sugarcane) and received lower farm business income per acre than the village average (Table 12). The two Rich capitalist farmers of the village owned rice mills in the nearest market town, K. M. Doddi, and this may be the reason they devoted a higher share of land to paddy cultivation. Income from the milling of rice is included in total household income and not in crop income.

Peasant 1 (rich peasant) households allocated a large share of their land to sugarcane cultivation (42 per cent of gross cropped area), but also to mango orchards (17 per cent). As incomes from mango cultivation were lowest in the village among all other cultivated crops, this brought down the overall farm business incomes from operational holdings for rich peasant households.

Thirdly, Peasant 4 households had the smallest share of land under sugarcane cultivation (only 30 per cent of gross cropped area), and devoted a relatively higher share of land to cereals (54 per cent) and mulberry crops (11 per cent). As we know, sugarcane cultivation requires plentiful supply of water and more capital investment than other crops. Limited access to irrigation, lack of capital and consumption needs of staple food "forced" poor peasants to cultivate cereals, which were less profitable than sugarcane.

One limitation of our analysis here is that incomes from mulberry cultivation have been treated as zero: mulberry leaves are taken as intermediate inputs in the production of silk cocoons, and income from cocoons is counted in household income. On the other hand, mulberry leaves are an intermediate product and are produced to feed the cocoons in sericulture cultivation. The net income from production of mulberry leaves has been taken as zero although it adds substantial value through sericulture cultivation. This has been included in total household income and not in income from crop production.

We now turn to the average farm business income per household by socio-economic class in Alabujanahalli. Table 13 shows that incomes per household from crop production were highest for Rich capitalist farmers (Rs 1,77,259), and these declined steeply as we moved from Peasant 1 households to Peasant 4 households. The income of a Peasant 4 household from crop production was only 8 per cent of the income earned by a Rich capitalist farmer from crop production. Not only that, income from crop production of almost half of all the cultivator households in the village was less than or equal to Rs 10,000. By contrast, 1 per cent of households – three Rich capitalist farmer households – obtained an annual crop income of more than Rs 200,001 each (Table 14).

**Table 11** *Average gross value of output (GVO), paid-out cost (cost A2), and farm business income (FBI) by operational holding and socio-economic class, Alabujanahalli, 2008–09* in Rs per acre

| Socio-economic class | Gross value of output | Cost A2 | Farm business income |
|---|---|---|---|
| Rich capitalist farmer | 21,238 | 13,531 | 7,707 |
| Peasant 1 | 22,128 | 13,521 | 8,608 |
| Peasant 2 | 28,147 | 16,254 | 11,894 |
| Peasant 3 | 24,067 | 14,916 | 9,151 |
| Peasant 4 | 23,688 | 16,638 | 7,049 |
| All classes | 24,746 | 15,717 | 9,030 |

*Source*: PARI survey data.

**Table 12** *Proportion of different crops in gross cropped area (GCA), by households belonging to different socio-economic classes, Alabujanahalli, 2008–09* in per cent

| Socio-economic class | Sugarcane | Orchard | Mulberry | Cereals | Fodder crops | All |
|---|---|---|---|---|---|---|
| Rich capitalist farmer | 30 | 2 | 0 | 57 | 9 | 100 |
| Peasant 1 | 42 | 17 | 2 | 41 | 3 | 100 |
| Peasant 2 | 40 | 3 | 7 | 47 | 2 | 100 |
| Peasant 3 | 37 | 2 | 8 | 48 | 5 | 100 |
| Peasant 4 | 30 | 3 | 11 | 54 | 3 | 100 |

*Source*: PARI survey data.

**Table 13** *Average annual incomes from crop production by socio-economic class, Alabujanahalli, 2008–09* in Rs per household

| Socio-economic class | Annual income from crop production |
|---|---|
| Rich capitalist farmer | 177,259 |
| Peasant 1 | 115,053 |
| Peasant 2 | 71,310 |
| Peasant 3 | 37,282 |
| Peasant 4 | 14,127 |
| All | 31,666 |

*Source*: PARI survey data.

**Table 14** *Number and proportion of cultivator households by size-class of crop income, Alabujanahalli, 2008–09*

| Crop income group (Rs) | Number of households | Proportion (per cent) |
|---|---|---|
| Up to 10,000 | 92 | 45 |
| 10,001–25,000 | 35 | 17 |
| 25,001–50,000 | 38 | 18 |
| 50,001–100,000 | 23 | 11 |
| 100,000–200,000 | 15 | 7 |
| More than 200,001 | 3 | 1 |
| All | 206 | 100 |

*Source*: PARI survey data.

# Siresandra Village, Kolar District

## Cropping Pattern

Siresandra village in Kolar district is located in the semi-arid south-eastern dry region of Karnataka. Almost 65 per cent of the operational land in the village was rainfed; the remaining got some supplementary irrigation from borewells during 2008–09. Drip irrigation was used for vegetable cultivation. Cropping intensity in the village was 117, which was slightly higher than the district average (103). The major crops grown were *ragi* (finger millet), mulberry, vegetables, and paddy. Finger millet was often intercropped with *sorghum*, pigeon pea (*thogari*), and carpet legume (*avare*). Intercropped finger millet accounted for 33 per cent of gross cropped area (GCA) in the village, followed by vegetables (22 per cent), mulberry (22 per cent), and *kharif* paddy (7 per cent). Vegetables included tomato, potato, carrot, ridge gourd, beetroot, and brinjal. One rich peasant household in the village also cultivated banana on 3 acres of land. Betel leaf, flowers like jasmine, and fodder crops were also cultivated on small plots of land.

Mulberry was cultivated in the village to feed cocoons for sericulture. Mulberry is a perennial crop and lasts for over 15 years in the field. It can be grown under a variety of agro-climatic conditions, and can survive poor rainfall conditions. The leaf yield of mulberry is in the order of 3,000–3,500 kilograms per hectare under low moisture conditions, whereas with assured irrigation, the yield can be stepped up to 30,000 kilograms per hectare (Government of Karnataka 2015). Sericulture was a very important

**Table 15** *Proportion of different crops in gross cropped area and total operated land, Siresandra, 2008–09*

| Crops | Area (acres) | As proportion of GCA (per cent) | As proportion of operational holdings (per cent) |
|---|---|---|---|
| Finger millet intercrop | 74.23 | 33 | 39 |
| Paddy | 15.13 | 7 | 8 |
| Finger millet mono-crop | 14.50 | 6 | 8 |
| Vegetables (*kharif*) | 9.25 | 4 | 5 |
| All *kharif* crops | 122.6 | 54 | 64 |
| Vegetables including potato (*rabi*) | 41.03 | 18 | 22 |
| All *rabi* crops | 51.03 | 23 | 27 |
| Mulberry | 48.94 | 22 | 25 |
| Banana | 3.00 | 1 | 2 |
| All annual crops | 52.49 | 23 | 27 |
| Gross cropped area (GCA) | 226.12 | 100 | 117 |
| Operational holding | 192.48 | na | 100 |

*Source*: PARI survey data.

| Cycle | Jun-08 | Jul-08 | Aug-08 | Sep-08 | Oct-08 | Nov-08 | Dec-08 | Jan-09 | Feb-09 | Mar-09 | Apr-09 | May-09 | Area |
|---|---|---|---|---|---|---|---|---|---|---|---|---|---|
| 1 | Finger millet intercrop | | | | | | | | | | | | 65.23 |
| 2 | Mulberry | | | | | | | | | | | | 48.94 |
| 3 | Paddy | | | | | | | | | | | | 9.63 |
| 4 | Finger millet mono-crop | | | | | | | | | | | | 9.50 |
| 5 | Vegetable | | | | | | Vegetable/fodder crops | | | | | | 9.25 |
| 6 | Paddy | | | | | | Vegetables | | | | | | 6.00 |
| 7 | Finger millet intercrop | | | | | | Vegetables | | | | | | 5.00 |
| 8 | Finger millet mono-crop | | | | | | Vegetables | | | | | | 5.00 |

**Graph 2** *Major crop cycles in Siresandra, 2008-09*
*Source:* PARI survey data.

economic activity in the village, and its scale depended on the availability of mulberry leaves.

Graph 2 shows the major crop cycles in Siresandra. The most important crop cycle was finger millet intercropped with coarse cereals, millet, and pulses in the *kharif* season, and land kept fellow in the *rabi* season. The

**Table 16** *Average yield of major crops, Siresandra, 2008–09* in kg per acre

| Crops | India | Karnataka State | Kolar district | Siresandra |
|---|---|---|---|---|
| Paddy (*kharif*) | 1,256 | 1,466 | 960 | 2,000 |
| Finger millet (*kharif*) | na | 673 | 656 | 1,000 |
| Tomato | 7,536 | na | na | 12,500 |
| Potato | 7,617 | na | na | 10,000 |
| Banana | 14,971 | na | 13,198 | 16,667 |

*Source*: PARI survey data for Siresandra; Directorate of Economics and Statistics website (http://aps.dac.gov.in/APY/Public_Report1.aspx) for Kolar district and Karnataka.

second most important crop cycle was mulberry, grown for mulberry leaves, throughout the year. The third and fourth crop cycles were cultivation of paddy or finger millet in the *kharif* season, and land kept fellow in the *rabi* season. On land with some access to borewell irrigation two crops a year were cultivated, including vegetables in the *rabi* season.

### Productivity/Yield of Major Crops

Intercropping, common in semi-arid agricultural systems, presents a challenge for measuring and interpreting data on crop yield. Unless the number of rows and the area devoted to each crop in the intercropping system is completely accounted for, individual crop yield data will be misleading. For these reasons, we are not presenting yield data for intercrops.

Table 16 shows the average yield of monocrops grown in Siresandra in 2008–09, and the corresponding official data for Kolar district, Karnataka, and India. Average yields of major monocrops in Siresandra were higher than the district and all-India averages. For example, in the case of *kharif* paddy, the average yield per acre was 2,000 kg for Siresandra; the corresponding figures were 960 kg for Kolar district, 1,466 kg for Karnataka, and 1,256 kg for all-India. All the crops listed in Table 16 together accounted for only 27 per cent of the gross cropped area in the village.

### Farm Business Incomes of Major Crops

Table 17 shows the average gross value of output, cost A2, and net income for major crops grown in Siresandra during 2008–09. Average farm business income per acre was highest for betel leaf (Rs 142,065 per acre), followed by banana (Rs 55,226 per acre), vegetables cultivated in the *kharif* season (Rs 41,324), vegetables cultivated in the *rabi* season (Rs 25,179), *kharif* paddy

**Table 17** *Average gross value of output (GVO), paid-out cost (cost A2), and farm business income (FBI), major crops, Siresandra, 2008–09* in Rs per acre

| Crop season | Crops | GVO | Cost A2 | FBI |
|---|---|---|---|---|
| *Kharif* | Finger millet intercrop | 9,092 | 6,191 | 2,900 |
| *Kharif* | Paddy | 16,021 | 11,785 | 4,237 |
| *Kharif* | Finger millet monocrop | 8,816 | 5,454 | 3,362 |
| *Kharif* | Vegetables | 74,885 | 33,561 | 41,324 |
| *Rabi* | Vegetables | 59,251 | 34,073 | 25,179 |
| Perennial | Banana | 75,000 | 19,774 | 55,226 |
| Perennial | Betel leaf | 170,000 | 27,935 | 142,065 |

**Table 18** *Average gross value of output (GVO), cost of production (cost A2), and farm business income (FBI) for finger millet intercrop by socio-economic classes, Siresandra, 2008–09* in Rs per acre

| Socio-economic classes | GVO | Cost A2 | FBI |
|---|---|---|---|
| Peasant 1 | 18,661 | 8,570 | 10,091 |
| Peasant 2 | 9,758 | 6,433 | 3,325 |
| Peasant 3 | 8,109 | 5,914 | 2,195 |
| All | 9,092 | 6,191 | 2,900 |

*Source*: PARI survey data.

(Rs 4,237), finger millet monocrop (Rs 3,362), and finger millet intercrop (Rs 2,900). It should be noted, however, that betel leaf and banana were cultivated by only 2–3 farmers in the village; these two crops together accounted for only 2 per cent of the total operated land in the village.

Table 18 presents data on average gross value of output, cost A2, and farm business income per acre for finger millet intercrop across different socio-economic classes in Siresandra. Other crops were cultivated by very few farmers in the village and therefore we are not presenting data for them. Table 18 shows that per acre farm business income for finger millet intercrop was Rs 10,091 for Peasant 1 households, followed by Rs 3,325 for Peasant 2 and Rs 2,195 for Peasant 3 households. Per acre farm business income for finger millet intercrop was almost three to four times higher for Peasant 1 cultivators as compared to the other cultivating classes in the village. This difference was mainly because of the higher gross value of output obtained by the Peasant 1 class, driven by higher yield on account of assured irrigation. On the other hand, Peasant 2 and Peasant 3 classes cultivated finger millet on unirrigated land and ended up with lower yields.

**Table 19** *Average expenditure on different cost items, finger millet intercrop, Siresandra, 2008–09* in Rs per acre

| Cost items | Peasant 1 | Peasant 2 | Peasant 3 |
|---|---|---|---|
| Seed | 453 | 326 | 338 |
| Manure | 734 | 1,027 | 1,213 |
| Fertilizer | 2,186 | 743 | 649 |
| Plant protection | 250 | 10 | 70 |
| Irrigation | 681 | 0 | 0 |
| Casual labour | 2,591 | 1,921 | 1,569 |
| Long-term workers | 0 | 0 | 0 |
| Animal labour | 213 | 1,369 | 844 |
| Machine labour | 541 | 733 | 933 |
| Rent | 0 | 0 | 27 |
| Other costs | 922 | 305 | 271 |
| Cost A2 | 8,570 | 6,433 | 5,914 |

*Source*: PARI survey data.

## Cost of Production of Finger Millet Intercrop

In this section, we examine the structure of cost of production of finger millet intercrop across socio-economic classes. Table 19 shows that Peasant 1 households spent Rs 8,570 per acre to cultivate finger millet intercrop on one acre of land; the corresponding amounts were Rs 6,433 for Peasant 2 and Rs 5,914 for Peasant 3 households. The higher cost of cultivation for Peasant 1 households was on account of higher costs incurred by them on chemical fertilizers, irrigation, and hired human labour. Even though rich peasants use more hired labour, they get higher yields and higher gross output by using higher doses of chemical fertilizer with assured irrigation.

## Farm Business Incomes from Operational Holdings

In Siresandra, average gross value of output per acre of operational holding, taking all seasons together, was Rs 26,831 in 2008–09 (Table 20). Average farm business income after deducting cost A2 was Rs 11,497. Variations across the main cultivating classes show that the average farm business income of Peasant 2 households was more than that of all other cultivators. Variations in per acre farm business income across classes are mainly explained by differences in cropping pattern. Peasant 1 and Peasant 2 households in the village allocated a higher proportion of land to high-value crops like banana,

**Table 20** *Average gross value of output (GVO), cost of production (cost A2), and farm business income (FBI) of operational holding by class, Siresandra, 2008–09 in Rs per acre*

| Socio-economic class | Gross value of output | Cost A2 | Farm business income |
|---|---|---|---|
| Peasant 1 | 26,095 | 13,438 | 12,656 |
| Peasant 2 | 35,282 | 18,522 | 16,759 |
| Peasant 3 | 15,642 | 12,297 | 3,345 |
| All | 26,831 | 15,334 | 11,497 |

*Source*: PARI survey data.

**Table 21** *Proportion of different crops in gross cropped area by households belonging to different classes, Siresandra, 2008–09 in per cent*

| Socio-economic class | Foodgrain | High-value crops | Mulberry | All crops |
|---|---|---|---|---|
| Peasant 1 | 28 | 43 | 29 | 100 |
| Peasant 2 | 46 | 29 | 24 | 100 |
| Peasant 3 | 77 | 9 | 14 | 100 |

*Source*: PARI survey data.

**Table 22** *Average annual income from crop production by socio-economic class, Siresandra, 2008–09 in Rs per household*

| Socio-economic class | Annual income |
|---|---|
| Peasant 1 | 168,040 |
| Peasant 2 | 47,083 |
| Peasant 3 | 5,555 |
| All | 30,394 |

*Source*: PARI survey data.

betel leaf, and vegetables. On the other hand, Peasant 3 households mainly cultivated foodgrains like finger millet (Table 21).

Not only that, income from crop production per household for Peasant 1 households was almost six times higher than the income of an average cultivator (Table 22). Income from crop production per household declined steeply as we moved from Peasant 1 to Peasant 3 households. Inequality in crop incomes across cultivator households was very high. Almost three-fourths of the total number of households earned less than Rs 10,000 in the survey year; at the same time, 5 per cent of households obtained more than Rs 200,000 a year (Table 23).

**Table 23** *Number and proportion of cultivator households by crop income group, Siresandra, 2008–09*

| Crop income (Rs) | Number of households | Proportion (per cent) |
|---|---|---|
| Up to 10,000 | 47 | 71 |
| 10,001–25,000 | 6 | 9 |
| 25,001–50,000 | 2 | 3 |
| 50,001–100,000 | 4 | 6 |
| 100,000–200,000 | 4 | 6 |
| More than 200,001 | 3 | 5 |
| All | 66 | 100 |

*Source*: PARI survey data.

## Zhapur Village in Kalaburagi District

### Cropping Pattern

Zhapur village in Kalaburagi district is located in the semi-arid Deccan Plateau region of Karnataka. The Deccan Plateau is located between two mountain ranges, the Western Ghats and the Eastern Ghats. The Western Ghats mountain range is very tall and blocks the Southwest monsoon from reaching the Deccan Plateau, so that the region receives very little rainfall.

Most of the farm land in Zhapur village has a relatively level surface and is usually raised above the adjoining land on at least one side, and often with one or more sides, with steep slopes. This kind of land terrain gives very limited scope for surface water flow and distribution. On the other hand, groundwater extraction through dug wells and borewells is also not easy due to the consolidated rocky structure of the aquifers. Given these characteristics of the land terrain, only 15 per cent of the farm land in the village received some supplementary borewell irrigation during 2008–09. Cropping intensity in Zhapur was 111, which was slightly lower than the district average (123). Cultivation was primarily unirrigated, and pigeon pea (*thogari* or *tur dal*) was the major crop grown in the village during the year 2008–09 (Table 24). Pigeon pea was grown both as a monocrop and an intercrop. In the *kharif* season (rainy season), pigeon pea was grown mixed with other pulses (like green gram and moth bean), millets (like pearl millet and *sorghum*), and oilseeds (like sunflower and safflower). Pigeon pea grown mixed with other crops accounted for 40 per cent of the gross cropped

**Table 24** *Proportion of different crops in gross cropped area (GCA) and total operated land, Zhapur, 2008–09*

| Crops | Area (acre) | As proportion of GCA (per cent) | As proportion of operational holdings (per cent) |
|---|---|---|---|
| Pigeon pea intercrop | 232.34 | 40 | 44 |
| Pigeon pea monocrop | 182.83 | 31 | 34 |
| Sunflower | 54.00 | 9 | 10 |
| *Sorghum* | 10.00 | 2 | 2 |
| All *kharif* crops (rainy season) | 487.58 | 83 | 92 |
| *Sorghum* monocrop | 68.00 | 12 | 13 |
| *Sorghum* intercrop | 24.25 | 4 | 5 |
| All *rabi* crops (winter season) | 98.25 | 17 | 18 |
| Banana | 2.00 | less than 1 | less than 1 |
| Gross cropped area (GCA) | 587.83 | 100 | 111 |
| Operational holding | 531.83 | NA | 100 |

*Source*: PARI survey data.

area (GCA) in the village; pigeon pea monocrop accounted for 31 per cent of GCA, followed by sunflower (9 per cent) and *sorghum* (2 per cent) in the *kharif* season. Although mixed cropping is practised in the cultivation of pulses in large parts of dryland agriculture in India, monocropping in pulses is very significant in this village. The share of monocropped pigeon pea in total pigeon pea area was much higher among landlord households as compared to other cultivator households.

*Sorghum* as a monocrop and *sorghum* mixed with safflower was grown in the *rabi* season. However, *rabi* crops constituted only 17 per cent of total GCA due to the non-availability of irrigation facilities. One household cultivated banana on 2 acres of land.

Graph 3 shows the major crop cycles in the village. The most important cropping pattern was pigeon pea mixed with other pulses, millets, and oilseeds, cultivated in the *kharif* season on rainfed land that was kept fallow in the *rabi* season. The second and third crop cycles in order of importance were pigeon pea or sunflower cultivated as monocrops in the *kharif* season, with the land left fallow in the *rabi* season. On land with access to borewell irrigation, *sorghum* was grown in the *rabi* season after cultivating pigeon pea in the *kharif* season.

| Cycle | Jun-08 | Jul-08 | Aug-08 | Sep-08 | Oct-08 | Nov-08 | Dec-08 | Jan-09 | Feb-09 | Mar-09 | Apr-09 | May-09 | Area |
|---|---|---|---|---|---|---|---|---|---|---|---|---|---|
| 1 | Pigeon pea intercrop | | | | | | | | | | | | 193.59 |
| 2 | Pigeon pea mono-crop | | | | | | | | | | | | 132.96 |
| 3 | Sunflower | | | | | | | | | | | | 54.00 |
| 4 | Pigeon pea mono-crop | | | | | | Sorghum (rabi) | | | | | | 46.25 |
| 5 | Pigeon pea intercrop | | | | | | Sorghum intercrop | | | . | | | 23.69 |
| 6 | Pigeon pea intercrop | | | | | | Sorghum (rabi) | | | | | | 10.00 |
| 7 | | | | | | | Sorghum (rabi) | | | | | | 10.00 |
| 8 | Sorghum (kharif) | | | | | | | | | | | | 10.00 |

**Graph 3** *Major crop cycles, 2008-09*

## Productivity/Yield of Major Crops

Like intercropping, a mixed cropping system also poses a challenge for measuring and interpreting data on individual crop yields. Several methods have been applied in the literature to calculate individual crop yields in a mixed cropping system. In the simplest of these methods, crop areas are divided by the number of crops grown on them. For example, if two crops are grown together on one acre of land, the area assigned to each crop would be 0.5 acre. In most cases, crops do not share the land equally, which seriously impairs the validity of this method. Slightly more complex methods involve using seed rates or crop densities to assign area across crops. Rather than make such assumptions, we measure the productivity performance of the mixed cropping system by calculating value of yield per acre for both mixed and monocropped fields in the next section.

Table 25 shows the average yield of monocrops grown in Zhapur in 2008–

**Table 25** *Average yields of major crops in Zhapur, Gulbarga district, Karnataka, and India, 2008–09* in kg per acre

| Crops | India | Karnataka | Gulbarga | Zhapur |
|---|---|---|---|---|
| Pigeon pea (*tur dal*) | 272 | 214 | 198 | 227 |
| Sunflower | 259 | 201 | 150 | 172 |
| *Sorghum* (*rabi*) | 389 | 477 | 413 | 253 |
| Banana | 14,971 | na | 6,972 | 19,000 |

*Source*: PARI survey data for Zhapur; Directorate of Economics and Statistics website (http://aps.dac.gov.in/APY/Public_Report1.aspx)a, Karnataka, and India.

**Table 26** *Average gross value of output (GVO), cost of production (cost A2), and farm busines income (FBI), major crops, Zhapur, 2008–09* in Rs per acre

| Crop season | Crops | GVO | Cost A2 | FBI |
|---|---|---|---|---|
| *Kharif* | Pigeon pea intercrop | 6,073 | 5,308 | 765 |
| *Kharif* | Pigeon pea monocrop | 8,851 | 4,516 | 4,335 |
| *Kharif* | Sunflower | 3,041 | 2,145 | 897 |
| *Rabi* | *Sorghum* | 3,682 | 3,200 | 482 |

*Source*: PARI survey data.

09, and the corresponding official data for Kalaburagi district, Karnataka, and India. The average yield of pigeon pea monocrop in Zhapur was higher than the district and State averages, but slightly lower than the all-India average. On the other hand, sunflower and *sorghum* yields in the village were lower than the State and all-India averages.

### Farm Business Incomes of Major Crops

Data for the major crops cultivated in Zhapur (Table 26) show that the average farm business income was highest for pigeon pea monocrop (Rs 4,335 per acre), followed by sunflower (Rs 897 per acre), pigeon pea intercrop (Rs 765 per acre), and *sorghum* (Rs 482 per acre). Of all the crops, farm business incomes were lowest for the cultivation of *sorghum*. Average cost A2 per acre for pigeon pea intercrop and pigeon pea monocrop was much higher than for sunflower and sorghum. However, farm business income per acre for pigeon pea monocrop was higher than farm business income for other crops on account of higher gross value of output (GVO).

### Cost of Production of Major Crops

This section disusses the structure of cost of cultivation of major crops in Zhapur. Table 27 shows average item-wise cost of cultivation for pigeon pea intercrop for households belonging to different socio-economic classes. The table brings out that Peasant 2 and Peasant 3 cultivators were in a disadvantageous position in respect of the cost they had to incur on major items like animal labour, rent for leased-in land, and plant protection. For example, while Peasant 1 households spent Rs 369 per acre on animal labour, the average expenditure on animal labour by Peasant 2 households was Rs 1,174 per acre, and Rs 1,418 per acre by Peasant 3 households. Note, again, that rent payments were not insignificant for Peasant 2 and Peasant 3 households.

Table 27 *Average expenditure on different cost items by socio-economic class, pigeon pea inter-crop, Zhapur, 2008–09* in Rs per acre

| Cost items | Peasant 1 | Peasant 2 | Peasant 3 |
|---|---|---|---|
| Seed | 153 | 166 | 230 |
| Manure | 0 | 157 | 204 |
| Fertilizer | 793 | 379 | 290 |
| Plant protection | 353 | 461 | 975 |
| Irrigation | 0 | 0 | 0 |
| Casual labour | 605 | 945 | 932 |
| Long-term workers | 0 | 0 | 0 |
| Animal labour | 369 | 1,174 | 1,418 |
| Machine labour | 35 | 174 | 244 |
| Rent | 0 | 1,538 | 720 |
| Other costs | 127 | 292 | 436 |
| Cost A2 | 2,436 | 5,285 | 5,448 |

*Source*: PARI survey data.

## Farm Business Incomes from Operational Holdings

Since agriculture is primarily rainfed in Zhapur, there was not much variation in crops cultivated by different strata, except for the fact that rich peasants could devote a larger share of land to pigeon pea monocrop, which was more profitable than intercropped pigeon pea. By cultivating pigeon pea as a monocrop on a larger share of their operational holding, rich peasant households were able to get higher incomes from per acre crop production than other households (Table 28).

Table 28 shows that the gross value of output (GVO) per acre declined steeply as we moved from Peasant 1 households to Peasant 2 and then Peasant 3 categories. On the other hand, variations in cost A2 per acre across different classes of households were much less. On balance, farm business income per acre was highest for Peasant 1 among all classes. For Peasant 3 households, farm business income per acre was twelve times lower than the average for Peasant 1 households.

We also see, from Table 29, that incomes from crop production per household declined steeply as we moved from Peasant 1 to Peasant 3 households. Inequality in crop incomes across cultivators was very high: 64 per cent of households obtained less than Rs 10,000 in the survey year; in

**Table 28** *Average gross value of output (GVO), cost of production (cost A2), and farm business income (FBI) of operational holding by class, Zhapur, 2008–09* in Rs per acre

| Socio-economic class | GVO | Cost A2 | FBI |
|---|---|---|---|
| Peasant 1 | 15,740 | 4,846 | 10,894 |
| Peasant 2 | 4,348 | 3,918 | 430 |
| Peasant 3 | 5,371 | 4,464 | 910 |
| All | 6,212 | 4,311 | 1,903 |

*Source*: PARI survey data.

**Table 29** *Average annual income from crop production by class, Zhapur, 2008–09* in Rs

| Socio-economic class | Annual income |
|---|---|
| Peasant 1 | 5,58,965 |
| Peasant 2 | 6,242 |
| Peasant 3 | 5,019 |
| All | 48,560 |

*Source*: PARI survey data.

**Table 30** *Number and proportion of cultivator households by size-class of crop income, Zhapur, 2008–09*

| Size-class of crop income (Rs) | Number of households | Proportion (per cent) |
|---|---|---|
| Up to 10,000 | 27 | 64 |
| 10,001–25,000 | 4 | 10 |
| 25,001–50,000 | 6 | 14 |
| 50,001–100,000 | 1 | 2 |
| 100,000–200,000 | 1 | 2 |
| More than 200,001 | 3 | 7 |
| All | 42 | 100 |

*Source*: PARI survey data.

contrast, the highest crop income earned by a household in the same year was around Rs 9 lakhs.

We calculated the gross value of output (GVO), cost of production and net incomes for pigeon pea using data for 2013–14 collected during our revisit of the village. Our calculation shows that to produce 1 quintal of pigeon pea, farmers had to incur almost Rs 3,500 (which includes all paid-out costs including imputed value of family labour).[1] If the farmers were able to sell the pigeon pea at the minimum support price (MSP), which was Rs 4,300, then they would get a return of Rs 800 per quintal. After five to six months of hard work, a cultivator could get, on average, Rs 5,000 to 6,000 per hectare, or Rs 1,000 per month from a hectare.

## Conclusions

India has no regular sources of official data on costs of and returns from crop production on operational holdings or at the household level. Data provided by the Ministry of Agriculture under the Comprehensive Scheme for Studying Cost of Cultivation or Production of Principal Crops (CCPC Scheme) only deal with selected crops at the plot level, and cannot be used to study crop incomes at the household level. The Situation Assessment Survey of Farmers conducted by the National Sample Survey Organisation (NSSO) gives data at the household level, but the methodology of the survey has serious limitations (Bakshi 2010; Sarkar 2015). A major criticism of the Situation Assessment Survey (SAS) is that it does not use the commonly accepted mehodology for derivation of crop incomes, as specified by the Indian Agricultural Statistics Research Institute. Our argument is that the SAS underestimates the costs of cultivation and consequently overestimates farm incomes. Notwithstanding these problems, the SAS 2002–03 showed that 43 per cent of farmers in Karnataka wanted to quit agriculture if given a choice, and 90 per cent of households that wanted to quit farming said farming was risky and not profitable.

In this context, the significance of this chapter lies in the fact that we have been able to arrive at realistic estimates of incomes from crop farming at the houseohld level, and examine variations in costs of and returns from crop production across agro-climatic regions and socio-economic classes. This chapter has extracted the relevent statistical information from a unique database created under the Project on Agrarian Studies in India (PARI) of the Foundation for Agrarian Studies (FAS). Data for three villages of Karnataka were collected in May–June 2009 for the agricultural year preceding the survey. We have used estimates of crop incomes over cost A2, a widely used cost concept to study the levels and variations in crop incomes.

---

[1] According to official data, the cost of cultivation was Rs 2,164 per quintal. Official data do not, of course, include rent paid for leased-in land, and they are likely to underestimate the costs of manure, fertilizer, and labour.

In this chapter, a cost–benefit analysis was undertaken for all major crops grown in the study villages: namely, sugarcane, paddy, and finger millet in the irrigated village of Alabujanahalli; finger millet and vegetables in Siresandra; and pulses and millets in Zhapur.

Among all the crops grown, average net incomes were highest for sugarcane (Rs 13,667 per acre) and vegetables like tomato (Rs 25,179 per acre). By contrast, pigeon pea and *sorghum* growers obtained a mere Rs 765 and Rs 482 per acre, respectively. However, if farmers cultivated pigeon pea as a monocrop under irrigated condition in Zhapur, they obtained a net income of Rs 4,335 per acre, close to that obtained by paddy growers in Alabujanahalli.

There was a systematic difference in returns as between planted and ratoon crops of sugarcane in Alabujanahalli. The difference was primarily on account of savings on the cost of seed and the cost of field preparation in the case of ratoon crops. So, despite the fact that ratoon crops had lower yields than planted crops, net returns were higher for ratoon crops.

For most crops, hired labour, organic and chemical fertilizers, draught and machine labour were the major items of costs. In the case of planted sugarcane, the cost of seed cane was also an important item of cost. Rent for leased-in land was a major item of cost for poor peasants in Zhapur, where tenancy was widespread.

Data on incomes from crop production show that average income per acre of operational holding was Rs 11,497 in Siresandra, followed by Rs 9,030 in Alabujanahalli and only Rs 1,903 in Zhapur. Zhapur is a village with no irrigation, and the main crops are unirrigated pulses, millets, and oilseeds. Cultivation of high-value crops (vegetables, banana, and betel leaf) by the well-off sections of the peasantry pushed up the per acre returns from crop production in Siresandra.

The chapter also analyses detailed data for three villages on variations in cropping pattern, structure of costs, output and net returns, in relation to socio-economic classes. The data show that in Zhapur, Peasant 1 households had the highest per acre income (Rs 10,894), with incomes declining sharply as one moved to Peasant 2 (Rs 430) and Peasant 3 households (Rs 910). In Alabujanahalli and Siresandra, we could not see the same systematic variation across socio-economic classes. Nevertheless, per acre crop income was always lower for poor peasants as compared to others. This was mainly because of lack of ownership of draught animals, machine power, and irrigation equipment among them, which pushed up their cost of cultivation. In addition, limited access to land, irrigation, and credit restricted their choice of a profitable crop mix.

The data also show that a substantial proportion of households in the study villages had very low crop incomes, less than Rs 10,000 a year. The proportion was highest in Siresandra (71 per cent), followed by Zhapur (64 per cent) and Alabujanahalli (45 per cent). The highest crop income earned by a household in a year was Rs 9,31,390 in Zhapur, followed by Siresandra (Rs 3,31,471) and Alabujanahalli (Rs 2,30,893).

The empirical evidence makes it clear that the majority of cultivator households in the study villages earned very low incomes from crop production. Disaggregated analysis shows that crop incomes varied across villages and socio-economic classes. The variations in crop income were mainly due to differences in access to land, technology, and ownership of means of production, and differential costs of production. To make agriculture more profitable, we need policies that can reduce the cost of cultivation for small cultivators, who comprise the majority of cultivators in village India.

# References

Chand, Ramesh, Saxena, Raka, and Rana, Simmi (2015), "Estimates and Analysis of Farm Income in India, 1983–84 to 2011–12," *Economic and Political Weekly*, vol. L, no. 22, May 30.

Deshpande, R. S., and Naika, T. Raveendra (2002), "Impact of Minimum Support Prices on Agricultural Economy: A Study in Karnataka," Agricultural Development and Rural Transformation Unit, Institute for Social and Economic Change.

Government of Karnataka, Department of Sericulture (2015) http://202.138.101.165/sericulture/English/Technologies/MulberryCultivation.aspx, accessed on June 3, 2015.

Kannan, Elumalai (2015), "Trends in Agricultural Incomes: An Analysis at the Select Crop and State Levels in India," *Journal of Agrarian Change*, vol. 15, no. 2, April, pp. 201–19.

Narayanamoorthy, A. (2013), "Profitability in Crops Cultivation in India: Some Evidence from Cost of Cultivation Survey Data," *Indian Journal of Agricultural Economics*, vol. 68, no. 1, January–March.

Ramachandran, V. K., Rawal, Vikas, and Swaminathan, Madhura (2010), *Socio-Economic Surveys of Three Villages in Andhra Pradesh: A Study of Agrarian Relations*, Tulika Books, New Delhi in asociation with Foundation for Agrarian Studies.

Sarkar, Biplab (2015), "Official Data Sources on Farm Income in India: a Critique," unpublished.

Sarkar, Biplab, Ramachandran, V. K., and Swaminathan, Madhura (2014), "Aspects of the Political Economy of Crop Incomes in India," *World Review of Political Economy*, vol. 5, no. 3, Fall.

Surjit, V. (2008), "Farm Business Incomes in India: A Study of Two Rice Growing Villages of Thanjavur Region, Tamil Nadu," thesis submitted to the University of Calcutta for the degree of Doctor of Philosophy (Science).

Vaidyanathan, A. (2005), "Report of the Analysis of Data of Cost of Cultivation Surveys," Indian Society of Agricultural Economics.

APPENDIX

# Shri Chamundeshwari Sugars Limited: A Note

*Arindam Das*

Chamundeshwari Sugars is part of the Sakthi group started by N. Mahalingam (Pollachi Mahalingam), a multi-crore conglomerate. The sugar factory at K. M. Doddi (Unit 1) was commissioned in 1974 with a cane crushing capacity of 1,200 tonnes per day (tpd). It has expanded over the years and its current capacity is 4,500 tpd. The current sucrose recovery rate is 9.6 per cent, i.e. 96 kg sugar from every 1,000 tonnes of cane that is crushed.[1]

Over the years, the factory has expanded. An integrated distillery unit that uses the molasses from the cane unit was started in 2003. The distillery produces industrial alcohol and has a capacity of 50 kilo litres per day. There is also a bio-compost unit using waste from the sugar factory, located about 30 kilometres away. A co-generation plant that uses bagasse for power generation, of 26 MW capacity, was commissioned three years ago. The power generated by this plant meets the needs of the company and the residential colony nearby, and also feeds into the power grid of the State Electricity Board. These plants operate for nine months in a year, and a three-month period of lean supply of cane is reserved for maintenance work. Electricity has to be imported during these months as the power plant is also shut down.

The company's Cane Development and Production Wing is the one that deals with cane producers. The sugarcane area under their jurisdiction is demarcated by the State Sugar Directorate. In 2009, they were allocated 184 villages in Malavalli taluk, 77 villages in Maddur taluk, and two *hobli* (cluster of villages) comprising 36 revenue villages in Chinnapatna taluk.

The Cane Development and Production Wing has 70 sections, each with a field assistant who is usually a qualified diploma holder in agriculture. Four to five sections make a divisional office headed by a cane development officer who is generally a graduate in agriculture. There are a total of 15 such divisions. The divisions come together under two zones, each headed by a senior agriculture officer in the managerial cadre. The Wing has a

---

[1] We interviewed the General Manager, co-generation division, and Deputy General Manager, cane division, at the time of our survey. We could not get an interview during the 2014 resurvey.

**Table 1** *Statutory minimum price of government and price offered by Chamundeswari Sugars in Rs per tonne*

| Year | Statutory minimum price of government | Price offered by Chamundeswari Sugars |
|---|---|---|
| 2007–08 | 811 | 836 |
| 2008–09 | 1298 | 1250 |
| 2009–10 | 1391 | 1950 |
| 2010–11 | 1450 | 1800 |

*Source*: Commission for Agricultural Costs and Prices (CACP), Government of India.

deputy general manager at its head office who oversees and is responsible for ensuring balanced and regular supply of cane to the mill.

Information on choice of sugarcane variety, seed material, and technical know-how such as weedicide application is given to farmers.[2] Financial assistance is arranged from the bank according to the eligible scale of finance, through a letter of recommendation from the company along with the application. The sale proceeds go towards clearing the loan first, and only the balance is credited to the farmer's account.

Sometimes, seed procured from seed producers is supplied to needy farmers on credit, to be adjusted against sale proceeds. The seed price is the prevailing price of cane. The cutting order is generated as per the crop's maturity date. The main crushing seasons are from July–August to April–May. The charges for harvesting and loading cane are fixed by the company, and were Rs 200 to 300 per tonne in 2008–09 and 2009–10. The transportation charges are also fixed within a 30-kilometre radius. In 2008–09, the rate was Rs 126. Any cost of transport beyond 30 kilometres was borne by the company.

The government announces a statutory minimum price for sugarcane every year. This is the base price. Following extensive negotiations with farmers, the company decides on the final price it will offer. This is generally valid for a year from October to September.

---

[2] After plantation, an agreement is entered into with the farmer whereby the variety sown, extent, date of planting, method, and other details are recorded, and the cutting date indicated. According to the management, the following is the planting practice for sugarcane: 12,000 sets of three eye budded cane saplings can be planted on one acre of land with a 3 feet gap. Each set is obtained from one metric tonne of seed. For tissue culture saplings, a gap of 5 feet width is recommended around a plant, with 2 feet between two plants. About 4,500 saplings would be required under this method per acre.

Cane prices for the last few years are shown in Table 1. The data in Table 1 suggest that the price offered by the sugar mill has been higher than the Statutory Minimum Price except in 2008–09.

One of the problems faced by sugarcane farmers of Karnataka is delay in payments by sugar factories. This can be critical for poor peasants (Peasant 3 and Peasant 4 classes) as they incur relatively high costs of production and would require payments for output at the earliest.

# 9

## Manual Workers in Rural Karnataka: Evidence from Three Villages

Niladri Sekhar Dhar, Arindam Das, and T. Sivamurugan

This chapter deals with the supply of manual workers to the village labour market, demand for wage labour generated in the village economy, especially in crop production, and realised number of days of employment obtained by manual workers belonging to the class of Manual worker households. As defined in chapter 4, Manual worker households are households whose major share of income comes from paid hired manual work outside the house; however, they do have other sources of income. These include income from crop production, animal resources, salaries, business and trade, rent, interest earnings, pensions, remittances, and scholarships. The data for analysis in this chapter come from the three villages of Alabujanahalli, Siresandra, and Zhapur, surveyed under the Project on Agrarian Relations in India (PARI) of the Foundation for Agrarian Studies (FAS).

The PARI village surveys collected data on the number of days of employment for each worker who had performed any wage work in crop production during the reference year. These data were collected on a disaggregated basis, that is, by season, then by crop, and finally by crop operation. Information pertaining to hours of work and number of days of employment for non-agricultural wage workers was also collected.[1] The number of labour-days of monthly-paid workers and of long-term workers was excluded from the calculation of the total number of days of employment. In the case of demand for labour, data on labour-days and length of work-hours were collected for all crops and crop combinations cultivated on all operational holdings, for all crop operations for each type

---

[1] The calculation here of the total number of days of employment does not include the number days of self-employed activity.

of labour (family labour, wage labour on daily wage payment, wage labour on piece-rate payment, exchange labour, long-term labour), and hours of machine labour utilised. The labour schedule also incorporated wages paid to hired labourers on both daily rate and piece rate, and hire/rental charges for machines. Data on actual work-hours were collected, but for our analysis, we converted calendar days into standard eight-hour labour-days.

## Size and Composition of Class of Manual Workers

The size of the class of Manual workers was substantial in the three study villages, especially in Alabujanahalli and Zhapur. In Zhapur, 46 per cent of households constituted the class of Manual workers. Further, on average, three members of each Manual worker household worked as manual workers in Zhapur. Siresandra is an aberration: it is a small village where only 16 per cent of households belonged to the class of Manual workers. However, if we combine Manual workers with Peasant 3 households, then they comprised 56 per cent of all households in Siresandra.

The data suggest that the worker to non-worker ratio (see Tables A1, A2, and A3) for persons aged 15 years and above was higher for the class of Manual workers as compared to other socio-economic classes. In Alabujanahalli, for example, the ratio of workers to non-workers for the class of Manual workers was as high as 2.4:1, as compared to 1:1 for Rich capitalist farmers and Peasant 1 households. As we move down the class ladder, the ratio of workers to non-workers increases. In Siresandra and Zhapur, the ratios of workers to non-workers for the class of Manual workers were 3.3:1 and 2.9:1 respectively.

Another pattern observed in the study villages (see Tables A1, A2, and A3) is that the ratio of workers to students in the age group of 15 years and above was extremely high for the class of Manual workers as compared to other

**Table 1** *Number of households and workers in Manual worker households, study villages, Karnataka, 2009–10*

| Village | Households | | Number of workers | | | No. of workers per household |
|---|---|---|---|---|---|---|
| | Number | As % of all | Female | Male | All workers | |
| Alabujanahalli | 73 | 30 | 79 | 82 | 161 | 2.2 |
| Siresandra | 13 | 16.5 | 13 | 15 | 28 | 2.2 |
| Zhapur | 50 | 46 | 50 | 86 | 136 | 2.8 |

*Source*: PARI survey data.

numerically significant socio-economic classes. In Alabujanahalli, the ratio of workers to students was 6.8:1 for the class of Manual workers, and ranged from 2.5:1 to 5.7:1 for the peasant classes. In Siresandra, the ratio of workers to students was as high as 10:1 among Manual workers, as compared to 4:1 for peasant households. In Zhapur, the worker to student ratio was 12.7:1 for Manual worker households and 6.2:1 for the peasant classes.

These ratios show that household members of the class of Manual workers cannot afford to be unemployed or pursue their education after 15 years of age. Given the lack of resources, especially land, more than one member of a Manual worker household has to participate in wage work.[2] Almost all the villages studied by FAS under PARI clearly indicate that, on average, at least two members of Manual worker households are required to work for wages to maintain a basic minimum standard of living.

### Caste Composition of Manual Worker Households

In the study villages, Scheduled Caste (SC) and Scheduled Tribe (ST) households were the largest constituents of the class of Manual workers (Tables A4 to A6). The share of SC households in the class of Manual workers was significantly higher than their representation in the population. In Alabujanahalli, SC households constituted 28.8 per cent of all Manual worker households, while they accounted for only 14.4 per cent of all households. Similar patterns were observed in Siresandra and Zhapur.

If we look at the number of Manual worker households among SC and ST households as a proportion of all households in the same social group, the ratio was substantially higher than among other caste groups. The proportions of SC households belonging to the class of hired Manual workers were 60 per cent in Alabujanahalli, 61 per cent in Zhapur, and 65 per cent in Siresandra. Thus, the majority of SC households in all three study villages belonged to the class of Manual workers.

## Labour Use in Crop Production

The major sources of employment for rural Manual workers in the study villages were crop production (in Alabujanahalli and Siresandra), sericulture

---

[2] Landlessness was very high among the Manual worker households in all three study villages. Of all Manual worker households, 45 per cent in Alabujanahalli and 46 per cent in Siresandra, respectively, were landless. In Zhapur, 74 per cent of all hired Manual worker households were landless.

**Table 2** *Distribution of labour use across seasons in the study villages, 2009–10* in per cent

| Village | Proportion of total labour use | | | |
| --- | --- | --- | --- | --- |
| | *Kharif* | *Rabi* | Annual | Total |
| Alabujanahalli | 30 | 14 | 56 | 100 |
| Siresandra | 67 | 16 | 17 | 100 |
| Zhapur | 85 | 14 | 1 | 100 |

*Source*: PARI survey data.

(in Alabujanahalli and Siresandra), and mining and stone quarrying (in Zhapur). In Alabujanahalli, the volume of labour use in crop production was much higher than in the other two villages. The reason for such a high volume of labour use was both extensive and intensive cultivation. The extent of land under cultivation (gross cropped area, or GCA) in Alabujanahalli was 715 acres, as compared to 226.1 acres in Siresandra and 587.83 acres in Zhapur. Crop production in Alabujanahalli was intensive and was undertaken round the year. In other words, the impact of seasonality in crop production was much less in Alabujanahalli than in Siresandra and Zhapur.

In Siresandra and Zhapur, labour use in crop production was concentrated in the *kharif* season. In Zhapur, the *kharif* crops absorbed as much as 85 per cent of total labour use in crop production. Labour absorption in crops produced in the *rabi* season was only 14 per cent of the total labour use. These two numbers indicate distinct and demarcated cropping seasons, with crop production being limited in the *rabi* season. In Siresandra, crops produced in the *kharif* season were labour-absorbing: about 67 per cent of total labour was utilised in producing *kharif* crops. Due to the presence of sericulture in Siresandra, cultivation of mulberry was done all round the year and labour absorption in mulberry was almost 17 per cent of total labour use.

### Use of Family Labour and Hired Labour in Crop Production

In all three study villages, the proportion of hired labour in total labour use was greater than the share of family labour. This indicates dependence on hired workers to perform crop operations. The custom of exchange labour has lost its relevance in all three study villages. The use of outside or hired workers in crop production was highest in the most agriculturally backward village, Zhapur, at 61 per cent of total labour use. The reason for this could be the availability of remunerative quarry work for men and availability of

**Table 3** *Composition of total labour use in study villages, 2009–10* in per cent

| Village | Family labour | Hired labour | Exchange labour | Total labour use |
|---|---|---|---|---|
| Alabujanahalli | 44 | 55 | 1 | 100 |
| Siresandra | 46 | 53 | 1 | 100 |
| Zhapur | 36 | 61 | 2 | 100 |

*Source*: PARI survey data.

cheap female workers in crop production. So, male members of cultivating households opted for work in the quarries and hired female wage workers performed the agricultural tasks.

Another striking feature of our data is the gender differences in family labour and hired labour. In Siresandra and Zhapur, male family labour provided 71 per cent and 65 per cent, respectively, of total family labour use. A diametrically opposite phenomenon was observed in the case of hired labour use in crop production: female wage workers provided 79 per cent of total hired labour in both the villages. It is imperative to mention here that in the case of gender division of hired labour in crop production, we have not considered the gender division of workers hired on piece-rated contracts, as methodologically, it is very difficult to estimate male and female labour use in crop operations done on a piece-rated basis.

Nevertheless, this feature of male workers dominating family labour and female workers dominating hired labour is an interesting one. This may be attributed to differences in the costs of hiring male and female workers (see the section below on "Wage Rates and Wage Earnings"), and the availability of non-farm remunerative employment for male workers and, at the same time, the scarcity of non-farm remunerative employment for female workers. The higher non-farm wage as compared to farm wage encourages male workers to leave farm work, and the resulting space created in crop production is filled by female workers. This would be advantageous for peasant households as the female reservation wage has always been low compared to the male reservation wage.

Two other patterns emerge from the data. First, the use of female family labour increased as we moved down the socio-economic class hierarchy. In Alabujanahalli, around 18 per cent of total family labour was female family labour for the class of Manual workers. On the other hand, households belonging to Rich capitalist farmer and Peasant 1 classes had not utilised any female family labour. This pattern is also observed in Siresandra and Zhapur. In Siresandra, Peasant 1 households did not use any female family

**Table 4** *Composition of family and hired labour use, by sex and socio-economic class, Alabujanahalli, 2009* in per cent

| Class | Family labour | | Hired labour | |
|---|---|---|---|---|
| | Males | Females | Males | Females |
| Rich capitalist farmer | 100 | 0 | 61.7 | 38.3 |
| Peasant 1 | 100 | 0 | 61.9 | 38.1 |
| Peasant 2 | 98.6 | 1.4 | 58.6 | 41.4 |
| Peasant 3 | 90.9 | 9.1 | 52.5 | 47.5 |
| Peasant 4 | 90.1 | 9.9 | 52 | 48 |
| Manual worker | 81.8 | 18.2 | 41.4 | 58.6 |
| Non-agriculture | 94.9 | 5.1 | 51.8 | 48.2 |
| All classes | 92.7 | 7.3 | 55.9 | 44.1 |

*Source*: PARI survey data.

**Table 5** *Composition of family and hired labour use, by sex and socio-economic class, Siresandra, 2009* in per cent

| Class | Family labour | | Hired labour | |
|---|---|---|---|---|
| | Males | Females | Males | Females |
| Peasant 1 | 100 | 0 | 34.7 | 65.3 |
| Peasant 2 | 73 | 27 | 20.1 | 79.9 |
| Peasant 3 | 66.7 | 33.3 | 13.3 | 86.7 |
| Non-agriculture | 41.9 | 58.1 | 15.1 | 84.9 |
| All classes | 71.2 | 28.8 | 20.9 | 79.1 |

*Source*: PARI survey data.

**Table 6** *Composition of family and hired labour use, by sex and socio-economic class, Zhapur, 2009* in per cent

| Class | Family labour | | Hired labour | |
|---|---|---|---|---|
| | Males | Females | Males | Females |
| Landlord | – | – | 55.3 | 44.7 |
| Peasant 1 | 92.3 | 7.7 | 22.5 | 77.5 |
| Peasant 2 | 73.6 | 26.4 | 15.6 | 84.4 |
| Peasant 3 | 57.6 | 42.4 | 15.2 | 84.8 |
| Non-agriculture | 70.7 | 29.3 | 38.1 | 61.9 |
| All classes | 64.7 | 35.3 | 20.7 | 79.3 |

*Source*: PARI survey data.

labour, while for Peasant 3 households, female family labour comprised 33 per cent of total family labour. For the non-agricultural classes, the ratio of female family labour to total family labour was 58 per cent. In Zhapur, the pattern was very similar.

Secondly, those higher in the hierarchy of socio-economic classes tended to use more hired wage workers to perform agricultural tasks. As we moved down the class ladder, the use of hired labour declined in all the study villages. Manual workers were hired on a daily and/or piece-rate basis. Peasant 3 and Peasant 4 households hired wage labour to perform some time-bound agricultural tasks like transplanting and harvesting. Most other agricultural operations were primarily done by family labour in Peasant 3 and Peasant 4 households.

# Number of Days of Employment

One of the key indices of employment, unemployment, and underemployment is the number of days of employment obtained by an individual and a household.

## Average Number of Days of Employment

We now turn to the number of days of agricultural and non-agricultural employment in the three villages (Tables 7, 8, and 9). In Alabujanahalli, both male and female workers were mainly employed in agriculture: more than 80 per cent of total employment was in agriculture during the survey year. This was a rice and sugarcane-growing village with irrigation, and, clearly, agricultural activities dominated the village economy.

In Siresandra, there was a clear male–female differential in terms of the composition of employment: female workers were confined to the agricultural sector while men found more employment in non-agricultural activities.

**Table 7** *Average number of days of wage employment obtained by Manual workers in agricultural and non-agricultural sectors, by sex, Alabujanahalli, 2009*

| Sex | Agriculture | Non-agriculture |
|---|---|---|
| Female | 105 | 22 |
| Male | 137 | 18 |
| All workers | 122 | 20 |

*Source*: PARI survey data.

**Table 8** *Average number of days of wage employment obtained by Manual workers in agricultural and non-agricultural sectors, by sex, Siresandra, 2009*

| Sex | Agriculture | Non-agriculture |
|---|---|---|
| Female | 103 | 41 |
| Male | 44 | 69 |
| All workers | 71 | 57 |

*Note*: In Siresandra, poor peasant households are included.
*Source*: PARI survey data.

**Table 9** *Average number of days of wage employment obtained by h Manual workers in agricultural and non-agricultural sectors, by sex, Zhapur, 2009*

| Sex | Agriculture | Non-agriculture |
|---|---|---|
| Female | 71 | 80 |
| Male | 29 | 161 |
| All workers | 47 | 126 |

*Source*: PARI survey data.

In Zhapur, both male and female workers received higher number of days of employment in non-agriculture than in agriculture. A female worker received around 80 days of employment in non-agricultural work out of 151 days of total work. For male workers, out of 190 days of wage employment, non-agricultural work provided 161 days of employment. Mining and quarrying in nearby areas was the major source of non-agricultural employment.

### Distribution of Workers by Number of Days of Employment

Tables 10, 11, and 12 give a better picture of the persistence of underemployment among workers belonging to Manual worker households. In all the study villages, a large proportion of workers received less than three months of wage employment in a production year: 45 to 54 per cent of female workers received wage employment for less than four months; and 26 to 38 per cent of all workers received employment for less than four months. On the other hand, 41 to 57 per cent of male workers received wage employment for more than six months. Among female workers, only 29 per cent of workers in Alabujanahalli and Zhapur, and 38 per cent of workers in Siresandra received wage employment for more than six months.

Thus, the persistence of underemployment among workers belonging

**Table 10** *Distribution of Manual workers by size-class of number of days of employment, by sex, Alabujanahalli, 2009*

| Size-class of number of days of employment | As per cent of all workers | | |
|---|---|---|---|
| | Males | Females | All workers |
| 1 to 60 days | 15 | 28 | 22 |
| 61 to 120 days | 23 | 26 | 24 |
| 121 to 180 days | 19 | 17 | 18 |
| Above 180 days | 43 | 29 | 36 |
| All | 100 | 100 | 100 |

*Source*: PARI survey data.

**Table 11** *Distribution of h Manual workers by size-class of number of days of employment, by sex, Siresandra, 2009*

| Size-class of number of days of employment | As per cent of all workers | | |
|---|---|---|---|
| | Males | Females | All workers |
| 1 to 60 days | 35 | 31 | 34 |
| 61 to 120 days | 12 | 15 | 13 |
| 121 to 180 days | 12 | 16 | 13 |
| Above 180 days | 41 | 38 | 40 |
| All | 100 | 100 | 100 |

*Source*: PARI survey data.

**Table 12** *Distribution of h Manual workers by size-class of number of days of employment, by sex, Zhapur, 2009*

| Size-class of number of days of employment | As per cent of all workers | | |
|---|---|---|---|
| | Males | Females | All workers |
| 1 to 60 days | 15 | 14 | 15 |
| 61 to 120 days | 11 | 31 | 20 |
| 121 to 180 days | 17 | 26 | 20 |
| Above 180 days | 57 | 29 | 45 |
| All | 100 | 100 | 100 |

*Source*: PARI survey data.

to the class of Manual workers was observed in all three study villages. The intensity of underemployment was more severe among female wage workers than among male wage workers. If we qualify these numbers using the definition of main and marginal workers provided by the Census of India, 71 per cent of female workers in Alabujanahalli and Zhapur, and 62 per cent of female workers in Siresandra were, in fact, marginal workers.[3] Among male workers, 43 per cent of workers in Alabujanahalli, 41 per cent in Siresandra, and about 57 per cent in Zhapur were main workers. This re-classification suggests that a large section of workers were marginal workers in the study villages.

### Access to Non-Agricultural Employment

The employment opportunities for unskilled manual workers in the non-agricultural sector were limited in two villages, especially for female workers. In Alabujanahalli, laundry work and work under the MGNREGS (Mahatma Gandhi National Rural Employment Guarantee Scheme) provided 35.3 per cent and 26.9 per cent respectively of the total number of days of employment generated in non-agricultural activities. In Siresandra, MGNREGS and sericulture were the major sources of non-agricultural employment; transport and other miscellaneous activities also provided a substantial number of days of employment. Zhapur was a different case. In Zhapur, mining work and construction-related work accounted for 82 per

**Table 13** *Distribution of days of non-agricultural employment by type of activity, study villages in Karnataka, 2009* in per cent

| Type of activity | Alabujanahalli | Siresandra | Zhapur |
|---|---|---|---|
| Construction-related work | 5.1 | 9 | 22.8 |
| Driving | 11.8 | NA | 16.2 |
| Laundry work | 35.3 | NA | NA |
| Mining sector | 0.1 | NA | 58.5 |
| MGNREGS | 26.9 | 22 | NA |
| Sericulture | 3.9 | 20 | NA |
| Transport-related activities | 9 | 11 | NA |
| Wood-cutting | NA | 16 | NA |
| Other work | 7.9 | 22 | 2.5 |
| Total days of non-agricultural employment | 100 | 100 | 100 |

*Note*: NA = not applicable.
*Source*: PARI survey data.

[3] A main worker is one who is employed for 181 days or more in a year.

---

**Box:** Quarry Workers

In Zhapur, the stone quarry is an important source of non-agricultural employment. The stone-quarrying and stone-crushing units are located at a distance of around 20 kilometres from the village. There are three quarry fields around the village. These fields give a substantial number of days of employment to Manual worker households in the village, particularly those belonging to more deprived sections of society: persons from Vaddara (Scheduled Caste), Beda (Scheduled Tribe), and Kabbaliga (Caste Hindu) households work in the quarry fields. These households reside at isolated areas in the village.

Manual worker households in Zhapur chose to participate in stone quarrying because of the low levels of employment in agriculture. The labourers worked in two shifts. The major operations performed in the quarries were breaking or crushing stones, and loading and unloading stones. Both males and females participated in quarry work, but in most cases, it was a family (husband and wife) that worked together. Employment is available throughout the year except in the rainy season. Wage rates may be piece-rated or daily-rated. The average daily wage rate for male workers was Rs 100–150 at the time of our survey in 2009, and for female workers it was Rs 50.

---

cent of the number of days of employment generated in the non-agricultural sector (see Box on "Quarry Workers"). No work under MGNREGS took place in Zhapur, a drought-prone village.

### Nature of Non-Agricultural Employment

In rural India, the non-agricultural sector is still considered to be only a secondary provider of employment, after the agricultural sector. The development of the non-agricultural sector in rural areas has been very slow, and it also lacks diversity. In villages where there is some diversity of non-agricultural employment, and where non-agricultural work is of a skilled type, the place of work is normally an urban area near the village.

Our survey data show that the employment opportunities for unskilled manual workers in the non-agricultural sector were limited in two of the three study villages, especially for female workers. Tables 14, 15, and 16 show the average number of days of employment for workers engaged in non-agricultural activities in the three villages.

Non-agricultural employment in Alabujanahalli was primarily obtained from the MGNREGS, with 47 female workers receiving, on average, 21 days of employment.

In Siresandra, an important non-crop source of employment was sericulture: 14 females received around two months of employment each in sericulture. Six male workers were engaged in construction-related work and they obtained around four months of employment. Under the MGNREGS, 18 males and 17 females received employment for around one month.

**Table 14** *Average number of days of non-agricultural employment by type of activity, Alabujanahalli, 2009*

| Type of activity | Males | | Females | |
|---|---|---|---|---|
| | No. of workers | No. of days of employment per worker | No. of workers | No. of days of employment per worker |
| Construction-related work | 9 | 22 | 2 | 24 |
| Tractor driver | 2 | 288 | – | – |
| Mining sector | 1 | 4 | – | – |
| MGNREGS | 27 | 11 | 47 | 21 |
| Sericulture | 4 | 8 | 15 | 10 |
| Transport-related work | 7 | 58 | 3 | 14 |
| Other work | 6 | 42 | 10 | 13 |
| All | 45 | 30 | 60 | 23 |

*Note*: Other work includes loading sand, dehusking coconuts, and painting houses.

**Table 15** *Average number of days of non-agricultural employment, by type of activity, Siresandra, 2009*

| Type of activity | Males | | Females | |
|---|---|---|---|---|
| | No. of workers | No. of days of employment per worker | No. of workers | No. of days of employment per worker |
| Construction-related work | 6 | 125 | 0 | – |
| MGNREGS | 17 | 35 | 18 | 41 |
| Other work | 4 | 158 | 3 | 59 |
| Sericulture | 17 | 31 | 14 | 58 |
| Transport-related activities | 1 | 360 | 0 | – |
| Wood-cutting | 7 | 93 | 0 | – |
| All | 37 | 95 | 28 | 62 |

*Note*: Other work includes employment in catering services, making stone slabs, etc.

**Table 16** *Average number of days of non-agricultural employment, by type of activity, Zhapur, 2009*

| Type of activity | Males | | Females | |
|---|---|---|---|---|
| | No. of workers | No. of days of employment per worker | No of workers | No. of days of employment per worker |
| Construction-related work | 22 | 176 | 2 | 69 |
| Driver | 12 | 238 | 0 | – |
| Mining sector | 33 | 196 | 20 | 193 |
| Other work | 7 | 12 | 0 | – |
| All | 67 | 151 | 21 | 190 |

*Note:* Other work includes cattle rearing, house painting, etc.

In Zhapur, mining, quarrying, and construction-related work generated around six months of employment for men and women. There was no employment under the MGNREGS. On an average, for those participating in non-agricultural work, about six months of employment per worker was available in the village.

## Wage Rates and Wage Earnings

This section deals with wage rates for agricultural and non-agricultural work, and the wage earnings of rural wage workers. The rural wage rate is a critical indicator of the well-being of labour. It also signifies the condition of the labour market and the demand for labour, and is a determinant of rural prosperity and poverty. Wage rates in agriculture vary by crop, crop operation, season, sex, and type of contract. There are two major types of contract prevailing in Indian villages: the time-rated contract (with the mode of payment being daily or annual) and the piece-rated contract. Specifically, this section looks at the agricultural wage rates for different operations of major crops and wage rates for non-agricultural tasks, the level of monetization of wage payment, the levels of wage earnings, and gender differentials in wage earnings.

### Wage Rates in Alabujanahalli

In Alabujanahalli, the major crops were sugarcane, paddy, and finger millet. The major operations of agriculture were not mechanized, and ploughing was done with bullocks. The wage rate ranged from Rs 100 to 400 for ploughing

**Table 17** *Daily wage rates for male and female workers by crop operation, Alabujanahalli, 2008–09* in Rs and number

| Crops | Crop operations | Males | | Females | |
|---|---|---|---|---|---|
| | | Cash | Kind | Cash | Kind |
| Sugarcane | Land preparation* | 100–150 | 3 meals + coffee | | |
| | Sowing | 100–120 | 3 meals + coffee | 50–60 | 1 coffee |
| | Weeding | 100–120 | 3 meals + coffee | 50–60 | 1 coffee |
| Paddy | Land preparation* | 100–150 | 3 meals + coffee | | |
| | Weeding | 100–120 | 3 meals + coffee | 50–80 | 1 coffee |
| | Harvesting and post-harvesting | 100–120 | 3 meals + coffee | 50–80 | 1 coffee |
| Finger millet | Land preparation* | 100–150 | 3 meals + coffee | | |
| | Weeding | 100–120 | 3 meals + coffee | 50–60 | 1 coffee |
| | Harvesting and post-harvesting | 100–120 | 3 meals + coffee | 50–60 | 1 coffee |

*Note*: * Rs 400 with bullocks.
*Source*: PARI survey data.

**Table 18** *Piece-rates for male and female workers by crop operation, Alabujanahalli, 2009* in Rs and number

| Crops | Crop operations | Cash | Kind |
|---|---|---|---|
| Sugarcane | Harvesting | 150/tonne | – |
| Sugarcane | Loading and transporting | 100/tonne | – |
| Paddy | Transplanting | 700–800/acre | 1 meal + 1 coffee* |
| Paddy | Harvesting and post-harvesting | 600–1200/acre | – |
| Finger millet | Sowing | 600/acre | 1 coffee |

*Note*: * Each member of the group gets 1 meal+1 coffee.
*Source*: PARI survey data.

**Table 19** *Daily wage rates for male and female workers in non-agricultural work, Alabujanahalli, 2009* in Rs and number

| Non-agricultural operations | Males | | Females | |
|---|---|---|---|---|
| | Cash | Kind | Cash | Kind |
| MGNREGS | 82 | – | 82 | – |
| Sericulture | | | 50 | 1 coffee |
| Coconut harvesting | Rs 10/tree | – | | |

*Source*: PARI survey data.

with bullocks, depending on who provided the bullocks. If the workers used their own bullocks, the wage rate was Rs 400; otherwise it was Rs 100. The prevailing wage rate for male workers was Rs 100 and for female workers, Rs 50 with cooked food. Other than ploughing, row-sowing for sugarcane was male-dominated work. Operations such as weeding, transplanting, and sowing were mostly performed by female workers.

Sowing operations for paddy and finger millet were completed by hired workers on piece-rated contracts. The piece-rate for this operation varied from Rs 600 to Rs 800 per acre. The most remunerative piece-rated wage was observed for sugarcane harvesting. Female workers participated in sericulture at a daily wage rate of Rs 50 with coffee.

Non-agricultural activities were not as important in Alabujanahalli, though the village was well connected to the town. The wage rate for MGNREGS workers was Rs 82 a day.

## Wage Rates in Siresandra

Siresandra belongs to the semi-dry rainfed region of Karnataka, and was known for vegetable cultivation. As it was a predominantly vegetable-growing area, the demand for female labour was higher than for male labour. However, the wage rate for female-specific operations was very low. Most of the operations were done on daily wage contracts. The total wage was paid in two components, cash and kind. The wage paid in kind, in most

Table 20 *Daily wage rates for male and female workers by crop operation, Siresandra, 2009* in Rs and number

| Crops | Crop operations | Males | | Females | |
|---|---|---|---|---|---|
| | | Cash | Kind | Cash | Kind |
| Vegetables | Ploughing* | 100 | – | | |
| | Sowing | 80–100 | 1 meal | 50–80 | 1 meal |
| | Weeding | 50 | 1 meal | 50–80 | 1 meal |
| | Harvesting | 80–100 | 1 meal | 50–80 | 1 meal |
| Finger millet | Ploughing* | 100 | – | | |
| | Sowing | 80–100 | 1 meal | 50 | 1 meal |
| | Weeding | 50 | 1 meal | 50–80 | 1 meal |
| | Harvesting | 70–100 | 1 meal | 50–80 | 1 meal |
| Mulberry | Harvesting | 100 | 1 meal | 50–60 | 1 meal |

*Note*: * Rs 200–300 for a worker with bullocks and Rs 100 for a worker without bullocks.
*Source*: PARI survey data.

Table 21 *Daily wage rates for male and female workers in non-agricultural activities, Siresandra, 2008–09* in Rs and number

| Non-agricultural activities | Males | | Females | |
|---|---|---|---|---|
| | Cash | Kind | Cash | Kind |
| MGNREGS | 82 | | 80 | |
| Wood-cutting (eucalyptus) | 100–150 | | | |
| Mason | 250 | | | |
| Construction worker | 150 | | | |
| Sericulture | 70–100 | 1 meal | 50 | 1 meal |
| | | | 3/*chandrik* | 1 meal |

*Note*: Chandrika or cocoonage is a circular basket with a spiral wall of about 5 cm width that acts as a mounting frame for ripe worms, providing support for the spinning of cocoons.
*Source*: PARI survey data.

cases, consisted of cooked food. For finger millet and vegetable cultivation, the daily wage rate for ploughing with bullocks was reported to be Rs 100. For sowing, male workers obtained wages between Rs 80 to Rs 100 a day along with one meal, while female workers received Rs 50 to Rs 100 a day with one meal. For harvesting, the wage rate for male workers ranged from Rs 50 to Rs 100, whereas female workers received Rs 50 to Rs 80 with one meal. In Siresandra, sericulture was an important source of income. For mulberry cultivation, male workers obtained a wage of Rs 100 per day, while female workers received a wage of Rs 60 to Rs 80.

Non-agricultural wages were higher than agricultural wages in Siresandra. The daily wage for masons was Rs 250 and construction workers earned Rs 150 a day.

## Wage Rates in Zhapur

The major crops grown in Zhapur were pigeon pea, sunflower, and *sorghum*. The wage rates for all major crop operations were as shown in Tables 22 and 23.

Daily-rated contracts were the norm for all major crop operations. Male workers worked on daily-rated contracts at a wage rate of Rs 100 a day. The floor wage rate for female workers in daily-rated contracts was Rs 30, going up to Rs 50. Wages for all operations were monetised except for *sorghum* harvesting. Harvesting of *sorghum* was paid for either in cash or kind – i.e. a fixed amount of *sorghum*. In Zhapur, cooked food was not provided along with a cash wage. Piece-rated operations were not prevalent in the village. Crop operations like sowing and weeding were dominated by female labour.

**Table 22** *Daily wage rates for male and female workers by crop operation, Zhapur, 2008–09 in Rs and kg*

| Crops | Crop operations | Males | | Females | |
|---|---|---|---|---|---|
| | | Cash | Kind | Cash | Kind |
| Pigeon pea and intercrop | Land preparation | 100 | | – | |
| | Sowing | 100 | | 30–50 | |
| | Weeding | 100 | | 30–50 | |
| | Harvesting and post-harvesting | 100 | | 50 | |
| Sorghum | Land preparation | 100 | | – | |
| | Sowing | 100 | | 40–50 | |
| | Weeding | 100 | | 30–50 | |
| | Harvesting and post-harvesting | 100 | 4.5 kg *sorghum* | 50* | 3.75–5 kg *sorghum* |
| Sunflower | Land preparation | 100 | | – | |
| | Sowing | 100 | | 40–50 | |
| | Weeding | – | | 30–50 | |
| | Harvesting and post-harvesting | 100 | | 50 | |
| Pearl millet | Land preparation | 100 | | – | |
| | Sowing | 100 | | 40–50 | |
| | Weeding | 100 | | 30–50 | |
| | Harvesting and post-harvesting | 100 | | 40–50 | |

*Source*: PARI survey data.

Non-farm employment was a very important source of income for wage workers in Zhapur. Male wage workers were engaged in construction work, and work in the quarry fields around the village. The wage rate for construction was Rs 100–150 a day, and for masons it was Rs 250. In the mining sector (quarry fields), the wage rates for male workers were between Rs 100 and Rs 150, depending on the tasks. It is important to note that women workers also participated in mining, working along with the men of their households.

Our major observations with respect to wage rates in the three study villages are as follows:

• First, daily-rated contracts were the norm for agricultural tasks in Zhapur

**Table 23** *Daily wage rates for male and female workers in non-agricultural activities, Zhapur, 2008–09 in Rs and kg*

| Non-agricultural activities | Males | | Females | |
|---|---|---|---|---|
| | Cash | Kind | Cash | Kind |
| Construction work | 100–150 | – | | – |
| Mason | 250 | – | | – |
| Mining work | 100–150 | – | 50 | – |
| MGNREGS | NA | – | NA | – |

*Source*: PARI survey data.

and Siresandra. However, in Alabujanahalli piece-rates were widespread, and covered the transplanting and sowing of paddy and finger millet, and harvesting of sugarcane.

- Secondly, a major part of the wages in all three villages was paid in cash, irrespective of the nature of crop operation. The exception was harvesting of *sorghum* in Zhapur. In Alabujanahalli and Siresandra, cooked food was provided along with cash payment, but in Zhapur, cooked food as part of the wage payment was not prevalent.
- Thirdly, other than agricultural tasks like ploughing, there was female participation in all operations. In some operations like sowing, weeding, and transplantation, female workers exceeded male workers. All three villages showed a persistent and large wage difference between males and females even when they worked on the same crop.

### Wage Earnings

We now turn to the wage earnings of rural manual workers in the three study villages. The average daily wage earning is calculated as total wage earnings from time-rated and piece-rated work, divided by the total number of days of employment. Wage payments received in kind have been given a cash value and added to the wage earning.

The average daily wage earning among male workers from Manual worker households was Rs 145 in Alabujanahalli, Rs 96 in Zhapur, and Rs 69 in Siresandra. As noted earlier, Alabujanahalli was a village with intensive cultivation. Sugarcane harvesting was the most remunerative task, as was ploughing with bullocks. Among female workers, the daily wage earning was almost equal across the three villages, at around Rs 60. The variation in male wage earnings across the three villages was high.

**Table 24** *Average wage earnings of workers in agricultural and non-agricultural wage work, study villages, 2009* in (Rs/day)

| Village | Agriculture | | Non-agriculture | |
|---|---|---|---|---|
| | Males | Females | Males | Females |
| Alabujanahalli | 134 | 61 | 95 | 80 |
| Siresandra | 69 | 65 | 108 | 76 |
| Zhapur | 96 | 61 | 122 | 56 |

*Source*: PARI survey data.

In the case of non-agricultural activities, the average daily wage earning for a male worker was Rs 122 in Zhapur, Rs 108 in Siresandra, and Rs 95 in Alabujanahalli. The daily wage earning for a female worker was Rs 80 in Alabujanahalli, Rs 76 in Siresandra, and Rs 56 in Zhapur. In Zhapur, male workers received employment in mining at a relatively high wage. Alabujanahalli was the only village where wages in non-agriculture were actually lower than in the agricultural sector.

The wage differential between male and female workers was remarkably high across the three villages, which is one of the general features of rural labour markets across India. In Alabujanahalli, on average, the wage earnings of female workers were less than half that of male workers. The situation was a little better in Siresandra. In non-agricultural wage employment too, we found wage differentials between male and female wage workers. The wage differential was highest in Zhapur: the daily wage earning of a female worker in this village was only 46 per cent of the wage earning of a male worker.

## Incidence of Poverty among Manual Worker Households

In this section, in order to understand the economic well-being of Manual worker households, we examine whether a typical household is able to obtain a minimum income from wage earnings. For purposes of simplicity, we have identified the minimum level of income in terms of India's official expenditure poverty line (the Tendulkar poverty line of 2008–09) and two international poverty lines: that of $1.5 PPP (purchasing power parity dollars) and $2 PPP. Table 25 presents the proportion of Manual worker households in the three villages whose annual incomes were below these three poverty lines.

Incidence of poverty among Manual worker households was highest in Zhapur, with 29.5 per cent of all Manual worker households having incomes below the $1 a day poverty line. In Siresandra the corresponding proportion was 15.4 per cent of all households, and in Alabujanahalli it was 20 per cent.

To put it differently, the low level of incomes among Manual worker households implies that they had to work a larger number of days at physically demanding manual work unless there was a rise in wage rates, in order to earn higher incomes.

## Conclusions

The class of Manual workers is a numerically significant section of the rural population. Scheduled Castes (SCs), Scheduled Tribes (STs), and Backward Classes (BCs) are over-represented in the class of Manual workers as compared to their representation in the village population. A large section of the class of Manual workers is resource-poor, especially in terms of cultivable land. Members of this class depend mainly on low-skill, low remunerative agricultural and non-agricultural wage work. Crop production continues to be an important source of employment in the study villages. The rural non-agricultural sector plays a secondary role in providing employment. Except for Zhapur, the non-agricultural sector did not generate employment opportunities for Manual workers resident in the village. Non-agricultural work in the villages lacked diversity. Opportunities for female workers in non-agriculture were even more limited. As male workers left agricultural wage employment and moved to more remunerative non-agricultural work, the women took up low-wage tasks in crop production.

While agriculture was the largest employer (in terms of sector of employment), the employment generated in crop production was not enough to absorb the entire work force of a village. Even in an agriculturally

**Table 25** *Proportion of Manual worker households with incomes below poverty, by different poverty lines, study villages*

| Village | Official poverty line (India) | $1.5 PPP (international) | $ 2 PPP (international) |
|---|---|---|---|
| Alabujanahalli | 19.2 | 20.5 | 39.7 |
| Siresandra | 15.4 | 15.4 | 38.5 |
| Zhapur | 27.5 | 29.4 | 51.0 |

*Note:* The international poverty lines are in purchasing power parity (PPP) dollars. They were converted to rupee equivalents at 2008–09 prices.
*Source:* PARI survey data.

prosperous village like Alabujanhalli, where crop production was round-the-year and the cropping pattern was highly labour-intensive, crop production failed to generate sufficient employment opportunities for workers belonging to the class of Manual workers.

The outcome was severe underemployment among Manual workers, especially female workers. A large section of workers received only three to four months of employment in a year. The MGNREGS was devised to address the crisis of rural unemployment by generating 100 days of employment per household. However, in the three villages studied, the MGNREGS failed to create adequate employment to address rural unemployment. In Alabujanahalli, in 2008–09, crop production generated 53,824 labour-days, whereas MGNREGS created only 1,313 labour-days. The labour-days generated under MGNREGS were only 2.4 per cent of the labour-days generated in the process of crop production. In Siresandra, the labour-days generated under MGNREGS were only 12.5 per cent of the labour-days generated in agricultural production. We may thus argue that the MGNREGS has not played a significant role in the rural production process, and has invariably failed to offset the effect of loss of employment in agricultural production. These data also show that the poverty of the class of Manual workers cannot be eradicated through state-sponsored programmes such as the MGNREGS. Eradication of poverty requires the creation of employment opportunities in the rural production process, and large-scale and long-term rural development programmes.

# Appendix Tables

**Appendix Table 1** *Ratio of worker to non-worker and worker to student by socio-economic class, Alabujanahalli*

| Socio-economic class | Ratio | |
|---|---|---|
| | Worker to non-worker | Worker to student |
| Rich capitalist farmer | 1.0:1 | 5.0:1 |
| Peasant 1 | 1.0:1 | 2.5:1 |
| Peasant 2 | 1.1:1 | 4.7:1 |
| Peasant 3 | 1.9:1 | 5.7:1 |
| Peasant 4 | 1.8:1 | 5.3:1 |
| Manual worker | 2.4:1 | 6.8:1 |
| All | 1.7:1 | 5.5:1 |

*Note*: Ratio is calculated for the population aged 15 years and above. Households dependent on rents and remittances, and salaries, were numerically insignificant and excluded.
*Source*: PARI survey data.

**Appendix Table 2** *Ratio of worker to non-worker and worker to student ratio by socio-economic class, Siresandra*

| Socio-economic class | Ratio | |
|---|---|---|
| | Worker to non-worker | Worker to student |
| Peasant 1 | 2.0:1 | 4.0:1 |
| Peasant 2 | 2.5:1 | 7.1:1 |
| Peasant 3 | 2.8:1 | 4.9:1 |
| Manual worker | 3.3:1 | 10.0:1 |
| All | 2.6:1 | 6.0:1 |

*Note*: Ratio is calculated for the population aged 15 years and above. Households in the category business/small self-employment are excluded.
*Source*: PARI survey data.

**Appendix Table 3** *Ratio of worker to non-worker and worker to student by socio-economic class, Zhapur*

| Socio-economic class | Ratio | |
|---|---|---|
| | Worker to non-worker | Worker to student |
| Landlord | 0.6:1 | 1.4:1 |
| Peasant | 2.6:1 | 6.2:1 |
| Manual worker | 2.9:1 | 12.7:1 |
| Business/self-employed | 1.8:1 | 10.0:1 |
| All | 2.3:1 | 7.9:1 |

*Notes*: Ratio is calculated for the population aged 15 years and above. Households dependent on rents and remittances, and salaries, were numerically insignificant and excluded.
*Source*: PARI survey data.

**Appendix Table 4** *Proportion of households from different social groups in all households and Manual worker households, Alabujanahalli, 2009* in per cent

| Social group | As proportion of all households | As proportion of Manual worker households | Share of Manual worker households in each social group |
|---|---|---|---|
| Caste Hindu | 85.2 | 69.8 | 24.6 |
| Scheduled Caste (SC) | 14.4 | 28.8 | 60 |
| Scheduled Tribe (ST) | 0.4 | 1.4 | 100 |
| All | 100 | 100 | 30 |

*Source*: PARI survey data.

**Appendix Table 5** *Proportion of households from different social groups in all households and Manual worker households, Siresandra, 2009* in per cent

| Social group | As proportion of all households | As proportion of Manual worker households | Share of Manual worker households in each social group |
|---|---|---|---|
| Scheduled Caste (SC) | 36.7 | 67.9 | 65.5 |
| Backward Class (BC) | 63.3 | 32.1 | 18 |
| All | 100 | 100 | 35.4 |

*Source*: PARI survey data.

**Appendix Table 6**  *Proportion of households from different social groups in all households and Manual worker households, Zhapur, 2009* in per cent

| Social group | As proportion of all households | As proportion of Manual worker households | Share of Manual worker households in each social group |
|---|---|---|---|
| Caste Hindu | 45 | 28 | 28.6 |
| Scheduled Caste (SC) | 42.2 | 56 | 60.9 |
| Scheduled Tribe (ST) | 12.8 | 16 | 57.1 |
| All | 100 | 100 | 45.9 |

*Source*: PARI survey data.

**Appendix Table 7**  *Distribution of days of non-agricultural employment, by type of activity and sex, Alabujanahalli, 2009* in per cent and number

| Type of activity | Males | Females | Total number of days of employment |
|---|---|---|---|
| Construction-related work | 80.6 | 19.4 | 247 |
| Driver | 100.0 | 0.0 | 576 |
| Laundry work | 61.7 | 38.3 | 1721 |
| Mining sector | 100.0 | 0.0 | 4 |
| MGNREGS | 23.5 | 76.5 | 1313 |
| Sericulture | 17.6 | 82.4 | 188 |
| Transport-related work | 90.6 | 9.4 | 449 |
| Other work | 65.1 | 34.9 | 384 |
| All | 58.1 | 41.9 | 4882 |

*Source*: PARI survey data.

**Appendix Table 8**  *Distribution of days of non-agricultural employment, by type of activity and sex, Siresandra, 2009* in per cent and number

| Type of activity | Females | Males | Total number of days of employment |
|---|---|---|---|
| Construction-related work | 0 | 100 | 615 |
| MGNREGS | 61 | 39 | 1500 |
| Sericulture | 61 | 39 | 1366 |
| Transport-related activities | 0 | 100 | 752 |
| Wood-cutting | 0 | 100 | 1093 |
| Other work | 22 | 78 | 1506 |
| All | 30 | 70 | 6832 |

*Source*: PARI survey data.

**Appendix Table 9** *Distribution of days of non-agricultural employment, by type of activity and sex, Zhapur, 2009* in per cent and number

| Type of activity | Males | Females | Total number of days of employment |
|---|---|---|---|
| Construction-related work | 97 | 3 | 4017 |
| Driver | 100 | 0 | 2853 |
| Mining sector | 63 | 38 | 10329 |
| Other work | 100 | 0 | 84 |
| All | 77 | 23 | 17283 |

*Source*: PARI survey data.

# 10

## Household Incomes in the Three Study Villages

Aparajita Bakshi and Arindam Das

## Introduction

In this chapter we describe the levels and patterns of household incomes in the three villages surveyed in Karnataka. In the first section, we briefly describe the methodology of calculating household incomes in the surveys conducted under the Project on Agrarian Relations in India (PARI) of the Foundation for Agrarian Studies (FAS). We then discuss, in the second section, the findings from the survey data. In the third section we describe the levels of income and income deprivation in the three villages. Then we discuss the patterns of household incomes in each village separately. We analyse the inequality in distribution of household incomes in each village – in particular, we analyse income disparities across caste groups and socio-economic classes. We also discuss the sources of incomes in the village, the income share from each source, and its implication for income differences across castes and classes.

## Estimation of Household Incomes

Estimates of household incomes in the PARI village surveys include all cash and kind incomes; they account for all cash and kind receipts other than from borrowing and from sale of assets (including cash transfers).[1] All incomes are net of costs incurred by the households in the process of production and income generation.

Incomes of households in the survey villages were estimated separately

---

[1] Transfers in kind such as food subsidies are not included.

for the following sources. The surveys used detailed modules on incomes from each of the following sources.

1. Crop production
2. Animal resources (including rental income from animals)
3. Wage labour
    i. Agricultural labour (casual)
    ii. Agricultural labour (long-term)
    iii. Non-agricultural labour (casual)
    iv. Non-agricultural labour (monthly/long-term)
4. Salaried jobs
    i. Government salaried jobs
    ii. Other salaried jobs
5. Business and trade
6. Moneylending
7. Income from savings in financial institutions and equity
8. Pensions and scholarships
9. Remittances and gifts
10. Rental income
    i. Rental income from agricultural land
    ii. Rental income from machinery
    iii. Rental income from other assets
11. Artisanal work and work at traditional caste calling
12. Any other sources.

Gross incomes net of paid-out costs from crop production were calculated for each individual crop or crop-mix. The definition here of cost of cultivation closely resembles the definition of the cost A2 category used under the Comprehensive Scheme for Studying Cost of Cultivation/ Production of Principal Crops (CCPC), of the Commission of Agricultural Costs and Prices (CACP), India. It includes, broadly speaking, the costs of all material inputs (purchased and home-produced), the cost of hired labour, rental payments, the imputed value of interest on working capital, and depreciation of owned fixed capital other than land. No cost is imputed for family labour and no rent is imputed for owned land. Conceptual and methodological problems in imputing the costs of family labour and owned land have been discussed at length in the writings on CCPC data (see Sen and Bhatia 2004, for a summary), and will not detain us here. We shall note, however, the consequences of exclusion of these items of cost from our calculations. As a result of exclusion of the cost of family labour, other factors being constant, a household using a greater share than others of family labour incurs a lower cost of cultivation than other households. Similarly, the cost of cultivation is higher for a tenant than for a landowner because rental payments of a tenant are included in the cost while no cost is imputed for owned land.

Similarly, for wage labour in agriculture, each worker was asked questions on the number of days of employment and on earnings (in cash, kind, or both), for each season, crop, and crop operation. In order systematically to record labour use and employment in different agricultural tasks, FAS has prepared a comprehensive list of all field operations and categorised them using a four-digit system of classification. Using this system of classification, the Foundation's survey team prepares, for each village, a separate set of survey codes covering all operations involved in the cultivation of each crop in the village. These village-specific survey codes take into account village-specific variations in production processes, techniques of production, and systems of hiring labour. When preparing these codes, care is taken to list all the tasks involved in the production of a crop. An appropriately disaggregated and comprehensive list of all the crop operations is crucial for collecting accurate data on labour use and employment.

On account of the detailed questionnaire, careful investigation, and processing, we argue that the FAS–PARI data on household incomes are reliable. Nevertheless, we know that incomes fluctuate substantially across households, over time. It is important to remember that our data on incomes pertain to a particular year and therefore give a cross-sectional picture of income generation. For further details of methodology, see FAS (2015).

## Levels of Household Incomes and Incidence of Poverty in the Three Villages

Tables 1 and 2 report the total and per capita annual household incomes estimated from the PARI survey data in the three Karnataka villages. The mean household income ranged from Rs 71,500 in unirrigated Zhapur, to Rs 89,968 in canal-irrigated Alabujanahalli and Rs 1, 33,000 in sericulture-dependent Siresandra.

In Zhapur about five households incurred losses in the year 2008–09, and in Alabujanahalli one household incurred a loss in net annual income. The negative annual returns were mainly on account of losses made in cultivation. Ten per cent of households in Alabujanahalli, 22 per cent of households in Siresandra, and 16 per cent of households in Zhapur incurred

**Table 1** *Descriptive statistics of total household income, study villages, 2008–09* in Rs

| Description | Alabujanahalli | Siresandra | Zhapur |
|---|---|---|---|
| Mean | 89,968 | 1,33,000 | 71,500 |
| Median | 57,095 | 82,300 | 51,600 |
| Maximum | 17,30,000 | 10,00,615 | 10,04,754 |
| Minimum | −15,400 | 3,430 | −1,64,515 |
| Number of households with negative income | 1 | 0 | 5 |

**Table 2** *Descriptive statistics of per capita household income, study villages, 2008–09* in Rs

| Description | Alabujanahalli | Siresandra | Zhapur |
|---|---|---|---|
| Mean | 17,543 | 22,600 | 12,500 |
| Median | 12,142 | 16,200 | 8,499 |
| Maximum | 2,46,934 | 1,10,423 | 2,32,415 |
| Minimum | −3,078 | 490 | −11,751 |

**Table 3** *Proportion of households below poverty line, study villages, Karnataka, 2008–09* in per cent

| Poverty line | Poverty line at 2008–09 prices (Rs per capita per annum) | Head count ratio | | |
|---|---|---|---|---|
| | | Alabujanahalli | Siresandra | Zhapur |
| Tendulkar poverty line, Karnataka, 2009–10 | 6719 | 19.8 | 13.9 | 34.9 |
| $2 PPP | 9402 | 34.2 | 22.8 | 56.9 |

losses in crop production. Households with alternate source of incomes, such as sericulture in Siresandra and Alabujanahalli, or agricultural labour and non-farm incomes in Alabujanahalli, could tide over their losses by supplementary incomes from other sources.

To understand the levels of income and economic well-being in the villages, we have compared household incomes with two income benchmarks used widely in policy research. First, we have compared household incomes with the Tendulkar poverty line for Karnataka, 2009–10, adjusted for 2008–09 prices using the consumer price index for agricultural labour (CPIAL). This works out to be Rs 6,719 per capita per annum in 2008–09. The Tendulkar poverty line is also very close to the internationally used $1.25 PPP (purchasing power parity) poverty line. The second benchmark we have used is the $2 (PPP) poverty line, which is approximately Rs 9,402 per capita per annum at 2008–09 prices. Households with incomes less than $2 a day are termed vulnerable. Table 3 presents the proportion of households in the three villages whose annual incomes were below the two poverty lines we have used.

Incidence of poverty was highest in Zhapur, with 34.9 per cent of households falling below the Tendulkar poverty line and 56.9 per cent categorized as vulnerable households. According to official estimates of poverty, 26.1 per cent of the rural population in Karnataka were below the Tendulkar poverty line in 2009–10. In comparison to the State average, incidence of poverty was low in Alabujanahalli and Siresandra.

In the following sections, we discuss the patterns of household incomes and income distribution in each of the three villages separately.

## Alabujanahalli, Mandya District

### Distribution of Household Incomes

Table 4 shows the distribution of total household incomes and per capita household incomes in Alabujanahalli, and some summary measures of

Table 4 *Distribution of total household income and per capita household income, by income decile, Alabujanahalli, 2008–09*

| Income deciles | Share in total households | Share in total household income | Share in per capita income |
|---|---|---|---|
| Poorest | 10 | 1.30 | 1.40 |
| 2 | 10 | 4.40 | 3.30 |
| 3 | 10 | 3.70 | 4.30 |
| 4 | 10 | 6.40 | 5.50 |
| 5 | 10 | 6.50 | 6.30 |
| 6 | 10 | 5.70 | 7.80 |
| 7 | 10 | 9.60 | 9.50 |
| 8 | 10 | 10.60 | 11.40 |
| 9 | 10 | 13.70 | 15.20 |
| Richest | 10 | 38.10 | 35.20 |
| Total | 100 | 100.00 | 100.00 |
| D10/D1 | 25 | | |
| D10/D9 | 2.3 | | |
| Gini coefficient of per capita household income | 0.453 | | |

income inequality. The Gini coefficient of per capita household income in the village was 0.453. While this is not very high compared to some of the other PARI villages (see Bakshi, Das, and Swaminathan 2014), we do observe concentration of incomes in the richest decile. Only 1.4 per cent of household incomes and per capita incomes accrued to the poorest 10 per cent households, while 38 per cent of total household incomes were in the hands of the richest decile. The income share of the richest decile was more than twice (2.3 times) that of the immediately preceding decile.

## Sources and Composition of Household Incomes

Alabujanahalli, situated in the Cauvery region of Karnataka, is irrigated by canals from the Krishnarajasagar dam. Paddy and sugarcane were the main crops in the village, along with finger millet. Mulberry was also cultivated for use in sericulture. The primary sector comprising agriculture, livestock, and sericulture was the major source of income and employment for households in the village. In the survey year, 98 per cent of households received incomes from the primary sector (Table 5). The primary sector contributed 58 per cent

Table 5 *Number and proportion of households receiving incomes from different sources, Alabujanahalli*

| Income source | No. of households | Percentage |
|---|---|---|
| Crop income | 204 | 84 |
| Animal resources | 189 | 78 |
| Sericulture | 87 | 36 |
| Agricultural labour | 101 | 42 |
| Rental income from agricultural land | 20 | 8 |
| Primary sector | 238 | 98 |
| Non-agricultural labour | 106 | 44 |
| Salaries | 34 | 14 |
| Business and trade | 46 | 19 |
| Rental income from machinery | 38 | 16 |
| Rental income from other assets | 24 | 10 |
| Secondary and tertiary sectors | 210 | 86 |
| Transfers and remittances | 81 | 33 |
| Other sources | 4 | 2 |
| All other sources | 84 | 35 |
| All households | 243 | 100 |

**Table 6** *Distribution of total household income by source, Alabujanahalli, 2008–09* in per cent

| Income sources | Share |
|---|---|
| Crop income | 30 |
| Animal resources | 7 |
| Sericulture income | 7 |
| Agricultural labour earnings | 12 |
| Earnings from long-term labour | 0 |
| Rental income from agricultural land | 1 |
| Primary sector | 58 |
| Non-agricultural casual labour | 2 |
| Non-agricultural monthly labour earnings | 0 |
| Government salaried job | 3 |
| Private salaried job | 6 |
| Business and trade earnings | 18 |
| Rental income from machinery | 3 |
| Rental income from other assets | 7 |
| Artisanal work and work at traditional caste calling | 0 |
| Secondary and tertiary sectors | 39 |
| Pension scholarship and insurance claim | 1.6 |
| Remittances | 1.4 |
| Other sources | 0 |
| All other sources | 3 |
| All households | 100 |

of the total household incomes of residents of the village (Table 6). Income from crop production constituted 30 per cent of net village household income in the survey year. Animal husbandry and sericulture each contributed 7 per cent of the annual household income. Earnings from agricultural labour were 12 per cent of annual household incomes in the village.

The major non-agricultural income was from business and trade. About 19 per cent of households were engaged in non-agricultural self-employment activities, which contributed to 18 per cent of household incomes. Another 14 per cent of households were engaged in salaried activities, primarily in the private sector in nearby towns and cities (including Bengaluru). However, income from salaried employment was not very high and constituted 12 per cent of total household income. Rental income from other assets, including houses and buildings in the village and nearby semi-urban areas, constituted

7 per cent of household incomes. Earnings from non-agricultural labour were not remunerative sources of income. While 44 per cent of households derived some non-agricultural labour earnings, these constituted only 2 per cent of household incomes.

### Income Disparities across Castes

The major caste group in Alabujanahalli was Vokkaliga (Backward Class, BC). Scheduled Caste (SC) households comprised 14 per cent of the population in the village. Households of Adi Karnataka caste were the major group among SCs. There was one Scheduled Tribe (ST) household in the village as well. (But we are not presenting the figures for this one ST household.)

Table 7 shows the wide disparity in average income levels between Caste Hindu and SC households. The mean per capita household income of SC households was half that of Caste Hindu households. The average income of Vokkaliga households was higher than that of other Caste Hindu households, such as Gangamatha/Besthar households, in the village. The Adi Karnataka (SC) households had the lowest incomes.

If we look closely at the distribution of per capita incomes, we find that SCs are over-represented in the bottom half: 50 per cent of SC households are in the bottom three deciles. At the other end of the distribution, there are no SC households in the richest two income deciles. The Caste Hindu households, by contrast, are more or less evenly spread across all income deciles, and are marginally over-represented in the top two income deciles.

The variations in income levels between Caste Hindu and SC households can be partially explained by the differences in the composition of incomes of the two groups (Table 9). SC households had limited access to self-employment opportunities within agriculture and outside. While 31 per cent of household incomes of Caste Hindu households originated from cultivation, and another 15 per cent from animal resources and sericulture, the share of crop incomes for SC households was a meagre 10 per cent, and another 8 per cent from animal husbandry and sericulture. Similarly,

**Table 7** *Mean and median per capita income, by caste group, Alabujanahalli, 2008–09* in Rs

| Caste group | Number of households | Mean | Median |
|---|---|---|---|
| Caste Hindu | 208 | 18,872 | 13,297 |
| Scheduled Caste (SC) | 34 | 9,479 | 8,851 |
| Total | 243* | 17543 | 12142 |

*Note:* *Includes one Scheduled Tribe household.

**Table 8** *Distribution of households, by caste, by per capita income deciles, Alabujanahalli, 2008–09*

| Per capita income (in Rs) deciles | Caste Hindu | | Scheduled Caste (SC) | | All | |
|---|---|---|---|---|---|---|
| | Number | Per cent | Number | Per cent | Number | Per cent |
| ≤4386 | 20 | 10 | 5 | 15 | 25 | 10 |
| 4386–6787 | 19 | 9 | 5 | 15 | 24 | 10 |
| 6787–8480 | 17 | 8 | 7 | 21 | 24 | 10 |
| 8480–10252 | 22 | 11 | 3 | 9 | 25 | 10 |
| 10252–12141 | 17 | 8 | 7 | 21 | 24 | 10 |
| 12141–15354 | 22 | 11 | 2 | 6 | 24 | 10 |
| 15354–17199 | 22 | 11 | 2 | 6 | 25 | 10 |
| 17199–22904 | 21 | 10 | 3 | 9 | 24 | 10 |
| 22904–31547 | 24 | 12 | 0 | 0 | 24 | 10 |
| 31547+ | 24 | 12 | 0 | 0 | 24 | 10 |
| Total | 208 | 100 | 34 | 100 | 243 | 100 |

**Table 9** *Composition of household income as percentage of total income, by caste, Alabujanahalli, 2008–09* in per cent

| Income source | Caste Hindu | Scheduled Caste (SC) |
|---|---|---|
| Crop income | 31 | 10 |
| Animal resources | 7 | 7 |
| Sericulture income | 8 | 1 |
| Agricultural labour | 9 | 50 |
| Rental income from agricultural land | 4 | 4 |
| Non-agricultural labour | 2 | 11 |
| Salaries | 9 | 6 |
| Business and trade | 19 | 1 |
| Transfer and remittances | 3 | 10 |
| Other sources | 7 | 1 |

while 19 per cent of incomes of Caste Hindu households originated from business and trade, the corresponding share for SC households was only 1 per cent. The pattern of household income composition is a reflection of SC households' lack of access to cultivable land and capital for investment. The major source of income for SCs was manual labour: agricultural wage incomes constituted 50 per cent of total household incomes, and non-agricultural wage incomes 11 per cent. As we have discussed earlier, these were the least remunerative sources of income in the village.

### Distribution of Household Incomes across Socio-economic Classes

Table 10 shows the distribution of household incomes across socio-economic classes. In our discussion on decile distribution of incomes, we had mentioned that there was concentration of incomes in the top decile. Table 10 reflects a similar pattern. The two Rich capitalist farmer households in the village (less than 1 per cent of the total 243 households) received 20 per cent of the total income in the village. The mean per capita annual income of Rich capitalist farmers was Rs 2,91,622 – manifold higher than the other classes in the village (Table 11). The other classes that received incomes considerably higher than their population share were the richer sections of the peasantry (Peasant 1 and 2), and households employed in business and trade. The per capita annual incomes of these classes ranged between Rs 24,000 and Rs 32,000. Drawing from our analysis on caste and income disparity, it is also abundantly clear that the classes of Rich capitalist farmers, rich peasants, and business and trade households are Caste Hindus. Manual workers comprised

**Table 10** *Distribution of total household income, by classes, Alabujanahalli, 2008–09*

| Class | Number of households | Share in households (per cent) | Share in total income (per cent) |
|---|---|---|---|
| Rich capitalist farmer | 2 | 1 | 20 |
| Peasant 1 | 9 | 4 | 8 |
| Peasant 2 | 39 | 16 | 24 |
| Peasant 3 | 30 | 12 | 10 |
| Peasant 4 | 58 | 24 | 11 |
| All peasants | 136 | 56 | 52 |
| Manual worker 1 | 40 | 17 | 9 |
| Manual worker 2 | 22 | 9 | 3 |
| Manual worker 3 | 11 | 5 | 3 |
| All manual workers | 73 | 30 | 15 |
| Business/ self-employment | 11 | 5 | 5 |
| Salaried persons | 14 | 6 | 6 |
| Rents/remittances | 7 | 3 | 3 |
| Total | 243 | 100 | 100 |

**Table 11** *Mean per capita annual income, by classes, Alabujanahalli, 2008–09* in Rs

| Class | Mean |
|---|---|
| Rich capitalist farmer | 2,91,622 |
| Peasant 1 | 31,078 |
| Peasant 2 | 24,955 |
| Peasant 3 | 15,381 |
| Peasant 4 | 10,330 |
| Manual worker 1 | 11,100 |
| Manual worker 2 | 11,838 |
| Manual worker 3 | 12,876 |
| Business/self-employment | 24,806 |
| Salaried persons | 24,289 |
| Rents/remittances | 14,578 |
| Total | 18,345 |

30 per cent of all households but received only 15 per cent of the village income. The mean per capita annual income of Manual workers ranged between Rs 11,000 and Rs 13,000. It is to be noted that poor peasants (Peasant 4) were the worst-off class in terms of annual income, and the average income of this class was marginally lower than even Manual workers.

### Changes in Household Incomes, 2008–09 to 2013–14

Case studies of 18 households in Alabujanahalli, conducted in October 2014, revealed some interesting changes in the village. However, it should be noted since these were case studies and not a statistically representative sample, the direction of change and figures quoted here are only indicative. In short, we are not presenting statistical estimates of income and income growth.

The case studies indicated that Rich capitalist farmer and rich peasant households had diversified further to non-agricultural sources of income, particularly incomes from business and trade (rice mills and shops in K. M. Doddi). The household income of the largest Rich capitalist farmer household doubled between 2009 and 2014, from Rs 1,930,790 to Rs 4,239,111. The source of the new income was non-agriculture – rental income from shops, income from rice mill, sale of seats in medical colleges, etc.

In general, peasant households were of the view that income from crop production of all farmers increased between 2009 and 2014 due to an increase in sugarcane prices. There was also an increase in sericulture production (about 20 per cent of households were engaged in sericulture). At the same time, there was a fall in the real incomes of agricultural workers. According to our calculations, there was an increase in nominal wages but a very small increase in real wages between 2009 and 2014: from Rs 189 to Rs 250 for all agricultural operations, deflated by CPIAL.

Thus, we can broadly say that in the five years since the main survey was conducted in 2009, differentiation in the countryside may have deepened and inequalities may have widened in Alabujanahalli. The richest few probably have accumulated more wealth by seizing new opportunities in the non-agricultural sector. However, it is interesting to note that a substantial part of these new income sources was actually constituted by rents from inflated real estate prices, and from leakages and corruption in the economic system (see Chapter 4). Differentiation within the peasantry may also have increased, with sugarcane farmers making higher gains than small peasants growing foodgrains. At the other extreme, wage workers seem to have been left out of the growth process. It is unclear whether the scope of non-agricultural wage employment increased in the intervening period.

## Siresandra, Kolar District

### Distribution of Household Incomes

The Gini coefficient for per capita household incomes in Siresandra was 0.456. Even in this predominantly unirrigated village, we find some concentration of incomes in the highest two deciles. The richest 10 per cent of households received 28 per cent of the total village income, while the ninth decile received 24 per cent of the total village income. Thus, we did not find a very small section of extremely wealthy households that was distinctly different from the rest in this village. The differences in income shares between the ninth and tenth decile was not so pronounced as in Alabujanahalli. This was also reflected in the class and caste disparities in the village, which will be discussed later.

The poorest 30 per cent of households in Siresandra received less than 10 per cent of the total income and per capita income in the village. The poorest 10 per cent received only 1 per cent of the total village income.

### Composition of Household Incomes

The main occupations of households in Siresandra were crop production and animal husbandry. All households in the village were engaged in crop

**Table 12** *Distribution of total household income and per capita household income, by income deciles, Siresandra, 2008–09*

| Income deciles | Share in total household income | Share in per capita income |
|---|---|---|
| Poorest | 1 | 1 |
| 2 | 3 | 3 |
| 3 | 4 | 5 |
| 4 | 7 | 6 |
| 5 | 7 | 7 |
| 6 | 7 | 8 |
| 7 | 8 | 8 |
| 8 | 11 | 11 |
| 9 | 24 | 22 |
| Richest | 28 | 31 |
| Total | 100 | 100 |
| D10/D1 | | 23.5 |
| D10/D9 | | 1.4 |
| Gini coefficient | | 0.456 |

production and 90 per cent of households were engaged in animal husbandry (Table 13). One-third of the households were also engaged in sericulture. Households in Siresandra practised sericulture and animal husbandry on a larger scale than households in Alabujanahalli. Being an unirrigated village, agricultural incomes were not very high; hence sericulture and animal husbandry played a vital role in the household economy. This is obvious from Table 14, which shows the composition of total household income by source of income. Crop production constituted 24.7 per cent of household incomes; sericulture and income from animal resources each constituted 20 per cent of total household income. Thus, these three sources were of equal importance in the household income portfolio. Income diversification within the agricultural sector, economies of scope between animal husbandry, crop production (which includes mulberry cropping), and sericulture, helped the household economy to mitigate instability in agricultural production.[2] During the survey year, 17 households incurred losses in crop income, but

---

[2] Economies of scope refer to the cost advantages in production of two goods together rather than each good separately.

**Table 13** *Number and proportion of households receiving incomes from different sources, Siresandra*

| Income source | No. of households | Percentage |
|---|---|---|
| Crop production | 79 | 100 |
| Animal resources | 71 | 90 |
| Sericulture | 26 | 33 |
| Agricultural wage | 38 | 48 |
| Primary sector | 79 | 100 |
| Non-agricultural wage | 38 | 48 |
| Salaries | 14 | 18 |
| Business and trade earnings | 12 | 15 |
| Rental income from machinery | 2 | 3 |
| Rental income from other assets | 5 | 6 |
| Artisanal work and work at traditional caste calling | 7 | 9 |
| Secondary and tertiary sectors | 58 | 73 |
| Transfer and others | 25 | 32 |
| All | 79 | 100 |

**Table 14** *Distribution of total household income, by source, Siresandra, 2008–09* in per cent

| Income source | Share |
|---|---|
| Crop production | 24.7 |
| Animal resources | 20.2 |
| Sericulture | 20.6 |
| Agricultural wage | 7.0 |
| Primary sector | 72.5 |
| Non-agricultural wage | 7.7 |
| Salaries | 5.7 |
| Business and trade earnings | 5.9 |
| Rental income from machinery | 3.1 |
| Rental income from other assets | 0.5 |
| Artisanal work and work at traditional caste calling | 3.0 |
| Secondary and tertiary sectors | 25.9 |
| Transfer and others | 1.5 |
| All | 100.0 |

no household made a net loss in annual income. This was due to positive net incomes from sericulture and animal resources.

Manual labour incomes were low in the village. Though 48 per cent of households received incomes from agricultural and non-agricultural wages, wages constituted only 14 per cent of total household incomes. Wage rates were in the range of Rs 80–100 for male agricultural wages, Rs 50–80 for female agricultural wages, Rs 150 for construction workers, and Rs 250 for masons (see Chapter 9). Income share from salaries and business and trade were also not very high in the village (5.7 per cent and 5.9 per cent, respectively, of total household income). The secondary and tertiary sectors made up only one-fourth of the total income of village residents.

### Income Disparities across Caste Groups

In spite of being a small and unirrigated village, caste disparities in household incomes were quite pronounced in Siresandra. The mean annual per capita income of Caste Hindu households (Rs 28,115) was more than double that of SC households (Rs 13,182). Most (46 out of 50) Caste Hindu households were Vokkaligas. The mean income of Vokkaliga households was much higher than the mean income of Kapu and Madivala households. Among the SCs, Adi Karnataka households received the lowest incomes on average (Rs 13,254). The mean per capita income of five Bhovi households was Rs 15,312.

Table 16 shows the highest concentration of SC households in the bottom four per capita income deciles of the village. Sixty nine per cent of SC households were concentrated among the poorest 40 per cent. Caste Hindu households were under-represented in the poorest four deciles, and more or less evenly distributed thereafter. There was one SC household in the richest decile – this household owned and rented a lorry.

The composition of household incomes of Caste Hindu and SC households in Siresandra showed similar patterns as those observed in the other villages. While Caste Hindu households received a major share of their household income from cultivation (30 per cent), animal resources and sericulture, SC households received their incomes from wages and self-employment

Table 15 *Mean and median annual per capita incomes, by caste, Siresandra, 2008–09* in Rs

| Caste group | Mean | Median |
|---|---|---|
| Caste Hindu | 28,115 | 18,558 |
| Scheduled Caste (SC) | 13,182 | 11,269 |

**Table 16** *Distribution of households, by caste, by per capita income deciles, Siresandra, 2008–09* in per cent

| Per capita income decile | Caste Hindu | Scheduled Caste (SC) |
|---|---|---|
| ≤4626 | 6.0 | 17.2 |
| 4627–8666 | 6.0 | 17.2 |
| 8667–11269 | 6.0 | 17.2 |
| 11270–13120 | 6.0 | 17.2 |
| 13121–16195 | 14.0 | 3.4 |
| 16196–17335 | 8.0 | 13.8 |
| 17336–19190 | 12.0 | 6.9 |
| 19191–29577 | 14.0 | 3.4 |
| 29578–62621 | 16.0 | 0.0 |
| 62622+ | 12.0 | 3.4 |

**Table 17** *Composition of total household income, by caste, Siresandra, 2009–10*

| Income source | Caste Hindu | Scheduled Caste (SC) |
|---|---|---|
| Crop production | 30 | 6 |
| Animal resources | 23 | 10 |
| Sericulture | 26 | 0 |
| Agricultural wage | 3 | 25 |
| Non-agricultural wage | 3 | 25 |
| Salaries | 6 | 3 |
| Business and trade earnings | 4 | 15 |
| Rental income from machinery | 4 | 0 |
| Rental income from other assets | 1 | 0 |
| Artisanal work and work at traditional caste calling | 0 | 15 |
| Transfer and others | 2 | 2 |
| Total income | 100 | 100 |

in non-agriculture. SC households in Siresandra engaged in carpentry and sculpture-making.

It is important to note that the SC households received only 6 per cent of their income from cultivation and none from sericulture. Sericulture was a very important economic activity; however, it was also dependent on access to land for mulberry cultivation. This was the main reason why SC households could not practise sericulture.

### Income Disparities across Socio-Economic Classes

While discussing the distribution of household incomes, we observed that concentration of incomes was not very pronounced in Siresandra. This was also reflected in the class structure of the village (Table 18). There were no landlord households in Siresandra. Peasant households comprised 76 per cent of all households in the village. There were three classes of peasants. Peasant 1 households comprised 5 per cent of all households, but received 24 per cent of total village income. Manual workers formed an undifferentiated category, as most workers were engaged in both agricultural and non-agricultural wage employment. This class constituted 16 per cent of all households and received only 6 per cent of total village income. Eight per cent of the households were self-employed in non-agriculture. There were no households that received a major part of their income from salaried employment.

Table 19 presents the mean per capita household incomes of different classes of households. The per capita household incomes of peasant households ranged from Rs 51358 for Peasant 1 households to Rs 16,438 for Peasant 3 households. Households in business and small self-employment received incomes similar to poor peasant households. Manual workers were the poorest in terms of mean incomes, receiving only Rs 11,389 per capita per annum. Manual workers did not receive incomes from sericulture and animal resources, whereas these two sources of income were crucial for Peasant 1 and Peasant 2 households (the share of sericulture and animal resources together in total household income of Peasant 1, Peasant 2, Peasant 3, and Manual worker households were 43, 46, 44, and 9 per cent, respectively) to cushion the effects of unstable agricultural production.

**Table 18** *Distribution of households and total household income, by socio-economic classes, Siresandra, 2009– 10* in per cent

| Class | No. of households | Share in total households | Share in total income |
|---|---|---|---|
| Peasant 1 | 4 | 5 | 24 |
| Peasant 2 | 24 | 30 | 42 |
| Peasant 3 | 32 | 41 | 23 |
| All peasants | 60 | 76 | 89 |
| Manual workers | 13 | 16 | 6 |
| Business/small self-employment | 6 | 8 | 6 |
| Total | 79 | 100 | 100 |

**Table 19** *Mean per capita annual household income, by socio-economic classes, Siresandra, 2009-10* in Rs

| Class | Mean per capita income |
|---|---|
| Peasant 1 | 51,358 |
| Peasant 2 | 33,795 |
| Peasant 3 | 16,438 |
| Manual workers | 11,389 |
| Business/small self-employment | 17,272 |
| Total | 22,712 |

### Changes in Household Incomes, 2008–09 to 2013–14

The case studies conducted in 2013–14 indicate that there was a decline in real incomes in Siresandra between 2008–09 and 2013–14. The reason for the decline was deterioration of groundwater irrigation due to a decline in the water table. Of the 20 borewells available for irrigation in 2009, only three were functional in 2014. Therefore, the production of horticultural crops was adversely affected. Sericulture and animal husbandry were the main sources of household income for most households in 2014. Crop land was now being used for plantations like that of eucalyptus trees due to lack of irrigation.

## Zhapur, Kalaburagi District

### Distribution of Household Incomes

Zhapur is a completely dry village. The problem of agriculture in the village is compounded by rocky soil. Thus, agricultural production is low and unstable. This is reflected in the fact that 16 per cent of households made losses in agriculture in the survey year, and the share of total household income of the poorest decile was negative (Table 20). These households were not necessarily the poorest in terms of assets; they were poor peasant households that made large losses in agriculture which could not be recovered from other sources of income.

The share in total household income of the bottom 50 per cent of households was only 15 per cent. On the other hand, the richest 10 per cent of households received 43 per cent of the total income. There was thus a very high concentration of wealth (see Chapter 7). The Gini coefficient of per capita household income in the village was 0.421. The richest decile

**Table 20** *Distribution of total household income and per capita household income, by income decile, Zhapur, 2008–09*

| Income decile | Share in total household income | Share in per capita income |
|---|---|---|
| Poorest | −2 | −1 |
| 2 | 2 | 3 |
| 3 | 4 | 4 |
| 4 | 5 | 6 |
| 5 | 6 | 7 |
| 6 | 8 | 8 |
| 7 | 9 | 9 |
| 8 | 11 | 11 |
| 9 | 15 | 15 |
| Richest | 43 | 40 |
| Total | 100 | 100 |
| D10/D2 = 14.8 | | |
| D10/D9 = 2.8 | | |
| Gini coefficient = 0.421 | | |

received 14.8 times more income than the second decile, and 2.8 times more than the ninth decile.

The richest households were large landowners, who received high incomes from leasing out land and from non-agricultural sources. Members of the largest landowning households did not live in the village. They resided in towns nearby having leased out most of their land, and derived large rental incomes from agricultural land.

## Sources and Composition of Household Incomes

Only 39 per cent of the households in Zhapur received incomes from crop production. Another 51 per cent of households received agricultural wage incomes. Incidence of tenancy was high in the village and 19 per cent of households received rental income from agricultural land. Animal husbandry was a common occupation and 68 per cent of households received small incomes from animal resources. However, unlike Alabujanahalli and Siresandra, there were few households that raised bovine animals in Zhapur; smaller animals like goats, sheep, and poultry were raised here. The primary sector contributed 47 per cent of total household incomes in the village (Table 22).

**Table 21** *Number and proportion of households receiving incomes from different sources, Zhapur*

| Source | No. of households | Percentage |
|---|---|---|
| Crop production | 43 | 39 |
| Animal resources | 74 | 68 |
| Agricultural labour | 56 | 51 |
| Rental income from agricultural land | 21 | 19 |
| Primary | 92 | 84 |
| Non-agricultural labour | 54 | 50 |
| Salaries | 20 | 18 |
| Business and trade earnings | 19 | 17 |
| Rental income from machinery | 3 | 3 |
| Rental income from other assets | 2 | 2 |
| Artisanal work and work at traditional caste calling | 1 | 1 |
| Other sources | 6 | 6 |
| Secondary and tertiary sectors | 79 | 73 |
| Transfers and remittances | 51 | 47 |
| Total household income | 109 | 100 |

**Table 22** *Distribution of total household income, by source, Zhapur, 2008–09* in per cent

| Source | Share |
|---|---|
| Crop production | 25 |
| Animal resources | 6 |
| Agricultural labour | 11 |
| Rental income from agricultural land | 6 |
| Primary | 47 |
| Non-agricultural labour | 31 |
| Salaries | 9 |
| Business and trade earnings | 7 |
| Rental income from machinery | 1 |
| Rental income from other assets | 0 |
| Artisanal work and work at traditional caste calling | 1 |
| Other sources | 0 |
| Secondary and tertiary sectors | 49 |
| Transfers and remittances | 4 |
| Total household income | 100 |

Non-agricultural sources of income played a vital role in the household economy. There was a stone quarry nearby and many workers in the village (including a few children) were employed in the quarry. Workers were also employed in non-agricultural wage employment in nearby villages and towns. Thus, 50 per cent of the households in Zhapur received incomes from non-agricultural wage employment. Non-agricultural wages were the single largest source of income in the village, contributing 31 per cent of the total village income. Average non-agricultural wage rates were Rs 122 per day for males, which was substantially higher than the agricultural wage rate of Rs 96 per day (Chapter 9).

Another 18 per cent of households were engaged in salaried employment, and 17 per cent in business and trade. These were petty jobs in the private sector such as that of lorry driver, machine operator, private schoolteacher and in small businesses. Hence, the share of incomes from salaries in total household income was only 9 per cent, and that from business and trade only 7 per cent.

The secondary and tertiary sectors constituted 49 per cent of total household incomes. Four per cent of the household incomes were sourced from transfers and remittances.

### Income Disparities across Castes

The population of Zhapur comprised Caste Hindus, SCs and STs. The mean per capita income of Caste Hindu households was higher than that of SC and ST households (Table 23). However, the median income levels show that Caste Hindu households had the lowest income among the three caste groups. There are two reasons for this apparent contradiction. First, Caste Hindus were a heterogeneous group; among them, the Lingayat households received higher incomes than the others. Secondly, Caste Hindus owned land and were engaged in crop production. As we can see from Table 25, while 45 per cent of the household income of this group accrued from crop production, SC and ST households received a much smaller income share from cultivation. We have discussed previously the problem of low and unstable agricultural production in Zhapur. Thus, many Caste Hindu households made losses in agriculture and this contributed to variations in income within the group. SC households received the lowest incomes on average, lower than ST households.

The distribution of households across per capita income deciles shows a picture that was very typical of the village (Table 24). Households in all caste groups were more or less evenly distributed across income deciles,

**Table 23** *Per capita household income, by caste, Zhapur, 2008–09* in Rs

| Caste group | Number of households | Mean | Median |
|---|---|---|---|
| Caste Hindu | 48 | 16,020 | 8,292 |
| Scheduled Caste (SC) | 46 | 9,415 | 8,773 |
| Scheduled Tribe (ST) | 14 | 10,732 | 10,750 |
| All | 109* | 12,494 | 8,499 |

*Note*: * The total number of households was 109; one Muslim household is included in "All."

**Table 24** *Distribution of households, by caste, by per capita income deciles, Zhapur, 2008–09* in per cent

| Decile | Caste Hindu | Scheduled Caste (SC) | Scheduled Tribe (ST) |
|---|---|---|---|
| ≤2118 | 15 | 4 | 14 |
| 2119–4109 | 10 | 11 | 7 |
| 4110–5565 | 10 | 11 | 7 |
| 5566–7476 | 6 | 13 | 14 |
| 7477–8499 | 15 | 9 | 0 |
| 8500–9938 | 4 | 17 | 0 |
| 9939–11693 | 10 | 7 | 21 |
| 11694–15716 | 6 | 15 | 7 |
| 15717–21086 | 6 | 13 | 14 |
| 21087+ | 17 | 0 | 14 |
| All | 100 | 100 | 100 |

except in the richest income decile. There were no SC households in the richest decile, whereas 17 per cent of Caste Hindu households and 14 per cent of ST households were in the top income decile.

Table 25 shows the composition of household incomes for each caste group. The major sources of income for Caste Hindus were crop production (45 per cent) and leasing out of agricultural land (10 per cent). They also received income from agricultural labour (12 per cent) and salaries (11 per cent). SC households earned the largest portion of their income from non-agricultural labour (62 per cent). They also received incomes from agricultural labour (17 per cent) and salaries (9 per cent). SC households were not engaged in cultivation, and only 1 per cent of their household income came from crop production. Non-agricultural labour (35 per cent), and business and trade (28 per cent) were the major sources of income for ST

**Table 25** *Composition of annual household income, by caste, Zhapur, 2009–10* in per cent

| Source | Caste Hindu | Scheduled Caste (SC) | Scheduled Tribe (ST) |
|---|---|---|---|
| Crop production | 45 | 1 | 2 |
| Animal resources | 6 | 5 | 10 |
| Agricultural labour | 6 | 17 | 17 |
| Rental income from agricultural land | 10 | 1 | 1 |
| Non-agricultural labour | 12 | 62 | 35 |
| Salaries | 11 | 9 | 0 |
| Business and trade earnings | 5 | 1 | 28 |
| Rental income from machinery | 1 | 0 | |
| Rental income from other assets | 0 | | |
| Artisanal work and work at traditional caste calling | | | 5 |
| Other sources | 0 | 0 | 0 |
| Transfers and remittances | 4 | 5 | 2 |
| Total household income | 100 | 100 | 100 |

households. The ST households in the top income decile received incomes from business and trade. Seventeen per cent of the household incomes of ST households were also sourced from agricultural labour. Thus we see some specialization of occupations across caste groups in the village. Caste Hindu households mostly received incomes from land – from cultivation and rent. SC households specialised in non-agricultural labour; ST households specialised in business and trade, and non-agricultural labour.

## Distribution of Household Incomes across Socio-economic Classes

Table 26 describes the incomes that accrued to different socio-economic classes in Zhapur village during the survey year. There were four large landowning households in the village in the class of Landlords. These households were among the richest, their share in total household income in the village being 22 per cent (Table 26). The largest landowner in the village had 60 acres of land. Apart from cultivation, his family also received rental incomes from land, salaried jobs, remittances, and business. The mean per capita annual income of this class was Rs 74,634. The Landlord class comprised a few households, constituting 2 per cent of total households, and received 7 per cent of the total income. The mean per capita income of Peasant 1 households in the village was Rs 44,737. Their income came from

**Table 26** *Distribution of annual household incomes, by socio-economic classes, Zhapur, 2008–09* in per cent

| Class | Share in total no. of households | Share in total incomes |
|---|---|---|
| Landlord | 4 | 22 |
| Peasant 1 | 2 | 7 |
| Peasant 2 | 6 | 4 |
| Peasant 3 | 26 | 12 |
| All peasants | 34 | 23 |
| Manual workers | 47 | 38 |
| Business activity/self-employed | 6 | 6 |
| Salaried persons | 6 | 6 |
| Rents and remittances | 5 | 6 |
| Total | 100 | 100 |

**Table 27** *Mean per capita annual income, by classes, Zhapur, 2008–09* in Rs

| Class | Mean |
|---|---|
| Landlord | 74,634 |
| Peasant 1 | 44,737 |
| Peasant 2 | 7,087 |
| Peasant 3 | 6,026 |
| Manual workers | 10,111 |
| Business activity/self-employed | 13,076 |
| Salaried persons | 12,909 |
| Rents and remittances | 16,775 |
| Total | 12,494 |

crops, rental income from machinery, petty business, and non-agricultural wage earnings.

Peasant 2 and Peasant 3 households received the lowest incomes in the village, Rs 7,087 and Rs 6,026 per capita per annum, respectively. Manual worker households received slightly higher incomes than poor peasant households (Rs 10,111). Manual worker households were engaged in both agricultural and non-agricultural wage employment. Salaried and self-employed households received incomes slightly higher than Manual workers, but much lower than rich peasant households.

Thus, the Landlord households in the village and the rich peasants clearly stood apart from the rest of the village. They had secured sources of incomes from agriculture due to large land holdings. These two classes constituted only 6 per cent of all households.

### Changes in Household Incomes, 2008–09 to 2013–14

Two major changes occurred in Zhapur between 2009 and 2014. First, Kalaburagi airport was constructed near Zhapur, which accelerated the process of urbanisation and deepened rural–urban linkages. Land prices increased and new opportunities opened up for non-agricultural employment. The incomes of Manual worker households increased due to the increase in the number of days of employment in quarry fields (now there are three quarry fields in the village) and in real wages (from Rs 236 to Rs 420 for mining work[3]). The second major change in the village was in irrigation, on account of a tubewell installed by an NGO. Instability of agricultural production is likely to have lessened due to the availability of irrigation, thus increasing agricultural output and incomes. Altogether, there was a perceptible increase of household incomes in the village over the last five years.

## Some Issues Concerning Household Incomes in the Study Villages

In this section we take up some issues that emerge from our analysis and that may have some implications for policies on incomes and livelihoods in the villages. We use the 2014 case studies to make our point. The issues we would like to focus on are: the crisis of agriculture and its implications for incomes of poor peasant households; the importance of income diversification, and how income diversification strategies are mediated through village hierarchies of caste and class; and the contribution of sericulture and dairy farming to household incomes.

### Crisis of Agriculture and Incomes of Poor Peasant Households

In each of the three villages studied, we found that the mean incomes of the poorer sections of the peasantry were substantially lower than the village mean. In Alabujanahalli and Zhapur poor peasant households received lower incomes than Manual worker households. This indicates a crisis of agricultural incomes particularly for the poor peasantry.

---

[3] Obtained after deflating by the Consumer Price Index for Agricultural Labourers (CPIAL).

Across the three villages, 12 to 48 per cent of poor peasant households incurred losses in crop production. In Alabujanahalli, out of 58 Peasant 4 households, 7 incurred losses in crop production; in Siresandra, 8 out of 33 Peasant 3 households incurred losses; and in Zhapur, 13 out of 28 Peasant 3 households incurred losses in crop production. In contrast, none of the Peasant 1 or rich peasant households in the three villages incurred losses in crop production during the survey year. The number of middle peasants incurring losses was also small, except in Zhapur. Thus, in a village like Zhapur where agriculture is unirrigated and risky, poor peasants were particularly vulnerable to income shocks arising out of losses in agriculture. The reasons for this are varied, and range from lack of access to irrigation and higher irrigation costs, to indivisibilities in input costs and lower output prices received by poor peasants (see Chapter 8). Poor peasant households received a significant share of their incomes from agricultural and non-agricultural manual labour. They were not able to diversify to high-end, non-farm sources of income generation due to their small asset base and lack of skills. We shall illustrate this with a few case studies.

The poorest peasant household in Alabujanahalli is a Vokkaliga household with 2 acres of land. The household cultivated summer paddy, winter paddy, sugarcane, and mulberry crops in the survey year, and made a net loss of Rs 21,480 from crop production due to low production and crop failure (due to excessive rain and disease). The household was able to earn Rs 6,089 from animal husbandry and non-agricultural labour, and had no other source of income. As a result, it had a negative income in 2008–09. The poorest peasant household in Siresandra was a Vokkaliga household with only 2 acres of land and an annual income of only Rs 3,443 from crop production. The household received Rs 9,158 from animal resources and had no other source of income. The poorest peasant household in Zhapur was a Madivala household with 2 acres of land. The household made a net loss of Rs 20,071 due to crop failure. The only other income it received was from animal resources (Rs 10,634). Total household income was negative during the survey year. In all three cases we see that the major source of vulnerability for poor peasant households was low income from crop production, and inability to diversify to other occupations and income sources.

Even the best-off among the poor peasants had very modest annual household incomes, slightly above Rs 2 lakhs in Alabujanahalli and Siresandra, and Rs 1 lakh in Zhapur. The major difference in the income composition of these better-off households from the poorest households was income received from sources *other than* crop production and animal husbandry.

**Table 28** *Income composition of lowest and highest income-receiving households among peasant households in the study villages, 2008–09* in Rs per annum

| Village | Caste group | Crop production | Animal resources | Other incomes | Total household income |
|---------|-------------|-----------------|------------------|---------------|------------------------|
| *Poorest* | | | | | |
| Alabujanahalli | Vokkaliga | −21480 | 1825 | 4264 | −15391 |
| Siresandra | Vokkaliga | 3443 | 9158 | 0 | 12601 |
| Zhapur | Madivala (Dhobi) | −20071 | 10634 | 585 | −8852 |
| *Richest* | | | | | |
| Alabujanahalli | Vokkaliga | 141436 | 13280 | 49368 | 204084 |
| Siresandra | Vokkaliga | −223 | 15412 | 209163 | 224352 |
| Zhapur | Vaddaru | 9076 | 0 | 100825 | 109901 |

The highest income-receiving peasant household in Alabujanahalli received Rs 34,526 from sericulture, Rs 10,000 from remittances, and Rs 4,842 from rents. The highest income-receiving peasant household in Siresandra received Rs 65,718 from sericulture and Rs 13,340 from rents. The highest income-receiving peasant household in Zhapur received Rs 86,250 from non-agricultural wages and Rs 14,450 from agricultural wages. Incomes received from these sources allowed the households to mitigate the effects of low agricultural incomes to the same extent.

## Income Diversification, Caste, and Class

The composition of household incomes, or how a household's income portfolio is diversified, determines the income levels of a household. At the same time, a household's access to different sources of income is mediated by its economic and social position in the village, that is, by caste and class. We discuss a few case studies to understand the relationship between household incomes, income composition, caste, and class.

Let us first consider the richest household in each of the three villages. In all three villages, the richest households were from the dominant caste in the respective village: Vokkaliga in Alabujanahalli and Siresandra, and Lingayat in Zhapur. In all three villages, the richest households belonged to the highest socio-economic class – Rich capitalist farmer in Alabujanahalli, and Peasant 1 in Siresandra and Zhapur – signifying that they owned relatively large land holdings and received substantial incomes from agriculture.

The richest households received incomes from the most remunerative sources available in the village. Even though incomes from land and agriculture formed the basis of their economic and social power, they have also diversified to other remunerative sources of income. The richest household in Alabujanahalli derived only 11 per cent of its total household income (Rs 2.14 lakhs) from agriculture and animal husbandry. The household did not engage in sericulture. The major income for this household came from business and trade (36.9 per cent), and rental income from other assets (37.2 per cent). The household owned a paddy mill and received income from sale of vehicles. One household member was a salaried employee. In Siresandra, the richest household received 73.4 per cent of its total household income from the primary sector, of which 36.7 per cent came from sericulture. This household received 19.9 per cent of household income from houses and buildings. The richest household in Zhapur received 93.4 per cent of its household income from agriculture and animal husbandry. The remaining income was rental income from tractors and threshing machine, and from a flour mill and shop. While the degree to which rich households diversified to other sources of income depended on the opportunities present in their location, it is clear that they diversified to asset-based and remunerative sources of incomes such as rental incomes from land and buildings, business and trade, which further strengthened their economic position. They were able to exploit the best opportunities outside agriculture available in the village and nearby due to their caste and class status, which gave them access to specific assets and social networks.

At the other extreme, it is also true that households that were not able to diversify outside agriculture were vulnerable to temporary income shocks in agriculture, as they were unable to make good their losses from incomes from other sources. Repeated shocks could deplete household savings and render these households poor in the medium to long term. Let us take the example of the resident Lingayat landlord household in Zhapur. The household owned 60 acres of land, of which 30 acres were rented out on share contract. In 2009–10, the household made a net loss of Rs 96,575 on the self-cultivated land and Rs 76,650 on the leased-out land. The household had a small positive income from animal resources and received no income from any other source. During the survey year, the household had the lowest income in the village due to the large agricultural loss.

Households with the lowest current incomes in the survey year in the three villages were either middle or poor peasant households that made losses in agriculture and had no other sources of income, or Manual worker

**Table 29** *Details of household income for lowest household incomes in 2008–09* in Rs

| Village | Class | Caste group | Total income | Major sources of income |
|---|---|---|---|---|
| Alabujanahalli | Peasant 2 | Vokkaliga | 4051 | Crop income (−14124), Animal resources (5393), Sericulture (12782) |
| Alabujanahalli | Peasant 4 | Vokkaliga | −15391 | Crop income (−21480), Animal resources (1825), non-agricultural labour (4264) |
| Alabujanahalli | Peasant 4 | Adi Karnataka (SC) | 6427 | Crop income (−1193), Non-agricultural labour (820), Transfers (6800) |
| Siresandra | Peasant 2 | Vokkaliga | 3430 | Crop income (−1043), Animal resources (3873) |
| Siresandra | Manual worker | Mala (SC) | 7092 | Manual labour (5592) |
| Zhapur | Manual worker | Kabbaliga | 500 | Agricultural labour (500) |
| Zhapur | Landlord | Lingayat | −164515 | Crop income (−96575), Rent from land (−76650), Animal resources (8710) |
| Zhapur | Manual worker | Vaddaru (SC) | 3800 | Manual labour (3800) |

households. Among the rich there was a very strong correlation between caste, class, and incomes. Lack of access to remunerative sources of income outside agriculture made households of all socio-economic categories vulnerable to income shocks and transitory poverty. This was due to the risky nature of agriculture in India, an uncertainty induced by both natural and market conditions.

## Allied Activities: Dairying and Sericulture

Activities allied to agriculture were often part of an integrated production system within the household as they presented economies of scope in concurrent use of inputs and outputs, and utilisation of family labour. Such activities also enabled households to earn supplementary incomes and mitigate risks in agriculture. Dairying and sericulture were two such activities in two of the villages that had well-developed markets and were in high demand, contributed significantly to household incomes, and were carried out primarily with family labour and female labour within the homestead.

*Income from dairy farming*

Income from animal resources, particularly dairying, was an important source of income for households in Alabujanahalli and Siresandra. About 7 and 10 per cent, respectively, of total household incomes in the two villages were obtained from animal resources.

In Alabujanahalli, animal resources were not an important source of income for the Rich peasant households, but most of the lower strata of peasantry received significant income from animal husbandry. The major types of animals reared were milch cows, buffaloes, and sheep. Most peasant households kept bullocks for ploughing and renting out bullock-carts. In Alabujanahalli, the mean income (net of expenses) from dairying for households that reared cows and buffaloes was Rs 10,089 per annum in 2008–09. PP, a poor peasant household, raised two milch cows, one calf, and a sheep. The total annual milk production was 1,750 litres and manure production was 10 carts. The total income from animal husbandry was Rs 41,878 net of all expenses. In 2014, as part of our case studies, we observed that the scale of milch cattle rearing in the village had increased because of the intervention of a dairy cooperative.

In Siresandra, the mean income (net of expenses) from dairying of households that reared cows and buffaloes was Rs 29,538 per annum in 2008–09. Households that reared sheep received incomes of about Rs 25,841 per annum. NG, a rich peasant household, raised two milch buffaloes, two milch cows, four calves, and 80 sheep. The total income from animal husbandry was Rs 2,19,400. Milk production from the cows was 20 litres per day per cow for 180 days, 18 litres per day per cow for 120 days, and 0 litre per day per cow for 60 days. Milk production from the buffaloes was 4 litres per day per buffalo for 180 days. Last year, the household sold 40 sheep, at Rs 2,500 per animal. The total manure production was reported to be 30 carts.

Hence, households that engaged in dairying were able to receive substantial incomes. However, as we have seen in the previous analysis, dairy farming also requires access to fodder, and hence landless, poor, and Dalit households were not able to rear dairy animals.

*Income from sericulture*

Sericulture is an important activity in Karnataka, and gives periodic income and employment opportunities to rural households, especially for women. Out of the three study village we studied, large and commercial-scale sericulture was practised in Siresandra, and small-scale sericulture was prevalent in Alabujanahalli. A detailed description of the sericulture in these two villages is presented as an Appendix to this chapter.

## Conclusions

This chapter has described the levels and sources of household incomes in the three study villages of Karnataka. The average per capita income in the three villages was Rs 17,543 in Alabujanahalli, Rs 22,600 in Siresandra, and Rs 12,500 in Zhapur, in 2008–09. The head-count ratio (HCR) of poverty was lower than the State HCR in Alabujanahalli, and higher in Zhapur. The data showed systematic differences in household incomes across caste groups and socio-economic classes in the three villages. The average incomes received by Dalit households were less than 60 per cent of average incomes received by Caste Hindu households. Though none of the three villages had a class of Landlords or Rich capitalist farmers, incomes received by the topmost classes of the peasantry were many times higher than incomes received by poor peasants and Manual workers.

The results also showed that though 84 to 100 per cent of households in the villages received incomes from the primary sector, incomes from non-agricultural sources played a very important role in the households' economic well-being. Incomes from secondary and tertiary sources constituted 27 per cent of all incomes in Siresandra, 42 per cent in Alabujanahalli, and 47 per cent in Zhapur. In Siresandra and Alabujanahalli, households were diversified within the primary sector as dairying and sericulture provided significant incomes.

Along with the changes taking place in agriculture, the nature of the non-agricultural sector in India also plays an interesting role in differentiation of the peasantry. Our case studies showed that the rich peasants in the three villages were able to diversify to remunerative, asset-based non-agricultural incomes and occupations, such as business and trade, rental incomes from land and buildings, and thus strengthen their economic position. On the other hand, peasant households who were unable to diversify to non-agricultural employment faced risks in agriculture, with periodic crop losses and adverse market conditions, and were particularly susceptible to recurrent income shocks. Thus, while new forms of non-agricultural incomes are creating a class of rich farmers with high stakes in these forms of rural non-agricultural incomes and employment, sections of the poor peasantry who are unable to find gainful non-agricultural employment are facing increasing risk of impoverishment.

# References

Bakshi, A., Das, A., and Swaminathan, M. (2014), "Household Incomes in Rural India: Results from PARI village Studies," paper presented at the Tenth Anniversary Conference of the Foundation for Agrarian Studies, Kochi, January 9 to 12, 2014.

Foundation for Agrarian Studies (FAS) (2015), "Calculation of Household Incomes: A Note on Methodology," available at http://fas.org.in/wp-content/themes/zakat/pdf/Survey-method-tool/Calculation%20of%20Household%20Incomes%20-%20A%20Note%20on%20Methodology.pdf, viewed on July 31, 2016.

Sen, Abhijit, and Bhatia, M. S. (2004), *State of the Indian Farmer: A Millennium Study*, vol. 14, *Cost of Cultivation and Farm Income*, Academic Publishers, New Delhi.

APPENDIX

# A Note on Sericulture in Two Study Villages

*Arindam Das*

Sericulture in Karnataka involves the cultivation of mulberry and rearing of silkworm for production of silk. The silkworm requires, on average, two months of preparation for harvesting of cocoons. Sericulture is mostly practised by small land holders. It is a labour-intensive activity and requires attention throughout the year. It gives employment to family labour throughout the year, and ensures periodic income to medium and small land holders. Sericulture was an important activity in two of the three study villages: Alabujanahalli in Mandya district, and Siresandra in Kolar district. Mulberry is a perennial crop and can be harvested for 10 years. So, ownership of land is an important prerequisite for undertaking sericulture. In this note, I examine the productivity of cocoons per 100 disease-free-layings(dfl) or disease-free silkworm eggs, cost of cultivation, and income from sericulture.

## Process of Sericulture

In Alabujanahalli, sericulture was practised by small and marginal farmers. Thirty-four per cent of households in the village derived incomes from sericulture, but most of these households belonged to medium and small peasant classes. Sericulture was a major activity in Siresandra village too, where it was undertaken on a commercial scale. All classes of farmers were engaged in sericulture in Siresandra, with rich peasant or Peasant 1 households undertaking sericulture on a large scale. In Alabujanahalli, most peasants cultivated CB gold and V1 varieties of silkworm. In Siresandra, peasants reared Kolar Gold, a multivoltine hybrid (MV), and China gold varieties of silkworm. The rearing started with the purchase of "disease-free-layings" (dfl) or larvae. In Alabujanahalli, most cultivators used larvae, but in Siresandra, most cultivators used eggs instead of larvae. The rearing of silkworms has to be undertaken in a separate place to ensure protection from disease. In the study villages, the majority of small farmers had separate sheds built within their homesteads. In Siresandra, large-scale cultivators had separate rearing sheds, some built with government subsidies. Apart from rearing sheds, specific equipment required for silkworm-rearing includes wooden trays (*meju*), bamboo-rearing stands, bamboo round trays, and *chandrike* (cocoonage). The scale of cultivation depends on the *meju*, a wooden tray containing the various stages of insects. The *meju* has four steps and a life of 15 to 20 years. *Chandrike* or cocoonage is a circular basket used to facilitate worms making their cocoons. For every 100 eggs, they need 50 to 55 *chandrike*. The life of a *chandrike* is two to three years. Sericulture is labour-intensive and family labour is largely used in this activity. Hired labour is mainly engaged for removing cocoons from the *chandrike*, and the wage for hired labour is usually piece-rated (per *chandrike*).

Normally, five to six cycles of production can be completed in one year. In the study villages, in summer, one cycle took 27 to 30 days, and in winter, it took 35 to 40 days. The yield per 100 eggs was 60 to 80 kg of cocoons. The silkworm is sensitive to climatic changes and suffers from many diseases, so protection by use of lime and other disinfectants was required.

### Landholding and Size of Operation

Land is a basic prerequisite for sericulture. The size of operation depends on the extent of cultivation of mulberry and the number of disease-free-layings eggs reared per batch. In Alabujanahalli, the average operational holding of silkworm rearers was 2.3 acres of land. Farmers with less than 1 acre of land constituted 21 per cent of all sericulture cultivators. This was not surprising as sericulture requires a large amount of family labour, and members of rich and medium households are reluctant to engage in sericulture. They have access to other sources of income (business) given the vicinity of towns. In Siresandra, about 20 per cent of households obtained incomes from sericulture. The majority of the farmers here practised sericulture on a large scale. The average land holding of a sericulture cultivator was 4.2 acres. The largest landholder in the village also practised large-scale sericulture.

Table 1 shows that 89 per cent of households had mulberry acreage equal to or less than 1 acre, indicating that the size of mulberry gardens was

Table 1 *Distribution of sericulture households by size of mulberry holding* in per cent

| Size of mulberry holdings (in acres) | Alabujanahalli | Siresandra |
| --- | --- | --- |
| Less than 1 | 89 | 30 |
| 1–2 | 11 | 33 |
| 2–3 | 0 | 19 |
| 3 and above | 0 | 19 |
| All | 100 | 100 |
| Average size | 0.5 | 1.81 |

**Table 2** *Distribution of households by scale of silkworm rearing in dfl per cycle* in number and per cent

| No of dfls/cycle | Alabujanahalli | | Siresandra | |
|---|---|---|---|---|
| | Number | Per cent | Number | Per cent |
| ≤ 100 | 82 | 94 | 10 | 38 |
| 100–200 | 4 | 4 | 8 | 31 |
| 200–300 | 1 | 2 | 3 | 12 |
| 300–500 | 0 | 0 | 5 | 19 |
| All | 87 | 100 | 26 | 100 |

predominantly small in Alabujanahalli. In Siresandra, about 60 per cent of households had less than 2 acres of land under mulberry cultivation, but 19 per cent had 3 acres or more and the largest land holding was 10 acres. The average size of mulberry holding was 0.5 acre in Alabujanahalli , whereas it was 1.81 acres in Siresandra.

In Alabujanahalli, 94 per cent of households reared less than 100 dfl of eggs, suggesting a picture of small-scale sericulture (Table 2). In Siresandra, 19 per cent of farmers reared 300 to 500 dfl of eggs in every batch.

## Cost of Cultivation

The cost of production or paid-out cost of rearing silkworms includes the cost of cultivation of mulberry, purchase of mulberry leaf (if required in excess of own production), cost of larvae/eggs, the value of chemicals, hired labour, cost of paper, costs of owned and hired machinery, interest on

**Table 3** *Average cost of cultivation of silkworm cocoons, by item and village per 100 dfl* in Rs

| Item | Alabujanahalli | | Siresandra | |
|---|---|---|---|---|
| | Cost | Per cent | Cost | Per cent |
| Larvae/eggs | 702 | 13 | 488 | 8 |
| Mulberry leaf | 3029 | 56 | 3217 | 55 |
| Disinfectants and other chemicals | 347 | 7 | 236 | 4 |
| Hired labour cost | 493 | 9 | 1228 | 21 |
| Rent for *chandrike* | 355 | 7 | 339 | 6 |
| Other costs | 389 | 7 | 371 | 6 |
| Total costs | 5317 | 100 | 6523 | 100 |

working capital, depreciation of own machinery, and insurance expenses.

There are two distinct activities and costs associated with sericulture. The first pertains to the production of mulberry leaf and the second to silkworm rearing, an indoor activity. The cost of cultivation of mulberry has been discussed in Chapter 8, as part of crop cultivation. Turning to the cost of cocoon production, the average cost of cultivation of 100 dfls was Rs 6,523 in Siresendra and it was Rs 5317 in Alabujanahalli. In terms of cost structure (Table 3), in Siresandra, mulberry leaves accounted for 55 per cent of the total cost of silkworm rearing, followed by labour costs (21 per cent) and other costs. In Alabujanahalli, the cost of mulberry accounted for 56 per cent of total costs. The share of purchased eggs/larvae in total cost was 13 per cent.

## Productivity and Income

I now turn to productivity and income from sericulture. The average yield of silk cocoons was found to be 74 kg per 100 dfl. Productivity was higher than the village average (78 kg per 100 dfl) among Peasant 1 households in Siresandra, and lower than the village average among Peasant 3 households. In Alabujanahalli, average productivity was similar to that in Siresandra, but most rearers were small or marginal cultivators and used family labour for sericulture. Here productivity was higher than the village average among Peasant 3 households.

The total income obtained in a year from sericulture was Rs 18,911 in Alabujanahalli. In Siresandra, the average income derived from sericulture was Rs 85,688. Among the socio-economic classes in Siresandra, Peasant 1 households derived an income of Rs 162,848, followed by Peasant 2 and Peasant 3 households (Tables 4 and 5).

Turning to per acre returns, the average income was Rs 56,374 per year in Siresandra and Rs 43,224 in Alabujanahalli. In Alabujanahalli, per acre returns were highest for Peasant 4 households and lowest for Peasant 1

**Table 4** *Average net income from sericulture, by socio-economic class, Siresandra* in Rs per year

| Class | Average net income |
|---|---|
| Peasant 1 | 162848 |
| Peasant 2 | 88203 |
| Peasant 3 | 48042 |
| All | 85688 |

**Table 5** *Average net income from sericulture, by socio-economic classes, Alabujanahalli* in Rs per year

| Socio-economic class | Mean income |
|---|---|
| Peasant 1 | 3665 |
| Peasant 2 | 26954 |
| Peasant 3 | 17663 |
| Peasant 4 | 18441 |
| Manual worker 1 | 11971 |
| Others | 14849 |
| All | 18912 |

**Table 6** *Average net income per acre of mulberry holding, Alabujanahalli* in Rs per year

| Class | Average income |
|---|---|
| Peasant 1 | 4311 |
| Peasant 2 | 35610 |
| Peasant 3 | 39634 |
| Peasant 4 | 55257 |
| Manual worker 1* | 42271 |
| Others | 31581 |
| All | 43224 |

*Note*: * Only one household

**Table 7** *Average net income per acre of mulberry holding, Siresandra* in rupees per year

| Class | Average income |
|---|---|
| Peasant 1 | 52394 |
| Peasant 2 | 59880 |
| Peasant 3 | 52015 |
| All | 56374 |

households (Table 6). In Siresandra, net income per acre was as high as Rs 59,880 for Peasant 2 households (Table 7).

## Conclusions

Sericulture was an important source of income for households in two study villages. It also provided substantial employment for women as it uses family labour. Land was the most important requirement for practising sericulture on a large scale. Sericulture was viable even for small and marginal farmers. Nevertheless, we observed during our revisit in 2014 that cultivators were uprooting mulberry and switching to other crops. There may be three reasons for the shift out of sericulture.

First, the major operation in sericulture is silkworm rearing, which requires utmost care and attention. A major constraint is the availability of labour. Most big farmers did not rear silkworms due to unavailability of family and hired labour. Secondly, the occurrence of diseases is a major problem for sericulture. A few households reported crop failure or low production due to diseases affecting silkworms. Thirdly, volatility of cocoon price is also a constraint for silkworm rearing. Cultivators are forced to sell cocoons at prevailing prices because once the moth is out of the cocoon, the cocoon becomes useless for reeling. When cocoons are sold at low prices, income falls and availability of capital for the next cycle falls.

# 11

## State of Rural Banking in Karnataka: With Special Reference to the Three Study Districts

### Pallavi Chavan

This chapter analyses the state of rural banking in Karnataka using secondary data on banking and rural households, with special reference to the three study districts: namely, Mandya, Kalaburagi, and Kolar.

Rural credit in India is provided by three major agencies: commercial banks, credit cooperatives, and regional rural banks (RRBs). The focus in this chapter is on rural credit provided by commercial banks and RRBs, given: (a) the lack of availability of updated data on rural cooperatives; and (b) the fact that commercial banks (including RRBs) have emerged as a more important source of rural credit in India in recent years (see Chavan 2013).

The policy on rural banking in India has undergone major changes since 1991, with the initiation of the policy of financial liberalisation. Studies on rural credit regard the decade of the 1990s and the first half of the 2000s as a period of reversal of many of the developmental measures instituted since the nationalisation of banks in 1969 (Shetty 2005; Ramachandran and Swaminathan 2005; and Chavan 2005). This reversal is reflected in the liberalisation of branch licensing policy and interest rate regulations, dilution of the definitions of priority sectors of lending, and also partial privatisation of public sector banks.[1] Studies on rural banking also note a striking decline in the spread of rural banking in India since the early 1990s. Further, there were distinct shifts in the distribution of bank credit across regions, socio-economic classes, and sectors of the economy in this period (Chavan 2012).

Geographically, the major losers in this period were States from the

---

[1] While the government did not dilute its stake in public sector banks completely, the share held by it was brought down close to a floor of 51 per cent; see Sathye (2003) and Chavan (2012).

underbanked regions in the country: the north-eastern, eastern and central regions. Sectorally, agriculture and micro and small enterprises (MSEs) lost out in terms of share in bank credit. The socially and economically backward classes including small and marginal cultivators, agricultural labourers, and Scheduled Castes and Scheduled Tribes (SCs and STs) too experienced increased marginalisation from the formal banking system (ibid.).

After 2005, however, there has been an emphasis on including the excluded sections/sectors into the fold of formal banking with the adoption of the policy of financial inclusion (ibid.). As a part of this policy, the branch authorisation policy was adopted, which gave freedom to banks to open branches according to an annual authorised plan but with the condition that at least 25 per cent of these branches had to be opened in unbanked rural centres. There was also a renewed commitment towards improving the allocation of bank credit to agriculture with the adoption of the Comprehensive Credit Policy in 2004–05 (see Ramakumar and Chavan 2014). Studies show some signs of revival in the spread of rural banking in India after 2005 (ibid.).

Karnataka belongs to the south of India, which is known to be a relatively well-banked region in the country. The State has often been described as the "cradle of banking" in India, given that the origins of many of the public sector banks in the country can be traced back to this State.

This chapter analyses trends in banking in general, and rural banking in particular, in Karnataka since the early 1990s. The discussion on Karnataka is based on the basic indicators of banking development, viz., branch intensity (persons per bank branch), bank credit per capita, bank deposit per capita, and sectoral distribution of bank credit and is presented in the first, second, and third sections of this chapter. Using similar indicators, in the fourth section, the chapter provides an analysis of rural banking in the three districts of Karnataka in which the three villages studied under the Project on Agrarian Relations in India (PARI) of the Foundation for Agrarian Studies (FAS) are located. The idea is to bring out the relative position of these three districts within the State as far as the development of rural banking is concerned. This section focuses on the trends during the 2000s in order to give a background to the discussion in the next chapter on the rural credit system in the study villages. The fifth section of this chapter provides concluding observations.

The major source of data used in this chapter is *Basic Statistical Returns of Scheduled Commercial Banks in India* (*BSR*), an annual publication on scheduled commercial banks brought out by the Reserve Bank of India (RBI). The *BSR* provides data on rural branches and the rural credit portfolio of scheduled commercial banks (including RRBs). The study also makes use of some information from the *All-India Debt and Investment Survey* (*AIDIS*) – a decennial survey conducted by the National Sample Survey Organisation (NSSO) – to give an overall perspective of the nature of the rural credit system in the State of Karnataka.

# Banking in Karnataka

Karnataka stands out as one of the States with a better reach of banking in India. In 2013, the branch intensity (persons per bank branch) in the State was 8,300 persons, as against the all-India average of 11,300 persons (Table 1). As already mentioned, there was a setback to the spread of banking in India after 1990. This can be seen from the rise in the number of persons per

**Table 1** *Population per bank branch, Karnataka and India, 1975–2013* '000 persons

| Year | Karnataka | India |
|------|-----------|-------|
| Phase of increase | | |
| 1975 | 18.5 | 32.5 |
| 1980 | 13.9 | 20.8 |
| 1985 | 10.4 | 14.3 |
| Phase of decline | | |
| 1990 | 10.2 | 13.8 |
| 1994 | 10.5 | 14.3 |
| 1995 | 10.8 | 14.4 |
| 2000 | 10.8 | 14.9 |
| 2005 | 10.9 | 15.5 |
| Phase of revival | | |
| 2006 | 11.0 | 15.6 |
| 2007 | 10.8 | 15.3 |
| 2008 | 10.4 | 14.7 |
| 2009 | 10.0 | 14.2 |
| 2010 | 9.6 | 13.6 |
| 2011 | 9.4 | 13.0 |
| 2012 | 8.7 | 12.1 |
| 2013 | 8.3 | 11.3 |

*Source*: Author's calculations based on *Basic Statistical Returns of Scheduled Commercial Banks in India*, various issues; Government of India (1991); Government of India (2001); and censusindia.gov.in.

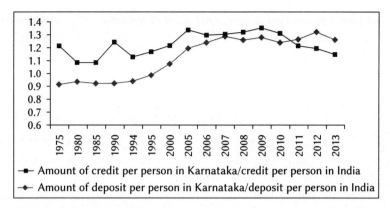

**Chart 1** *Amount of credit/deposit per person, Karnataka and India, 1975–2013*
*Source:* Author's calculations, based on *Basic Statistical Returns of Scheduled Commercial Banks in India,* various issues; Government of India (1991); Government of India (2001); and <censusindia.gov.in>.

bank branch in this period. This decline, however, was reversed after 2005 and the branch intensity across India once again registered an increase. A similar trend can also be seen in the case of Karnataka.

On account of better intensity of banking, the average availability of bank credit per person in Karnataka was generally higher than the all-India average. Similarly, the average amount of bank deposits mobilised per person in the State too had picked up and was seen to be greater than the all-India average in recent years (Chart 1).

## Banking in Rural Karnataka

Rural areas of the State too had a well-developed banking infrastructure.[2] The branch intensity in rural Karnataka was greater than that in rural India as a whole (Table 2). The trends of increase, decline, and then revival in branch intensity as seen at the all-India level could also be seen in rural Karnataka.

Further, the gap between branch intensity of banks in rural and urban Karnataka narrowed significantly from 1975 through the early 1990s (Table 3), suggesting a sharper expansion of branch network in rural Karnataka as compared to urban Karnataka. However, the gap widened in the second half

[2] This is also borne out by the data on debt profiles of rural households. See [Appendix Table 1] for details about the debt profiles of rural households. This information is only available up to 2002 and hence has not been discussed as part of the main chapter.

**Table 2** *Rural population per bank branch, Karnataka and India, 1975 to 2013* in '000 persons

| Rural population per branch | Karnataka | India |
|---|---|---|
| 1975 | 33.1 | 64.3 |
| 1980 | 14.8 | 22.8 |
| 1985 | 10.2 | 14.6 |
| 1990 | 10.0 | 14.0 |
| 1994 | 10.3 | 14.4 |
| 1995 | 10.5 | 14.6 |
| 2000 | 11.2 | 15.7 |
| 2005 | 11.5 | 16.5 |
| 2006 | 12.5 | 17.2 |
| 2007 | 12.1 | 17.2 |
| 2008 | 11.8 | 16.7 |
| 2009 | 11.5 | 16.2 |
| 2010 | 11.4 | 15.7 |
| 2011 | 11.0 | 15.0 |
| 2012 | 10.0 | 13.8 |
| 2013 | 9.2 | 12.7 |

*Notes:* 1. The separation of the years using shaded bars indicates the years that are comparable with each other after accounting for changes in the definition of rural/semi-urban and urban centres in the *BSR*. These phases should not be confused with the phases highlighted in Table 3.
2. "Rural" refers to the total of rural and semi-urban branches, and "urban" refers to the total of urban and metropolitan branches, as reported in the *BSR*.

of the 1990s and up to 2010, after accounting for changes in the definition of centres in this period; and it once again narrowed after 2010. Comparing the data in Tables 1, 2, and 3, it can be said that while the branch intensity in Karnataka increased after 2005, this increase was limited to urban areas. The increase in branch intensity in the rural areas started a little later, and was initially at a slower pace than in urban areas. The relative amount of credit per capita in rural areas as compared to urban areas of the State, although higher than the all-India level, was never more than 25 per cent (Table 4). This underlined the general deprivation of the rural areas in the State in terms of the allocation of bank credit, in comparison with urban areas.

**Table 3** *Rural and urban population per bank branch, Karnataka, 1975 to 2013* in '000 persons

| Year | Rural Karnataka | Urban Karnataka | Gap (rural–urban) |
|------|-----------------|-----------------|-------------------|
| 1975 | 33.1 | 7.8 | 25.3 |
| 1980 | 14.8 | 11.7 | 3.1 |
| 1985 | 10.2 | 10.8 | −0.5 |
| 1990 | 10.0 | 10.7 | −0.7 |
| 1994 | 10.3 | 11.2 | −0.9 |
| 1995 | 10.5 | 11.5 | −1.0 |
| 2000 | 11.2 | 10.1 | 1.1 |
| 2005 | 11.5 | 10.0 | 1.5 |
| 2006 | 12.5 | 8.7 | 3.8 |
| 2007 | 12.1 | 9.0 | 3.1 |
| 2008 | 11.8 | 8.5 | 3.3 |
| 2009 | 11.5 | 8.1 | 3.3 |
| 2010 | 11.4 | 7.6 | 3.8 |
| 2011 | 11.0 | 7.5 | 3.6 |
| 2012 | 10.0 | 7.1 | 2.9 |
| 2013 | 9.2 | 8.5 | 0.8 |

*Notes:* Same as for Table 2.

The changes in branch intensity translated into similar changes in credit availability in the rural areas of Karnataka. There was a decline in the relative allocation of credit to rural areas of the State from 1990 till 2009. Thereafter, there was a revival in the relative amount of credit allocated to rural areas.

## Credit to Agriculture in Karnataka

Credit to agriculture, both total and direct, accounted for a larger share of total bank credit in Karnataka as compared to India (Table 5).[3] Total credit

[3] Direct agricultural credit refers to credit given directly to cultivators and producers in allied activities. Indirect agricultural credit refers to credit given to institutions that support cultivation and production in allied activities. Total agricultural credit refers to the total of both direct and indirect agricultural credit.

**Table 4** *Ratio of credit per capita in rural areas to urban areas, Karnataka and India, 1975 to 2013* in per cent

| Year | Karnataka | India |
|------|-----------|-------|
| 1975 | 14.8 | 6.6 |
| 1980 | 17.8 | 9.8 |
| 1985 | 26.8 | 13.8 |
| 1990 | 24.5 | 14.7 |
| 1994 | 23.5 | 12.4 |
| 1995 | 22.5 | 12.0 |
| 2000 | 22.6 | 10.4 |
| 2005 | 16.5 | 12.4 |
| 2006 | 11.7 | 10.0 |
| 2007 | 12.3 | 9.5 |
| 2008 | 12.3 | 9.3 |
| 2009 | 11.6 | 9.2 |
| 2010 | 12.0 | 9.6 |
| 2011 | 12.7 | 9.4 |
| 2012 | 13.7 | 9.2 |
| 2013 | 16.3 | 9.8 |

*Notes:* Same as for Table 2.

to agriculture accounted for about 15 per cent of total bank credit in the State in 2013. The share of agriculture in total credit in the State, however, was on a general decline after 1990. The share of agricultural credit showed some signs of revival after 2010 but still remained at a level far lower than that reached in 1990. This trend was similar to that witnessed at the all-India level and in most other States, as shown by earlier studies (see Chavan 2005).

Furthermore, studies have shown a growing dominance of urban and metropolitan areas in the distribution of agricultural credit in the country, in the period of economic reforms (Chavan 2010). This shift towards urban and metropolitan areas, and away from rural areas, can be explained by changes in the definition of priority sector lending by the Reserve Bank of India in recent decades, whereby various indirect forms of financing agriculture – such as input dealers and warehouse operators located not

**Table 5** *Share of agriculture in total bank credit, Karnataka and India, 1990 to 2013* in per cent

| Year | Karnataka | India |
|------|-----------|-------|
| 1990 | 22.5 | 15.9 |
| 1994 | 20.8 | 13.0 |
| 1995 | 19.7 | 11.8 |
| 2000 | 17.6 | 9.9 |
| 2005 | 14.5 | 10.8 |
| 2006 | 12.5 | 11.4 |
| 2010 | 13.3 | 11.7 |
| 2011 | 14.0 | 11.3 |
| 2012 | 14.7 | 11.7 |
| 2013 | 15.4 | 14.1 |

*Source: Basic Statistical Returns of Scheduled Commercial Banks in India* (2013).

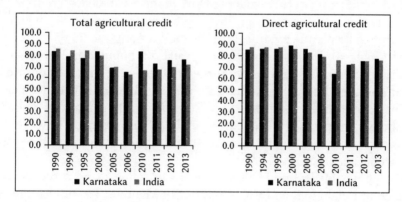

**Chart 2** *Share of rural areas in total/direct agricultural credit, Karnataka and India* in per cent

*Note:* In 1994 and 2005, there was a change in the definition of rural/semi-urban and urban centres in the *BSR*. Hence, a direct comparison is only possible between 1990 and 1994, 1995 and 2005, and for years from 2006 onwards.

*Source:* Author's calculations based on *Basic Statistical Returns of Scheduled Commercial Banks in India,* various issues.

just in rural areas, but also urban and metropolitan areas – were included as part of priority sector credit. However, such a shift could also be seen in the case of direct agricultural credit. In part, this could also be explained by the changes in the definition of agricultural credit, whereby loans up to a stipulated credit limit given to corporates and joint stock companies engaged in agricultural production were made eligible to be a part of direct agricultural credit (see Ramakumar and Chavan 2014).

For Karnataka too, a shift away from rural areas was evident in the case of total and direct agricultural credit. There was a welcome, though marginal increase in the share of rural areas in the distribution of both total and direct agricultural credit after 2010 in the State. In 2013, about 76 per cent of total agricultural credit in the State was outstanding in rural areas; and the share of rural areas was about 79 per cent for direct agricultural credit (Chart 2).

## Banking in the Three Study Districts

In terms of the development of overall banking, the three study districts – Kalaburagi, Mandya, and Kolar – were below the State average. When ranked in the order of their share in bank branches and bank credit in 2013, Kalaburagi was at the tenth position, followed by Mandya at seventeenth position and Kolar at twenty-third position among the 28 districts of the State (Table 6). When normalised by size of population, however, the intensity of branches in Mandya turned out to be the highest, followed by Kolar and then Kalaburagi (Chart 3). In 2013, Mandya had 11,500 persons per bank branch, as compared to 13,200 and 14,000 persons in Kolar and Kalaburagi, respectively. The corresponding State average, however, was 8,300 persons, indicating the limited spread of branches in the three study districts.

The phases of decline in branch intensity followed by a revival could be seen in Kalaburagi and Kolar, but not in Mandya. The branch intensity in Mandya showed a slow but steady increase after 1990. By contrast, Kalaburagi showed a striking fall in branch intensity in the 1990s. The revival after 2005 was quite slow in comparison to the earlier decline. Kolar was the worst affected among the three, with the branch intensity declining in the 1990s and up to 2010. Again, the revival after 2010 was rather moderate in comparison with the earlier decline.

From 1990, there has been a trend decline in the relative amount of credit available per person in all three districts. The gap in terms of credit availability between the three districts narrowed over time and had almost vanished by 2013. Moreover, the amount of credit in each of these districts was generally found to be lower than the State average (Chart 4).

**Table 6** *Share of districts in total number of branches and bank credit, Karnataka, 2013* in per cent

| District | Share in number of bank branches | Share in bank credit |
|---|---|---|
| Bangalore Urban | 24.3 | 64.0 |
| Dakshin Kannad | 6.4 | 3.7 |
| Mysore | 4.9 | 3.2 |
| Belgaum | 6.2 | 3.0 |
| Dharwad | 4.1 | 2.8 |
| Bellary | 3.2 | 2.7 |
| Udipi | 3.9 | 1.7 |
| Tumkur | 3.0 | 1.4 |
| Bagalkot | 2.5 | 1.4 |
| *Kalaburagi* | *3.2* | *0.4* |
| Shimoga | 3.0 | 1.2 |
| Davangere | 2.2 | 1.2 |
| Hassan | 2.9 | 1.1 |
| Raichur | 2.2 | 1.1 |
| Bijapur | 2.3 | 1.1 |
| Chikmagalur | 2.3 | 0.9 |
| *Mandya* | *2.0* | *0.8* |
| Chitradurga | 2.1 | 0.7 |
| Bangalore Rural | 1.8 | 0.7 |
| Koppal | 1.6 | 0.7 |
| Ramanagara | 1.6 | 0.7 |
| Haveri | 2.0 | 0.7 |
| *Kolar* | *3.1* | *0.6* |
| Uttar Kannad | 3.0 | 0.6 |
| Gadag | 1.6 | 0.5 |
| Kodagu | 1.7 | 0.5 |
| Bidar | 1.6 | 0.5 |
| Chamrajanagar | 1.2 | 0.4 |
| *Karnataka* | *100.0* | *100.0* |

*Source: Basic Statistical Returns of Scheduled Commercial Banks in India* (2013).

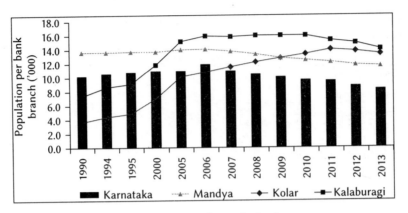

**Chart 3** *Population per bank branch in Karnataka, study districts*
*Source:* Author's calculations based on *Basic Statistical Returns of Scheduled Commercial Banks in India*, various issues; Government of India (1991); Government of India (2001); and censusindia.gov.in.

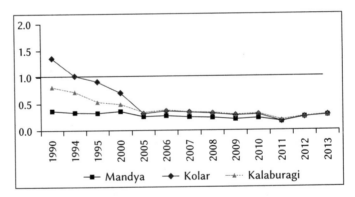

**Chart 4** *Amount of credit per capita in each district as a ratio of credit per capita in Karnataka*
*Source:* Author's calculations based on *Basic Statistical Returns of Scheduled Commercial Banks in India*, various issues; Government of India (1991); Government of India (2001); and censusindia.gov.in.

## Development of Rural Banking in the Three Study Districts

The branch network in all three districts was largely rural; it was more so in the case of Kolar (Table 7). In terms of the intensity of rural banking, Kalaburagi ranked the lowest among the three districts (Table 8). Rural branch intensity was the highest in Kolar, followed by Mandya.

**Table 7** *Share of rural branches in total branches, three study districts, 2013* in per cent

| District | Share of rural branches in total branches (2013) |
|----------|--------------------------------------------------|
| Kolar | 90.5 |
| Mandya | 82.3 |
| Kalaburagi | 72.1 |

*Source: Basic Statistical Returns of Scheduled Commercial Banks in India* (2013).

**Table 8** *Rural population per bank branch, three study districts, 1990 to 2013* in '000 persons

| Year | Mandya | Kolar | Kalaburagi |
|------|--------|-------|------------|
| 1990 | 13.7 | 2.5 | 5.9 |
| 1994 | 13.5 | 3.1 | 7.3 |
| 1995 | 13.5 | 3.3 | 7.7 |
| 2000 | 13.6 | 5.0 | 10.5 |
| 2005 | 13.7 | 7.2 | 14.0 |
| 2006 | 13.7 | 8.5 | 14.9 |
| 2007 | 13.7 | 9.1 | 15.2 |
| 2008 | 13.4 | 9.7 | 15.9 |
| 2009 | 13.1 | 10.2 | 16.0 |
| 2010 | 12.5 | 10.6 | 16.4 |
| 2011 | 12.2 | 11.0 | 15.5 |
| 2012 | 11.9 | 11.0 | 15.2 |
| 2013 | 11.6 | 10.7 | 14.1 |

*Notes:* Same as for Table 2.
*Source:* Author's calculations based on *Basic Statistical Returns of Scheduled Commercial Banks in India,* various issues; Government of India (1991); Government of India (2001); and censusindia.gov.in.

In the early 1990s, there was a wide gap in branch intensity in the rural areas of these three districts, with Kolar at the top, followed by Kalaburagi and then Mandya. This gap narrowed over time with the rural branch network shrinking significantly in Kolar and Kalaburagi, and almost stagnating in Mandya. Kolar, the district where the branch network was primarily rural in nature, was evidently the worst affected during this period. The revival in branch intensity after 2005 – as seen at the State level – was weak and delayed in the case of Kolar as well as Kalaburagi.

# Conclusions

Karnataka is a relatively well-banked State in India. Rural areas of the State are better endowed in terms of bank branches than the rural areas of most other States.

Karnataka, like all the other States of India, showed signs of weakening of bank branch intensity – owing mainly to the decline in rural branch network – in the 1990s and early 2000s, following the initiation of financial sector reforms. However, with the adoption of the policy of financial inclusion with an explicit emphasis on opening rural branches, the branch intensity in the State, including in its rural areas, showed an increase after 2005.

The changes in branch intensity translated into similar changes in credit availability in the rural areas of Karnataka in the second half of the 2000s, although these gains were much smaller than the losses incurred during the previous decade. Also, notwithstanding these gains, the amount of bank credit per capita in rural areas as a percentage of bank credit per capita in urban areas never exceeded 25 per cent, indicating the highly lopsided distribution of bank credit in the State favouring urban areas.

In terms of banking development, Mandya, Kolar, and Kalaburagi can be broadly categorised as underbanked districts of the State. Of these three districts, banking in general, and rural banking in particular, suffered adversely in Kolar and Kalaburagi during the 1990s and early 2000s. Moreover, there was only a marginal increase in branch intensity in the two districts in the second half of the 2000s. The turnaround for these two districts came about only after 2010 and was delayed when compared to the State as a whole. Mandya, which was an underbanked district to begin with, showed signs of stagnation or at best a moderate increase in its branch intensity over the 1990s and 2000s.

# Appendix Tables

**Appendix Table 1** *Share of sources in total debt of rural households, Karnataka and India, AIDIS, 2002* in per cent

| Source | Karnataka | India |
|---|---|---|
| *Formal sources* | **66.7** | **57.2** |
| of which, Commercial banks | 28.9 | 22.7 |
| *Informal sources* | **33.3** | **42.8** |
| of which, Moneylenders | 23.5 | 30.2 |

*Source*: National Sample Survey Organisation (2005).

**Appendix Table 2** *Share of debt from formal sources in total debt of rural households, all States, AIDIS, 1971 and 2002* in per cent

| State | 1971 | 1981 | 1991 | 2002 |
|---|---|---|---|---|
| Maharashtra | 67 | 86 | 82 | 85 |
| Kerala | 44 | 79 | 92 | 81 |
| Himachal Pradesh | 24 | 75 | 62 | 74 |
| Orissa | 30 | 81 | 80 | 74 |
| Jammu & Kashmir | 20 | 44 | 76 | 73 |
| West Bengal | 31 | 66 | 82 | 68 |
| Gujarat | 47 | 70 | 75 | 67 |
| *Karnataka* | *30* | *78* | *78* | *67* |
| Madhya Pradesh | 32 | 66 | 73 | 59 |
| Assam | 35 | 31 | 66 | 58 |
| Punjab | 36 | 74 | 79 | 56 |
| Uttar Pradesh | 23 | 55 | 69 | 56 |
| Haryana | 26 | 76 | 73 | 50 |
| Tamil Nadu | 22 | 44 | 58 | 47 |
| Bihar | 11 | 47 | 73 | 37 |
| Rajasthan | 9 | 41 | 40 | 34 |
| Andhra Pradesh | 14 | 41 | 34 | 27 |
| *India* | *29* | *61* | *64* | *57* |

*Note*: States are ranked in descending order based on the figures for 2002.
*Source*: National Sample Survey Organisation (1998); National Sample Survey Organisation (2005).

# References

Chavan, Pallavi (2005), "Banking Sector Reforms and Growth and Distribution of Rural Banking in India," in V. K. Ramachandran and Madhura Swaminathan, eds., *Financial Liberalisation and Rural Credit*, Tulika Books, New Delhi.

Chavan, Pallavi (2010), "How Rural is India's Agricultural Credit?" *The Hindu*, August 13.

Chavan, Pallavi (2012), "Public Banks and Financial Intermediation in India: The Phases of Nationalisation, Liberalisation, and Inclusion", unpublished note.

Chavan, Pallavi (2013), "Credit and Capital Formation in Agriculture: A Growing Disconnect," *Social Scientist*, September–November.

Government of India (GoI) (1991), *Final Population Totals – Series 1*, New Delhi.

Government of India (GoI) (2001), *Provisional Population Totals: Rural and Urban Distribution for India and States/Union Territories*, New Delhi.

National Sample Survey Organisation (NSSO) (1998), "Note on Household Assets and Liabilities as on 30.06.91: NSS 48th Round (Jan–Dec 1992)," *Sarvekshana*, vol. 22, no. 2, October to December.

National Sample Survey Organisation (NSSO) (2005), *Household Indebtedness in India as on 30-06-2002: Report No. 501*, New Delhi.

Ramachandran, V. K. and Swaminathan, Madhura (2005), "Introduction," in V. K. Ramachandran and Madhura Swaminathan, eds., *Financial Liberalisation and Rural Credit*, Tulika Books, New Delhi.

Ramakumar, R. and Chavan, Pallavi (2014), "Agricultural Credit in India in the 2000s: Dissecting the Revival," *Review of Agrarian Studies*, vol. 4, no. 1, February–June.

Reserve Bank of India (RBI), *Banking Statistics/Basic Statistical Returns of Scheduled Commercial Banks in India*, Mumbai, various issues.

*Sathye, Milind (2003), "Privatisation, Performance and Efficiency: A Study of Indian Banks," paper presented at* World Bank Conference on Bank Privatisation, Washington D. C., October.

Shetty, S. L. (2005), "Regional, Sectoral and Functional Distribution of Bank Credit," in V. K. Ramachandran and Madhura Swaminathan, eds., *Financial Liberalisation and Rural Credit*, Tulika Books, New Delhi.

# 12

## Rural Indebtedness in Karnataka: Findings from Three Village Surveys

R. V. Bhavani

This chapter examines patterns of indebtedness of households in the three Karnataka villages surveyed under the Project on Agrarian Relations in India (PARI) of the Foundation for Agrarian Studies (FAS). It examines their outstanding debts by source, purpose, and rate of interest.

### Incidence of Debt

More than 70 per cent of households in all three villages reported some borrowing during the reference year. Table 1 gives the number and percentage of indebted households in each village.

In all three villages, both the proportion of number of loans and loan amounts outstanding from the informal sector were higher than from the formal sector. The average proportion of number of loans from the formal sector across the three villages was just 18 per cent. Table 2 shows that formal sector loans accounted for just 29 per cent of the loan amount outstanding in Zhapur, 34 per cent in Siresandra, and 50 per cent in Alabujanahalli. The 50 per cent share in the case of Alabujanahalli was due to two high-value loans availed by a Rich capitalist farmer household during the year of survey.

A majority of households in the three villages (60 per cent and above) had borrowings only from the informal sector, as seen in Table 3. Further, this pattern was found to be similar across all social groups. In all three villages, it was the Backward Class (BC) households that had relatively more borrowings from the formal sector as compared to Scheduled Caste (SC) households.

Commercial banks and regional rural banks (RRBs) were the main formal

**Table 1** *Indebtedness in the study villages, 2008–09*

| District | Village | Total no. of households | No. of indebted households | Percentage of indebted households |
|---|---|---|---|---|
| Mandya | Alabujanahalli | 243 | 201 | 83 |
| Kolar | Siresandra | 79 | 60 | 76 |
| Kalaburagi | Zhapur | 109 | 78 | 72 |
| Total | All villages | 431 | 339 | 79 |

*Source*: PARI survey data.

**Table 2** *Share of formal and informal sector loans, 2008–09* in per cent

| Village | Outstanding debt from formal sector | Outstanding debt from informal sector | No. of loans from formal sector (per cent) | No. of loans from informal sector (per cent) |
|---|---|---|---|---|
| Alabujanahalli | 50 | 50 | 21 | 79 |
| Siresandra | 34 | 66 | 17 | 83 |
| Zhapur | 29 | 71 | 18 | 82 |

*Source*: PARI survey data.

**Table 3** *Number of households borrowing from formal–informal sectors, three study villages, 2008–09*

| Village | No. of indebted households | Households with only formal sector borrowing | | Households with only informal sector borrowing | | Households with borrowing from both sectors | |
|---|---|---|---|---|---|---|---|
| | | No. | per cent | No. | per cent | No. | per cent |
| Alabujanahalli | 201 | 28 | 14 | 120 | 60 | 53 | 26 |
| Siresandra | 60 | 8 | 13 | 45 | 75 | 7 | 12 |
| Zhapur | 78 | 11 | 14 | 53 | 68 | 14 | 18 |

*Source*: PARI survey data.

sector institutions accessed by households in the three villages; there was no borrowing at all from primary cooperative societies in Siresandra. Formal sector borrowing in Alabujanahalli was reported from Vijaya Bank (the lead bank in Mandya district), State Bank of Mysore, Visveshvaraya Grameena Bank (RRB), State Bank of India, Mandya District Cooperative Credit Bank, Primary Cooperative Agricultural and Rural Development Bank at Maddur, Primary Agricultural Cooperative Credit Societies (PACS), Karnataka State Finance Corporation, ICICI Bank, and CitiBank. The last two agencies accounted for two high-value loans to the same household, for a road roller and a rice mill respectively.

In Siresandra, formal sector borrowing by households was reported from Canara Bank (the lead bank in Kolar district), State Bank of Mysore, State Bank of India branches in neighbouring villages, Pragathi Krishna Gramin Bank (RRB), and the Primary Cooperative Agricultural and Rural Development Bank at Bangarpet.

In Zhapur, households reported formal sector borrowing from State Bank of India (the lead bank in Kalaburagi district), Corporation Bank, Canara Bank, Bank of Maharashtra, Pragathi Krishna Gramin Bank (RRB), and Kalaburagi District Central Cooperative Bank (DCCB).

Landlords, peasants, and professional moneylenders comprised the main informal sector lenders in all three villages. Professional moneylenders were seen to be relatively more important in Siresandra, accounting for 23 per cent of loan accounts, in comparison to Zhapur (8 per cent) and Alabujanahalli (11 per cent). While borrowing from self help groups (SHG) was observed in all three villages, it accounted for a fifth of borrowings in terms of number of loans in both Alabujanahalli and Siresandra. Borrowing from pawn shops and chit funds was found in Alabujanahalli. Some of these pawn shops were managed by Marwaris who came from Rajasthan many years ago. In Zhapur borrowing from private microfinance companies was observed, accounting for 11 per cent of the number of loan accounts; this may be attributed to Kalaburagi's proximity to Andhra Pradesh, a state with a profusion of microfinance institutions. The amount outstanding with microfinance companies, however, accounted for only 1 per cent of the loan amounts outstanding, indicating the small size of these loans. In Alabujanahalli private finance companies were primarily chit funds and 2 per cent of the loan amount outstanding was accounted for by them.

Self help groups supported by PACs, DCCB, the regional rural bank, Vijaya Bank, and State Bank of Mysore were functioning in Alabujanahalli village (see Box). In Siresandra, SHGs in operation were supported by the RRB and Canara Bank. In the case of Zhapur, the majority of SHGs were linked to Corporation Bank. Loans from SHGs have also been categorised under the head 'informal', given that the groups are free to charge the rate of interest they wish – and it is generally found to be in the range of 24 per cent, much higher than the rate of interest charged by formal credit agencies.

Borrowing for production purposes included recurrent agricultural expenses, purchase of land, animal resources, business and trade, purchase

**Box:** Self Help Groups (SHGs) in Alabujanahalli

Access to formal credit and banking services in rural India has been a perennial problem along with high levels of rural indebtedness. Apart from micro finance institutions (MFIs), self help groups (SHGs) have played a pivotal role in expanding access to micro-credit for the rural poor. Since 1998, the Reserve Bank of India (RBI) allows SHGs to operate savings bank (SB) accounts in the name of the SHG.

In Alabujanahalli, 67 per cent of all households (164 out of 243 households) had at least one household member participating in an SHG. The median size of an SHG was 20 members, with the smallest group consisting of 10 members and the largest being 200 strong.

Members of SHGs generally met once a week and contributed small amounts to the common pool, which was subsequently deposited into bank accounts and advanced as loans to members. Public sector banks (PSBs) too offered loans to women SHGs at a significantly lower rate of interest of 7 per cent per annum, at par with agricultural credit. The median savings or contribution of members of SHGs in Alabujanahalli was Rs 50 per month.

Membership in an SHG is a long-term commitment and members of SHGs often tend to share common interests. In Alabujanahalli, the median period of membership of individual was 36 months or three years. The longest serving member in a SHG in the village was Chennamma. She was a member of two SHGs: one for 10 years and another for seven years. Chennamma, 45 years old, was a mother of three boys, and belonged to the Vokkaliga (Gowda) community. She was a social worker, notwithstanding the fact that she could only sign her name, and could not read or write. Her household was a middle peasant household and owned 5.5 acres of land, no part of which was registered in her name.

The median total savings of individuals in SHGs was Rs 1,800 per member, ranging from Rs 120 to Rs 19,200. At times, apart from the periodic contributions, some members tended to advance loans to the group. Rajamma was one such member who had advanced a loan of Rs 25,000 at an interest of 24 per cent per annum. Her family owned only a small plot of land (0.2 acre), and cultivated paddy and sugarcane on their own as wells as leased-in land.

*Source:* Jagannath (2016).

and maintenance of productive durable assets like tractor and bullock cart. A loan is characterised as multipurpose when the same loan is utilised for more than one of the purposes mentioned above. The bulk of borrowing for productive purposes was for agricultural expenses in Alabujanahalli, while it was in the category of purchase and maintenance of productive

**Table 4** *Descriptive statistics of interest rates, study villages, 2008–09* in per cent per annum

| Village | Modal rate of interest | Weighted rate of interest | Simple Average rate of interest | Minimum rate of interest | Maximum rate of interest |
|---------|------|------|------|------|------|
| Alabujanahalli | 36 | 20.6 | 24.1 | 0 | 120 |
| Siresandra | 36 | 22.9 | 27.2 | 0 | 120 |
| Zhapur | 36 | 24.8 | 24.8 | 0 | 36 |

*Source*: PARI survey data.

durable assets in both Siresandra and Zhapur. Borrowing for education and medical purposes, as also for purchase and construction or repair of house, are included under consumption loans. The other heads in this category are borrowing for day-to-day expenses, for marriages and other ceremonies, purchase and maintenance of domestic durable assets, and repayment of old loans. The bulk of borrowing under the consumption category was found to be for marriages and other social ceremonies in all three villages.

The modal rate of interest in all three villages was 36 per cent per annum, the rate generally charged by professional moneylenders, landlords, and peasants. While lending by friends and relatives was at a zero rate of interest, 120 per cent was recorded as the highest rate of interest in both Alabujanahalli and Siresandra. The average interest rate ranged from 24 per cent in Alabujanahalli to 27 per cent in Siresandra, with Zhapur in between at 25 per cent. Table 4 gives the picture of rates of interest across the three villages.

The share of loans contracted at more than 24 per cent per annum was 44 per cent in Alabujanahalli, 45 per cent in Siresandra, and 53 per cent in Zhapur. From 2007 onwards, agricultural loans have been extended at 7 per cent per annum by commercial banks and cooperative credit institutions as per government directive, with a further 3 per cent subvention on timely repayment. The share of loans in the $0 \leq r \leq 10$ per cent interest band was, however, only 17 per cent in Alabujanahalli, 7 per cent in Siresandra, and 14 per cent in Zhapur. Tables 8, 12, and 16 give the details of loans at different interest rates in Alabujanahalli, Siresandra, and Zhapur respectively.

Evidence of debt tied to labour was observed in the study villages. While it involved just one household in Siresandra, there were two households in Zhapur and ten households in Alabujanahalli that reported debt tied to labour. All these households were Manual worker households, save one poor peasant household in the case of both Alabujanahalli and Zhapur.

Loans were for taken consumption purposes as well as for education, house construction, marriage, medical expenses, and repayment of old loans. The borrower either had to work for free in return for the loan, or at a lower wage rate than the prevalent village wage towards repayment of the loan. The lender was a Landlord/Rich capitalist farmer or peasant either from the village itself or a neighbouring village. An implicit rate of interest was tied to these loans. The prevalence of such instances of tied debt pointed to the lack of availability of formal sources of credit to meet the household needs of poor households dependent on manual labour income, and with little or no assets to offer as collateral.

Next, the situation of indebtedness in each village is examined separately by socio-economic classes.

### Alabujanahalli

The average amount of loan outstanding in this village was highest in the Rich capitalist farmer category. Table 5 shows the indebtedness and debt–asset ratio of indebted households by socio-economic class. The high amount outstanding in the Rich capitalist farmer category was primarily accounted for by one Rich Capitalist farmer household owning 25 acres of land. This household had borrowed Rs 22 lakhs from a foreign bank during the year of the PARI survey to purchase a road roller. The same household had also borrowed Rs 14 lakhs from the State Finance Corporation to set up a rice mill. These two loans accounted for the fact that the loan amount outstanding from formal institutions was 50 per cent, even as the number of loans from the former accounted for only a 21 per cent share in the total loan portfolio, as seen in Table 2. Excluding these two large loans, the amount outstanding from the formal sector accounted for 38 per cent of total loan outstanding. The debt to asset ratio was the highest for the business/self-employment category of households.

Households in the Peasant 3 and Peasant 4 categories, Manual worker households, business and self-employed households, and households dependent on rents and remittances had the greater share of their borrowings from the informal sector, as revealed by both the number of loans and amount outstanding (Table 6). The dependence was observed to be the highest in the case of Manual worker households, and households dependent on income from business and self-employment. The reverse was the case for households in the category of Rich capitalist farmer and Peasant 1. Households dependent on salary incomes had a high share of loans (72 per cent) from the informal sector, but the shares of the amount outstanding

**Table 5** *Amount outstanding and debt to asset ratio of indebted households by socio-economic class, Alabujanahalli, 2008–09*

| Class | No. of households | No. of indebted households | Share of total amount outstanding | Average amount outstanding (Rs. per household) | Debt–asset ratio (per cent) |
|---|---|---|---|---|---|
| Rich capitalist farmer | 2 | 2 | 20 | 2705234 | 7.3 |
| Peasant 1 | 9 | 8 | 6.8 | 234675 | 3.7 |
| Peasant 2 | 39 | 31 | 27.8 | 246631 | 8.4 |
| Peasant 3 | 30 | 26 | 7.8 | 82161 | 5.5 |
| Peasant 4 | 58 | 47 | 13.7 | 80385 | 13.6 |
| Manual worker 1 | 40 | 36 | 7.2 | 54842 | 17.1 |
| Manual worker 2 | 22 | 14 | 1.7 | 33254 | 15.2 |
| Manual worker 3 | 11 | 10 | 1.8 | 49575 | 29.7 |
| Rents/ Remittances | 7 | 7 | 2.1 | 81677 | 6.8 |
| Salaried persons | 14 | 12 | 4.7 | 106765 | 5.4 |
| Business/ self-employed | 11 | 8 | 6.7 | 228559 | 38.8 |
| All | 243 | 201 | 100 | 136640 | 8.2 |

*Source*: PARI survey data.

from both formal and informal sectors were quite close – at 51 and 49 per cent, respectively.

Table 7 shows the class-wise share of debt outstanding by purpose. The bulk of borrowings by Manual worker households (79 per cent and above), households dependent on income from business and self-employment (78 per cent), and households in Peasant 4 category (72 per cent) was for consumption purposes. The entire debt of the two Rich capitalist farmer households was for productive purposes.

Table 8 presents the rates of interest at which loans were contracted by households. The bulk of the loans of Manual worker households (66 per cent), households dependent on rents and remittances (61 per cent), and households dependent on salary incomes (56 per cent) were contracted at interest rates of

**Table 6** *Percentage share of number and amount of loan outstanding sector-wise by class, Alabujanahalli*

| Class | Amount outstanding from formal sector (per cent) | Amount outstanding from informal sector (per cent) | No. of loans from formal sector (per cent) | No. of loans from informal sector (per cent) |
|---|---|---|---|---|
| Rich capitalist farmer | 95 | 5 | 83 | 17 |
| Peasant 1 | 74 | 26 | 44 | 56 |
| Peasant 2 | 62 | 38 | 40 | 60 |
| Peasant 3 | 39 | 61 | 30 | 70 |
| Peasant 4 | 19 | 81 | 16 | 84 |
| Manual worker 1 | 4 | 96 | 4 | 96 |
| Manual worker 2 | – | 100 | – | 100 |
| Manual worker 3 | 11 | 89 | 11 | 89 |
| Rents/ Remittances | 24 | 76 | 9 | 91 |
| Salaried persons | 51 | 49 | 28 | 72 |
| Business/ Self-employed | 8 | 92 | 18 | 82 |

*Source*: PARI survey data.

**Table 7** *Share of amount of debt outstanding by purpose and socio-economic class, Alabujanahalli* in per cent

| Class | Production | Consumption | Multi-purpose (production and consumption) |
|---|---|---|---|
| Rich capitalist farmer | 100 | – | – |
| Peasant 1 | 63 | 21 | 16 |
| Peasant 2 | 41 | 51 | 8 |
| Peasant 3 | 38 | 57 | 5 |
| Peasant 4 | 19 | 72 | 9 |
| Manual worker 1 | 17 | 79 | 4 |
| Manual worker 2 | 13 | 87 | |
| Manual worker 3 | – | 92 | 8 |
| Rents/Remittances | 44 | 53 | 3 |
| Salaried persons | 35 | 53 | 12 |
| Business/Self-employed | 22 | 78 | – |

*Source*: PARI survey data.

**Table 8** *Distribution of number of loans by socio-economic class and annual interest rate, Alabujanahalli* in per cent

| Class | Interest rate | | | | | | | |
|---|---|---|---|---|---|---|---|---|
| | No. of loans | 0 | 0–≤10 | 10–≤15 | 15–≤24 | 24–≤36 | >36 | Total |
| Rich capitalist farmer | 6 | 16 | – | 67 | 17 | – | – | 100 |
| Peasant 1 | 18 | 11 | 33 | 11 | 28 | 17 | – | 100 |
| Peasant 2 | 73 | 1 | 26 | 27 | 19 | 25 | 1 | 100 |
| Peasant 3 | 53 | 6 | 24 | 15 | 15 | 40 | – | 100 |
| Peasant 4 | 107 | 5 | 19 | 6 | 28 | 40 | 2 | 100 |
| Manual worker 1 | 76 | 13 | 11 | 4 | 13 | 47 | 12 | 100 |
| Manual worker 2 | 30 | 3 | 3 | 7 | 40 | 43 | 4 | 100 |
| Manual worker 3 | 18 | 17 | 5 | | 17 | 56 | 5 | 100 |
| Rents/ Remittances | 24 | – | 4 | 18 | 17 | 52 | 9 | 100 |
| Salaried persons | 36 | 6 | 19 | 11 | 8 | 50 | 6 | 100 |
| Business/ Self-employed | 22 | 5 | 14 | 9 | 32 | 36 | 5 | 100 |
| All | 463 | 6 | 17 | 12 | 21 | 40 | 4 | 100 |

*Source*: PARI survey data.

more than 24 per cent. Only 17 per cent of the loans were contracted at rates less than 10 per cent, the bulk of them by peasants – ranging from 33 per cent among Peasant 1 households to 19 per cent among Peasant 4 households.

## Siresandra

Table 9 shows the debt profile of households in Siresandra. The average amount of loan outstanding was highest in the Peasant 1 category. The debt to asset ratio was highest in the Manual worker category, followed by households in the business/self-employment category. The bulk of the share of total debt outstanding (51 per cent) was accounted for by the Peasant 2 class, with an average debt–asset ratio of 5.

Table 10 shows the source of borrowing. Households in the Peasant 1 class had an equal proportion of loans from formal and informal sectors in terms of number of loans, but the bulk of loan outstanding (89 per cent) was from the formal sector. Commercial banks and the RRBs were the main sources of formal sector borrowing. No borrowing was reported from cooperative credit societies.

**Table 9** *Amount outstanding and debt to asset ratio of indebted households by socio-economic class, Siresandra, 2008–09*

| Class | No. of households | No. of indebted households | Share of total amount outstanding (per cent) | Average amount outstanding Rs/household | Debt–asset ratio (per cent) |
|---|---|---|---|---|---|
| Peasant 1 | 4 | 2 | 9 | 277577 | 2.2 |
| Peasant 2 | 25 | 21 | 51 | 150038 | 5.0 |
| Peasant 3 | 31 | 22 | 25 | 70055 | 8.2 |
| Manual workers | 13 | 10 | 9 | 55187 | 20.3 |
| Business/ Self-employed | 6 | 5 | 6 | 69080 | 13.3 |
| All | 79 | 60 | 100 | 102407 | 5.5 |

*Source*: PARI survey data.

**Table 10** *Percentage share of number and amount of loan outstanding by sector and socio-economic class, Siresandra*

| Class | Amount outstanding from formal sector (per cent) | Amount outstanding from informal sector (per cent) | No. of loans from formal sector (per cent) | No. of loans from informal sector (per cent) |
|---|---|---|---|---|
| Peasant 1 | 89 | 11 | 50 | 50 |
| Peasant 2 | 35 | 65 | 17 | 83 |
| Peasant 3 | 04 | 96 | 07 | 93 |
| Manual workers | 71 | 29 | 24 | 76 |
| Business/ Self-employed | 7 | 93 | 20 | 80 |

*Source*: PARI survey data.

Peasant 3 households showed the highest dependence on the informal sector both in terms of number of loans (93 per cent) and percentage share of loans outstanding (96 per cent). They were followed by the business and self-employed class of households: 80 per cent of their loans and 93 per cent of the amount outstanding were from the informal sector. Among Manual worker households, 71 per cent of the outstanding debt was from the formal sector, although this accounted for only 24 per cent of the number of loans.

**Table 11** *Share of amount of debt outstanding by purpose and socio-economic class, Siresandra* in per cent

| Class | Production | Consumption | Multi-purpose (production and consumption) |
|---|---|---|---|
| Peasant 1 | 100 | – | – |
| Peasant 2 | 47 | 53 | – |
| Peasant 3 | 40 | 60 | – |
| Manual workers | 12 | 88 | – |
| Business/Self-employed | 79 | 20 | 1 |

*Source*: PARI survey data.

**Table 12** *Distribution of number of loans by socio-economic class and annual interest rate, Siresandra* in per cent per annum

| Class | | Interest rate | | | | | | |
|---|---|---|---|---|---|---|---|---|
| | No. of loans | 0 | 0–≤10 | 10–≤15 | 15–≤24 | 24–≤36 | >36 | Total |
| Peasant 1 | 04 | – | 25 | 25 | 25 | 25 | – | 100 |
| Peasant 2 | 35 | 03 | 14 | 06 | 17 | 49 | 11 | 100 |
| Peasant 3 | 28 | 14 | 04 | 11 | 28 | 32 | 11 | 100 |
| Manual workers | 17 | 24 | – | 29 | 23 | 12 | 12 | 100 |
| Business/ Self-employed | 10 | 10 | – | 20 | 30 | 20 | 20 | 100 |
| All | 94 | 11 | 07 | 14 | 23 | 33 | 12 | 100 |

*Source*: Survey data

Table 11 shows the borrowing by households across different socio-economic classes by purpose. The bulk of the borrowing by Manual worker households (88 per cent) was for consumption purposes. For poor peasant (Peasant 3) households, 60 per cent of the borrowing was for consumption purposes. The entire borrowing of Peasant 1 households was for production purposes.

Table 12 shows the distribution of loans by the rates of interest at which they were contracted. The bulk of the loans of Peasant 2 households (60 per cent) were contracted at interest rates of more than 4 per cent. Low-interest loans – that is, loans contracted at rates below 10 per cent – were mainly taken by rich peasant (Peasant 1) households.

### *Zhapur*

Table 13 gives information on the indebtedness of households across different socio-economic classes. The average amount of loan outstanding was highest in the Landlord class: there were two indebted households, and their debt accounted for 20 per cent of the total outstanding debt. The debt to asset ratio was highest in the business/self-employment class. The Peasant 3 class, with an average debt to asset ratio of 15, accounted for the highest share (25 per cent) of total debt outstanding.

All classes of households including the Rich capitalist farmer/Landlord class borrowed primarily from the informal sector both in terms of the number of loans and the percentage share of loan amount outstanding. Table 14 presents the data on borrowing from formal and informal sectors by households in different socio-economic classes. Ninety per cent of the loans of households in the Manual worker class were from the informal sector. The two indebted Landlord households accounted for 78 per cent of loans outstanding to the informal sector. Fifteen households reported borrowing from micro-finance institutions (MFIs). The rate of interest was 13 per cent per annum and repayment was in weekly instalments over 50 weeks. The size of loan was usually Rs 10,000 or less.

**Table 13** *Amount outstanding and debt to asset ratio of indebted households by socio-economic class, Zhapur*

| Class | No. of households | No. of indebted households | Share of total amount outstanding (per cent) | Average amount outstanding Rs/household | Debt–asset ratio (per cent) |
|---|---|---|---|---|---|
| Landlord | 4 | 2 | 20 | 649128 | 6.9 |
| Peasant 1 | 2 | 1 | 07 | 464250 | 7.4 |
| Peasant 2 | 7 | 5 | 07 | 90996 | 6.3 |
| Peasant 3 | 28 | 20 | 25 | 79699 | 16.7 |
| Manual workers | 51 | 38 | 22 | 37355 | 16.7 |
| Rents/ Remittances | 5 | 2 | 02 | 50541 | 2.4 |
| Salaried persons | 6 | 4 | 01 | 18129 | 1.2 |
| Business/ Self-employed | 6 | 6 | 15 | 158225 | 43.6 |
| All | 109 | 78 | | 81460 | 10.2 |

*Source*: PARI survey data.

**Table 14** *Share of number and amount of loan outstanding sector-wise by socio-economic class, Zhapur* in per cent

| Class | Amount outstanding from formal sector | Amount outstanding from informal sector | No. of loans from formal sector | No. of loans from informal sector |
|---|---|---|---|---|
| Landlords | 22 | 78 | 33 | 67 |
| Peasant 1 | 100 | – | 100 | – |
| Peasant 2 | 29 | 71 | 25 | 75 |
| Peasant 3 | 33 | 67 | 18 | 82 |
| Manual workers | 11 | 89 | 10 | 90 |
| Rents/ Remittances | 100 | 0 | 100 | 0 |
| Salaried persons | 41 | 59 | 40 | 60 |
| Business/ Self-employed | 16 | 84 | 14 | 86 |

*Source*: PARI survey data.

**Table 15** *Percentage share of amount of debt outstanding by purpose and socio-economic class, Zhapur*

| Class | Production | Consumption | Multi-purpose (production and consumption) |
|---|---|---|---|
| Landlords | 27 | 73 | – |
| Peasant 1 | 100 | – | – |
| Peasant 2 | 15 | 85 | – |
| Peasant 3 | 46 | 15 | 39 |
| Manual workers | 39 | 02 | 59 |
| Rents/Remittances | – | 100 | – |
| Salaried persons | 41 | 59 | – |
| Business/Self-employed | 18 | 82 | – |

*Source*: PARI survey data.

Table 15 shows the share of debt outstanding by purpose of borrowing. The bulk of borrowing by Peasant 2 households (85 per cent) was for consumption purposes. Borrowing for consumption was high in the business/ self-employment class (82 per cent) and the Rich capitalist farmer/Landlord class (73 per cent). Interestingly, the entire borrowing of the two households in the rent and remittance class was for consumption purposes, and was from the formal sector. The bulk of loans of Manual worker households

**Table 16** *Distribution of number of loans by socio-economic class and annual interest rate, Zhapur* in per cent per annum

| Class | No. of loans | Interest rate | | | | | | |
|---|---|---|---|---|---|---|---|---|
| | | 0 | 0–≤10 | 10–≤15 | 15–≤24 | 24–≤36 | >36 | Total |
| Landlords | 6 | – | 33 | – | – | 67 | – | 100 |
| Peasant 1 | 2 | – | 100 | – | – | – | – | 100 |
| Peasant 2 | 12 | 17 | 08 | 17 | – | 58 | – | 100 |
| Peasant 3 | 45 | 04 | 07 | 18 | 20 | 49 | 02 | 100 |
| Manual workers | 69 | 06 | 13 | 19 | 09 | 52 | 01 | 100 |
| Rents/Remittances | 2 | – | 50 | 50 | – | – | – | 100 |
| Salaried persons | 5 | – | 20 | 20 | – | 60 | – | 100 |
| Business/Self-employed | 14 | 14 | 14 | | 15 | 57 | – | 100 |
| All | 155 | 06 | 14 | 16 | 11 | 52 | 01 | 100 |

*Source*: PARI survey data.

(59 per cent) were multi-purpose, i.e. for both production and consumption purposes.

Table 16 shows the distribution of loans by the interest rates at which they were borrowed. The entire borrowing of households in the Peasant 1 class was at less than 10 per cent rate of interest. All the other classes had the bulk of their borrowings at rates of interest above 24 per cent.

Village-wise details of distribution of debt outstanding by socio-economic class, and source and purpose are given in Appendix Tables 1 to 6.

## Conclusions

Overall, one finds that a characteristic feature across the three villages is a high level of dependence on the informal sector for borrowing. However, among the three villages, Alabujanahalli village, and Mandya district, appeared to be a little better off in terms of banking development. Seventy per cent or more of the households in the three villages reported outstanding debts. Sixty per cent or more of the indebted households in all three villages had borrowed only from the informal sector. The main sources of borrowing in the informal sector were moneylenders, middle and rich peasants, and landlords. The modal rate of interest in all three villages was a high 36 per cent, the rate charged by moneylenders, and small and middle peasants.

Borrowing from the formal sector was largely by households with large landholdings and a bigger asset base. Among the formal sector agencies, commercial banks were the most popular source of credit. The larger share of borrowings by poor peasant and Manual worker households was from the informal sector. The major purpose of borrowing by households in these two socio-economic classes was for consumption.

High debt to asset ratios or a high burden of servicing debt was visible among Manual worker households and the business/self-employed category of households in all three villages. The latter were households engaged in small petty businesses like running a shop. In one village, the evidence of debt tied to labour indicated the persistence of inter-linked loans.

# Appendix Tables

**Appendix Table 1** *Distribution of debt outstanding by socio-economic class and source, Alabujanahalli, 2009* in per cent

| Class | All formal sources | Commercial banks | Regional rural banks (RRBs) |
|---|---|---|---|
| Rich capitalist farmer | 95 | 59 | |
| Peasant 1 | 74 | 46 | |
| Peasant 2 | 62 | 51 | |
| Peasant 3 | 39 | 20 | 4 |
| Peasant 4 | 19 | 11 | 8 |
| Manual worker 1 | 4 | 2 | |
| Manual worker 2 | – | – | |
| Manual worker 3 | 11 | | |
| Rents/Remittances | 24 | 03 | |
| Salaried persons | 51 | 43 | 3 |
| Business/Self-employed | 8 | 3 | |

| Class | All informal sources | Friends and relatives | Landlord/ rich peasant | Professional moneylender | Small and medium peasant | Salaried person |
|---|---|---|---|---|---|---|
| Rich capitalist farmer | 5 | 5 | | | | |
| Peasant 1 | 26 | 3 | | | 7 | |
| Peasant 2 | 38 | 2 | 0.3 | 15 | 6 | 1 |
| Peasant 3 | 61 | 2 | 9 | 25 | 12 | |
| Peasant 4 | 81 | 2.4 | 0.1 | 13.3 | 24 | 0.2 |
| Manual worker 1 | 96 | 1 | 24.5 | 15 | 29 | 0.3 |
| Manual worker 2 | 100 | | 8 | 6 | 1 | |
| Manual worker 3 | 89 | 22 | 4 | | 10 | |
| Rents/Remittances | 76 | 23 | 2 | 8 | 10 | |
| Salaried persons | 49 | 3 | 6 | 3 | 26 | |
| Business/ Self-employed | 92 | 1 | 3 | 10 | 67 | 3 |

**Appendix Table 1** *(continued)*

| Cooperative banks | Cooperative societies | Primary cooperative agricultural and rural development bank | Other formal financial institutions |
|---|---|---|---|
| | 10 | | 26 |
| 2 | 26 | | |
| 2 | 08 | | 1 |
| 3 | 12 | | |
| | 0.3 | | |
| 1 | 1 | | |
| | | 8 | 3 |
| | 21 | | |
| 1 | 4 | | |
| | 5 | | |

| SHG | Pawn shop | Private finance companies/ chit fund | Trader/ other service provider | Sugar factory | Other unspecified informal sources | Worker |
|---|---|---|---|---|---|---|
| 1 | | | 15 | | | |
| 0.5 | | 2 | 7 | 2 | 1 | |
| 6 | | 1 | 4 | | 2 | |
| 4 | 1 | 5 | 4 | | 27 | |
| 8 | | 1 | 2.5 | 0.1 | 15 | |
| 33 | 1 | 6 | 4 | | 41 | |
| 12 | | 1 | | | 40 | |
| 9 | | | | | 21 | 3 |
| 6 | | 0.5 | | | 4 | 0.5 |
| 5 | | 3 | | | | |

**Appendix Table 2** *Distribution of debt outstanding by socio-economic class and source, Zhapur, 2009* in per cent

| Class | All formal sources | Commercial banks | Regional rural banks (RRBs) |
|---|---|---|---|
| Landlords | 22 | 22 | |
| Peasant 1 | 100 | 100 | |
| Peasant 2 | 29 | 15 | 14 |
| Peasant 3 | 33 | 30 | |
| Manual workers | 11 | 11 | |
| Rents/Remittances | 100 | 81 | |
| Salaried persons | 41 | 7 | 34 |
| Business/Self-employed | 16 | 16 | |

| Class | All informal sources | Friends and relatives | Landlord/ rich peasant | Professional moneylender | Small and medium peasant | Salaried person |
|---|---|---|---|---|---|---|
| Landlord | 78 | 19 | | 54 | | |
| Peasant 1 | – | | | | | |
| Peasant 2 | 71 | 42 | | 9 | 5 | |
| Peasant 3 | 67 | | 16 | 10 | 18 | 2 |
| Manual workers | 89 | 3 | 37 | 4 | 11 | |
| Rents/ Remittances | – | | | | | |
| Salaried persons | 59 | | 28 | 21 | | |
| Business/ Self-employed | 84 | 3 | 5 | 3.5 | 18 | |

**Appendix Table 2** *(continued)*

| Cooperative banks | Cooperative societies | Primary cooperative agricultural and rural development bank | Other formal financial institutions |
|---|---|---|---|
| | | | |
| 2 | 1 | | |
| 19 | | | |

| SHG | Pawn shop | Private finance companies/chit fund | Traders/other service provider | Sugar factory | Other unspecified informal sources |
|---|---|---|---|---|---|
| | | | 5 | | |
| 1 | | | 6 | 8 | |
| | 1 | 1 | 19 | | |
| 5 | | 6 | 1 | 10 | 12 |
| 10 | | | | | |
| 1.5 | | | 10 | 42 | 1 |

**Appendix Table 3** *Distribution of debt outstanding by socio-economic class and source, Siresandra, 2009 in per cent*

| Class | All formal sources | Commercial banks | Regional rural banks (RRBs) | Cooperative banks | Cooperative societies | Primary cooperative agricultural and rural development bank | Other formal financial institutions |
|---|---|---|---|---|---|---|---|
| Peasant 1 | 89 | 63 | | | | 26 | |
| Peasant 2 | 35 | 21 | 14 | | | | |
| Peasant 3 | 4 | | 1 | | | 3 | |
| Manual workers | 71 | 70 | 1 | | | | |
| Business/Self-employed | 7 | 1 | 6 | | | | |

| Class | All informal sources | Friends and relatives | Landlord/rich peasant | Professional moneylender | Small and medium peasant | Salaried person | SHG | Pawn shop | Private finance companies/chit fund | Trader/other service provider |
|---|---|---|---|---|---|---|---|---|---|---|
| Peasant 1 | 11 | | | 10.6 | | | 0.4 | | | |
| Peasant 2 | 65 | 0.5 | 0.5 | 40 | 13 | 3 | 1 | 4 | 3 | |
| Peasant 3 | 96 | 19 | 12 | 26 | 15 | | 3 | | | 21 |
| Manual workers | 29 | 3 | 2 | 7 | 6 | | 2 | | | 9 |
| Business/Self-employed | 93 | | | 69 | 7 | | 2 | | 15 | |

**Appendix Table 4** *Distribution of debt outstanding by socio-economic class and purpose of loan, Alabujanahalli, 2009 in per cent*

| Class | Production-related | Recurring agricultural expense | Animal husbandry | Productive durable asset | Business and trade | Land purchase | Multi-purpose production | Multi-purpose production and consumption |
|---|---|---|---|---|---|---|---|---|
| Rich capitalist farmer | 100 | 30 | – | – | 26 | – | 44 | – |
| Peasant 1 | 63 | 25 | | 6 | | 3 | 29 | 16 |
| Peasant 2 | 41 | 21 | 2 | 2 | 3 | | 15 | 8 |
| Peasant 3 | 38 | 25.5 | 2 | 0.3 | | 1.2 | 9 | 5 |
| Peasant 4 | 19 | 9 | 1 | 2 | | | 7 | 9 |
| Manual worker 1 | 17 | 12.5 | 3 | 1.5 | | | | 4 |
| Manual worker 2 | 13 | | 4 | | | | 9 | – |
| Manual worker 3 | – | – | – | – | – | – | – | 8 |
| Rents | 44 | | 1 | 2 | 42 | | | 3 |
| Salaried persons | 35 | 34 | 1 | | | | | 12 |
| Business | 21 | | 1 | 7 | 13 | | | |
| Total | 43 | 19 | 1 | 2 | 7 | | 14 | 6 |

(continued)

**Appendix Table 4** *(Continued) Distribution of debt outstanding by socio-economic class and purpose of loan, Alabujanahalli, 2009 in per cent*

| Class | Consumption-related | Day-to-day expenses | Marriage and ceremonies | Education | Medical expenses | Domestic durable assets | Repay loans | House repair/ construction | Unspecified consumption | Multi-purpose consumption |
|---|---|---|---|---|---|---|---|---|---|---|
| Rich capitalist farmer | – | – | – | – | – | – | – | | – | – |
| Peasant 1 | **21** | 1 | | | | | | 20 | | |
| Peasant 2 | **51** | 3 | 25 | | | 0.3 | 4 | 13 | 1 | 4 |
| Peasant 3 | **57** | 4 | 18 | | 3 | | 2 | 1 | 6 | 23 |
| Peasant 4 | **72** | 2 | 34 | | 5 | | 2 | 20 | 6 | 3 |
| Manual worker 1 | **79** | 5 | 25 | 3 | 10 | | 2 | 21 | 5 | 8 |
| Manual worker 2 | **87** | 1 | 8 | | 8 | | 4 | 63 | 2 | 1 |
| Manual worker 3 | **92** | 5 | 4 | | 18 | | 6 | 52 | 7 | |
| Rents | **53** | 2 | 19 | | 4 | | 2 | 22 | 4 | |
| Salaried persons | **53** | 3 | 18 | | | | 6 | 22 | 1 | 3 |
| Business | **79** | | | | | | 3 | 72 | 1 | 3 |
| Total | **51** | 2 | 19 | | 3 | | 2 | 17 | 3 | 5 |

**Appendix Table 5** *Distribution of debt outstanding by socio- economic class and purpose of loan, Zhapur, 2009 in per cent*

| Class | Production-related | Recurring agricultural expense | Animal husbandry | Productive durable asset | Business and trade | Land purchase | Multi-purpose production |
|---|---|---|---|---|---|---|---|
| Rich capitalist farmer | 27 | 27 | | | | | – |
| Peasant 1 | 100 | | | 100 | | | – |
| Peasant 2 | 15 | 1 | 5 | | | 9 | – |
| Peasant 3 | 46 | 16 | 1 | 29 | | | 15 |
| Manual worker 1 | 38 | 6 | | 12 | | 21 | 3 |
| Rents | | | | | | | – |
| Salaried persons | 41 | 34 | | | 7 | | – |
| Business | 18 | 5 | 1 | 11 | 1 | | – |
| Total | 37 | 12 | 1 | 19 | | 5 | 4 |

| Class | Consumption-related | Day-to-day expenses | Marriage and ceremonies | Education | Medical expenses | Domestic durable assets | Repay loans | House repair/ construction | Land rents | Unspecified | Multi-purpose consumption |
|---|---|---|---|---|---|---|---|---|---|---|---|
| Rich capitalist farmer | 73 | | 54 | | | | | | | | 19 |
| Peasant 2 | 85 | 19 | 40 | | 8 | | 14 | | 4 | | |
| Peasant 3 | 39 | 11 | 11 | | | | 3 | | | 14 | |
| Manual worker 1 | 59 | 10 | 13 | 1 | 13 | 1 | 13 | 1 | | 3 | 4 |
| Rents | 100 | | 81 | | 19 | | | | | | |
| Salaried persons | 59 | | 11 | | | | | 48 | | | |
| Business | 82 | 1 | 60 | 7 | 11 | | | | | 1 | 2 |
| Total | 59 | 6 | 30 | 1 | 5 | | 4 | 2 | | 5 | 5 |

**Appendix Table 6** *Distribution of debt outstanding by socio-economic class and purpose of loan, Siresandra, 2009 in per cent*

| Class | Production-related | Recurring agricultural expense | Animal husbandry | Productive durable assets | Business and trade | Multi-purpose production | Land purchase | Unspecified production | Multi-purpose production and consumption |
|---|---|---|---|---|---|---|---|---|---|
| Peasant 1 | 100 | | | 63 | | 37 | | | – |
| Peasant 2 | 47 | 12 | 1 | 22 | 12 | | | | – |
| Peasant 3 | 40 | | | 37 | | | 1 | 2 | – |
| Manual workers | 12 | | 8 | | 2 | | 2 | | – |
| Business | 79 | | 1 | 72 | 6 | | | | 1 |
| Total | 49 | 6 | 1 | 31 | 7 | 3 | | 1 | – |

| Class | Consumption-related | Day-to-day expenses | Marriage and ceremonies | Education | Medical expenses | Repay loans | House repair/ construction | Unspecified consumption |
|---|---|---|---|---|---|---|---|---|
| Peasant 1 | – | | | | | | | |
| Peasant 2 | 53 | 1 | 22 | | | 14 | 13 | 3 |
| Peasant 3 | 60 | 5 | 37 | 2 | | 5 | 11 | |
| Manual workers | 88 | 1 | 3 | | 1 | 9 | 74 | |
| Business | 20 | 5 | | | | | | 15 |
| Total | 51 | 2 | 21 | 1 | | 9 | 16 | 2 |

# 13

## Condition of Housing and Access to Basic Household Amenities

### Shamsher Singh

This chapter discusses the conditions of housing and the access of households in the three study villages to basic household amenities such as electricity, drinking water, and lavatories.

The indicators examined are ownership of a dwelling; availability of homestead land; type of house structure; fuel used for cooking and provision of kitchen; and availability of living space measured in terms of number of rooms and persons per room. With respect to access to basic household amenities, the chapter discusses availability of electricity; source of drinking water; ownership and location of source of drinking water; and access to a lavatory. Special emphasis has been given to households belonging to different social groups and socio-economic classes. We also report wherever figures from the Census of India 2011 are comparable with the survey data of the Project on Agrarian Relations in India (PARI).

## Housing

### Ownership of Dwelling

Ownership status of dwellings is one of the important indicators of housing conditions. Our data show that more than 90 per cent of households across the study villages were residing in their own dwellings. In most Indian villages, the proportion of households owning a dwelling is close to 100 per cent. This was the case in Alabujanahalli and Siresandra villages too. In Zhapur, the proportion was 91 per cent in aggregate, and 89 per cent among Scheduled Castes (SCs). A close look at the data reveals that Zhapur village, unusually, had a rental market for housing because of the demand

**Table 1** *Proportion of households owning houses, by social group, study villages, 2009*
in per cent

| Village | Scheduled Caste (SC) | Backward Class (BC) | All | Census 2011 |
|---|---|---|---|---|
| Alabujanahalli | 94 | 98 | 97 | 95 |
| Siresandra | 100 | 96 | 97 | 97 |
| Zhapur | 89 | 93 | 91 | 92 |

*Source*: PARI survey data and Census of India 2011.

for housing from Manual worker households who came to work in the nearby stone quarries. Data from Census 2011 corroborate this observation.

### Quality of the Structure

The quality of a dwelling structure depends on the type of material used in constructing its roof, walls, and floors. In Tables 2 and 3, we have reported the proportion of households who were living in fully *pucca*/permanent structures, i.e. dwellings which had roofs, walls, and floors made of *pucca*/ permanent materials. It is important to note that this definition is different from that used by the Census of India and the National Sample Survey Organisation (NSSO), as these agencies take into consideration only the materials used in construction of roofs and walls.

In the study villages, more than three-fourths of the households were living in fully *pucca* houses. The proportion of such households was the highest, 81 per cent, in Zhapur village. In Alabujanahalli, the proportion of SC households who were residing in fully *pucca* houses was almost half that of Backward Class (BC) households. In Siresandra also there was inequality in this regard between SC and BC households. The least inequality was observed in Zhapur. In this village, a relatively high proportion of households across all socio-economic groups had *pucca* houses. Because of the existence of stone quarries around the village, the villagers had easy access to stone, which was used in constructing houses.

Our data show that the use of locally made tiles, called Mangalore tiles, which were less costly than conventional construction materials, had improved the quality of roofing in dwellings across all social groups in Alabujanahalli village. In Siresandra, the majority of households used metal and asbestos sheets for constructing a roof. In many countries, asbestos sheets are not permitted because of their harmful effects on the health of residents.

Table 3 shows the disparities across different socio-economic classes. A higher proportion of Landlord households and other sections of the

**Table 2** *Proportion of households owning fully "pucca" houses, by social group, study villages, 2009* in per cent

| Village | Scheduled Caste (SC) | Backward Class (BC) | All |
|---|---|---|---|
| Alabujanahalli | 44 | 82 | 76 |
| Siresandra | 61 | 82 | 75 |
| Zhapur | 77 | 82 | 81 |

*Notes*: The classification of construction material is the same as that used by the Census of India and NSSO. These agencies classify the following as *pucca*/permanent materials: cement, concrete, oven-burnt bricks, hollow cement/ash bricks, stone, stone blocks, jack boards (cement-plastered reeds), iron, zinc or other metal sheets, timber, tiles, slate, corrugated iron, asbestos cement sheet, veneer, plywood, artificial wood of synthetic material and polyvinyl chloride (PVC) material.
*Source*: PARI survey data.

**Table 3** *Proportion of households owning fully "pucca" houses, by socio-economic classes, study villages, 2009,* in per cent

| Village | Landlord/Rich capitalist farmer | Peasant 1 and Peasant 2 | Peasant 3 and Peasant 4 | Manual worker |
|---|---|---|---|---|
| Alabujanahalli | 100 | 90 | 82 | 60 |
| Siresandra | – | 86 | 74 | 54 |
| Zhapur | 100 | 67 | 86 | 76 |

*Source*: PARI survey data.

peasantry lived in fully *pucca* structures than Manual worker households across all three villages. Peasant 1 and 2 households in Zhapur were the only exception to this. Of nine households in these two classes, three households had a *kutcha* floor.

## Availability of Homestead Land and Living Space

The extent of homestead land was a crucial determinant of the quality of housing. We found large-scale disparities between SC and BC households in Alabujanahalli and Siresandra villages in terms of the extent of homestead land. On average, a BC household in Alabujanahalli owned 4,000 square feet of homestead land. In Zhapur village, one SC household owned a large homestead plot; hence, use of an average figure would be misleading. If we take the median, the size of homestead plots was higher among BC households than SC households.

Disparities as between peasant and Manual worker households were

**Table 4** *Ownership of homestead land by social group, study villages, 2009* in square feet

| Village | Scheduled Caste (SC) | | Backward Class (BC) | |
|---|---|---|---|---|
| | Average | Maximum | Average | Maximum |
| Alabujanahalli | 2649 | 22346 | 4008 | 34848 |
| Siresandra | 1139 | 3507 | 3478 | 21780 |
| Zhapur* | 1200 | 21780 | 1375 | 8482 |

*Note:* * Average refers to median value in Zhapur.
*Source*: PARI survey data.

**Table 5** *Proportion of households owning single-room structures, by social group, study villages, 2009* in per cent

| Village | Scheduled Caste (SC) | Backward Class (BC) | All | Census 2011 |
|---|---|---|---|---|
| Alabujanahalli | 38 | 15 | 18 | 22 |
| Siresandra | 42 | 29 | 33 | 32 |
| Zhapur | 53 | 37 | 48 | 41 |

*Source*: PARI survey data and Census of India 2011.

stark. The average homestead land owned by a Manual worker household was substantially less than that owned by a Landlord or peasant household in all three villages. Peasant households with ownership of agricultural land also had more homestead land than Manual worker households.

Following ILO (1961), we examine two indicators of crowdedness: the proportion of households living in single-room structures, and the proportion of households accommodating more than two persons per room.[1] Data in Table 5 show that almost one-fifth of all households in Alabujanahalli, one-third in Siresandra, and one-half in Zhapur lived in houses with a single room. The situation among SC households was worse than the village averages. In Zhapur, although the majority of SC households lived in fully *pucca* structures, more than half of them lived in single-room structures. Data from Census 2011 show a similar situation.

No Rich capitalist farmer or Landlord household lived in a single-room

---

[1] The adequacy of living space in a dwelling can be measured in terms of the number of rooms available, floor or carpet area, and covered area. Internationally, the number of rooms and persons per room are considered better indicators to measure living space and crowdedness in dwellings than floor or carpet area. The International Labour Organisation (ILO) workers' housing recommendations, 1961, put forth three criteria for measuring space per person or per family: floor area; cubic volume; size and number of rooms (ILO 1961).

**Table 6** *Proportion of households owning single-room structures, by socio-economic classes, study villages, 2009* in per cent

| Village | Landlord/Rich capitalist farmer | Peasant 1 and Peasant 2 | Peasant 3 and Peasant 4 | Manual workers |
|---|---|---|---|---|
| Alabujanahalli | 0 | 4 | 11 | 36 |
| Siresandra | – | 31 | 34 | 40 |
| Zhapur | 0 | 11 | 48 | 62 |

*Source:* PARI survey data.

**Table 7** *Proportion of households with more than two persons per room, by social group, study villages, 2009* in per cent

| Village | Scheduled Caste (SC) | Backward Class (BC) | All |
|---|---|---|---|
| Alabujanahalli | 62 | 33 | 37 |
| Siresandra | 79 | 60 | 67 |
| Zhapur | 84 | 77 | 83 |

*Source:* PARI survey data.

structure in Alabujanahalli or Zhapur, respectively. On the other hand, a significant proportion of Manual worker households in all three villages lived in single-room houses. In Siresandra and Zhapur, a significant proportion of poor peasant (Peasant 3 and Peasant 4) households lived in single-room structures.

Data in Table 7 show that the majority of households in Siresandra and Zhapur, and more than one-third of all households in Alabujanahalli, accommodated more than two persons per room. This is the norm mentioned by the United Nations Housing Programme (UNHRP) (UN 2003). In all three villages, the situation was worse among SCs with respect to this indicator. In Zhapur, 80 per cent of SC households had more than two persons per room.

Baswaraj, 55 years old, an SC small peasant and daily labourer from Zhapur, lives in a single-room house. His house is fully *pucca* with stone walls, roof, and floor. There are 12 members in his household: Baswaraj and Milamma have five sons, one daughter, two daughter-in-laws, and two grandsons. The house has a kitchen which is also used for sleeping. Most of the adult family members work on their own land and also labour out. The household does not have enough resources to purchase more homestead land and construct extra rooms in their dwelling.

## Availability of Kitchen and Type of Fuel Used for Cooking

In Alabujanahalli and Siresandra, a majority of households have separate kitchens in their houses (Table 8). In Alabujanahalli, the traditional house construction style seems to have played a role in ensuring the availability of a kitchen. Among Vokkaliga households, the kitchen is usually situated next to the prayer room/area. In Zhapur, the proportion of households with kitchens in their houses was less than half. A higher proportion of SC households in Alabujanahalli and Zhapur had kitchens than BC households.

In Alabujanahalli and Siresandra, data from the Census of India 2011 are similar to our survey data, but there is a huge difference between the two data-sets in the case of Zhapur. According to the Census, only 1 per cent of households in this village had a kitchen. This discrepancy could be due to an error in the village-level Census data. According to the Kalaburagi (rural) district and tehsil Census data, the proportion of households with kitchens is 67 per cent and 65 per cent, respectively.

One reason for more SC households having kitchens than BC households in Alabujanahalli and Zhapur was that almost 90 per cent of SC households in Alabujanahalli and all SC households in Zhapur used unclean fuel for cooking, though this proportion was also high among BC households in both the villages. The use of unclean fuel such as firewood, dung cakes, leaves, and crop residue has harmful effects on the health of the person who cooks. In case there is no provision of a separate kitchen in the dwelling, smoke generated from the use of unclean fuel affects the health of all residents. Clean fuels such as liquefied petroleum gas (LPG), biogas, and electricity are smokeless and safe for the health of the dwellers, especially the women of the household as they are mainly engaged in cooking. Provision of a separate kitchen is also important from the point of view of hygiene.

Table 8 *Proportion of households having a separate kitchen, by social group, study villages, 2009* in per cent

| Village | Scheduled Caste (SC) | Backward Class (BC) | All | Census 2011 |
|---|---|---|---|---|
| Alabujanahalli | 91 | 84 | 85 | 92 |
| Siresandra | 67 | 86 | 79 | 85 |
| Zhapur | 53 | 45 | 48 | 1 |

*Note:* Kitchen is defined as a separate room used for either storing cooking materials, or cooking, or both, and not for any other purpose.
*Source:* PARI survey data and Census of India 2011.

**Table 9** *Proportion of households using clean fuel for cooking, by social group, study villages, 2009* in per cent

| Village | Scheduled Caste (SC) | Backward Class (BC) | All |
|---|---|---|---|
| Alabujanahalli | 6 | 11 | 10 |
| Siresandra | 0 | 2 | 1 |
| Zhapur | 0 | 0 | 0 |

*Notes:* Classification of fuels into clean and unclean is based on the classification used by the IIPS (2014), NFHS 4.
*Source:* PARI survey data.

Unclean fuels include firewood, dung cakes, coal/charcoal, crop residue, leaves, and kerosene. Clean fuels include LPG, biogas, and electricity. In cases where more than one fuels were reported, the first (and most used) reported fuel was considered as the primary fuel.

Table 9 shows that only a small proportion of households in Alabujanahalli used clean fuel and an overwhelming majority of all households used unclean fuels. Only a small proportion, 2 per cent, of BC households used clean fuel in Siresandra, and this proportion was zero in Zhapur. Strikingly, no SC household in Siresandra and Zhapur used clean fuels, and only a very small section in Alabujanahalli did so.

## Electricity, Drinking Water And Lavatories

### Electricity

The majority of households across all social groups in the three study villages had access to domestic electricity, but in none of the villages did all the households have access to electricity. The proportion of SC households with electricity connections was lower than the proportion of BC households with electricity connections in Alabujanahalli and Zhapur villages.

Siresandra was different. All SC households in this village had an electricity connection. "In September 1979, the State government introduced the Bhagya Jyothi scheme with the objective of providing electricity (one lamp a house) to poor households, particularly Scheduled Caste and Scheduled Tribe households. Each household had to pay a total of Rs 200, in instalments, over a period of 15 years" (Government of Karnataka 2012, p. 14). Under this scheme the beneficiary household was allowed to use only one bulb for lighting purposes.

**Table 10** *Proportion of households with access to electricity, by social group, study villages, 2009* in per cent

| Village | Scheduled Caste (SC) | Backward Class (BC) | All | Census 2011 |
|---|---|---|---|---|
| Alabujanahalli | 86 | 93 | 92 | 88 |
| Siresandra | 100 | 98 | 99 | 89 |
| Zhapur | 83 | 89 | 88 | 74 |

*Source*: PARI survey data and Census of India 2011.

Six households in Siresandra benefited, of which one was a SC household. Even with the Bhagya Jyothi scheme in place for 30 years, not all households had access to electricity.

### Access to Drinking Water

There are three important aspects of the issue of access to sources of drinking water. These are: first, type or quality of source/s used for drinking water, i.e. whether the source is open or covered; secondly, whether access to the source is personal or common/public; and thirdly, distance of the source from the house.[2]

Our village-level data showed that all households in Siresandra and 97 per cent of all households in Alabujanahalli had access to covered sources of water. As shown in Table 11, three-fourths of all households in Zhapur had access to a covered source of water. According to the Census of India 2011, only 1 per cent of households in Zhapur had access to a covered source of drinking water. The proportion of SC households who had access to covered sources was higher than BC households in Zhapur. There is a conceptual problem here in classifying the covered sources as safe or better sources. This classification is misleading as it is not necessary that the quality of water from covered sources is always better when water from open sources is of poor quality and unsafe. Zhapur village is an example of this.

Zhapur had a panchayat-operated water supply mechanism. Many BC households here reported that the water supplied by the common system was not suitable for drinking, and these households used a community well for drinking water while the panchayat supplied water for cleaning and bathing purposes. SC households were not allowed to use the "community"

---

[2] Since we do not have information on the quality of water used for drinking purpose, we use type of source, i.e. open or closed source, as a proxy for quality of water. In this classification closed sources are considered safe and open sources unsafe.

**Table 11** *Proportion of households with access to covered sources of drinking water, by social group, Zhapur village, 2009* in per cent

| Village | Scheduled Caste (SC) | Backward Class (BC) | All | Census 2011 |
|---------|---------------------|---------------------|-----|-------------|
| Zhapur | 96 | 67 | 75 | 1 |

*Note:* Covered water sources are sources where water is either supplied through pipes from an overhead tank or a water reservoir, or directly from the source (handpump/tubewell/borewell).
*Source:* PARI survey data and Census of India 2011.

**Table 12** *Proportion of households with personal access to source of drinking water, by social group, study villages, 2009* in per cent

| Village | Scheduled Caste (SC) | Backward Class (BC) | All |
|---------|---------------------|---------------------|-----|
| Alabujanahalli | 18 | 58 | 49 |
| Siresandra | 7 | 10 | 6 |
| Zhapur | 4 | 2 | 3 |

*Note:* Personal access is defined as sources owned (exclusively or jointly with other household/s) and personal connections to common water supply.
*Source:* PARI survey data.

**Table 13** *Proportion of households with source of drinking water within homestead or just outside, by social group, study villages, 2009* in per cent

| Village | Scheduled Caste (SC) | Backward Class (BC) | All | Census 2011 |
|---------|---------------------|---------------------|-----|-------------|
| Alabujanahalli | 9 | 44 | 39 | 43 |
| Siresandra | 0 | 6 | 4 | 8 |
| Zhapur | 4 | 4 | 4 | 1 |

*Source:* PARI survey data and Census of India 2011.

well. As a result, SC households did not have a choice but to use sub-standard and inferior-quality piped water. Though the water was supplied through pipes and was covered, it was not as good as the water from an open source. Water supply was not regular from the panchayat-operated mechanism.

In Siresandra and Alabujanahalli there were panchayat-operated water supply mechanisms, and the water was supplied through pipes. Further examination of the data shows that in Alabujanahalli a few BC households owned wells and used water from these wells – which, according to them, was better in taste and quality, and more convenient than the piped water supplied by the panchayat – for drinking purposes.

The second aspect of sources of drinking water was ownership, i.e. whether access was private/personal or public/common.

The data show that in Alabujanahalli, 50 per cent of all households had access to a personal source of drinking water. In Siresandra and Zhapur, however, the majority of households were dependent on public/common sources or sources owned by other persons.

In Alabujanahalli there was a village water supply mechanism, but a common reason for SC households not to take a personal connection was that they could not afford to pay the installation charges and monthly/ yearly user charges.

Table 13 shows the proportion of households with a source of drinking water within or just outside the homestead. This is an important aspect of access to source of drinking water. It gives an idea of the time and hardship involved in fetching water.

Table 12 shows that in Alabujanahalli, 44 per cent of BC households and 9 per cent of SC households had access to a source of drinking water within the homestead. In Siresandra and Zhapur, it was rare to have a source of drinking water within or just outside the homestead. In Siresandra, no SC household had a source of drinking water inside or just outside the homestead. The situation was similar in Zhapur, where only 4 per cent of SC households had a source of drinking water inside or just outside their houses. Data from the Census of India 2011 paint a similar picture.

Not having a source of drinking water within or just outside the homestead results in some household members spending time and energy in fetching water from sources located at a distance.

### Access to Lavatories

Table 14 presents a dismal picture in respect of access to lavatories. One-half of the households in Alabujanahalli, more than 90 per cent of households

Table 14 *Proportion of households without access to lavatories, by social group, study villages, 2009* in per cent

| Village | Scheduled Caste (SC) | Backward Class (BC) | All | Census 2011 |
|---|---|---|---|---|
| Alabujanahalli | 80 | 44 | 50 | 44 |
| Siresandra | 100 | 88 | 92 | 92 |
| Zhapur | 100 | 100 | 99 | 91 |

*Source*: PARI survey data and Census of India 2011.

in Siresandra, and all except one (a Muslim business household) household in Zhapur did not have access to a lavatory. The situation of SC households was worse than that of others. In Siresandra and Zhapur, no SC household had access to a lavatory. This large-scale absence of lavatories had serious socio-economic and environmental consequences. A similar picture emerges from the Census of India 2011.

It is clear from the data that even households with *pucca* houses and electricity lacked access to lavatories.

## Integrated Housing

Various international agencies advocate a broader approach towards defining housing, which goes beyond four walls and a roof (see United Nations 1991 for more details on adequate housing). In Singh, Swaminathan, and Ramachandran (2013), we proposed a set of criteria based on basic and minimal norms for housing to gauge the quality of housing in an integrated way. A house that met the following criteria was defined as adequate: "(1) pucca roofs, walls, and floors; (2) two rooms; (3) a source of water inside

**Table 15** *Proportion of households with fully "pucca" house, two or more rooms, electricity connection, source of drinking water within homestead or just outside, and access to lavatory, by social group, study villages, 2009* in per cent

| Village | Scheduled Caste (SC) | Backward Class (BC) | All |
|---|---|---|---|
| Alabujanahalli | 3 | 32 | 28 |
| Siresandra | 0 | 2 | 1 |
| Zhapur | 0 | 0 | 0 |

*Source*: PARI survey data.

**Table 16** *Proportion of households with fully "pucca" house, two or more rooms, electricity connection, source of drinking water within homestead or just outside, and access to lavatory, by socio-economic classes, study villages, 2009* in per cent

| Village | Landlord/Rich capitalist farmer | Peasant 1 and Peasant 2 | Peasant 3 and Peasant 4 | Manual workers |
|---|---|---|---|---|
| Alabujanahalli | 50 | 62 | 25 | 2 |
| Siresandra | – | 0 | 4 | 0 |
| Zhapur | 0 | 0 | 0 | 0 |

*Source*: PARI survey data.

or immediately outside the house; (4) an electricity connection (authorised or unauthorised); and (5) a functioning latrine" (Singh, Swaminathan, and Ramachandran 2013, p. 64).

The data in Table 15 speak for themselves. In Alabujanahalli 28 per cent of all households fulfilled the above-mentioned criteria, whereas fulfillment of criteria was almost nil in the other two villages. Even in Alabujanahalli village, the majority of households that met these criteria were BC households, and only 3 per cent of SC households met the criteria. This large-scale deprivation with respect to a minimum standard of housing needs arose mainly due to the absence of lavatories, and non-availability of drinking water sources within or just outside the homestead.

Table 16 shows the levels of deprivation in terms of access to basic housing and household amenities across different socio-economic classes. It is clear that there was overall deprivation in terms of access to the selected indicators, but this deprivation was very high among Manual worker households across the three villages. Only 2 per cent of Manual worker households in Alabujanahalli had access to these minimum levels of housing and amenities.

## Access to Selected Consumer Goods

Table 17 shows the proportion of households that owned a television (TV) set in the three villages. More than half of all households in Alabujanahalli and Siresandra owned a TV. Both these villages also showed sharp inequalities between SC and BC households. A closer examination shows that in Alabaujanahalli and Siresandra, where the incidence of TV ownership was generally high, the overall incidence of TV ownership was 57 per cent and 63 per cent, respectively. Only one-fourth of SC households in Alabujahanalli and a little over one-third of households in Siresandra possessed TVs; 62 per cent and 77 per cent of BC households in the respective villages owned TVs.

However, the disparity among BC households on the one hand, and SC households on the other, was markedly lower in Zhapur: 48 per cent of BC households and 40 per cent of SC households had a TV.

Table 18 shows that a very small proportion of households, one-fifth or less, across the three villages owned a transistor or radio. A higher proportion of SC households in Siresandra and Zhapur owned a transistor/radio than BC households. This could be because a transistor/radio is cheaper and more affordable than a TV, but still serves as a medium of information. However, the overall low incidence of ownership of a transistor/radio could also be

**Table 17** *Proportion of households owning television sets, by social group, study villages, 2009* in per cent

| Village | Scheduled Caste (SC) | Backward Class (BC) | All |
|---|---|---|---|
| Alabujanahalli | 25 | 62 | 57 |
| Siresandra | 36 | 77 | 63 |
| Zhapur | 40 | 48 | 43 |

*Source:* PARI survey data.

**Table 18** *Proportion of households owning transistors/radios, by social group, study villages, 2009* in per cent

| Village | Scheduled Caste (SC) | Backward Class (BC) | All |
|---|---|---|---|
| Alabujanahalli | 19 | 21 | 20 |
| Siresandra | 25 | 15 | 18 |
| Zhapur | 16 | 13 | 14 |

*Source:* PARI survey data.

**Table 19** *Proportion of households owning mobile/landline telephones, by social group, study villages, 2009* in per cent

| Village | Scheduled Caste (SC) | Backward Class (BC) | All |
|---|---|---|---|
| Alabujanahalli | 39 | 73 | 69 |
| Siresandra | 43 | 74 | 63 |
| Zhapur | 38 | 39 | 36 |

*Source:* PARI survey data.

due to its outdatedness in times when modern mediums of information and entertainment are available.

Table 19 shows the availability of mobile phones or landline phones in the study villages. A majority of households in Alabujanahalli and Siresandra had a mobile or landline telephone, while this proportion was a little more than one-third in Zhapur. In Alabujanahalli and Siresandra, where the overall ownership of telephones was higher, disparities among SC and BC households was also more striking, whereas this inequality was almost negligible in Zhapur with overall lower ownership of telephones. In Alabujanahalli and Siresandra, around three-fourths of BC households owned a mobile or landline telephone, but only 39 and 43 per cent, respectively, of SC households did so.

## Conditions of Scheduled Tribe Households

In Zhapur village there were 14 Scheduled Tribe (ST) households, and we describe their conditions of housing and access to basic amenities in this section.

Out of all 14 ST households in Zhapur, 12 lived in their own dwellings and only two households lived in non-*pucca* structures. The conditions of housing were relatively better in this village due to the availability of cheap stone in the area, as discussed earlier. A little more than one-third of the households had a separate cooking space/kitchen. The majority of ST households in the village, eight out of 14, lived in single-room dwellings. All the households had domestic electricity connections, but none had a source of water within the house or just outside it. None of the households had access to a lavatory. Thus no ST household lived in houses with our five selected components of integrated housing.

The availability of selected consumer durable items was also very low. Table 20 shows that only two ST households owned a transistor/radio, four households owned a TV set, and three households had a mobile or landline telephone.

**Table 20** *Conditions of housing, and access to basic household amenities and selected consumer durable items among Scheduled Tribe (ST) households, Zhapur, 2009* in numbers

| | |
|---|---|
| Households living in own dwellings | 12* |
| Households living in *kutcha* wall houses | 0 |
| Households living in *kutcha* roof houses | 0 |
| Households living in *kutcha* floor houses | 2 |
| Households living in fully *pucca* houses | 12 |
| Households living in single-room houses | 8 |
| Households with access to domestic electricity | 14 |
| Households with access to water within premises of or just outside the house | 0 |
| Households with access to lavatories | 0 |
| Households using clean fuel for cooking | 0 |
| Households owning transistor/radio | 2 |
| Households owning television set | 4 |
| Households owning mobile/landline telephone | 3 |

*Note*: *Information for two households was not available.
*Source*: PARI survey data.

## Box: Public Distribution System

This section deals with various aspects of the functioning of the public distribution system (PDS) in the three villages surveyed in Karnataka.

### *Alabujanahalli*

In Alabujanahalli, of the total 243 households, 238 households had PDS cards. The coverage of cards was near-universal (98 per cent) in this village. The total number of PDS cards issued was 259: the reason for the existence of more PDS ration cards than the total number of households in the village was that some households held multiple cards.

The total number of above poverty line (APL) cards was 125, while there were 96 below poverty line (BPL) cards. Antyodaya Anna Yojana (AAY) cards are issued to the poorest of the poor, and 16 such cards were issued in Alabujanahalli. A few

**Table 1** *Category-wise distribution of PDS cards, Alabujananhalli, 2009* in per cent

| Card category | No. of cards | Per cent of cards |
|---|---|---|
| APL (above poverty line) | 125 | 49 |
| BPL (below poverty line) | 96 | 37.1 |
| AAY (Antyodaya Anna Yojana) | 16 | 6.2 |
| AAR (Akshaya Anila Rahita) | 14 | 5.4 |
| No information | 6 | 2.3 |
| Total number of cards | 257 | 100 |

*Source*: FAS survey data.

**Table 2** *Type of ration card by socio-economic class, Alabujanahalli, 2009*

| Socio-economic class | Type of card | | | | |
|---|---|---|---|---|---|
| | APL | BPL | AAY | Others | Total |
| Rich capitalist farmer | 2 | 0 | 0 | 0 | 2 |
| Peasant | 47 | 4 | 0 | 1 | 52 |
| Poor peasant | 44 | 33 | 2 | 10 | 89 |
| Manual worker | 20 | 44 | 9 | 6 | 79 |
| Others | 12 | 15 | 5 | 3 | 35 |
| Total | 125 | 96 | 16 | 20 | 257 |

*Note*: We have grouped Peasant 1 and Peasant 2 under the "peasant" class, and Peasant 3 and Peasant 4 under the "poor peasant" class.
*Source*: PARI survey data.

card holders held temporary cards or Akshaya Anila Rahita (AAR) cards. These AAR cards have different entitlements based upon the category of the card holder.

Table 2 helps to understand errors in PDS targeting. There were two Rich capitalist farmer households in Alabujanahalli, and both had APL cards. Ninety per cent of peasant class households had APL cards, and none of them had an AAY card. As we moved down the socio-economic class hierarchy, the proportion of BPL cards increased, from 8 per cent in the peasant class to 56 per cent among Manual worker card holders. Sixty nine per cent of AAY cards were issued to poor peasants and Manual workers.

There were limited errors of wrong inclusion, but errors of exclusion were present. For example, one-fourth of Manual worker households had APL cards.

**Table 3** *Average purchase of various commodities by card holders who bought from PDS shops in reference month, Alabujanahalli, 2009* in kilograms and litres

| Card category | Commodity | | | |
|---|---|---|---|---|
| | Rice (kg) | Wheat (kg) | Kerosene (litres) | Sugar (kg) |
| APL | 17 | 3 | 3 | 1.5 |
| BPL | 14 | 3 | 3 | 1 |
| AAY | 30 | 6 | 3 | 1 |
| AAR | 17 | 4 | 4 | 0.5 |

*Source*: PARI survey data.

The average monthly quantity of rice purchased by APL card holders was 17 kg, compared to only 14 kg purchased by BPL card holders. The highest monthly purchase of rice and wheat was by Antyodaya (AAY) card holders.

### Siresandra

**Table 4** *Category-wise distribution of PDS cards, Siresandra, 2009* in per cent

| Card category | No. of cards | Per cent of cards |
|---|---|---|
| APL (above poverty line) | 20 | 23 |
| BPL (below poverty line) | 46 | 53 |
| AAY (Antyodaya Anna Yojana) | 5 | 6 |
| AAR (Akshaya Anila Rahita) | 12 | 14 |
| No information | 4 | 4 |
| Total number of cards | 87 | 100 |

*Source*: PARI survey data.

Of the total cards issued in Siresandra, 53 per cent were issued to the BPL category while 23 per cent were issued to the APL category. Only 6 per cent of cards issued were of the AAY category. Almost all (78 of 79) households in this village possessed a ration card.

**Table 5** *Type of ration card by socio-economic class, Siresandra, 2009*

| Socio-economic class | Type of card | | | |
|---|---|---|---|---|
| | APL | BPL | Others | Total |
| Rich peasant | 2 | 1 | 3 | 6 |
| Middle peasant | 17 | 35 | 11 | 63 |
| Manual worker | 0 | 10 | 2 | 12 |
| Others | 1 | 5 | 0 | 6 |
| Total | 20 | 51 | 16 | 87 |

*Note*: The Manual worker class here includes Peasant 3 and manual workers, and Antyodaya (AAY) cards are combined with BPL cards.
*Source*: PARI survey data.

Table 5 shows the distribution of PDS cards in Siresandra across socio-economic classes. The proportion of BPL and AAY card holders increased as we moved down the class hierarchy. While 56 per cent of Peasant 2 households held BPL cards, an overwhelming 83 per cent of Manual worker households had BPL cards. It is also worth noting that no Manual worker household had an APL card.

Compared to Alabujanahalli, Siresandra had lower errors of exclusion and inclusion. Of 29 card holders in the Peasant 2 class, 11 had APL cards and nine had BPL cards. However, 16 out of 87 cards were temporary cards, which we were unable to classify properly.

Despite a sizeable number of APL card holders belonging to the Peasant 2 class (85 per cent), no purchases were made by them from the PDS shops. Siresandra was the only village of the three villages surveyed in Karnataka where APL households did not make any purchases from PDS shops. There were 20 APL card holders, out of which 17 were held by Peasant 2 households, and none of them had reported any purchase from PDS shops.

Table 6 shows the average quantity of commodities purchased from PDS shops. Among all BPL card holders, the average quantity of rice purchased in a month was 15 kg, along with 4 kg of wheat, 1 kg of sugar, and 3 litres of kerosene. Antyodaya (AAY) card holders purchased 28 kg of rice and 6 kg of wheat every month from PDS shops.

**Table 6** *Average purchase of various commodities by card holders who bought from PDS shops in reference month, Siresandra, 2009* in kilograms and litres

| Card category | Commodities | | | |
|---|---|---|---|---|
| | Rice (kg) | Wheat (kg) | Kerosene (litres) | Sugar (kg) |
| APL | 0 | 0 | 0 | 0 |
| BPL | 15 | 4 | 3 | 1 |
| AAY | 28 | 6 | 3 | 1 |
| AAR | 20 | 2 | 3 | 0 |

*Source*: PARI survey data.

## Zhapur

**Table 7** *Category-wise distribution of PDS cards, Zhapur, 2009*

| Card category | No. of cards | Per cent of cards |
|---|---|---|
| APL (above poverty line) | 23 | 20.6 |
| BPL (below poverty line) | 45 | 40.5 |
| AAY (Antyodaya Anna Yojana) | 22 | 20 |
| AAR (Akshaya Anila Rahita) | 13 | 11.7 |
| No information | 8 | 7.2 |
| Total number of card holders | 111 | 100 |

*Source*: PARI survey data.

In Zhapur, of the 109 households, 102 households had PDS cards. The coverage of cards was near-universal (93.5 per cent) in this village. The total number of PDS card holders in the village was 111, out of which 23 were APL card holders, 45 were BPL card holders, and 22 card holders were under the AAY scheme. Around 40 per cent of all cards issued in the village were BPL cards, whereas 11.7 per cent of all cards were temporary or under the Akshaya Anila Rahita (AAR) scheme.

Table 8 gives a picture of PDS card distribution in Zhapur by socio-economic class. Manual worker households were the largest class category in Zhapur: 38 per cent of them held BPL cards, while 23 per cent had AAY cards. Forty three per cent of Peasant households had BPL cards, as compared to 38 per cent among Manual worker households. When it came to AAY cards, the distribution was almost identical: 23 per cent of Manual workers and 22 per cent of peasants had AAY cards.

It is interesting to note that out of six Landlord or Rich capitalist farmer households in this village, two held BPL cards while two did not report the type of card they possessed. Ravishankar Patil was a landlord who owned 35 acres of

**Table 8** *Type of ration card by socio-economic class, Zhapur, 2009*

| Socio-economic class | Type of card | | | | |
|---|---|---|---|---|---|
| | APL | BPL | AAY | Others | Total |
| Landlord | 2 | 2 | 0 | 2 | 6 |
| Peasant | 5 | 16 | 8 | 8 | 37 |
| Manual worker | 9 | 18 | 11 | 10 | 48 |
| Others | 7 | 9 | 3 | 1 | 20 |
| Total | 23 | 45 | 22 | 21 | 111 |

*Note*: We have grouped Peasant 2 and Peasant 3 households together as "Peasant," and grouped Peasant 1 households with and Landlord households.
*Source*: PARI survey data.

land. He was one of the two landlords who did not report the type of card he held; the other landlord household that did not report was that of Basavaraj Patil who owned 60 acres of land.

Gangamma was a quarry worker who was also the head of her household. Her family had moved to Zhapur a month ago in 2008, paying a rent of Rs 100 per month for the house they lived in. Gangamma had been in possession of a PDS card in Erapur, Kalaburagi, from where they had migrated to Zhapur. A quarter of the ration cards in Zhapur were classified as "other." This included persons/ households with no cards.

**Table 9** *Average purchase of various commodities by card holders who bought from PDS shops in reference month, Zhapur, 2009* in kilograms and litres

| Card category | Commodities | | | |
|---|---|---|---|---|
| | Rice (kg) | Wheat (kg) | Kerosene (litres) | Sugar (kg) |
| APL | 17 | 3 | 3 | 1 |
| BPL | 20 | 3 | 3 | 1 |
| AAY | 28 | 0 | 0 | 0 |
| AAR | 16 | 3 | 4 | 1 |

*Source*: PARI survey data.

Table 9 shows the average quantity of various commodities purchased from PDS shops in Zhapur. APL card holders on average purchased 17 kg of rice every month, along with 3 kg of wheat and 3 litres of kerosene. The 45 BPL households in the village on average purchased 20 kg of rice from PDS shops, along with 3 kg of wheat and 3 litres of kerosene. Antyodaya Anna Yojana (AAY) card holders on average purchased 28 kg of rice in a month. It is interesting to note that AAY card holders in Zhapur did not purchase anything apart from rice from PDS shops.

### Concluding Remarks

In the three villages surveyed in Karnataka, the percentage of households that had PDS cards was high, with more than 90 per cent of households in possession of at least one card. Amongst the three villages, Siresandra had the highest coverage with 99 per cent of households in possession of at least one ration card.

Amongst the three villages, Alabujanahalli had the largest population with 243 households, as compared to 79 and 109 households in Siresandra and Zhapur, respectively. In Alabujanahalli, 37.1 per cent of all card holders had BPL cards, compared to 53 and 40.5 per cent, respectively, in Siresandra and Zhapur. Twenty-three per cent of card holders in Siresandra had APL ration cards, compared to 49 and 20.6 per cent, respectively, in Alabujanahalli and Zhapur.

APL households in Zhapur and Alabujanahalli on average purchased 17 kg of rice in a month, while in Siresandra no APL household purchased any commodity from PDS shops. In Siresandra and Zhapur, BPL households purchased more rice than APL households, while APL households in Alabujanahalli bought 17 kg of rice from PDS shops as compared to 14 kg of rice bought by BPL households.

**Subhajit Patra and R. Jagannath**

# Concluding Remarks

This chapter has examined the conditions of housing, and the coverage and availability of basic household amenities such as domestic electricity connection, source of drinking water, and sanitation facilities, in the three study villages of Karnataka. The focus of the discussion is on inequalities between Scheduled Caste (SC) and Backward Class (BC) households, and households belonging to different socio-economic classes, with respect to housing and basic amenities.

Our analysis shows that a majority of households in the villages lived in their own dwellings. Zhapur was the only village where 10 per cent of SC Manual worker households lived in rental accommodation.

More than three-fourths of households in the three study villages lived in fully *pucca*/permanent houses, with Zhapur having the highest proportion of such households. Easy availability of stone as construction material in this village was one reason for this. There were sharp inequalities in

Alabujanahalli village between SC and BC households in this respect, and similarly between Manual worker households, and Landlords and other sections of the peasantry.

There were large inequalities in terms of ownership of homestead land between SC and BC households, and Manual worker households and households belonging to different strata of the peasantry. SC households owned smaller homesteads in comparison to BC households in Alabujanahalli and Siresandra villages. As a result of lack of adequate homestead land and economic resources to construct an adequate number of rooms, 38 per cent of SC households in Alabujanahalli, 42 per cent households in Siresandra, and more than half the households in Zhapur lived in single-room structures. Homes were highly crowded in general, and in particular among SC households.

An overwhelming majority of households across different socio-economic classes in all three study villages had access to domestic electricity connections in their dwellings, but it was still not 100 per cent in any of the villages. The majority of households also had access to covered sources of drinking water. SC households were not allowed to access BC community wells in Zhapur for drinking water, and they relied on sub-standard piped drinking water. The proportion of households with personal access to a source of drinking water source was negligible in Siresandra and Zhapur.

Access to lavatories was highly inadequate in all three villages. Not a single SC or Manual worker household in Siresandra and Zhapur had access to lavatories. In all of Zhapur village there was only one household with a lavatory!

On the whole, our data show large-scale deprivation and particularly acute deprivation among SC and Manual worker households. Even going by a minimal definition of adequate housing and basic amenities (a fully *pucca* house, two or more rooms, electricity connection, source of drinking water within homestead or just outside, and access to a lavatory), only 28 per cent of the households in Alabujanahlli, one household in Siresandra, and none in Zhapur village met these standards. Among SC and Manual worker households in Alabujanahalli this proportion was negligible; and no SC and Manual worker household in Siresandra and Zhapur met these basic standards of adequate housing and basic amenities. The situation of Scheduled Tribe (ST) households was also poor.

While more than half of all households in Alabujanahalli and Siresandra owned a television and mobile or landline telephone, the inequalities between SC and BC households in these villages were striking, In Zhapur overall ownership levels of such modern amenities were lower, and inequalities were also lower.

Our revisit to these three villages in 2014 showed that little had changed after four years with respect to housing and basic amenities. In Alabujanahalli some improvement in housing and individual water connections along with access to lavatories was noticed at the time of the revisit in November 2014. There was some improvement in access to lavatories in Siresandra village, but the situation with regard to individual water connections remained the same as earlier. There was no change in respect of sanitation facilities and individual water connections in Zhapur.

# References

Census of India (2011), Houselisting and Housing Data, Percentage of Households to Total Households by Amenities and Assets (India and States/UTs – Village and Ward Level), Karnataka State; available at http://www.censusindia.gov.in/2011census/HLO/HL_PCA/Houselisting-housing-Kar.html, viewed on July 31, 2016.

Government of Karnataka (2012), http://karnatakavarthe.org/wp-content/publications/August-2012.pdf, viewed on July 31, 2016.

Indian Institute of Population Studies (IIPS) (2014), National Family Health Survey, India 2015–16 (NFHS 4), Household Questionnaire, November, Mumbai; available at http://rchiips.org/NFHS/NFHS4/schedules/NFHS-4Household.pdf, viewed on July 31, 2016.

International Labour Organisation (ILO) (1961), *R115 – Workers' Housing Recommendation, 1961 (No. 115)*, Geneva; available at http://www.ilo.org/dyn/normlex/en/f?p=NORMLEXPUB:12100:0::NO:12100:P12100_INSTRUMENT_ID:312453:NO, viewed on July 25, 2016.

National Sample Survey Organisation (NSSO) (2010), *Report No. 535: Housing Condition and Amenities in India, 65th Round, 2008–09,* Ministry of Statistics and Programme Implementation, Government of India, New Delhi.

Singh, Shamsher, Swaminathan, Madhura, and Ramachandran, V. K. (2013), "Housing Shortages in Rural India," *Review of Agrarian Studies,* vol. 3, no. 2, pp. 54–72.

United Nations (UN) (1991), *The Right to Adequate Housing (1991), Article 11(1) of the Covenant on Economic, Social and Cultural Rights (ICESCR),* General Comment 4, Sixth Session, Office of the High Commissioner for Human Rights, Geneva.

United Nations Human Rights Programme (UNHRP) (2003), *Monitoring Housing Rights: Developing a Set of Indicators to Monitor the Full and Progressive Realisation of the Human Right to Adequate Housing,* Background report for Expert Group Meeting on Housing Rights Monitoring, Working Paper No. 1, Geneva, November.

# Contributors

ATHREYA, VENKATESH, Consultant, M. S. Swaminathan Research Foundation, Chennai

BAKSHI, APARAJITA, Assistant Professor, School of Development Studies, Tata Institute of Social Sciences, Mumbai

BHAVANI, R. V., Project Manager, Leveraging Agriculture for Nutrition in South Asia (LANSA), M. S. Swaminathan Research Foundation, Chennai

CHANDRASHEKAR, H., Consultant, Karnataka Agricultural Prices Commission, Bengaluru

CHAVAN, PALLAVI, researcher on rural credit based in Mumbai

DAS, ARINDAM, Senior Programme Manager, Foundation for Agrarian Studies, Bengaluru

DAS, YASODHARA, Senior Economist, Foundation for Agrarian Studies, Bengaluru

DEEPAK KUMAR, Ph.D. scholar, Yokohama National University, Yokohama, Japan

DHAR, NILADRI SEKHAR, Assistant Professor, School of Rural Development, Tata Institute of Social Sciences, Tuljapur

GIREESH P. S., Technical Assistant, Karnataka Agricultural Prices Commission, Bengaluru

JAGANNATH, R., Student, National Law School of India University, Bengaluru

KAMMARDI, T. N. PRAKASH, Chairman, Karnataka Agricultural Prices Commission, Bengaluru

NAGENDRA, Technical Assistant, Karnataka Agricultural Prices Commission, Bengaluru

PARAMESHWARAPPA, K. J., Consultant, Karnataka Agricultural Prices Commission, Bengaluru

PATRA, SUBHAJIT, Data Analyst, Foundation for Agrarian Studies, Bengaluru

RAMACHANDRAN, V. K., Vice-Chairman, State Planning Board, Kerala, and Professor, Economic Analysis Unit, Indian Statistical Institute, Bengaluru

RAMAKUMAR, R., Professor and Dean, School of Development Studies, Tata Institute of Social Sciences, Mumbai

SARKAR, BIPLAB, Senior Research Fellow, Indian Statistical Institute, Bengaluru

SINGH, SHAMSHER, Post-doctoral Fellow, Indian Institute of Management, Ahmedabad

SIVAMURUGAN, T., Programme Manager, Foundation for Agrarian Studies, Bengaluru

SWAMINATHAN, MADHURA, Professor and Head, Economic Analysis Unit, Indian Statistical Institute, Bangalore Centre

TORGAL, HARSHA V., Technical Assistant, Karnataka Agricultural Prices Commission, Bengaluru

USAMI, YOSHIFUMI, Research Fellow, University of Tokyo, Japan

VIJAY KUMAR, MALI PATIL, Technical Assistant, Karnataka Agricultural Prices Commission, Bengaluru